Sudden Deaths and Inquiries in S Law, Policy and Practice

Sudden Deaths and Fatal Accident Inquiries in Scotland: Law, Policy and Practice

Gillian Mawdsley

Bloomsbury Professional

LONDON • DUBLIN • EDINBURGH • NEW YORK • NEW DELHI • SYDNEY

BLOOMSBURY PROFESSIONAL
Bloomsbury Publishing Plc

50 Bedford Square, London, WC1B 3DP, UK
1385 Broadway, New York, NY 10018, USA
29 Earlsfort Terrace, Dublin 2, Ireland

BLOOMSBURY and the Diana logo are trademarks of Bloomsbury Publishing Plc

© Bloomsbury Professional 2023

British Library Cataloguing-in-Publication Data

A catalogue record for this book is available from the British Library.

ISBN – Paper:	978 1 52651 903 0
ISBN – Epdf:	978 1 52651 905 4
ISBN – Epub:	978 1 52651 904 7

Typeset by Evolution Design and Digital (Kent)
Printed and bound by CPI Group (UK) Ltd, Croydon, CR0 4YY

To find out more about our authors and books visit www.bloomsburyprofessional.com. Here you will find extracts, author information, details of forthcoming events and the option to sign up for our newsletters

Foreword

In introducing this book "Sudden Deaths and Fatal Accident Inquiries in Scotland: Law Policy and Practice" I adopt a phrase from the Game of Thrones: "death is certain, the time is not." That appropriately outlines the background to this book. When sudden, unexpected, unexplained or suspicious deaths occur, there is need for immediate investigations to take place.

I have spent times throughout my career, with the Crown Office and Procurator Fiscal Service (COPFS), from procurator fiscal depute to Crown Agent and more recently as a Sheriff, immersed in Fatal Accident Inquiry procedure and actual Inquiries and many notable Inquiries of the last 40 years or so are etched on my experience.

What has long been apparent to me is that the families of the deceased often have had no prior understanding of the sudden death system into which they were plunged at a time of enormous grief and which has sometimes played out under intense media scrutiny. They had little knowledge, if any, of the role of COPFS, regarding that organisation, if at all, as simply the Scottish criminal prosecution service.

The role of the Procurator Fiscal and COPFS is unique as regards death investigation, with a very long tradition of exercising, in private, many of the traditional functions of the coroner in other common law jurisdictions and, now for well over a century, the role of assembling and presenting the evidence in public inquiries into sudden unexpected, unexplained and suspicious deaths in Scotland. The investigation of such deaths is essential when considering the interest of the public in learning lessons from the facts and circumstances of the death. Relatives need to be able seek out answers and have reassurance that other families will not suffer from the same mistakes that have resulted in a death and to know when changes can and should be made.

Some Fatal Accident Inquiries have been conducted under the full glare of publicity – such as these held in connection with the disasters at Ibrox, Lockerbie, Dunblane, and Cairngorm – all dominating the headlines of their day. But each death is a tragedy for the relatives involved, no less so in the vast bulk of inquiries which proceed without press interest. It is a crucial part of the role of COPFS and of the Lord Advocate as the head of the system of investigation of deaths to ensure that a fair, effective, independent judicial inquiry is held into such deaths, where appropriate.

One of the more positive innovations in recent years, addressed in this book, is the publication on the internet of all fatal accident inquiry determinations. Those researching fatal accident inquiries in future will, to that extent at least, be spared the labours which the author has exercised in researching all but the most recent Inquiries.

This book examines the Scottish system in depth from the initial investigation and reporting of the sudden death to the conclusion of the Fatal Accident Inquiry. Its scope is wider than that, as it includes the historical development of Fatal Accident Inquiries brought up to date with the operation of Inquiries under the current legislation, the Inquiries into Fatal Accidents and Sudden Deaths etc. (Scotland) Act 2016. It looks at the State's requirement to investigate sudden deaths under Article 2 of the European Convention on Human Rights. It considers the role of Fatal Accident Inquiries in relation to inquiries such as Piper Alpha which are now instructed under the Inquiries Act 2005.

Although a Scottish process, the purpose of holding Fatal Accident Inquiries is replicated in other UK and international systems in investigating deaths where a comparative perspective is provided, focused mainly on the coroner and inquest system. The background is covered of cases where deaths occur in Scotland of those normally resident elsewhere as well as deaths occurring abroad which may now give rise to the holding of a Fatal Accident Inquiry in Scotland.

In recognising the importance of the Fatal Accident Inquiry system, the author includes examples of historical as well as current inquires to show how the nature of such deaths being investigated has changed over the years. She also seeks to inform the public on how to access such records principally through the National Libraries of Scotland.

This book aims to appeal to an audience beyond that of the legal practitioner who is involved in Fatal Accident Inquiries. With the diffidence of such a reader, it seems to me that the author admirably succeeds, drawing on her own experience in conducting a number of complex inquires, not only in providing useful information and context for those who find themselves appearing in court in connection with any such deaths, but also in providing, in a highly readable way, a wealth of information for interested members of the public; and that includes those affected by sudden death investigations or inquiries, but also more broadly, researchers, historians and comparative lawyers.

The author does not shy away from criticising and commenting on practice and policy and this book should be of interest to any reader who is interested in there being a sudden death and fatal accident inquiry system in Scotland which achieves equality, ensures accountability and demonstrates fairness – as well as fulfilling procedural and legal transparency when a death has occurred.

Gillian Mawdsley is to be commended for producing a book which is eminently readable, yet learned and which is insightful, yet highly practical.

Sheriff Norman McFadyen, CBE, FSA Scot
Edinburgh

Contents

Contents

Glossary of Terms

ACPOS   Association of Chief Police Officers in Scotland

COPFS   Crown Office and Procurator Fiscal Service

CPS   Crown Prosecution Service

CVF   Combined voice and flight data information

DIPLAR   Death in Prison Learning Audit and Review

ECHR   European Convention on Human Rights

EU   European Union

FAI   Fatal Accident Inquiry

FER   Forward Electronic Registrar

FOI   Freedom of Information

GMC   General Medical Council

HIS   Healthcare Improvement Scotland

HMCIPS   Her Majesty's Chief Inspector of Prisons for Scotland

JIS   Judicial Institute for Scotland

MCCD   Medical Certificate of the Cause of Death

MRHA   Medicines and Healthcare Products Regulatory Agency

NAME   National Association of Medical Examiners

NCIS   National Coroners Information System

NRS   National Records of Scotland

ONR   Office for Nuclear Regulation

OPC   Operational Performance Committee

PFD	Prevention of Further Death
PIR	Pre-inquest review
POW	Prisoner of War
SAE	Serious Adverse Events
SAER	Serious Adverse Event Review
SCA	Scottish Courts Administration
SCTS	Scottish Courts and Tribunals Service
SFIU	Scottish Fatalities Investigation Unit
SLAB	Scottish Legal Aid Board
SNOD	Specialist Nurse for Organ Donation
SPS	Scottish Prison Service
SUDI	Sudden Unexpected Death in Infancy
VIA	Victim Information and Advice
WHO	World Health Organisation

Table of Statutes

All references are to paragraph number

Table of Cases

All references are to paragraph number

Table of Fatal Accident Inquiries

All references are to paragraph number

OTHER INQUIRIES AND INQUESTS

Introduction

For every sudden death in Scotland, there are bereaved relatives. At the outset, no book discussing the system in Scotland for investigating sudden deaths can start without acknowledging the family of the deceased person and their role which lies at the centre of the fatal accident inquiry process. The need for society to learn from the death is often partly initiated by the families' determination to identify lessons to be learnt from the death 'so this does not happen to anyone else'. That need for society to learn and to move forward provides the motivation in exploring the unique Scottish system that deals with investigations into deaths. The families must not be forgotten in the process with sympathy expressed to them. Their dignity and respect at all times shines through.

My second acknowledgement lies with Ian HB Carmichael's seminal book on *Sudden Deaths and Fatal Accident Inquiries*. This was published in the wake of the Fatal Accidents and Sudden Deaths Inquiry (Scotland) Act 1976 and provided a detailed account of this unique Scottish system of investigating sudden deaths. It identified the importance of the process within the Scottish justice system. This book hopefully builds on his innovative work.

This book starts by considering sudden deaths in Scotland. The main focus considers how the Scottish justice system has evolved to deal with the formal investigation of deaths under the Fatal Accident Inquiries (FAIs) system. It considers the historical development of FAIs, a statutory administrative law hearing which has developed over time. It is now governed under the Inquiries into Fatal Accidents and Sudden Deaths etc. (Scotland) Act 2016 ('the 2016 Act'). That Act, along with the Rules[1] that were created to support the functioning of the process, provide the framework in terms of which FAIs are held today.

The FAI system can be seen to have two objectives. First, the State, in representing society, must be able to discharge its obligations in ascertaining how sudden deaths have occurred by means of investigations. Second, consideration is given to learning

---

1   Act of Sederunt (Fatal Accident Inquiry Rules) 2017.

how such deaths may or should be avoided in future. In other words, what lessons can be learnt to avoid a repeat of systemic failure, errors, omissions or otherwise that caused the death. In Scotland, the FAI system provides the means by which Scotland undertakes that process, complies with and discharges its obligations under Art 2 of the European Convention on Human Rights (ECHR) in respecting the right to life.

FAIs where the Crown initiates and leads the evidence in court have been in existence since the nineteenth century. As society has changed, so have FAIs to an extent in their form and certainly in the complexity of their subject matter, thinking now of the FAIs held into offshore North Sea operations, such as Piper Alpha and the terrorist bombing at Lockerbie. The style too has changed, as since 1976 juries are no longer required.

FAIs continue to examine deaths in custody and those arising during the course of employment. However, the range of the circumstances of other deaths examined through the FAIs process is open-ended, and varied: they include the deaths of German prisoners of war in 1946; in a hotel at Loch Maree from food poisoning in 1921; in a gas explosion at Clarkston in 1971; and in a road traffic accident with a bin lorry in Glasgow in 2014. The purpose of this book is not to focus purely on their history and specific FAIs, though a number of examples are discussed to illustrate how the system works. Their historical development is important in demonstrating why there is a system of holding investigations into deaths in Scotland and how that has evolved.

Inevitably, when FAIs are mentioned, there are names associated with disasters with which they are synonymous. These include examples such as Lockerbie, Ibrox, Dunblane, Piper Alpha and the Clutha pub. Important though as each of these FAIs definitely were, all deaths and indeed all FAIs when held are just as important, whether there are a number of victims or just one death. It is essential to investigate the cause of such deaths and to ensure the transparency of the investigation in relation to certain deaths. We need to recognise that investigation into a death comes at a time when families are grieving and is quite intrusive. There is a need to recognise why that investigation is necessary, or indeed justified, as the FAI process may help to make improvements to eliminate the conditions or circumstances that caused or directly led to the death.

For the FAI process to achieve these objectives, the process of selection of the deaths to be investigated that result in an FAI must be effective, so, that selection must be followed by successful evidence gathering and presentation processes in court, led principally by the Crown, and then by the other parties to the FAI. Then, there needs to be respect for the independence of the judge's conclusion issued in a determination as to the date, cause and the time of death. Judges issue their determination and, if appropriate, make recommendations. A robust and thorough investigation process must take place, with all parties involved in understanding and undertaking each of their significant roles effectively. The bereaved families need to be included in the process at all stages, whether by legal or their personal representation, and effective participation and/or presence.

The FAIs system is unique to Scotland. Other jurisdictions have their own form of investigations into deaths, where many follow the coronial inquest system derived from the system in England and Wales. These systems in England and Wales, other common law countries and Europe, are explored to provide a comparative perspective with Scotland. Scotland's examination of deaths within the FAIs system has much in common with that coronial process, though there are fundamental and significant differences, principally in the role of the Crown Office and Procurator Fiscal Service (COPFS). Though COPFS may be better known as the sole, independent criminal prosecution service in Scotland, their role in FAIs is crucial. They are in charge of the investigation into the death. The Lord Advocate as the head of COPFS is responsible for using their discretion as to holding discretionary FAIs in the public interest. Thereafter, COPFS is responsible for leading evidence in the FAI in court on behalf of the State. Any examination of the FAI process must fully consider that role and promote an understanding as to how that underpins the operation of the FAI system in Scotland.

Any examination of the FAI system must start with the death. Sudden, unexpected, unexplained and suspicious deaths fall to be reported to COPFS. Thereafter, investigation into certain types of deaths will inevitably, under the 2016 Act, ensure that an FAI takes place in due course. Other deaths, though reportable to COPFS, may require only an investigation to be undertaken and then conclude with no FAI process. These will not result in any FAI being held, though decisions on the circumstances of other deaths may result in further examination with the conclusion that a discretionary FAI should be held.

There is a need to recognise that there are a range of organisations operating within the FAI system. The medical profession certifies the death and may well go to provide expert medical evidence. They need to know when and to whom to report any death. As emphasised above, that is crucial to ensure the process works successfully from the start. If the death is not reported or the medical profession are unaware of the need to report a death, as seen in the FAI into the death of Norma Haq,[2] these delays may well seek to impede the successful administration of justice.

Inevitably, over time, the legislation, including the procedure and processes under which FAIs are held, has changed. The current position in relation to FAIs is examined, where criticism from a range of sources such as families, the public and MSPs can be seen, not least due to what appear to be long delays in undertaking FAIs. A much greater focus today can be identified on investigating the deaths of persons in custody that make up the majority of the FAIs currently being held. FAIs too have not been immune from the effects of the Covid-19 pandemic, with some being held remotely, using technology never previously envisaged to good effect in keeping the system of justice going.

---

2   A finding made in the FAI was to the effect that 'the death ought to have been reported to the procurator fiscal in terms of the literature "Death and the Procurator Fiscal"': 2011 FAI 34: *www.scotcourts.gov.uk/search-judgments/judgment?id=4c5386a6-8980-69d2-b500-ff0000d74aa7* [accessed on 14 March 2023].

The public interest and knowledge of FAIs has possibly increased with the incidence and reporting of some of the major FAIs mentioned earlier. However, that knowledge about FAIs tends to remain poor, perhaps not infrequently derived from TV dramas where reference is made wrongly to inquest verdicts applying to deaths arising in Scotland. For the families themselves, there is a lack of awareness and understanding of what an FAI may achieve, as well as what it cannot achieve under its relatively limited statutory framework. Locating information about investigation into deaths, the role of COPFS and the court processes at times appears to lack the cohesion and join-up to allow members of the public to find or locate the relevant information.

A framework exists which provides a mechanism under which to investigate deaths. That tends to be rather piecemeal in its approach, lacking consistency as to timescales and indeed how FAIs are conducted. There is an evolving practice for FAIs to rely on Joint Minutes, a procedure for agreeing evidence, rather than leading evidence through oral testimony of witnesses in court. That has reduced the court time that FAIs take, but does not permit on occasion as robust an examination process as such death investigations may require.

If the circumstances of the death are not fully investigated, there is the risk of a failure to make changes that eliminate or reduce the risk of another death. There are common factors seen in the rising number of deaths in prison, such as the incarceration of young persons, mental health issues and illicit drug consumption. This may support the holding of an inquiry into multiple deaths or a speedier resolution of the number of the outstanding FAIs.

However, before changes can be identified and made, at the outset, there is a need to understand the context of the role of FAIs – one which stresses their importance within Scotland's legal framework and how they should provide the means to meet the challenges of investigating deaths occurring within Scotland's dynamic and ever-changing environment. Much could be achieved by provision of better information for all, for the medical profession to the public, in a centralised, consistent manner and as an initial step, ensuring the public have greater awareness of what the death investigation process and what FAIs can achieve for the families and the public to make Scotland a safer place in the 21st century.

My thanks are due to Fran Fullarton of Edinburgh University Law Library, Fiona Homewood of the National Library of Scotland and the Scottish Courts and Tribunals Service for their help in locating and advice on sources. Thanks are also due for the support and advice of former colleagues, friends and family. Robert Shiels who originally inspired me in writing and provided essential historical research and context in relation to early FAIs, Fiona Millar and Michael Clancy OBE who provided helpful comments. Finally, to Robyn for her creative input, Michael for his stoicism and finally, Evan, 'non lawyer', without whom this book simply could not have existed.

Chapter 1

Reporting of Sudden Deaths in Scotland: Introduction

1. WHAT TRIGGERS A DEATH REPORT?

1.01 The public tend to be unaware of the death reporting system in Scotland until they are themselves involved in an actual death that is required to be reported. A number of organisations are involved in that process, such as the medical and legal profession whose roles and responsibilities will be covered subsequently. Meanwhile the public may already be familiar with the following type of news reports that appear in the media. These appear in relation to all manner of deaths and are in similar terms:

'Police said settled weather and longer hours of daylight were welcome signs for outdoor pursuits enthusiasts. But ... Police Scotland Mountain rescue coordinator said, "We would urge those seeking to venture into the outdoors to take extra care. Challenging winter conditions still prevail in the hills with large areas totally covered in snow and ice. Often these areas are completely unavoidable, and snow may be rock hard with a high likelihood of a fall unless crampons and an ice axe are carried and most importantly, the group has a knowledge in how and when to use them...... *Police said the death on Ben Nevis was not suspicious and a report would be submitted to the Procurator Fiscal.'*[1] (italics added)

1.02   This chapter will discuss why a report on this death would be sent to the procurator fiscal. There is an issue in that members of the public who are aware of the procurator fiscal commonly associate that role only with murders and criminal investigations/prosecutions. They do not fully appreciate that the procurator fiscal has much wider societal responsibilities extending well beyond criminal law.

1.03   There is of course an inevitable overlap between suspicious deaths and other deaths – as a death in a fire may not have been caused on purpose, but negligence by the owner may result in a prosecution for a death under the relevant legislation, such as health and safety. This type of death can be seen, by example, in the case of two students, James Fraser and Daniel Heron, who died in a tenement fire in Glasgow in March 1999, where there were no working smoke detectors, and the landlord was later to be prosecuted for perjury for the evidence given by him at the Fatal Accident Inquiry (FAI).[2]

1.04   The procurator fiscal's responsibilities therefore extend to inquiring into all sudden, suspicious, accidental or unexplained deaths in Scotland. The categories of death that fall to be reported (reportable deaths) to the procurator fiscal are outlined below.[3]

2.   WHAT ARE REPORTABLE DEATHS?

Reportable deaths: unnatural cause of death

1.05   These include any death which cannot be entirely attributed to natural causes (whether as the primary cause or a contributing factor). These include:

- suspicious deaths – ie where homicide cannot be ruled out;

---

1   BBC News, *www.bbc.co.uk/news/uk-scotland-highlands-islands-60675661* (accessed on 21 February 2023).
2   *www.scotcourts.gov.uk/search-judgments/judgment?id=72aa87a6-8980-69d2-b500-ff0000d74aa7* (accessed on 21 February 2023).
3   *https://view.officeapps.live.com/op/view.aspx?src=https%3A%2F%2Fwww.copfs.gov.uk %2Fmedia%2Fnzlpzgzh%2Freporting-deaths-information-for-medical-practitioners. docx&wdOrigin=BROWSELINK* (accessed on 21 February 2023).

- drug related deaths – including deaths due to adverse drug reactions that are reportable under the Medicines and Healthcare Products Regulatory Agency (MHRA) (Yellow Card Scheme);[4]
- accidental deaths (including those resulting from falls);
- deaths resulting from an accident in the course of employment;
- deaths of children from overlaying or suffocation;
- deaths where the circumstances indicate the possibility of suicide.

Reportable deaths: natural cause of death

1.06   Deaths are reported which may be due in whole or part to natural causes where the cause of death cannot be identified by a medical practitioner to the best of their knowledge and belief.

1.07   There is no need for mathematical certainty. Old age is accepted now as a cause of death but it is indicated that it should 'only be given as the sole cause of death in very limited circumstances'. There is no reason that the death should be investigated where the doctor can certify and that they have personally cared for the deceased over a long period (such as years or many months).[5] **Appendix 1** includes the death certificate of the Queen in September 2022 as an example showing the information which is provided and has been recorded. Natural causes include the following:

- deaths which occur as a result of neglect/fault;
- any death which may be related to a suggestion of neglect (including self-neglect) or exposure or where there is an allegation or possibility of fault on the part of another person, body or organisation;
- any death of a child which is a sudden, unexpected and unexplained perinatal death, where the body of a new-born is found, where the death may be categorised as a sudden unexpected death in infancy (SUDI), or which arises following a concealed pregnancy;
- any death of a child or young person under the age of 18 years who is 'looked after' by a local authority, including:
  (a) a child whose name is on the Child Protection Register;
  (b) a child who is subject to a supervision requirement made by a Children's Hearing;
  (c) a child who is subject to an order, authorisation or warrant made by a court or Children's Hearing (eg a child being accommodated by a local

---

4   There is a need to report suspected side effects to medicines, vaccines, e-cigarettes, medical device incidents, defective or falsified (fake) products to ensure safe and effective use: *https://yellowcard. mhra.gov.uk/* (accessed on 21 February 2023).

5   The Queen's death was certified as natural causes: *www.bbc.co.uk/news/uk-63078676* (accessed on 21 February 2023).

authority in foster care, kinship care, residential accommodation or secure accommodation);

(d) a child who is otherwise being accommodated by a local authority.

Reportable deaths: deaths from notifiable industrial/infectious diseases

1.08   The death is due to a notifiable industrial disease or disease acquired as a consequence of the deceased's occupation in reference to reg 8 (occupational diseases) of the Reporting of Injuries, Diseases and Dangerous Occurrences Regulations 2013, SI 2013/1471.

1.09   These include those relating to asbestosis, mesothelioma and asbestos-related lung cancer or reg 9 (exposure to carcinogens, mutagens and biological agents) of the Reporting of Injuries, Diseases and Dangerous Occurrences Regulations 2013, SI 2013/1471.[6]

1.10   Deaths resulting from asbestos are important in Scotland with its extensive history of shipbuilding. Many families do not appreciate that these form a category of reportable deaths. Those who have been diagnosed with an asbestos-related disease may be unaware of a former employer's potential liability for causing it due to exposure to asbestos, even though exposure may well have occurred some considerable time ago.[7]

- Deaths which pose an acute and serious risk to public health due to either a notifiable infectious disease or organism in terms of Sch 1 to the Public Heath (Scotland) Act 2008[8] or any other infectious disease or syndrome.

---

6   SI 2013/1471. Chapter 10 of *The Reporting of Deaths to the Procurator Fiscal Information and Guidance to Medical Practitioners updated May 2019* (*www.copfs.gov.uk/publications/reporting-deaths/* (accessed on 21 February 2023)) refers to an acquisition of an industrial disease following asbestos exposure, such as asbestosis, mesothelioma and asbestos-related lung cancer, as these may give rise to a civil claim for compensation. A number of industrial diseases, including asbestosis, mesothelioma and asbestos-related lung cancer can be accurately diagnosed in life. If offered as a cause of death, this can be accepted without a post mortem examination. If no conclusive diagnosis is made during the patient's life, the procurator fiscal will instruct a post mortem examination to establish the cause of death and to preserve the necessary evidence, in the event that the nearest relatives wish to pursue a claim in relation to the industrial disease caused by previous asbestos exposure. The doctor who reports the death must complete Pt 3 of the Mesothelioma Pro Forma: *www.sehd.scot.nhs.uk/cmo/CMO(2014)07.pdf* (accessed on 21 February 2023).
7   *www.clydesideactiononasbestos.org.uk/information-for-the-medical-profession/posthumous-claims* (accessed on 21 February 2023).
8   *www.legislation.gov.uk/asp/2008/5/schedule/1* (accessed on 21 February 2023).

1.11   Such deaths include the 1996 e-coli outbreak in Lanarkshire where an FAI was held into the circumstances of the 21 deaths caused by eating infected butcher meat.[9]

Reportable deaths: deaths under medical or dental care[10]

1.12   These include any death:

- where the circumstances of which are the subject of concern to, or complaint by, the nearest relatives of the deceased about the medical treatment given to the deceased, with a suggestion that the medical treatment may have contributed to the death of the patient;
- where the circumstances of which might indicate fault or neglect on the part of medical staff or where medical staff have concerns regarding the circumstances of death;
- where the circumstances of which indicate that the failure of a piece of equipment may have caused or contributed to the death;
- where the circumstances of which are likely to be subject to a Significant Adverse Event Review (SAER) defined by Healthcare Improvement Scotland as 'an event that could have caused, or did result in, harm to people or groups of people';[11]
- where, at any time, a death certificate has been issued and a complaint is later received by a doctor or by the Health Board, which suggests that an act or omission by medical staff caused or contributed to the death;
- caused by the withdrawal of life sustaining treatment or other medical treatment to a patient in a permanent vegetative state (whether with or without the authority of the Court of Session);[12]
- which occurs in circumstances raising issues of public safety.

1.13   There are many deaths reported under this category which do not merit further investigation especially where the Hospital Trust has held a Significant Adverse Event Review which have brought in the necessary changes to their

---

9   Determination by Graham L Cox, QC, Sheriff Principal of Sheriffdom of South Strathclyde Dumfrles and Galloway into the E-coli 0 157 Fatal Accident Inquiry, *https://mars.northlanarkshire.gov.uk/ egenda/images/att10103.pdf* (accessed on 21 February 2023).
10   The *Reporting Deaths to the Procurator Fiscal. Information and Guidance to Medical Practitioners* (updated May 2019), Ch 9 refers to most deaths under medical care representing an unfortunate outcome where every reasonable care has been taken. However, some deaths associated with the provision of medical care may involve fault or negligence on the part of medical or paramedical staff and may give rise to questions of public safety and, in rare cases, may be associated with criminality. Medical care includes surgical, anaesthetic, nursing or other care/treatment, whether provided in a healthcare or non-healthcare setting.
11   *www.healthcareimprovementscotland.org/our_work/governance_and_assurance/management of udverse_events/national_framework.aspx* (accessed on 21 February 2023).
12   *Law Hospital NHS Trust v Lord Advocate* 1996 SLT 848.

processes and procedures. However there are a range of FAIs which examine the background of medical care such as the FAI into the death of Sharman Weir, a maternal death from pre-eclampsia.[13] **Appendix 2 Part C** includes an example of a medical related FAI.

Reportable deaths: deaths while subject to compulsory treatment under mental health legislation

1.14   These include:

- Any death of a person who was, at the time of death, detained or liable to be detained under the Mental Health (Care and Treatment) (Scotland) Act 2003 or Pt VI of the Criminal Procedure (Scotland) Act 1995 or subject to a community based compulsory treatment order or compulsion order.

- Any death not falling into any of the foregoing categories where the circumstances surrounding the death may cause public anxiety.

Reportable deaths: deaths in legal custody

1.15   Any death of a person subject to legal custody must be reported. This includes (but is not restricted to) all persons:

- detained in prison;
- arrested or detained in police offices;
- in the course of transportation to and from prisons, police offices or otherwise beyond custodial premises, such as a prisoner who has been admitted to hospital or a prisoner on home leave.

1.16   These deaths also lead to the holding of a mandatory FAI, as is discussed later (in **Chapter 7**). There should not be any delay in the reporting of such deaths, though the FAI into the death of Thomas Lamb Cooper Campbell left an unexplained gap between the death occurring on 24 November 2019 and the reporting of the death to the procurator fiscal on 5 December 2019.[14] This gap in time seems somewhat surprising, but more surprising that it did not merit comment in the FAI. The timely reporting of such deaths in custody is important and sheriffs should be aware of, and query, any gap in time to satisfy the issue of public concern.

---

13   *www.scotcourts.gov.uk/search-judgments/judgment?id=13c286a6-8980-69d2-b500-ff0000d74aa7* (accessed on 21 February 2023).
14   [2022] FAI 13.

3.   DEATHS WHICH DO NOT NEED TO BE REPORTED

1.17   In the COPFS guidance,[15] they state that the categories of reportable deaths are non-exhaustive. That is the right approach, as where there is any doubt the death should be reported. What COPFS has produced is their guidance that sets out where some common misunderstandings may exist as to certain circumstances of death that are required to be reported. These include that:[16]

- the death occurred within 24 hours (or any other timescale) of admission to hospital;
- the death occurred within 24 hours (or any other timescale) of an operation;
- the deceased, who had a terminal illness, died earlier than expected;
- the deceased had not been seen by a GP for some time; or
- a consultant has instructed that the death be reported without specifying the reasons why.

1.18   This illustrates why it is so important that the reporting of the death is undertaken by the best person qualified to do so. Where that role is delegated, questions may not be able to be competently answered, resulting in the decision that a post mortem should be carried out. That uses resources and time, as well as being an intrusion to the family where that post mortem may not have been required had the death been appropriately reported and the relevant questions answered. This forms part of effective communications from when the death occurs to the family and the procurator fiscal. That need for effective communication is echoed throughout the reporting process that follows. The medical profession need to be aware of the role of the procurator fiscal. This should be included in their basic medical education so they recognise when to report a death. For example, where a death may be due to a medical mishap or potentially so, subject to a complaint from relatives:

'Perceived poor communications (and understanding) with medical professionals [is required] from the outset. That stresses the importance of the initial communication with and the disclosure of information to the deceased's relatives immediately after death.'[17]

15   *Reporting Deaths to the Procurator Fiscal. Information and Guidance to Medical Practitioners* (updated May 2019), *www.copfs.gov.uk/publications/reporting-deaths/* (accessed on 21 February 2023).
16   *Reporting Deaths to the Procurator Fiscal. Information and Guidance to Medical Practitioners* (updated May 2019), 4. Common misconceptions. *www.copfs.gov.uk/publications/reporting-deaths/* (accessed on 21 February 2023).
17   Mawdsley, *Fatal Accident Inquiries: Raising awareness of their role in relation to the medical profession in Scotland.* J R Coll Physicians Edinb 2016; 46: 254–9.

4.   PROCESS OF REPORTING A DEATH

1.19   A medical practitioner should identify a cause of death to the best of their knowledge and belief. As highlighted above, absolute certainty as to the certification of the cause of death is not required. However, the consultant in charge, rather than the junior doctor, should report in complex cases as they are the person familiar with the facts. The reporting should not be left to a junior doctor because they happened to be on duty 'in the morning' but were not previously involved.

That is in line too with the medical practitioner's responsibility to complete the Medical Certificate of the Cause of Death (MCCD or Form 11) accurately to the best of their knowledge and belief. Guidance is issued periodically by Healthcare Improvement Scotland as to how such forms should be completed.[18] A review process outlined in section 5 below has now been put in place.

Once the cause of death has been ascertained, the death certificate can be issued in accordance with s 24 of the Registration of Births, Deaths and Marriages (Scotland) Act 1965 as amended by the Certification of Death (Scotland) Act 2011. The MCCD provides the permanent legal record of the fact of death. It enables the family to register the death and to make arrangements for the disposal of the body. It is also used to allow the deceased's estate to be settled. It provides a record of causes of death for public health reasons and various other statistical purposes.[19]

1.20   Deaths prior to certification are often likely to be discussed with the procurator fiscal's office to explain the likely cause of death and to clarify the absence of any suspicious circumstances. This allows the death certificate to be issued with no post-mortem examination then being required.

1.21   There is advice available from the COPFS to doctors in *Reporting deaths to the Procurator Fiscal. Information and Guidance for Medical Practitioners.*[20] This may be somewhat out of date but appears to be the only publicly available guidance accessible on the internet. It outlines when doctors should report any deaths which fall into the categories of reportable deaths outlined above. This information should be provided to doctors as part of their undergraduate training and repeated when they are doctors in training in Scotland, bearing in mind that many doctors will not have

---

18   *www.healthcareimprovementscotland.org/our_work/governance_and_assurance/ death_certification/questions_and_answers.aspx#:~:text=What%20is%20death%20 certification%3F,including%20the%20cause%20of%20death)* (accessed on 21 February 2023).

19   '1.2.3 Information from death certificates is used to measure the relative contributions of different diseases to mortality in Scotland. Statistical information on the underlying causes of death is important for monitoring the health of the population; designing and evaluating public health interventions; recognising priorities for medical research and health services; planning health services and assessing the effectiveness of those services. Death certificate data is extensively used in research into the health effects of exposure to a wide range of risk factors through the environment, work, medical and surgical care, psychosocial, and other sources': *www.gov.scot/publications/ certification-death-scotland-act-2011-statutory-guidance/* (accessed on 21 February 2023).

20   *www.copfs.gov.uk/publications/reporting-deaths/* (accessed on 21 February 2023)

qualified in Scotland or be aware of the role of the procurator fiscal. Their training should be refreshed periodically so they are kept up to date as to their responsibilities

1.22 The failure to report a death timeously was the focus of the FAI held into the death of Norma Haq.[21] Her death was not reported at the time to the procurator fiscal. The sheriff's determination under s 6(1)(e) of the Fatal Accidents and Sudden Deaths Inquiry (Scotland) Act 1976 (now repealed) outlined that 'the death ought to have been reported to the procurator fiscal in terms of the literature "Death and the Procurator Fiscal". That literature ought to be sent by the [Scottish Government] to managers of private hospitals in addition to NHS hospitals. Management in NHS and private hospitals should ensure that all doctors treating patients are aware of the terms of 'Death' and the 'Procurator Fiscal.'[22] Whether the review process that now exists would have helped avoid that type of case occurring is unknown, but that review does provide an additional layer of scrutiny.

1.23 Deaths which require discussion with the procurator fiscal however should be differentiated from deaths where the cause of death can at least initially be ascertained. Some deaths will always require a post-mortem examination because the cause of death cannot be ascertained. It is important to note that even after a post-mortem examination is completed the cause of death may still remain unascertained. There may be a requirement for toxicology and other investigations still to be carried out. Some deaths still remain unascertained even after the FAI is held. Paragraph 4 of the FAI into the death of Tammi Bruce states, in terms of s 26(2)(c) of the Inquiries into Fatal Accidents and Sudden Deaths etc. (Scotland) Act 2016, that the death was due to an unascertained cause or causes.[23]

5. REVIEW OF MEDICAL CERTIFICATES OF CAUSE OF DEATH

Background to the review

1.24 The purpose of the Certification of Death (Scotland) Act 2011 was to update the certification of death process. Scotland's burial and cremation legislation was by then over 100 years old and did not then reflect 21st century life. There was also increased sensitivity over the death certification given the problems that had arisen in relation to the case of Dr Harold Shipman[24] in England and Wales. The Shipman Inquiry Third Report under Dame Janet Smith, published in 2003, considered in depth the death certification processes and the investigation of deaths by coroners which

---

21 [2011] FAI 34, *www.scotcourts.gov.uk/search-judgments/judgment?id=4c5386a6-8980-69d2-b500-ff0000d74aa7* (accessed on 21 February 2023).

22 2011 FAI 34.

23 [2020] FAI 12.

24 *The Shipman Inquiry,* Third Report, Cm 5854, *https://assets.publishing.service.gov.uk/government/uploads/system/uploads/attachment_data/file/273227/5854.pdf* (accessed on 21 February 2023).

of course applied only in England and Wales. However, it recommended a need to improve public health information and strengthen clinical governance in relation to deaths. These conclusions provided some emphasis as a 'driver for change'[25] behind the review that was subsequently undertaken in Scotland. Guidance on the operation of the 2011 Act has been produced by Scottish Government. This also refers to the roles undertaken by other parties involved in the process of the review of deaths. This includes the functions of the National Records of Scotland, local authority registrars, cremation and burial authorities, funeral directors and NHS Education for Scotland.[26]

1.25   Specifically, the 2011 Act provides that, where concerns with the death have been identified, the review service can carry out a review of a series of certificates written by an individual certifying doctor. That can be in relation to a specified number of certificates or for an agreed length of time which is known as a 'For cause' review.[27] This directly addressed the sort of issues that arose with the Shipman case where Dr Shipman had certified deaths of a number of elderly patients who had been healthy shortly before their death and their encounter with him. There had been no inquiry conducted into the number of similar types of death certification arising in the area in which Dr Shipman operated.

1.26   What now exists in Scotland is a single system of independent and effective scrutiny applicable to deaths that runs parallel to an extent to the procurator fiscal's processes outlined above. These deaths that fall under a review do not require a procurator fiscal investigation.

1.27   The review process has improved the quality and accuracy of the MCCDs along with the provision of better public health information. It has strengthened clinical governance in relation to deaths. As highlighted above, the Death Certification Review Service is organised under Healthcare Improvement Scotland.[28]

The review process

1.28   As well as 'For cause' reviews, a random proportionate number of MCCDs now fall to be reviewed[29] as part of that process of assessing the quality of information, that is being provided by the medical profession. The content of the MCCDs are reviewed, by considering whether the information that is supplied is accurate. It also considers governance so that relatives can understand what has happened to their deceased relative.

---

25   Paragraph 17 of the Certification of Death (Scotland) Bill Policy Memorandum.
26   *Certification of Death (Scotland) Act 2011: statutory guidance* (19 August 2015), *www.gov.scot/ publications/certification-death-scotland-act-2011-statutory-guidance/* (accessed on 21 February 2023).
27   No 'For cause' reviews were undertaken by the service in 2020/2021.
28   *www.healthcareimprovementscotland.org/about_us.aspx* (accessed on 21 February 2023).
29   Certification of Death (Scotland) Act 2011, s 24A.

1.29   The review is undertaken by an appointed medical reviewer within a specific timescale, depending on the nature of the review that has been undertaken. There are two levels of review:

- Level 1 covers the vast majority of reviews. These involve checking the MCCD and a discussion being undertaken with the certifying doctor. These reviews are expected to be completed within one working day.
- Level 2 covers fewer reviews. These involve an additional, more detailed review of the clinical information provided about the death of the deceased and the issue of the MCCD. This may involve discussions with another doctor or a clinical member of the medical team with knowledge of the case and/or access to the clinical records of the deceased. These reviews are expected to be completed within three working days. There are powers provided to the medical examiner so that they can 'require any person who is able, in the opinion of the medical reviewer, to produce relevant documents (including health records), to do so.'[30]

1.30   The medical reviewer may report any death to the procurator fiscal. They can also report a number of deaths, presumably if they give rise to similar causes of concern. This might occur where there is any suspicion of criminality having occurred in Scotland. Presumably this would include, though not stated, where there was a public interest in looking into these deaths and where criminal prosecution was not appropriate.

1.31   The cases for review are selected at random when the registration of death is made by the informant in the registrar's office, during or following the input of the applicable MCCD details into the Forward Electronic Registrar (FER)[31] or when the electronic MCCD is transmitted to the FER.

1.32   There is provision too for an interested person review[32] to be undertaken which provides a further measure of public and professional reassurance. It should be noted that certain conditions operate in relation to such deaths that can then fall to be reviewed. Reviews cannot be conducted where the death pre-dated the implementation of the 2011 Act. They have to be requested within three years of the date of death and these reviews can only be conducted where the case has not already been reviewed by the procurator fiscal. These are therefore rare occurrences.

1.33   These reviews need to be raised by the interested person directly with the medical examiners, rather than via the registrar. There is a duty to inform the Registrar General in the case of any such review being undertaken by the medical reviewers. It is important to understand that an interested person review request is a

---

30   Certification of Death (Scotland) Act 2011, s 14.
31   The registrar enters the relevant information into the National Records of Scotland registration system.
32   Certification of Death (Scotland) Act 2011, s 14.

request for the review of the contents of the MCCD. It is not about any inquiry into the care provided to the deceased prior to their death.

1.34   Such concerns over care prior to death should be referred to the appropriate hospital trust. In these circumstances, such deaths could give rise to the holding of an FAI where it was deemed appropriate by the Lord Advocate. If the medical reviewer considers that an application for an interested person review is vexatious, they have the power to reject such a request. It is expected that interested person reviews will be completed within a maximum of 15 working days.

1.35   Where an MCCD has been the subject of random selection, a medical reviewer can agree to allow the registration of the death to proceed before the review is complete. The registrar will complete the registration and issue the Certificate of Registration of Death (Form 14). The body can then be released, and the funeral can proceed whilst the formal Level 1 or Level 2 review, as originally randomly selected, continues to take place. If the body is released, this means that no post-mortem examination would be possible in the future.

1.36   Arrangements should be in place for the rare situations where there is a need and a clear rationale for a funeral to proceed within a specific timescale, and where that timescale may not be met if the standard review procedure is followed. A 'Request to Not Stay' Registration form (advance registration application form) must be used by the informants, requesting that registration not be stayed. Once a request has been made it is for the medical reviewer to make a decision as to whether or not to allow registration to continue before the review is completed, based on the information available in the form, from the MCCD and from any other sources they consider appropriate.

There are three categories of circumstances where not staying registration might be appropriate. These include:

- religious or cultural reasons: some religious traditions require burial within 24 hours, and some communities have a tradition of burial within three days;
- compassionate reasons: where the death of a child under 16 years or a neo-natal death is involved, a delay may cause significant additional distress;
- administrative or practical reasons: where the family does not reside in Scotland and the deceased is to be transferred to another part of the UK or to international destinations for a funeral.

It is expected that the decision as to whether or not to stay registration should be made within two hours of the request. If the medical reviewer agrees to allow the registration to proceed before the review is complete, the registrar will complete the registration and issue the Certificate of Registration of Death (Form 14). The body is then released. The funeral will proceed while the formal Level 1 or Level 2 review, as originally randomly selected, continues to take place. Any further examination of the deceased, if considered necessary at a later stage, such as a post-mortem, would not then be possible.

1.37   The medical reviewer will then consider whether or not to stay registration.

1.38   In conclusion, a range of mechanisms for review of death certification exist, all of which are designed to enhance patient safety. To support the enforcement of the 2011 Act, an offence was created under s 25 of the 2011 Act which arises if any persons having charge of a cemetery or crematorium were to dispose of a body without the required documentation.

6. INVESTIGATION INTO DEATHS OCCURRING OUTSIDE SCOTLAND

1.39   In deaths that occurred outside the UK, the document required for disposal of the body will be a certificate issued by a medical reviewer. Anyone wishing to arrange the burial or cremation of a body in such a case must apply to the medical reviewer. A medical reviewer must, on the request of a relevant person such as the next of kin or a funeral director, determine whether the documentation relating to an individual's death is in order.

1.40   Medical reviewers check whether the relevant documents that are submitted are authentic and equivalent to the documentation which would be required to dispose of the body of a person who died in Scotland. If they are, they will issue a certificate of death. Unless requested to do otherwise by the medical reviewer, certified copies of the original documents can be provided instead of the original documents. Any copies should be certified by a third party in a professional capacity, presumably similar to the notarisation process.[33]

1.41   The medical reviewer will carry out a level 2 review of the documentation related to the death of the individual who has died abroad. Where the deceased does not have a care record held within Scotland, it will not be possible to carry out a level 2 review. The medical reviewer would then contact the deceased's GP elsewhere in the UK and/or the Foreign and Commonwealth Office or equivalent to obtain the relevant information.

1.42   Medical reviewers have the additional function of ensuring that it is safe to cremate the body of anyone who dies overseas and who is to be cremated in Scotland. Where it is determined that it is not safe for the deceased to be cremated, a certificate of disposal specifying burial as a requirement will be issued. In all cases of repatriation, medical reviewers will check whether the body of the deceased poses a risk to public health and provide appropriate advice.

---

33   Certified copies must be signed and dated by a person described above and should be a true copy of the original. To certify, the applicant should take the photocopied and original copy of the certificate or document to the person certifying who should write 'Certified to be a true copy of the original seen by me', sign and date it, print their name under the signature and add their occupation, address and telephone number.

1.43   The 2011 Act includes provisions which enable medical reviewers to assist in arranging for a post-mortem examination to be carried out on an individual who has died outside the UK and where a cause of death cannot be ascertained, despite reasonable attempts to do so. A request for post-mortem examinations on individuals who meet the criteria set down in s 19(1) of the 2011 Act should be made on the specified form (the Request for Post-Mortem Form)[34].

7.   CROSS-BORDER DEATHS AND TRANSFERS

1.44   Where a death is registered in another part of the UK, and the deceased is then moved to Scotland for the funeral, that cause of death will have already been reviewed in that country. Further review in Scotland will therefore not be required.

1.45   Where a death is registered in Scotland, and the deceased is to be moved to another UK country for the funeral, the MCCD can be subject to review at either level or will not have been selected for review. The registrar will complete the registration and issue the Certificate of Registration of Death (Form 14). Once Form 14 is issued by the registrar, the informant or relatives can make arrangements with the relevant funeral director for the transfer of the deceased to other parts of the UK.

1.46   Where it is determined that it is not safe for the deceased to be cremated, a certificate of disposal specifying burial will be issued. In all cases of repatriation, medical reviewers will check whether the body of the deceased poses a risk to public health and advise any relevant person as necessary.

8.   MEDICAL CERTIFICATION OF THE CAUSE OF DEATH REVIEW REPORTING REQUIREMENTS

1.47   Section 23 of the 2011 Act provides that the senior medical reviewer is responsible for preparing and sending an Annual Report to Scottish Ministers for each financial year on the activities of the medical reviewers and to provide such further information as Scottish Ministers may require.[35] They also arrange for the Report to be published. Under s 23(3) of the 2011 Act Scottish Ministers have reserved regulation-making powers to make further provision regarding the information to be contained in the report information, require more frequent reports and specify other persons to whom such a report should be sent. That report includes a summary of key monitoring information, an analysis of any trends or issues identified and actions taken, and proposals with action plans for the improvement and developments in the service for the coming year.

---

34   The Certification of Death (Scotland) Act 2011 (Post-Mortem Examinations – Death Outwith United Kingdom) Regulations 2015 (SSI 2015/165).
35   Healthcare Improvement Scotland Death Certification Review Service Annual Report 2020–2021.

1.48   In the Death Certification Review Service Annual Report: 2020–2021,[36] 4,364 deaths were subject to randomised reviews including:

- hybrid level 1 (65%);[37]
- standard level 1 and level 2 (32.7%);
- advance registration reviews (0.9%).

Of the deaths reported, 68.3% of these were approved, as the MCCD appeared to be substantially in order. 31.7% were declined. These were declined either because the review was already complete or was nearing completion and the death was required to be reported to the procurator fiscal.

1.49   In 2020–21, MCCDs were deemed 'not in order' if the certifying doctor made a clinical or administrative error. A total of 904 (20.4%) of all MCCD reviews were found to be 'not in order'. 69% were found to have a clinical closure error recorded. The most common recorded was that the cause of death was too vague (at 55%).

1.50   Some of the deaths under review were required to be formally reported to the procurator fiscal. Where it became apparent that the death fell within the criteria for reporting to the procurator fiscal, as outlined above, the certifying doctor then made a formal report.

1.51   The average number of deaths identified by the review service, which failed to be reported to the procurator fiscal, remained at around 2.4% per month. Concerns were expressed about that failure. There was also duplication in that 50 MCCDs were received for review when deaths had already been reported to the procurator fiscal. The certifying doctor had not completed the MCCD correctly.

---

36   *www.healthcareimprovementscotland.org/our_work/governance_and_assurance/death_ certification/dcrs_annual_report_2020-2021.aspx* (accessed on 21 February 2023).

37   This was in response to the Covid-19 pandemic. Changes from the 'normal' service were put in place to support families and give public reassurance, Health Boards and reduce pressure on acute clinical staff and certifying doctors, COPFS to manage reports on deaths from Covid-19, registrars to manage the significant increase in death registrations, and funeral directors to allow funerals to proceed quickly. Following a period of suspension at the start of the pandemic, a 'hybrid' Level 1 review was implemented in May 2020. The 'hybrid' review allowed the medical reviewer to scrutinise the Key Information Summary (KIS), reducing the requirement for hospital and general practice administrative staff sending patient medical records, supported certifying doctors by agreeing minor changes to MCCDs verbally and the service medical reviewer confirming these with the local authority registrars, and continued to offer escalation to a full level 2 review. From 31 August 2020 to 23 November 2020, the service returned to normal reviews. At the request of Scottish Government, whilst using the 'hybrid' review, changes were made to the number of MCCDs selected for review. This varied from 4% at the peak of the pandemic, to 12% when the number of deaths being reported had reduced significantly. *www.healthcareimprovementscotland.org/ our_work/governance_and_assurance/death_certification/dcrs_annual_report_2020-2021.aspx* (accessed on 21 February 2023).

1.52   Review numbers for 'interested persons' review were low, comprising eight in 2020–21. Six were received from members of the public and two were registrar referrals.

1.53   The analysis conducted in the review report provides useful information on the certification of death processes and seeks to provide some public reassurance.

1.54   In conclusion, there may be ways in which the information regarding the deaths which are required to be reported to the procurator fiscal should be updated annually. There could also be a useful review of the range of circumstances where doctors appear to have been unaware that a death should be reported. This could usefully be factored in at all levels of training, though it is appreciated that Healthcare Improvement Scotland do issue guidance, the most recent of which was September 2022.[38]

9.   COVID-19 DEATHS

1.55   Consideration of the mechanisms for reporting of deaths cannot ignore the recent Covid-19 pandemic. On 13 May 2020, the Lord Advocate indicated that in view of public anxiety, two categories of deaths should be reported:

- All Covid-19, or presumed Covid-19, deaths where the deceased may have contracted the virus in the course of their employment or occupation (on the basis that the deaths of care home workers, front-line National Health Service (NHS) staff, public transport employees and emergency services personnel were included in the reporting requirements which links in with the scope of the mandatory nature of FAIs in the course of employment).
- All Covid-19, or presumed Covid-19, deaths where the deceased was resident in a care home when the virus was contracted.

1.56   Interestingly this did not include deaths of prisoners in custody from Covid-19. This is discussed in full in **Chapter 6**: Deaths in Custody.

1.57   This guidance represented a change in position from the Lord Advocate. Previously, they had only required reporting if there was some other substantive reason for reporting the death. That had been consistent in the past with other outbreaks of infectious diseases. These deaths had not been reported in order to reduce the demands on the medical profession and to respect the overall integrity of the system for reporting and investigating of deaths.

1.58   This decision was also retrospective, in that deaths falling within these two categories that arose prior to May 2020 were now to be reported. The effect was also to ensure that such deaths could be investigated, which partly provided the precursor

---

38   *www.sehd.scot.nhs.uk/cmo/CMO(2022)33.pdf* (accessed on 21 February 2023).

and evidence base for the public inquiry which is to be conducted in Scotland into Covid-19 deaths.[39]

1.59   In conclusion to including a specific category of deaths related to the Covid-19 pandemic, it is helpful to remember why changes to the reporting of deaths were required. The main reason was to preserve relevant data for the purposes of accurate record keeping to ensure that the implications and effect of the pandemic could be considered in due course. It was seen to be a volatile and changing landscape.

1.60   The effect of the original changes was still for deaths to be registered in Scotland within eight days of their occurrence unless the death was one to be reported to the procurator fiscal. Healthcare Improvement Scotland recognised that prompt and accurate certification of death was 'essential and crucially important' since the MCCD provided the family with an explanation of how and why their relative died.

1.61   The doctor issuing the MCCD is required to state what they believed to be the most likely cause of death based on their knowledge of the patient, the events surrounding the death, the medical history and the result of any investigations that were available. There was a lack of comprehensive Covid-19 swab testing of individuals in the community, so an emphasis was placed on the clinical accuracy of the cause of death based on the doctors' clinical opinion.[40]

1.62   Reflective too of the changing nature of the Covid-19 pandemic, the Lord Advocate has since directed that Covid-19-related care home and worker deaths are no longer required to be reported to the procurator fiscal.[41]

1.63   What exactly the Covid-19 inquiries being conducted in both the UK and Scotland will reveal about the reporting of deaths will not be ascertained for some considerable time.

1.64   As at December 2022, COPFS advised that they have received over 5,500 death reports.[42]

39   Scottish Government, Publication – factsheet, *Covid-19 Inquiry*, *www.gov.scot/publications/Covid-19-inquiry/* (accessed 21 February 2023).
40   Joint statement from Care Quality Commission, General Medical Council and Healthcare Improvement Scotland on death certification during the Covid-19 pandemic, *www.healthcareimprovementscotland.org/our_work/governance_and_assurance/death_certification/Covid-19_useful_information.aspx* (accessed 21 February 2023).
41   Scottish Government, 'Updated Guidance to Medical Practitioners For Death Certification and Reporting Deaths to the Procurator Fiscal During the Recovery From Covid-19 Disease Pandemic' (21 December 2022), *www.sehd.scot.nhs.uk/cmo/CMO(2022)40.pdf* (accessed 21 February 2023).
42   Scottish Government, 'Updated Guidance to Medical Practitioners For Death Certification and Reporting Deaths to the Procurator Fiscal During the Recovery From Covid-19 Disease Pandemic' (21 December 2022), *www.sehd.scot.nhs.uk/cmo/CMO(2022)40.pdf* (accessed 21 February 2023).

10.   WHERE TO REPORT A DEATH IN SCOTLAND

1.65   When a death is reportable, it now falls to be reported to the Scottish Fatalities Investigation Unit (SFIU)[43] branch of COPFS. This was set up as a specialist unit, whereas historically deaths were reported to the local procurator fiscal's office. The SFIU has the responsibility for receiving reports of the relevant deaths occurring in Scotland. It is divided into three areas shown below.

1.66   Scottish Fatalities Investigation Unit Teams and Contact Details

- ■ North
- ■ East
- □ West

- SFIU NORTH, telephone: 0300 020 2387, email: SFIUNorth@copfs.gov.uk
- SFIU EAST, telephone: 0300 020 3702, email: SFIUEast@copfs.gov.uk
- SFIU WEST, telephone: 0300 020 1798, email: SFIUWest@copfs.gov.uk.

---

43   Crown Office and Procurator Fiscal Service (last updated 23 January 2023), *www.copfs.gov.uk/ investigating-deaths/our-role-in-investigating-deaths#:~:text=Within%20COPFS%2C%20the%20 Scottish%20Fatalities,and%20West%20(SFIU%20West)* (accessed on 21 February 2023).

1.67   Within the SFIU, procurator fiscal deputes (PFD) deal with the reports. Once a death has been reported, the procurator fiscal is legally responsible for the death until such time they decide that the body is cleared.

1.68   All reportable deaths as outlined above must be notified to the procurator fiscal as soon as possible after their occurrence and before any steps are taken to issue a death certificate. If a death certificate has been issued to the family and the procurator fiscal declines to accept the cause of death, this certificate will have to be retrieved from the family, which could cause distress. Death reports will be made during office hours, though there is an out of hours service which can deal with emergency reports, usually only utilised where religious rites are required to be observed.

11.   WHAT HAPPENS ONCE A REPORT IS MADE TO THE PROCURATOR FISCAL

1.69   As discussed above, the person making the report of the death to the procurator fiscal should be able to give all relevant details and information as to the deceased's medical background and the circumstances of the death. The type of information required by the Notification of Death Form (eF5) is shown in **Appendix 1**. From then, there are a range of possible actions for the procurator fiscal to take.

To accept the death certificate as to the cause of a reportable death

1.70   This will arise where the procurator fiscal is satisfied as to the medical background that has been provided and the circumstances of death that have been reported. The death will have occurred due to natural causes. The death will not be required to be investigated further.

Example

The deceased had complained of recent chest pains. They had a history of angina and were on relevant medication. A family member saw them in the afternoon when they were going upstairs for a rest. When they did not appear, the family investigated and found them in bed unresponsive. The local GP attended and was prepared to issue a death certificate, recording the death as a myocardium infarction. There were no suspicious circumstances or medical concerns expressed from the family as to the cause of death. The death certificate is accepted.

To issue consent to a hospital (non-PF) post mortem examination

1.71   There may be some circumstances where a reportable death that took place in hospital is due to natural causes but has not been certified. The doctor may seek a hospital post mortem examination for the sole purpose of achieving a more accurate certification. Consent from the nearest relatives will be required. The cause of death will be provided to the procurator fiscal following the hospital's post mortem examination.

Example

There are no family complaints about the medical treatment. The circumstances have been fully explained to the relatives who have consented to a post mortem examination. The post mortem examination is completed and the cause of death ascertained. The death certificate is accepted.

To request a police report

1.72   Where the cause of death has not been ascertained or further information is required, a police report will be requested. The procurator fiscal does not undertake their own investigation but will instruct the police. This does not mean that there are any untoward circumstances, but it can ascertain if there were any concerns being expressed from the relatives. It provides more details to allow an assessment of the relevant information to be made. A police report is likely to be requested in any case where it is likely that a post mortem examination will thereafter be instructed.

1.73   The police will be involved in the investigation which may be distressing for the families. Paragraph 1.2 of the Police Scotland's Standard Operating Procedures recognises that deaths occur in society on a very regular basis and arise in hospital settings. Paragraph 1.4 recognises that the deceased relatives must be treated with dignity, compassion and respect throughout. The police will take statements and submit a report as part of the investigation process with initial findings to COPFS as part of that process.[44]

Example

The deceased did not turn up to a family lunch. Investigation found them dead at home with no suspicious circumstances. The death has been certified but there is no

---

44   *www.scotland.police.uk/access-to-information/policies-and-procedures/standard-operating-procedures/* (accessed on 21 February 2023).

known medical history of disease or illness. A post mortem examination is going to be required as the doctor is not able to certify the cause of death. A police report can outline any cause of concern, such as any sign of a break-in, illicit drugs or any concerns from the family as to any suspicious circumstances.

To undertake 'a view and grant' examination

1.74   In some circumstances, a 'view and grant' examination may be carried out where one pathologist examines the deceased's body. This is a non-invasive examination which requires only an external examination. The pathologist can also consider the medical history and the circumstances of death and is able to grant a death certificate, certifying the cause of death without the need to undertake a full invasive post mortem examination.

1.75   To provide a perspective on numbers, in 2013–14, out of 9,549 death reports received, 5,060 post mortem examinations were instructed, with 864 'view and grant' examinations conducted. Clearly, if a 'view and grant' examination can be carried out, this is much less distressing for relatives. It also avoids delay in accepting the cause of death.

To instruct a post mortem examination

1.76   Where there is no-one able to certify the case of death or if the procurator fiscal is not prepared to accept the cause of death (and they can seek advice from the local forensic pathologists), a post mortem examination will be instructed to ascertain what the cause of death is. It is a matter for the procurator fiscal, based on the facts and circumstances, whether and what type of post mortem examination should be instructed and carried out. They also instruct the forensic pathologists to carry out the post mortem examination on their behalf. In cases that appear to have potentially suspicious circumstances, a two-doctor post mortem examination will be instructed for the purpose of satisfying the requirements of evidential rule of corroboration in Scots criminal law, should the death thereafter turn out to be suspicious.

Example

The deceased was at home with their partner. Their partner went next door to give a neighbour some dinner. On their return, they found their partner dead. An ambulance was called. There were signs of scratches on their throat. Possible suffocation or suspicious circumstances were suspected. A two-doctor post mortem examination was carried out. Following the post mortem report, a piece of ham was found stuck in the deceased's throat. They had choked and asphyxiated. The scratches were consistent with them trying to free their throat. It was not a suspicious death.

1.77   Where a full post mortem examination is necessary, the procurator fiscal, acting in the public interest and fulfilling their role under Art 2 of the ECHR can instruct a post mortem examination. There is no need for consent from relatives as their decision overrides any objection from relatives. There is benefit in communicating that decision in a suitable fashion to the relatives.

1.78   In all circumstances, it is important for COPFS to liaise with the family and to keep them informed as to the processes involved in death investigations. Once the post mortem examination is carried out and the cause of death ascertained, the death certificate will be issued. The deceased's body at that time will normally be released, allowing the funeral to take place. Where the pathologist wishes to consider the findings of their examination and to receive the results of blood/tissue/organ analysis, or any other tests which were carried out before certifying a final cause of death, a provisional cause of death may be issued to enable the family to proceed with funeral arrangements. Once the results of the further examinations are received, the pathologist may amend the final cause of death. This could provide, eg the level of intoxication or indeed, identification of the drugs ingested and the relevant levels.

1.79   Where consideration is being given as to a possible prosecution, or to the holding of an FAI, further investigations will follow the post mortem examination. The staff from the COPFS 'Victim Information and Advice' (VIA) will contact the family to provide information about the progress of the case and put relatives in touch with relevant support agencies.

1.80   Relatives are invited to meet with the procurator fiscal when there is the possibility of criminal proceedings, the holding of an FAI or where the death involves a road traffic collision. Throughout the subsequent investigations, the procurator fiscal will liaise with the nearest relatives of the deceased's family to ensure that they are kept fully informed of any progress and that their views are carefully considered as and when any decision regarding the holding of an FAI is made. In a criminal case, the Lord Advocate will take the decision to prosecute based on an assessment of the evidence and being satisfied that prosecution is in the public interest.

Suspicious deaths

1.81   In cases of homicide, the deceased's body will not be released. This allows the accused[45] and their defence team an opportunity to arrange for the examination of the body if required for evidential purposes. A recent review recognised that there was a professional obligation on the defence to ensure that they investigate the accused's defence. This may include instructing a defence post mortem examination. This is in effect instructing that a second post mortem examination is carried out.

---

45   Scottish term for the defendant.

A Consultation Protocol[46] has been published to inform the defence in order to consider whether a second post mortem examination is actually required, as a means in which to reduce the number of these defence post mortem examinations being carried out. This was also undertaken with a view to reducing the delays in releasing the deceased's body to the relatives, which is a contentious and vexed subject.

1.82   The delay in releasing bodies following a suspicious death has remained an issue of considerable public concern. A Members' Bill was introduced to the Scottish Parliament on 21 May 2020 which proposed to introduce a time limit on bodies being retained. This would have affected the existing right of the defence to instruct a post mortem examination for the purposes of the person's defence (in addition to the post-mortem examination carried out at the instruction of the procurator fiscal), where a person has been charged with an offence in connection with causing or contributing to a death.[47] The Bill was ultimately not successful, though as part of the Consultation Protocol COPFS undertook to monitor these timescales.

Where cremation is required

1.83   Regulation 8 of the Cremation (Scotland) Regulations 2019[48] provides that where the death of a person has been investigated by the procurator fiscal, a certificate in the form of Form E1 as set out in Sch 8 (Form E1) is necessary. It confirms that the remains of the deceased may be cremated for the purpose of s 27A(2)(a) of the Registration of Births, Deaths and Marriages (Scotland) Act 1965. It is required before the disposal of the remains of that person can take place by cremation.

1.84   An E1 Form should only be produced by the procurator fiscal when the cause of death has been ascertained and there are no grounds for believing that destruction of the remains will be detrimental to any further investigations that are required, such as in the case of a murder or culpable homicide. The E1 Form is sent by the procurator fiscal to the nominated crematorium to confirm that the procurator fiscal is satisfied that there are no circumstances which render it necessary that any further examination of the deceased's body take place. Funeral arrangements can then be undertaken by the relatives in consultation with the crematorium and their funeral directors.

1.85   As set out under reg 1(4)(a) of the Cremation (Scotland) Regulations 2019, this permits the transfer of E1 Forms with an electronic signature. The Head of

---

46   Crown Office and Procurator Fiscal Service, *Forensic Pathologist Consultation Protocol* (last updated 1 October 2018), *www.copfs.gov.uk/publications/forensic-pathologist-consultation-protocol/* (accessed 21 February 2023).

47   Post-Mortem Examinations (Defence Time Limit) Scotland Bill, *https://archive2021.parliament. scot/parliamentarybusiness/CurrentCommittees/116138.aspx* (accessed on 21 February 2023).

48   SSI 2019/36.

SFIU electronic signature is added, and the E1 Form is emailed to the appropriate crematorium.

1.86   This process was brought in to simplify the unnecessary steps for funeral directors or other family representatives having to attend a procurator fiscal's office in person to uplift the E1 Form. The change minimised disruption and distress and eliminated unnecessary cost to relatives. It was an unpopular action, as highlighted earlier, as the procurator fiscal's office was associated with criminal proceedings.

12.   ORGAN TRANSPLANTATION

1.87   Organ and tissue transplantation are authorised under the Human Tissue (Scotland) Act 2006 as amended by the Human Tissue (Authorisation) (Scotland) Act 2019.[49] That Act sets out the process of authorisation underpinning the organ and tissue transplantation system and changed the process quite radically in that it set up a 'deemed authorisation' or 'opt out' system of organs and tissue donation for transplantation. Donations can now proceed where a person[50] was not known to have had any objection to donation.

Section 3(1)[51] of the 2006 Act provides that part of the body of a deceased person can be used for (a) transplantation, (b) research, (c) education or training or (d) audit or quality assurance provided that the removal and use for the purpose is authorised in accordance with the provisions of the 2006 Act.[52]

The removal of organs and tissues must be carried out in accordance with s 1 of the 2006 Act that sets out the requirements for the process of organ and/or tissue retention to ensure that the process is legal and acceptable. There must be public confidence relating to the process of the certification of death before organ or tissue donation is considered.

1.88   The 2019 Act as such does not alter the role of the procurator fiscal in giving consent or in the process of removal of organs. The procurator fiscal's consent for organ donation may be required before death occurs. This does not apply in the case of tissue donation, as tissue can be retrieved up until 48 hours (24 hours for cornea donation) after death.

1.89   The COPFS and the Scottish Donation and Transport Group Agreement[53] (updated December 2017) set out the respective responsibilities relating to organ

---

49   The system came into effect on 26 March 2021.
50   Protections exist for adults without capacity as well as adults resident in Scotland for under 12 months and children who are aged under 16.
51   As amended by the Human Tissue (Authorisation) (Scotland) Act 2019.
52   Human Transplant (Scotland) Act 2006, s 3(20).
53   This Agreement originated in 2004 and has been since updated: *www.gov.scot/publications/ agreement-between-crown-office-procurator-fiscal-service-scottish-donation-transplant/* (accessed on 21 February 2023).

and tissue donation and still apply. It recognises the medical urgency required in connection with the importance of having processes in place to obtain the necessary consent and to achieve successful organ transplants.

1.90 The consent of the procurator fiscal is required for the removal of any body part 'where a person knows, or has reason to believe, that an examination of the body of a deceased person is, or may be, required for the purposes of the functions of the procurator fiscal'.[54] That consent can be given verbally and is to be confirmed in writing as soon as is reasonably practicable.[55] The procurator fiscal will normally permit the removal of organs and/or tissue, provided that evidence is preserved for the purpose of any possible criminal proceedings and/or any FAI. Corneas can be donated up to 24 hours after death, while tendons, heart valves and other tissue can be donated up to 48 hours after death.

1.91 As organs must be retrieved soon after death if they are to be viable, the procurator fiscal may instruct the police to make enquiries into the circumstances of the death to allow them to give the appropriate consent. Discussions may take place with the doctor in charge, the Specialist Nurse for Organ Donation (SNOD) or the on-call pathologist. If there is uncertainty as to whether the retrieval operation could affect potential evidence and future proceedings, discussions may take place with the senior transplant surgeon on the organ retrieval team. Advice may also be sought from the on-call forensic pathologist.

1.92 The hospital procedure requires that the retrieval procedure will not be commenced until the brain-stem death of the potential donor has been established by two senior doctors, acting independently of the transplant team. These doctors will, if required, give evidence to that effect, that the death of the donor was not caused by the retrieval operation. The retrieval surgeon will detail the operative procedure and any other findings in the patient's medical records, which will be available for the post mortem pathologist should they wish to see them. The surgeon who is thereafter to retrieve the body parts must also be satisfied that life is extinct.[56]

1.93 In the majority of cases, patients will have been admitted to an intensive care unit and given full life support. Where further treatment is not in the patient's overall best interests, with the agreement of the family, a decision may then be taken to withdraw all life-sustaining treatment. Once life-sustaining treatment has been withdrawn, cardiorespiratory arrest will occur after an interval, following which death can be pronounced.

1.94 It is also possible for organ and/or tissue donation to occur from children and even babies from the age of at least 36 weeks corrected gestational age. Like adults, children and babies can potentially be donors and the procedures to be followed

---

54 Human Transplant (Scotland) Act 2006, s 5(1).
55 Human Transplant (Scotland) Act 2006, s 5(2).
56 Human Transplant (Scotland) Act 2006, s 11(4).

in seeking consent from the procurator fiscal for paediatric or neonatal donation to proceed are the same as those set out above for adult potential donors.

1.95   Mention should also be made of the Anatomy Act 1984 as amended by the 2006 Act, so that individuals over 12 years of age can request to bequeath their body to universities 'for the purposes of teaching or studying, or training in or researching into, the gross structure of the human body'. Currently, five Scottish universities[57] run body donation programmes. A bequeathal request must be in writing and signed by the person concerned in the presence of a witness (or two in the case of those aged between 12 and 16). Following the death, under s 4(2) of the Anatomy Act 1984, the person lawfully in possession of the body can authorise the request.

1.96   These rights are over-ridden in cases where deaths have been reported to the procurator fiscal as outlined above. Possession will in effect be under their control until the release of the body is authorised. Where such circumstances regarding a body donation arise, early communication processes are required with the procurator fiscal.

13.   PERSISTENT VEGETATIVE STATE AND WITHDRAWAL OF LIFE SUPPORT FACILITIES

1.97   In *Law Hospital NHS Trust v Lord Advocate*,[58] a patient had suffered from irreversible damage to the cerebral cortex, falling into a persistent vegetative state. She remained alive only because of artificial feeding and hydration and the provision of nursing care. There were no further medical routes to explore to assist her recovery. The patient was herself unable to consent to her treatment being terminated, with her family agreeing all medical treatment should stop.

1.98   The Law Hospital NHS Trust sought a declarator to confirm that it was not unlawful if all medical treatment was stopped. The then Lord President, Lord Hope recognised the importance of the issues as given medical advances, there was a possibility of increased incidence of this type of case. He considered that 'it is possible to nourish the body and preserve it from disease so that life in the clinical sense may be continued indefinitely'.[59] The court could not declare whether the proposed action was or was not criminal as these were matters for the declarator power of the High Court of Justiciary or the Lord Advocate. There was a difficulty that 'the criminal law was ill-suited to control the conduct of doctors in the exercise of their skill and judgment, especially when they had acted in accordance with proper professional practice, but the threat of a criminal sanction and of the devastating effects which that might have on the accused and his family was a real one so that

---

57   Aberdeen, Dundee, Edinburgh, Glasgow and St Andrews.
58   1996 SLT 301.
59   *Law Hospital NHS Trust v Lord Advocate* 1996 SC 301.

the medical profession was entitled to look to the courts in Scotland to provide to doctors, by declaration, clear rulings as to whether the course they proposed to adopt was or was not lawful'.[60]

1.99   The Court of Session held that treatment could be withdrawn by applying the test of the patient's best interests. Continuing treatment was not in her best interests so the court authorised that life sustaining and medical treatment should discontinue.[61]

1.100   The Lord Advocate has since issued guidance to establish where a hospital which has care of a patient who is in a persistent vegetative state, or any relative of that patient, seeks withdrawal of treatment, an application should be made to the Court of Session to authorise that treatment can be discontinued. Any qualified medical practitioner (or any person acting upon the instructions of such a practitioner) who, acting in good faith and with the authority of the Court of Session, withdraws or otherwise causes to be discontinued life sustaining treatment or other medical treatment from a patient in a persistent, or permanent, vegetative state, with the result that the patient dies, will not be prosecuted.

1.101   Where medical practitioners withdraw life sustaining treatment from a patient in a persistent or permanent vegetative state without court authority, they are not immune from prosecution. The Lord Advocate has stated that if doctors and those acting on their instructions were acting in accordance with accepted medical practice and had exercised the proper degree of care expected of them, it would be very unlikely that any prosecution in the public interest would be brought against them.

1.102   Any death of a patient in a permanent vegetative state as a result of the withdrawal of life sustaining treatment or other medical treatment (whether with or without the authority of the Court of Session) must be reported to the procurator fiscal as soon as it occurs.[62] Relatively few cases have arisen in Scotland since 1996. This may be as a result of the absence of legal funding (legal aid constraints) to challenge medical decisions and indeed, in relevant cases, that doctors have obtained the prior necessary court authority.

1.103   However, distress and delay does arise in undertaking the legal formalities in obtaining the relevant court declarator. Were this not required, the process would be simpler. In the English case of *An NHS Trust and others (Respondents) v Y (by his litigation friend, the Official Solicitor) and another (Appellants)*[63] this issue was discussed. It remains to be seen how this might be followed in Scotland.

60   Ibid.
61   *Law Hospital NHS Trust v Lord Advocate (No.2)* 1996 SLT 869.
62   *Reporting Deaths to the Procurator Fiscal. Information and Guidance to Medical Practitioners* (updated May 2019), *www.copfs.gov.uk/publications/reporting-deaths/* (accessed on 21 February 2023).
63   [2018] UKSC 46, *www.supremecourt.uk/cases/docs/uksc-2017-0202-judgment.pdf* (accessed on 21 February 2023).

1.104   The Supreme Court decided that there was no requirement under common law or ECHR that it was mandatory to involve a court in deciding on the best interests of every patient in cases where the withdrawal of life support processes were being considered. Where 'at the end of the medical process, it is apparent that the way forward is finely balanced, or there is a difference of medical opinion, or a lack of agreement to a proposed course of action from those with an interest in the patient's welfare, a court application can and should be made'. The 'possibility of approaching a court in the event of doubts as to the best interests of the patient is an essential part of the protection of human rights' should be followed.

1.105   This decision has been broadly welcomed by the charity Compassion in Dying as it brings clarity to doctors and relatives of those who are in a vegetative or minimally conscious state, following severe illness or injury. Much will depend on the facts and circumstances of each case. 'The court's decision also recognises the fact that sometimes, sadly, it is in someone's best interests to withdraw treatment. It will allow those closest to a person – their loved ones and medical team – to feel supported and empowered to make the right decision for the person, even when it is a difficult one.'[64]

Children

1.106   Two recent well-publicised English cases have focused on the right to withdraw treatment involving young children and have generated considerable public interest. These were the cases of Charlie Gard[65] and Alfie Evans,[66] which ultimately involved the withdrawal of artificial ventilation with both children dying as a result. The various court proceedings took approximately five months in each case, involving a number of appeals to various courts. These cases involved a child who lacked capacity, meaning that the parents had the right to consent to treatment on behalf of their child, provided that the treatment was in the child's best interests. The Scottish courts have not as yet been involved in such a high-profile case where the role of overriding the parents' views remains a problem. In Scotland too, no expedited procedure exists for the type of petition that is required, so that the process would need to include the appointment of a curator ad litem which itself would take several months, no doubt causing continuing anguish and delay to the family.

---

64   Ibid.
65   *Great Ormond Street Hospital and (1) Constance Yates Respondents (2) Christopher Gard (3) Charlie Gard (by his Guardian)* [2017] EWHC 1909 (Fam).
66   *Alder Hey Children's NHS Foundation Trust Applicant and (1) Mr Thomas Evans (2) Ms Kate James (3) Alfie Evans (A Child by his Guardian CAFCASS Legal)* [2018] EWHC 308 (Fam).

Lack of capacity

1.107 In Scotland, Pt 5 (Medical Treatment and Research) of the Adults with Incapacity (Scotland) Act 2000 applies.[67] It provides for medical treatment and concerns of issues of consent where the patient lacks capacity. It does not specifically deal with decisions to be made regarding the withdrawal of treatment.

1.108 The Mental Welfare Commission for Scotland issued a Good Practice Guide in February 2022[68] as to assistance on how to take decisions concerning medical treatment. By recourse to the courts, this ensures that all parties are provided with protection from complaints and claims as well as any potential allegations of professional negligence to the General Medical Council (GMC), any civil claims or criminal charges.

Right to life

1.109 This remains an unresolved emotive topic. A private member's Bill was introduced to the Scottish Parliament by Liam McArthur MSP following a public consultation that closed in December 2021. The Assisted Dying for Terminally Ill Adults (Scotland) Bill[69] provides for competent adults who are terminally ill to be provided with assistance to end their life at their request.

14. FAMILY LIAISON

1.110 In all deaths involving the procurator fiscal, following advice from the police or the relevant doctor, the procurator fiscal provide the family with the necessary information. Further information is set out in the COPFS *Family Liaison*

---

67 The Scottish Government has consulted on potential changes to the 2000 Act: Adults with incapacity (Scotland) Act 2000: proposals for reform (31 January 2018), *www.gov.scot/publications/adults-incapacity-scotland-act-2000-proposals-reform/* (accessed on 21 February 2023).

68 Mental Welfare Commission for Scotland, *Right to treat? Delivering physical healthcare to people who lack capacity and refuse or resist treatment Good practice guide* (February 2022): *www.mwcscot.org.uk/sites/default/files/2022-08/RightToTreat-Guide-February2022.pdf* (accessed on 21 February 2023).

69 Assisted Dying for Terminally Ill Adults (Scotland) Bill (22 September 2021), *www.parliament.scot/-/media/files/legislation/proposed-members-bills/assisted-dying-for-terminally-ill-adults-scotland-consultation-2021-final.pdf* (accessed on 21 February 2023). Mr McArthur published the outcome of his public consultation on assisted dying, which achieved 14,038 responses. Some 76% of people who responded expressed full support, with a further 2% partially supporting a change in the law. He will now work with the Scottish Parliament's Non-Governmental Bills Unit (NGBU) to draft a bill, aimed at introduction to the Scottish parliament in early 2023.

Charter: Charter to Bereaved Families: Access to Information and Liaison with the Procurator Fiscal,[70] published in 2016.

1.111   The Charter sets out how staff will liaise with the family of a person in relation to whose death an FAI may be or is to be held. It sets out the different stages of the investigation process, the information which will be provided to bereaved families and the timescales for giving information. Insofar as it is possible to do so, additional information is to be provided at any stage of the investigation upon request.[71]

1.112   FAIs investigations, and if further family members are identified, the procurator fiscal should consider providing them with the relevant information. Normally information can be provided to a nominated point of contact within a family. There will be circumstances where a family liaison officer may be appointed by the police, where the procurator fiscal will communicate with them when appropriate.

1.113   The diagram on the following page shows the process that is involved where a death is reported to the procurator fiscal.

---

70   Crown Office and Procurator Fiscal Service, *Family Liaison Charter* (September 2016), *www.copfs.gov.uk/publications/the-family-liaison-charter/* (accessed on 21 February 2023).
71   It applies to any death reported to COPFS on or after 1 September 2016 and to any FAI applied for on or after 1 September 2016. It will also apply to deaths reported earlier than 1 September 2016 if the bereaved family specifically ask COPFS for the Charter to apply.

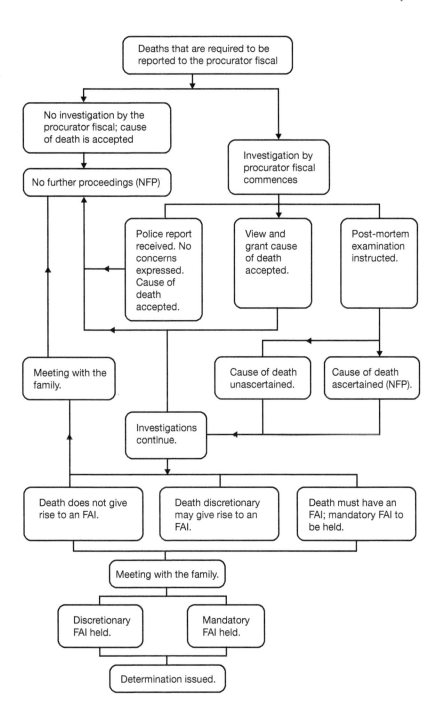

Chapter 2

An Introduction to the FAI system

1. BACKGROUND TO FAIs

2.01   This chapter looks at the process as well as the background to FAIs to understand what their role is and how they have evolved. FAIs are, primarily, a product of statute, therefore created through law. They have been described by the Right Honourable Lord Cameron of Lochbroom KC, His Majesty's Advocate, as forming part of a 'somewhat arcane corner of administrative law'.[1] From the public perspective that appears to be true, in so far as any real understanding of how their role fits in with the Scottish justice system. That should not be the actual position. The public should be able to understand the role of an FAI in relation to sudden, unexpected, unexplained and suspicious deaths. That means what an FAI is, and equally what it is not. It should not be some "arcane" process only familiar to those who may commonly appear, such as the police, prison staff and medical professionals.

2.02   There are a number of reasons why the public do not understand what an FAI is and why one is to be held. They will, if asked about an FAI, most likely recall the Lockerbie or Dunblane FAIs, but if asked exactly why these were held will demonstrate their lack of awareness of why, and also what, they set out to achieve.

---

1   Carmichael, Ian HB, *Sudden Deaths and Fatal Accident Inquiries* (2nd edition, Edinburgh, W. Green Sweet & Maxwell, 1993).

2.03 This lack of awareness may be partly argued to be the fault of the legal profession. They do not promote an understanding of who is involved in advising on an FAI. There is perhaps a mistaken belief that FAIs are merely the focus of lawyers who specialise in civil court work. Civil lawyers are frequently involved in FAIs as many of these deaths that go onto the holding of an FAI may also involve a claim for personal injury or damages. But it is a quite different process as an FAI will not determine criminal, or indeed civil, liability. When viewing the nature of the deaths covered by FAIs, those with regulatory roles for organisations will commonly be involved. Depending on the nature of the death, FAIs will frequently include the medical defence unions representing doctors, Central Legal Office[2] representing the hospital trusts, union representatives in health and safety cases and marine or air specialists, prison services and so on.

2.04 However, the greater confusion may be caused by the law on FAIs being complicated as the responsibility for undertaking FAIs lies squarely for the time being with the Crown Office and Procurator Fiscal Service (COPFS). Their role is normally seen as in being the independent Crown prosecution service in Scotland. There is therefore no real understanding of their specific role discussed in **Chapter 1** in receiving sudden death reports, instructing post mortems, discharging bodies and then in undertaking death investigations. They have the important role of discharging Scotland's responsibility in conducting death investigations in relation to the European Convention on Human Rights (ECHR), Art 2, as outlined below. It is a parallel role to that undertaken by the Coroner[3] in England and Wales in discharging that identical responsibility.

2.05 Better understanding of the FAI system in Scotland could be achieved by developing or growing awareness of the role. Much greater scrutiny of a wide range of deaths is now demanded, calling for accountability where someone has died, and requiring robust investigations to be made into the circumstances of these deaths. There is a demand from the public then of exactly when, why, and into what kind of deaths, investigations may or must be merited. With the lack of understanding, there may be some room for misunderstanding where FAIs are thought to form a 'preliminary hearing' or 'precursor' for any criminal or civil case to follow. FAIs do not exclude any criminal proceedings or indeed civil action taking place, but under statute, do not assign fault.

2.06 The FAI is a form of inquiry that only applies to Scotland, and which has potential implications for those involved, whether as individuals or when working within organisations. The subject matter of deaths that require investigations to

2   The Central Legal Office is the organisation that provides NHS Scotland with legal advice and assistance in every area of law relevant to the health service. It is one of the Strategic Business Units of NHS National Services Scotland.
3   CPS, *Coroners* (updated 2 February 2021), *www.cps.gov.uk/legal-guidance/ coroners#:~:text=Inquests%20are%20legal%20inquiries%20into,Coroners%20and%20 Justice%20Act%202009* (accessed on 21 February 2023).

be undertaken to ascertain the facts and circumstances is not of course unique. International jurisdictions have similar means of public scrutiny into sudden deaths, though their processes and structures, of course, vary. These will be examined in **Chapter 7**: Death Investigations in England and Wales and **Chapter 8**: Sudden Death Investigations Abroad – Process and Practice.

2.   WHERE ARE FAIs TODAY

2.07   Administrative law is a brand of public as opposed to private law. It is that aspect of 'public' on which attention is focused. The interest in FAIs being held and the determinations that fall to be issued, following the conclusion to the FAI, primarily concern those persons central to the process, namely the deceased's family. However, the ambit of an FAI is much wider.

2.08   FAIs include the interest of the public which can be seen from the FAIs which have been conducted in relation to all types of deaths. Their historical development can be tracked to show their origins which culminate in the form in which they are held today. They are held under the Inquiries into Fatal Accidents and Sudden Deaths etc. (Scotland) Act 2016 (asp 2) which provides a framework for FAIs to be held. The 2016 Act states that it has 'provision for holding *public* inquiries in respect of certain deaths' (emphasis provided). It is public as it is held in the interests of society in identifying the nature of facts and circumstances and the cause of the death and in exploring if lessons can be learnt to avoid any such death arising again. It is held in public with transparency for all who can both hear and observe the proceedings.

2.09   The public in Scotland may have become more aware of FAIs over the last few years. There has been some public disquiet expressed as to the considerable delays that have arisen with them being held. The Solicitor General, Ruth Charteris KC, has apologised for the delay in holding the FAI into the prison death of Katie Allan.[4] These concerns in delays in holding FAIs were echoed in the findings of the Independent Review of Responses to Deaths in Prison Custody[5] published in October 2021. It stated that 'promptness – while recognising the logistical challenges facing [Crown Office and Procurator Fiscal Service] (COPFS) and [the Scottish Fatalities Investigation Unit] (SFIU)], the delays currently incurred do not meet this test and leave families without closure for far too long'.[6] That closure for families is important, but is not the primary objective in holding an FAI.

---

4   Scottish Legal News, *Solicitor General Apologises for Delays into Katie Allan Inquiry* (5 August 2021), *www.scottishlegal.com/articles/solicitor-general-apologises-for-delays-into-katie-allan-inquiry* (accessed on 25 November 2022).

5   Independent Review of the Response to Deaths in Prison Custody (November 2021), *www.prisonsinspectoratescotland.gov.uk/sites/default/files/publication_files/Independent%20Review%20of%20the%20Response%20to%20Deaths%20in%20Prison%20Custody%20p6%20%281%29%20WEB%20PDF.pdf* (accessed on 21 February 2023).

6   Ibid, Chapter 6, Overarching Conclusions and Recommendations.

2.10   Any such delays now arising have inevitably been exacerbated by the effects of the Covid-19 pandemic, in common with other delays caused to all court cases being held within the Scottish court system by the Scottish Courts and Tribunals Service. The effects of the pandemic can also be seen in the changes that have resulted in the ability for FAIs now to be held remotely by means of teleconferences in light of the Covid-19 constraints.[7] That has come a long way from the holding of the early FAIs dating back to the 19th century.

2.11   Another factor promoting more public awareness of FAIs and the opportunities presented by them has been the list of recent high-profile inquiries. These have included the helicopter crash on the Clutha Bar in Glasgow, resulting in a number of deaths, both within the bar and of the personnel in the helicopter,[8] and the deaths of pedestrians in Glasgow where a bin lorry driver lost control of his vehicle.[9] Historically, other FAIs have been synonymous with globally significant incidents, such as the Pan-Am bombing at Lockerbie[10] (1990-91), the classroom shooting at Dunblane (1996) and the crush on the stairs at the Rangers/Celtic football match at Ibrox (1971).

2.12   There is therefore a need to ensure that those involved in the FAI process understand what its purpose is. What does need emphasised is that they neither offer a panacea to the bereaved relatives nor a means of convicting those allegedly responsible for the death. Crucially, FAIs do not now, as will be explained later, make any finding of guilt or indeed seek to determine criminal or civil liability which are excluded under s 1(4) of 2016 Act.

2.13   The families also need to be aware that the circumstances of a death may indeed not give rise to the holding of any FAI but could lead to the lodging of a complaint, for instance, in a medical case, which would be dealt with by the relevant NHS Hospital Trust.[11] The death of Amanda Cox illustrated a case where Lothian Hospital NHS Trust undertook a report into her death in the maternity hospital where COPFS determined that there was nothing more to be gained from holding an FAI. The Serious Adverse Event Review (SAER) held into her death resulted in

---

7   FAI into death of Lee Tortolano [2020] FAI 39 (remand prison death). Scottish Courts and Tribunals, *Access to remote Fatal Accident Inquiry hearings, www.scotcourts.gov.uk/the-courts/sheriff-court/ preliminary-hearings-and-dates-of-inquiry/access-to-remote-fatal-accident-inquiry-hearings* (accessed on 21 February 2023).

8   *www.scotcourts.gov.uk/search-judgments/judgment-search?indexCatalogue=fatal%2Daccident%2 Djudgments& searchQuery=Clutha&wordsMode=0* (accessed on 21 February 2023): [2019] FAI 46.

9   *www.scotcourts.gov.uk/search-judgments/judgment?id=e916fba6-8980-69d2-b500-ff0000d74aa7* (accessed on 21 February 2023): [2015] FAI 31.

10   *www.vetpath.co.uk/lockerbie/fai.pdf* (accessed on 21 February 2023).

11   NHS inform, *Making a Complaint about your NHS care or treatment, www.nhsinform.scot/care-support-and-rights/health-rights/feedback-and-complaints/complain-about-a-gp-pharmacy-dentist-or-hospital-in-scotland* (accessed on 21 February 2023).

the necessary changes in processes having taken place at the hospital.[12] In effect, holding an FAI was not going to explore any circumstances that had not already been investigated and been changed.

3. WHO HAS THE RESPONSIBILITY FOR INSTRUCTING AND HOLDING FAIs?

2.14   At common law, it is the responsibility of the COPFS through the procurator fiscal to investigate sudden, unexplained, unexpected or suspicious deaths. The Lord Advocate is the ministerial head of the COPFS, appointed by the King on the recommendation of the First Minister, and with the agreement of the Scottish Parliament. They[13] act as the principal legal adviser. Their role in respect of independent decision-taking about criminal prosecutions in Scotland is well known. However, what is perhaps less understood is their role in heading investigations into such deaths. Fundamentally, that investigation is undertaken by them as part of their responsibility of the State under Art 2 the Right to Life – of the European Convention on Human Rights (ECHR).

2.15   Considering the role of ECHR Art 2 and European jurisprudence is essential and provides a good starting point as to how important the FAI role is and why the responsibilities incumbent on COPFS need to be discharged effectively. There should be a robust framework in which to investigate relevant deaths and to ensure that FAIs are held, expeditiously where appropriate.

4. THE STATE AND THE INTERACTION WITH ARTICLE 2 OF THE ECHR

2.16   Article 2 (an absolute right) of the ECHR states that:

'1. Everyone's right to life shall be protected by law. No one shall be deprived of his life intentionally save in the execution of a sentence of a court following his conviction of a crime for which this penalty is provided by law.[14]

2. Deprivation of life shall not be regarded as inflicted in contravention of this article when it results from the use of force which is more than absolutely necessary:

---

12   NHS Lothian, Statement, *Statement on the Death of Amanda Cox at the Royal Infirmary of Edinburgh, 10 December 2018* (14 March 2022), *https://news.nhslothian.scot/2022/03/14/statement-on-the-death-of-amanda-cox-at-the-royal-infirmary-of-edinburgh-10-december-2018/* (accessed on 21 February 2023).

13   Deliberately it has been referred to as 'they' to support gender neutral drafting.

14   Protocol 6 was ratified by the UK in January 1999 where it banned the death penalty in peacetime and Protocol 13 was signed by the UK in May 2002 in wartime.

   (a)   in defence of any person from unlawful violence
   (b)   in order to effect lawful arrest or prevent the escape of a person lawfully detained;
   (c)   in action lawfully taken for quelling a riot or insurrection.'

2.17   Protocol 6 banned the death penalty in peacetime[15] and Protocol 13 in wartime.[16] Its operation can be seen by interpretating Art 2, where the European Court of Human Rights has inferred that positive obligations lie with States to establish and enforce a general framework of procedures to ensure that the lives of individuals within their jurisdictions are protected. These rights have been refined over time.

2.18   *Osman v UK*[17] establishes a positive obligation on the State authorities to take preventive operational measures to protect an individual whose life is at risk from the criminal acts of another individual. In *LCB v UK*,[18] there was an obligation established where there was a failure to warn the applicant's parents of the possible risk to her health caused by her father's participation in nuclear tests, and to monitor her father's radiation dose levels.

2.19   There was a similar obligation to carry out effective investigation into a death where an individual had died in custody or detention, as seen in *Salman v Turkey*.[19] The State authorities in Turkey were required to account for the deceased's treatment in custody which had been particularly stringent. They failed to provide a satisfactory and convincing explanation for the death since he had been in apparent good health, before his detention, without any pre-existing injuries or active illness.

2.20   This right to investigation into a death is wider and will arise even where there is no suggestion as to any State involvement in the death or any specific failure on the part of the State to prevent the death occurring.

2.21   One of the inquests included as an example of the coroner system in England and Wales is the inquest into the death of Ella Adoo-Kissi-Debrah[20] from asthma,[21] which found that air pollution had been a factor in her death. Though ECHR, Art 2 was not cited, looking to where observance of climate change may go, in 2019, the

---

15   Council of Europe, Protocol No. 6 to the Convention for the Protection of Human Rights and Fundamental Freedoms Concerning the Abolition of the Death Penalty, as Amended by Protocol No. 11, *www.echr.coe.int/Documents/Library_Collection_P6_ETS114E_ENG.pdf* (accessed on 21 February 2023).
16   Council of Europe, Protocol No. 13 to the Convention for the Protection of Human Rights and Fundamental Freedoms Concerning the Abolition of the Death Penalty in all circumstances, *www.echr.coe.int/Documents/Library_Collection_P13_ETS187E_ENG.pdf* (accessed on 21 February 2023).
17   (1998) 29 EHRR 245.
18   (1999) 27 EHRR 212.
19   (2002) 34 EHRR 425.
20   Blackstone Chambers, Inquest into the death of Ella Adoo-Kissi-Debrah (17 December 2020), *www.blackstonechambers.com/news/inquest-death-ella-adoo-kissi-debrah/#:~:text=In%20 a%20landmark%20case%20 2C%20H.M.,and%20%E2%80%9Cair%20pollution%20 exposure%E2%80%9D* (accessed on 21 February 2023).
21   See **Chapter 7**.

Supreme Court of the Netherlands cited ECHR, Art 2 in stating that the government must limit climate change in order to protect human health.[22] The possible extension of ECHR, Art 2 can perhaps be seen in relation to future deaths which may be attributed to the effects of climate change.

What does Article 2 of the ECHR mean for Scotland?

2.22   In Scotland, Scottish Ministers and the Lord Advocate are required to respect the norms of customary international law in as far as they create international obligations on the UK. Powers devolved to them in terms of s 58 of the Scotland Act 1998 should not be exercised in a manner which would place the UK in breach of its international obligations. Paragraph 7(2)(a) of Sch 5 to the Scotland Act 1998 provides that it is within devolved competence for the Scottish Ministers (and Lord Advocate) to observe and implement 'international obligations, obligations under the Human Rights Convention[23] and obligations under international law'. There is a legitimate expectation that actions of the devolved institutions should be compatible with the UK's 'international obligations under ECHR'.

2.23   The 2016 Act provides the framework for an FAI to be held, and the holding of an FAI should comply with Scotland's responsibility for investigations being held into deaths. The petition of *Rosaleen Kennedy and Jean Black v Lord Advocate*[24] set out that position quite clearly. That petition involved a judicial review of the Lord Advocate's decision not to hold an FAI in the case of Hepatitis C deaths that had resulted from contaminated blood transfusions. Public concerns had arisen over the deaths of Mrs O'Hara and Mr Black when they had become infected with the Hepatitis C virus. The families claimed that an FAI would be able to look at the wider issues of public concern, surrounding the prevalence of the Hepatitis C virus, its isolation, the development of a screening test and the management of infected patients.

2.24   The Lord Advocate had argued that these matters were unlikely to be considered fully within the remit of an FAI (which can be quite narrow). These were issues that had been examined elsewhere so that the responsibilities of the State and ECHR, Art 2 had been fully complied with, recognising that 'the actual nature of the process required, if Article 2 rights are engaged, varies according to context'. It should be noted that this was not a death which involved the State directly or had arisen through any violence.

---

22   *Urgenda Foundation v State of the Netherlands* [2015] HAZA C/09/00456689: *http:// climatecasechart.com/non-us-case/urgenda-foundation-v-kingdom-of-the-netherlands/* (accessed on 21 February 2023).

23   Scotland Act 1998, s 126(1) as being the ECHR and its protocols as they have effect for the time being in the UK.

24   Rosaleen Kennedy & Jean Black v Lord Advocate: *https://scotcourts.gov.uk* (accessed on 21 February 2023).

2.25   The court found that the Lord Advocate's decision in not holding an FAI which was discretionary had erred in law. The issue was whether anything could and should have been done to prevent the deaths from having occurred. He had failed to comply with the ECHR, Art 2 obligations, as the Lord Advocate should know or ought to have appreciated that the holding of an FAI would be one way in which the UK could initiate the public inquiry necessary to provide a practical and effective investigation into the facts of a particular death in Scotland. By holding an FAI, that would have therefore ensured the UK complied with its obligations under Art 2 in respect of these deaths. The exercise of the Lord Advocate's discretion should have been guided by the existence of those obligations. Lord Mackay concluded that the only means by which a practical and effective investigation into these deaths was to initiate a public inquiry. That could be done by the Lord Advocate seeking the holding of an FAI before a Sheriff or by the Scottish Ministers setting up a public inquiry under the provisions of the Inquiries Act 2005.

2.26   There was also criticism of a failure to give adequate notice of the materials on which the decision had been based. They had pre-judged the likely outcome of any FAI, as well as having failed to outline what 'the existence of other remedies available to the parties' meant.

2.27   Lord Hope of Craighead took the opportunity to consider Scots law in relation to Art 2 obligations in the case of the death of Zahid Mubarek in prison: he was murdered by another prisoner. He reiterated that in Scotland the responsibility for death investigations rested with the public prosecutor (COPFS) and the sheriff. There was no doubt, as he expressed that undertaking an FAI[25] would satisfy the procedural obligation to carry out an effective investigation imposed on the UK by Art 2.[26] The Court of Appeal also outlined that 'the procedural obligation introduced by Article 2 has three interlocking aims: to minimise the risk of future like deaths, to give the beginnings of justice to the bereaved, and to assuage the anxieties of the public'.[27] It goes on to add that 'What is required by way of an investigation cannot be reduced to a catechism of rules; a flexible approach is needed, responsive to the dictates of the facts, case by case.'[28]

2.28   In contrast, where the circumstances of the death had been fully explored within the context of a criminal trial for murder, the Lord Advocate's decision not to hold an FAI was upheld in Niven Petitioner.[29] A similar ECHR, Art 2 challenge had been made but there was no wider public interest element or significant additional information justifying ordering such an inquiry.

---

25   Held then under the 1976 Act.
26   *R (Amin) v Secretary of State for the Home Department* [2003] UKHL 51 at [60], per Lord Hope, *https://publications.parliament.uk/pa/ld200203/ldjudgmt/jd031016/amin-1.htm* (accessed on 21 February 2023).
27   As observed by the Court of Appeal in *R (Khan) v Secretary of State for Health* [2004] 1 WLR 971 at [67] of the judgment of the court.
28   As observed by the Court of Appeal in *R (Khan) v Secretary of State for Health* [2004] 1 WLR 971 at [67] of the judgment of the court.
29   2009 SLT 876.

2.29   Effectively, the Lord Advocate's decision whether to hold a discretionary FAI may be quite narrow but there is a remedy in that their decision may be judicially reviewed. The need to ensure that lessons can be learnt from a death is vital but where other internal or external review processes have been undertaken, there may be no public justification in holding an FAI. It is about achieving balance. There must be care that there is not an acceptance that where reviews of deaths have been undertaken by SPS, by means of a DIPLAR (discussed more fully in **Chapter 6**) or the NHS by way of a SAER, and any recommendations implemented that does necessarily mean that an FAI is not required.

2.30   For years in Scotland, FAIs have provided the route for allowing deaths to be publicly investigated before an independent judicial tribunal. There is an opportunity for the deceased's relatives to participate but there is evidence to suggest that they do not necessarily participate: exactly why seems not to have been fully explored.[30] The FAI seeks to ascertain the full facts surrounding the death, with any unsafe and dangerous practices and procedures being explored and identified. What is needed from the FAI is to understand what happened and why did it happen and that no other family will go through that loss.

2.31   No one route exists as to fulfilling how deaths should be investigated as European jurisprudence affords flexibility as to the method adopted, though minimum standards must be met. These standards include that the public examination of the facts has to be practical and effective.

2.32   The State should take all reasonable steps to secure evidence regarding the death. Any deficiency in the investigation by COPFS who is responsible for fulfilling these functions and those acting under its instructions will undermine the ability to establish the cause of death or identify the person(s) responsible. The FAI will not comply with the required standards for ensuring an effective inquiry is completed, nor comply with the State's obligations under Art 2.

2.33   Finally, to understand what is meant by an inquiry into the death of any 'person', in Scotland whether this includes a foetus falls within a legal debate as to when the right to life begins. The court authority indicates that 'the issue of when the right to life begins comes within the margin of appreciation which the Court generally considers that States should enjoy in this sphere'.[31] Whether an FAI involving a foetus were to be held would fall within the margin of appreciation[32] and therefore lies within the Lord Advocate's discretion.

---

30   See **Chapter 6** 'Nothing to See Here' where researchers reported families were only present in 31% of FAIs and only 16% had legal representation. Just 17% gave evidence at the hearings: *Nothing to See Here? www.sccjr.ac.uk/project/deaths-in-custody-15-years/* (accessed on 21 February 2023).
31   *Evans v UK* (2006) (*Evans v UK* (2006) 43 EHRR 21 as affirmed in *Evans v UK* (2008) 46 EHRR 34).
32   *Evans v UK* (2006) (*Evans v UK* (2006) 43 EHRR 21 as affirmed in *Evans v UK* (2008) 46 EHRR 34).

2.34 FAIs are not the only route to investigations into deaths as public inquiries can be set up to consider the terms of the deaths. These are discussed fully in **Chapter 10**.

Apologies (Scotland) Act 2016

2.35 The role of the Apologies (Scotland) Act 2016 also needs to be considered. As highlighted already, deaths are investigated much more fully now, with relatives keen for FAIs to be held so that they understand and learn from the facts and circumstances of the death. Much of the purpose of holding an FAI is so that lessons can be learnt from any mistakes. As part of that climate and growing public accountability, the Apologies (Scotland) Act 2016[33] was passed and is now in force.

2.36 The Apologies (Scotland) Act 2016 does not affect the responsibility of the Lord Advocate in relation to the investigation of deaths as outlined here and their decision into the holding of an FAI. However, it is important to acknowledge that there is a connection between an FAI being held and an apology given in terms of the Act in relation to a death.

2.37 The Apologies (Scotland) Act 2016 is aimed at encouraging apologies to be given in cases to discourage the use of extensive and expensive litigation. It includes, but is not restricted to, medical cases. An apology is inadmissible in most civil proceedings, including FAIs under s 2(1)(c), as to evidence relevant to the determination of any liability. An apology cannot otherwise be used to the prejudice of the person or organisation making the apology.

2.38 Apologies can be given orally or in writing to acknowledge that mistakes were made and to seek to deliver a successful outcome. An apology does not 'include statements of fact or admissions of fault' and it is only the apology that is inadmissible as to evidence of liability. An apology may include an undertaking to look at the circumstances that gave rise to the act, omission or outcome with a view to preventing a recurrence. There may be an undertaking to review the circumstances of the incident with a view to making improvements or learning lessons. The overlap with consideration as to the background when assessing whether to hold an FAI into a death can therefore be understood.

2.39 The Lord Advocate may decide that there is no reason to hold an FAI if lessons have been learnt already and steps have been put in place to avoid any recurrence of the circumstances leading to the death. These may be factors when considering how relatives respond where mistakes have been made, which are discussed in the *National Law Review* that states:

---

33   19 June 2017.

'Physicians typically recall, with stunning clarity, the moment a patient's treatment went wrong. Following an adverse event, physicians often are tormented by competing desires to apologize and instincts to forge ahead without acknowledgement. *A patient's decision to file a malpractice action may be triggered by the physician's response to a problem—or lack thereof...* Apologies may decrease feelings of frustration and anger that drive some plaintiffs to file lawsuits.'[34] (italics added)

2.40 An apology may influence the decision regarding holding an FAI but should not be the defining factor.

5. RETRIEVAL OF INFORMATION

2.41 In order that the Lord Advocate can fully investigate the circumstances of the death, they need full information. In most cases, this will be relatively straightforward to put together. It will include the relevant accident reports and medical records. Difficulties arose in relation to the retrieval of the combined voice and flight data information (CVF) in relation to the off-shore helicopter crash on 23 August 2013 near Sumburgh Airport, Shetland Islands in which four passengers died. The CVF included a number of communications between the pilots, radio transmissions and announcements to passengers.[35] The CVF is described as a 'vital investigative tool for accident investigators'. However, it may contain information that the pilot and crew may not wish to be made public, including their personal discussions. The concern was that the aircrew might interfere with the operation of the CVF if they were concerned about what might be recorded.

2.42 Though the Air Accidents Investigation Branch were responsible for investigating the accident, the Lord Advocate requested that information to help with their investigation into the circumstances of the deaths. No technical fault with the aircraft had been established as causing the accident. Consequently, the Lord Advocate had asked for an expert report to look at the crew's actions. In order to do so, access to the CVF was required. The Air Accidents Investigation Branch refused to release this information without a court order being obtained.[36]

2.43 The court's decision focused on the balance between the public interest in obtaining the information contained within the CVF as compared to any adverse implications that might result from that disclosure in relation to their investigation. There were concerns that this might act as a precedent in relation to other future

---

34 B Ackerman, 'You had me at "I'm Sorry": The Impact of Physicians' Apologies on Medical Malpractice Litigation', *The National Law Review* (6 November 2018), *www.natlawreview. com/article/you-had-me-i-m-sorry-impact-physicians-apologies-medical-malpractice-litigation* (accessed on 21 February 2023).
35 Air Navigation Order 2009 (SI 2009/3015), Art 37 and Sch 4.
36 Paragraphs 1 and 2 of Art 14 of Regulation EU 996/2010 on the Investigation and Prevention of Accidents and Incidents in Civil Aviation.

investigations, as this may inhibit pilots and staff in conversations that were vital to issues such as considerations of public safety. A Memorandum of Understanding exists between the AAIB, COPFS,[37] the Marine Accident Investigation Branch, and the Association of Chief Police Officers in Scotland (ACPOS).

2.44 The Memorandum sets out that 'the principles for effective liaison, communication and cooperation between these parties so that air and marine accidents, and related criminal incidents and deaths, can be independently investigated, as necessary, by each party, in parallel with each other, whilst also ensuring that legitimate public expectations are met'.[38]

The AAIB will investigate the circumstances of the accident and will then conclude with the publication of a report which will include any safety recommendations that may be appropriate. The CVF will only be used for the accident investigation and will not be disclosed to third parties for litigation or any disciplinary purposes.

2.45 In this case, the right of the Lord Advocate was upheld in seeking the disclosure of the CVF. The Lord Advocate's obligations extended to both criminal [39]and death investigations, both functions being exercised in the public interest and the interests of justice. The recovery of the CVF would provide 'relevant, accurate and reliable evidence … to assist him in his investigation of the circumstances of the death of the four passengers whose lives were lost, and his decision whether and, if so, against whom to launch a prosecution. For that reason, the disclosure of the [CVF] will bring benefits for the purpose of the Lord Advocate's investigation.'[40]

2.46 The benefits of disclosure were held to 'outweigh the adverse domestic and international impact that disclosure may have on the current [internal air] investigation and any future safety investigation'.[41] This may have implications in other cases regarding obtaining access to necessary evidence as to the over-riding authority of the Lord Advocate and their responsibility for discharging in respect of death investigations.

---

37 Marine Accident Investigation Branch and Air Accidents Investigation Branch, *MOU Between AAIB, MAIB, COPFS and ACPOS* (11 January 2008), *www.gov.uk/government/publications/mou-between-aaib-maib-copfs-and-acpos* (accessed on 21 February 2023).

38 Marine Accident Investigation Branch and Air Accidents Investigation Branch, Policy paper, Air and marine investigations in Scotland (11 January 2008), *www.gov.uk/government/publications/mou-between-aaib-maib-copfs-and-acpos/air-and-marine-investigations-in-scotland* (accessed on 21 February 2023).

39 *Boyle v HMA* (1976) JC 32: 'It is for him to decide when and against whom to launch prosecution and upon what charges. It is for him to decide in which Court they shall be prosecuted. It is for him to decide what pleas of guilt he will accept and it is for him to decide when to withdraw or abandon proceedings. Not only so, even when a verdict of guilt has been returned and recorded it still lies with the Lord Advocate whether to move the Court to pronounce sentence, and without that motion no sentence can be pronounced or imposed. In the exercise of these formidable responsibilities the Lord Advocate has at his disposal the fullest available machinery of inquiry and investigation.'

40 *Lord Advocate For an Order in Terms of Regulation 18 of the Civil Aviation Investigation of Air Accidents and Incidents Regulations 1996* [2015] CSOH 80 at [45].

41 Ibid at [45].

Chapter 3

The Historical Development of the FAI system

1. INTRODUCTION

3.01   This section focuses on how the FAI system has evolved and developed.

3.02   FAIs, as will be seen with the discussion on inquests, are quasi-judicial proceedings that, once held, result in the issue of a determination to comply with statutory requirements by making findings as to the cause and manner of the death. Both FAIs and inquests are features of the common law system. Yet, they are an inquisitorial process conducted in a 'stereotypically adversarial common law system'.[1] Their very nature may provide some background to why the FAI system is not as effective as it might be, as the differences in approach are not fully appreciated by those involved in the court processes.

3.03   The FAI system is a product of administrative law which has evolved mainly from 1895. It formed part of the development of a specialist system of tribunals, recognising that there was a need (and legislation then followed) for greater regulation, consistency and control in relation to investigations into deaths.

---

1   McMahan, *The Inquest and Virtues of the Soft Adjudication*, The Yale Law & Policy Review, *https:// ylpr.yule.edu/sites/default/files/YLPR/33.2_article_-_mcmahon_final.pdf* (accessed on 21 February 2023).

3.04 Determinations issued by judges undertaking FAIs affect no one's rights. These rights fall to be determined in other actions that may go on to take place, whether within the civil or criminal process. The conclusions in FAIs may still be highly 'consequential'[2] and may go on to influence the relevant parties' attitudes certainly in respect of subsequent civil court actions. That should mean that FAIs can 'aim more squarely than other legal proceedings at establishing the truth about a contested event'[3] as there should be no sides, other than achieving that of satisfying the public interest.

3.05 FAIs have the aspiration to achieve much for society, providing 'accountability for wrongful deaths, for collection and dissemination of information about risky activities and helping the deceased's family come to terms with a traumatic death'.[4] The procurator fiscal under COPFS adopts the leading role in the investigation, the precursor to the judicial proceedings that follow, and in the conduct of the FAI. This required statutory mechanisms[5] to set out, the then, recognised processes which respected societal interest. FAIs were to be held in the public interest and to provide a state-based system of investigating deaths. Later on, they have ensured compliance with the operation of ECHR, Art 2.

3.06 FAIs now form and are recognised as part of the Scottish established court process. Unlike the coroner in England and Wales, much investigation of deaths is completed without any deaths reaching the court to be investigated. COPFS will decide on the deaths which do fall to be investigated further in in discretionary cases in court (mandatory categories of deaths will go to court as discussed later.) What that means is only a limited number of deaths fall under the judicial scrutiny provided by means of an FAI, the majority of which will be as a result of the mandatory inquiries into deaths. Of course any decisions not to hold an FAI in discretionary cases are subject to review by means of judicial review within the court process.

3.07 The legislative development of the FAI system in Scotland can be shown in the following time line over five periods. The brief historical overview that follows culminates with the commencement of the 1976 Act. That allows for a closer examination of the Fatal Accidents and Sudden Deaths Inquiry (Scotland) Act 1976 as it requires a greater scrutiny to consider the practices that were adopted from that Act and have been developed into the statutory form of FAIs that are now held today.

2   Ibid.
3   Ibid.
4   McMahan P, *The Inquest and Virtues of the Soft Adjudication*, The Yale Law & Policy Review, *https://ylpr.yale.edu/sites/default/files/YLPR/33.2_article_-_mcmahon_final.pdf* (accessed on 21 February 2023).
5   Lord Clyde, Public Law in Scotland. The full address by Lord Clyde to the conference held by the Murray Stable Public Law Group on 10 November 2008 (edited version: Journal, December 2008, 18), *www.lawscot.org.uk/members/journal/issues/vol-54-issue-01/public-law-in-scotland/* (accessed on 25 November 2022).

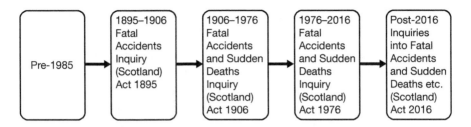

2. PRE-1895

3.08   In the early 19th century, there was no actual authority for holding any public inquiry into the death of any individual. The investigation into the death was undertaken by a procurator fiscal. Robert Shiels[6] has provided some background to the procedures in referencing Henry Brown, the then procurator fiscal at Elgin, from *The Procedure in Accident Inquiries and Investigations according to the Law of Scotland*,[7] where the outline looks similar to what still takes place today, nearly 130 years later, and can be looked at in stages:

> Investigation to Report: 'Every occurrence in Scotland which has caused loss of life or serious injury to person or property is made the subject of a careful inquiry by the local police constable so soon as it comes to his knowledge. This is usually the first step in the investigation. The constable reports the facts to his superior officer, who examines the report, and, if satisfied that it is as complete as circumstances permit, transmits it to the [p]rocurator [f]iscal of the county or district in which the casualty has taken place.'[8]

> Report to the procurator fiscal: 'The procurator fiscal: […] is bound to investigate every fatal accident, of whatever description it may be, which happens within his jurisdiction.'[9]

> '[T]he Procurator Fiscal may investigate either by personal inquiry on the spot, or, if he deems it advisable, by a formal precognition. As it may be necessary to compel the attendance of witnesses for examination, he presents a petition to the Sheriff, obtains a warrant, fixes a convenient place and time for holding the inquiry, and cites witnesses to attend at it. Unless the witnesses are few in number, or there is sufficient cause for making a different arrangement,

---

6   Shiels, *The opposition of lawyers to the introduction of fatal accident inquiries* 2014 SLT 179–184.
7   Brown, *The Procedure in Accident Inquiries and Investigations according to the Law of Scotland* (Edinburgh, 1897).
8   Brown, *The Procedure in Accident Inquiries and Investigations according to the Law of Scotland* (Edinburgh, 1897), p 7.
9   Brown, *The Procedure in Accident Inquiries and Investigations according to the Law of Scotland* (Edinburgh, 1897), p 7.

precognitions are held as near as possible to the scene of the accident. In every case the locus ought to be visited by the [p]rocurator [f]iscal.'[10]

3.09   The visit to the scene by the procurator fiscal continues in practice today. In sudden or suspicious deaths, the procurator fiscal is in charge and will attend soon after the initial reports are obtained.

3.10   Procurators fiscal were then appointed to their role (which continues to be the practice) and it helps to provide some context as to their role.

3.11   Procurators fiscal then and now (once of course they fulfil the requirements of interview etc by COPFS as they are now civil service positions as Scottish Government solicitors) are appointed by a judge, usually a sheriff. They are appointed to a sheriffdom, following a letter of appointment signed by or on behalf of the Crown Agent. This is then presented to the appropriate court when they take up their appointment and where they take an oath of office. Once a procurator fiscal depute has taken their oath before any sheriff from the sheriffdom, they may appear in any sheriff court in that sheriffdom.

3.12   That position, with regard to their role and death investigations, was recognised in *Bell's Dictionary and Digest of the Law of Scotland*.[11] It can be contrasted with the role of a coroner which is covered in **Chapter 7**:

'... there being no coroner in Scotland it is the duty of the sheriff and procurator fiscal in cases where there is reason to suspect that any individual has met his death by violence or from other natural causes immediately to have the body examined by medical men and to take a precognition regarding the circumstances of the case. And where murder fire-raising or any of the greater crimes have been committed these officers frequently repair to the spot, for the purpose of better ascertaining, and of being able to report upon the different circumstances and appearances which the case may exhibit ... Although appointed by the sheriffs, the procurators fiscal of countries from their cumulative and extensive jurisdiction over the whole county are accountable to Crown Counsel for proper discharge of their duties: and in all cases of difficulty it is their duty to communicate with the Crown Agent, for the advice of the Crown Counsel; all correspondence of the fiscals being through the Crown Agent.'[12]

3.13   In effect, as Robert Shiels states, referencing Brown,[13] 'the law and practice ...envisaged a private inquiry by a public official'. There was a personal inquiry

---

10   Brown, *The Procedure in Accident Inquiries and Investigations according to the Law of Scotland* (Edinburgh, 1897), p 12.
11   Watson (ed), *Bell's Dictionary and Digest of the Law of Scotland* (7th edn, Bell & Bradfute, 1890).
12   Watson (ed), *Bell's Dictionary and Digest of the Law of Scotland* (7th edn, Bell & Bradfute, 1890)
13   Shields, *The opposition of lawyers to the introduction of fatal accident inquiries* 2014 SLT 179–184.

undertaken where there was no doubt or difficulty about the facts, but if the death was suspicious of foul play or criminal recklessness, a full precognition was led.[14]

3.14 This practice is largely followed today by Crown counsel and the staff of COPFS. The procurator fiscal carries out their duties in relation to criminal and death investigations. Their work by way of precognition[15] is reported with recommendations about proceedings being made to COPFS, with Crown counsel responsible, under the auspices of the Lord Advocate, in making decisions as to the next steps. Where appropriate, in criminal cases, prosecution on indictment will follow. In death investigations, when the circumstances of the death merit, the instruction will be given to hold an FAI.

3.15 Mention should also be made, as Robert Shiels reflects,[16] to the role of the Book of Regulations, of which the first[17] was issued in July 1868. That Book of Regulations provided depute fiscals with 'a logical, coherent, comprehensive and systematic statement of prosecutorial policy'. (The Book of Regulations is still issued by COPFS today to allow for that promotion of consistency of practice, though it is not necessarily all made publicly available.[18]) This, along with the extent of discretion exercised by the Lord Advocate in relation to deaths, was then enshrined in statute in 1895 and enhanced in 1906.

3.16 However, evolution of the practices relating to deaths in prison falls to be considered separately. These are of course deaths that now result in the holding of a mandatory FAI.[19] The practice of investigation into such deaths evolved from those cases where after a criminal trial there was the imposition of the death penalty when a capital charge was proved. Executions had been held previously in public on the authority of a judicial warrant. This was changed by the Capital Punishment Amendment Act 1868 which abolished public hanging.

3.17 Section 5 of the 1868 Act required the coroner to hold an inquiry within 24 hours of the execution which was modified by s 13 of the 1868 Act to ensure its application to Scotland as follows:

'The Procurator Fiscal of the jurisdiction within which the prison is situated [where the] sentence of death is executed on any offender shall within twenty-four hours after the execution hold a public inquiry before the [sheriff principal

---

14 Brown, *The Procedure in Accident Inquiries and Investigations According to the Law of Scotland* (Edinburgh, T&T Clark, 1897); reviewed at (1897) 13 SL Rev 151.

15 A record of statements, Reports analysis of evidence and recommendations made to COPFS.

16 Shiels, *The Emerging Authority Of Crown Office In The Imperial Age: A Discussion Paper*, Crime and History (2018) 1, *www.lawcrimehistory.org/journal/vol.8%20issue1%202018/shield%20Crown%20office.pdf* (accessed on 21 February 2023).

17 Crown Agent, TG Murray, although necessarily on the authority of the Lord Advocate.

18 Chapter 12 is understood to refer to reporting of deaths but is not currently available. It was obtained on 3 November 2022 (R-06586-22) by means of an FoI request but is out of date in that all references are to the 1976 Act.

19 **Chapter 6**.

or sheriff[20]] of the county on the body of the offender and in particular shall inquire into and ascertain the identity of the body, and whether sentence of death was duly executed on the offender.'

3.18   Thereafter a report or 'deliverance' in duplicate and an original was to be delivered to the lord provost or provost, or magistrate(s), responsible for ensuring the sentence of death had been carried into effect.

3.19   Section 4 of the 1868 Act dealt with the important formalities that:

'as soon as may be after judgment of death has been executed on the offender, the surgeon of the prison shall examine the body of the offender, and shall ascertain the fact of death, and shall sign a certificate thereof, and deliver the same to the sheriff. The sheriff, and the gaoler and chaplain of the prison, and such justices and other persons present (if any) as the sheriff requires or allows, shall also sign a declaration to the effect that judgment of death has been executed on the offender.'

3.20   Section 10 of the 1868 Act required all paperwork including the certificate, declaration and the duplicate of the inquisition to be sent 'with all convenient speed' by the sheriff to one of Her Majesty's Principal Secretaries of State. A notification requirement required that printed copies of the documents were exhibited as soon as possible and for at least 24 hours kept exhibited on or near the principal entrance of the prison where the death sentence was carried out.

3.21   What was clear was that the procurator fiscal had an important role to establish the cause of death and that the implementation of the sentence was completed in accordance with the law ie complying with the judicial warrant.

3.22   The inquiries were of a rather limited nature completed in private before the sheriff with no representations from any other party. Though there was an inquiry into the death, what can be seen is that challenge was in effect not really possible except in theory. It did not then extend to deaths in prison from other causes such as natural causes.

3.23   Later, s 53 of the Prisons (Scotland) Act 1877 widened these investigations so it provided that:

'it shall be the duty of the procurator fiscal of the jurisdiction within which a prison is situated to hold a public inquiry before the sheriff or sheriff-substitute of the county on the body of every prisoner who may die within such prison. Where it is practicable, time shall intervene between the day of the death prison. and the day of the holding the inquiry, to allow the attendance of the next of kin to the deceased.'

20   Sheriff Courts (Scotland) Act 1971, s 4.

3.24   Under s 25(1) of the Prisons (Scotland) Act 1952, which repealed the 1877 Act, there was an obligation on the governor of a prison, in the event of the death of a prisoner, to give immediate notice thereof to the procurator fiscal within whose area the prison in situated, and to the visiting committee, and, where practicable, to the nearest relative of the prisoner. Section 25(2) obliged the procurator fiscal to 'hold a public inquiry before the sheriff into the death of any prisoner in a prison within his area, and where practicable sufficient time between the death and the holding of the inquiry shall intervene to allow the attendance of the next of kin of the prisoner'.

3.25   The system into investigations into deaths in custody was therefore conducted separately alongside the operation of investigations into other deaths until 1976 when all investigations into deaths were included within the 1976 Act. That set out the basis for holding mandatory and discretionary FAIs as discussed in section 5 below.

3.   1895–1906

3.26   For practical purposes, the Fatal Accidents Inquiry (Scotland) Act 1895[21] ('the 1895 Act') is taken as the statutory starting point for the framework of the FAI system. The 1895 Act's purpose was to 'to make provision for Public Inquiry in regard to Fatal Accidents occurring in Industrial Employments or Occupations in Scotland'. Under s 2 of the 1895 Act, the public inquiry referred to cases of death of any person or persons, whether employers or employed, engaged in any industrial employment or occupation in Scotland, due or reasonably believed to be due to an accident occurring in the course of such employment or occupation.[22]

3.27   There was no definition of what an industrial employment, occupation and accident were, which were terms on which discussions thereafter ensued. FAIs were only mandatory where they related to an accident resulting in death and not for accidents where there was only injury, no matter how significant. Deaths too from non-industrial accidents are dealt with separately, as this did not include deaths that resulted from natural causes such as from floods or storms.

3.28   Section 4(2) of the 1895 Act provided that:

'(i)n any case in which it is competent for any official or department of Her Majesty's Government to cause public inquiry to be made into the … accident under the provisions of any statute in force for the time being, then such intimation [by the Sheriff Clerk] shall also be made to such official or department.'

---

21   58 & 59 Vict Ch 36.
22   1895 Act, s 2.

3.29   These FAIs were held in front of a sheriff and jury under s 4(4) of the 1895 Act. Under ss (5), the jury was to consist of five common and two special jurors. Questions were to arise as to the role of the jury over whether they could find any culpability in the circumstances. Mr Graham Murray, Solicitor General, in responding to a question in the UK Parliament, indicated that 'the jury could "find culpability in any individual, [which] leaves it open to them to do so if they choose'.[23] This was to be clarified by the 1906 Act.

4.   1906–1976

3.30   The Fatal Accidents and Sudden Deaths Inquiry (Scotland) Act 1906 set out under s 7 that where the verdicts were to be returned that:

'the jury, after hearing the evidence and the persons, if they so desire, appearing thereon, including any person duly authorised by any trades union or friendly society of which the deceased was a member, and the summing up by the sheriff, if he shall consider such summing up necessary or proper, shall return a verdict setting forth, so far as such particulars have been proved, when and where the accident and the death or deaths to which the inquiry relates took place, the cause or causes of such accident or death or deaths, the person or persons, if any, to whose fault or negligence the accident is attributable, the precautions, if any, by which it might have been avoided, any defects in the system or mode of working which contributed to the accident, and any other facts disclosed by the evidence which, in the opinion of the jury, are relevant to the inquiry.'

3.31   Section 3 of the 1906 Act also widened the scope of FAIs to provide that 'in any case of sudden or suspicious death in Scotland, the Lord Advocate may, whenever it appears to him to be expedient in the public interest, direct that a public inquiry into such death and the circumstances thereof shall be held; and the public interest directed to be held shall take place according to the forms and procedure prescribed by [the 1895 Act].' Wide discretion in holding FAIs was now afforded to the procurator fiscal.

3.32   Under s 5(3) of the 1895 Act, the right to appear at an FAI was quite wide. It was competent for the wife or husband of the deceased spouse 'and to the relatives' and to the various employers of the deceased person who has lost their life in the accident. It is interesting perhaps to reflect too that the legislation did take account of working women, though there were few FAIs into the death of women. **Appendix 2** goes on to highlight one of the earliest records of an FAI into the death of a woman: that of Jessie Cargill or Jamieson in October 1915.

---

23   HC Deb 5 August 1898 Vol 64 cc 281–2.

3.33   The section goes on to give a perspective of what type of accidents were commonplace at this time as it refers to 'an accident in or about a mine to an inspector of mines', and to 'an accident in a factory or workshop to an inspector of factories and workshops', and also to any persons engaged under the same employers as the deceased person. A catchall allows any other persons whom the sheriff may consider, to have a just interest in the inquiry, to appear at, and take part in, and adduce evidence at, such inquiry, either by themselves or by counsel or agents, or by any other person or persons whom the sheriff may allow to appear on their behalf.

3.34   An early inquiry held under the 1906 Act was the Elliott Junction railway accident at Arbroath on 28 December 1906. This involved a collision on the Arbroath to Dundee-bound section of two trains, resulting in 22 casualties. Two inquiries were held. One was conducted by the Board of Trade under Major JW Pringle published on 26 February 1907. Given the death of a number of railway employees in the course of their employment, the procurator fiscal also held a five-day public inquiry at Arbroath Courthouse before Sheriff James Ferguson in January 1907. Allegations of alcohol being a factor in relation to the driver Mr Gourlay were made at the public inquiry, as there must be an explanation for the accident which was described as 'unusual carelessness' and even having consumed two half glasses of whisky at Arbroath should not have affected him to that extent. The report outlined the opinion that 'lack of intelligence, or of caution and alertness, displayed by the driver, Gourlay on this occasion were in part at all events induced by drink, the effects of which may possibly have been accentuated after he left Arbroath by exposure to the weather'.[24]

3.35   Among the casualties was Alexander William Black, MP, a Liberal party member, who was severely injured in the crash and died later. Interestingly, a criminal prosecution of the driver was also held resulting in his conviction for culpable homicide.

3.36   What might be of passing interest for comparison purposes were the numbers of FAIs held in 1964–1966 shown in the table below:

Number of FAIs	1964	1965	1966
Road traffic accidents	43	46	40
Industrial accidents	152	159	158
Other (This includes accidents in the home)	43	63	27
Total	238	268	225

---

24   *Accident Returns, Extract for Accident at Elliot Junction on 28th December 1906, www. railwaysarchive.co.uk/docsummary.php?docID=176* (accessed on 21 February 2023).

3.37   These represent a very different number of FAIs being held in comparison to an estimated 50 or so FAIs being held annually by COPFS[25] as referenced at the time when the 2016 Bill was introduced.

5.   1976–2016

3.38   With the implementation of the 1895 and 1906 Acts, this meant that the FAI system remained relatively unchanged. This was the FAI system in place until the 1976 Act was passed. The importance of the exercise of the Lord Advocate's discretion was stressed under the provisions of the 1906 Act, while respecting the privacy of the families' interest in the death. The ultimate decision as to holding an FAI remained then, as today, that of the Lord Advocate. Mr William Ross MP Secretary of State for Scotland in 1967 who, in response to a question from Mr Dewar MP stated that:

> 'in any case of a sudden or suspicious death which does not come within the scope of [the 1895 Act] and in which, although there is no appearance of criminal responsibility, the information available suggests that the occurrence was directly or indirectly connected with the actions of a third party; or in which there is a desire locally for a public inquiry into the circumstances; or where the procurator fiscal considers that such an inquiry is expedient in the public interest, the views of the relatives of the deceased are taken into account in deciding whether an inquiry should be held in … The relatives are informed, however, that the final decision on the matter rests with the Lord Advocate.'[26]

3.39   For the period of World War 2, the requirement to hold an FAI with a jury was removed unless a sheriff so directed.[27] Consequential modifications followed as to the procedures that might be necessary where there was no jury. In effect, this removed the need to empanel jurors when many had been called up or were undertaking war service. After the war, juries were reinstated. Though consideration had been given in World War 1 to that exact change being made, no legislation was forthcoming to resolve 'the waste of time and inconvenience caused by summoning jurors to attend inquiries under the Fatal Accidents Inquiry (Scotland) Acts'.[28]

3.40   The debate as to the use of juries in FAIs was to resurface and was finally resolved when the Fatal Accidents and Sudden Deaths Inquiry (Scotland) Act 1976 (c.14) was passed. It followed the Grant Committee Report recommendations that indicated that the use of juries in such inquiries had ceased to be useful, 'with the jury merely rubber-stamping a verdict dictated by the sheriff'. They did:

---

25   *https://archive2021.parliament.scot/S4_Bills/Fatal%20Accidents%20(Scotland)%20Bill/b63s4-introd-pm.pdf* (accessed on 21 February 2023).
26   Vol 741: debated on Tuesday 14 February 1967.
27   Administration of Justice (Emergency Provisions) (Scotland) Act 1939, s 4(3).
28   *Hansard* Debate 5 February 1918.

'no more than give effect to a verdict dictated to them by the sheriff or sheriff-substitute, which merely records the cause of death … on balance, we [that is, the Grant Committee] take the view that what is important is the public inquiry and the hearing of evidence, and not the form of the verdict. We have also had in mind that the time of jurymen is at present needlessly occupied, and we note that during the last war fatal accident inquiries were conducted without juries, without any ill effects of which we are aware.'[29]

3.41 Their removal would effect a considerable saving of time and expense. This practice lies directly contrary to the position maintained in England and Wales with public scrutiny provided by the use of juries in inquests that continues today.

3.42 A number of very significant FAIs were indeed held with a jury whose verdict was then recorded. These include the FAI into the Ibrox disaster in 1971 into the 66 deaths which occurred at the New Year's Day match between Rangers and Celtic. This was held in February 1972 at Pollokshaws Burgh Hall in front of Sheriff Allan Walker and lasted for seven days.[30] An extract of a death certificate is included below:

3.43 Another FAI in this period with a jury was the Cairngorm Plateau disaster where school children died on 21 and 22 November 1971. This FAI is included in **Appendix 2** that outlines the importance and significance of this FAI.

3.44 What these FAIs illustrate are the lessons that were learnt from these deaths which led to changes that were made by way of legislation resulting from the Ibrox disaster about football safety. That introduced the Safety of Sports Grounds Act 1975.[31] Following the Cairngorm disaster, a number of changes were made to trips for school parties which included obtaining the relevant parental

29 Column 839, Lord Kirkhill, *https://hansard.parliament.uk/Lords/1975-12-09/OOc4bOee-cf90-4ec6-94f2-e8bc90dfcda0/FatalAccidentsandSuddenDeathsInquiry(Scotland)BillHl* (accessed on 21 February 2023).

30 Scotlands People, *Our Records: The Ibrox Disaster of 1971* (6 January 2022), *www.scotlandspeople.gov.uk/article/our-records-ibrox-disaster-1971* (accessed on 21 February 2023).

31 Under the Safety of Sports Grounds Act 1975, which brought about the introduction of the safety certificate, the local authority is responsible for both issuing and enforcing a safety certificate in respect of sports grounds designated by the Secretary of State.

consent to the activities being undertaken. A fuller discussion of that FAI is included under **Appendix 2**.

3.45   However, the FAI may not itself result in any actual legislation changes but has as much a role in raising awareness of the relevant dangers. By 1971, the time of these disasters, this was much more apparent as media reporting was now able to cover these disasters in a visual way, through television. The significance for the country as a whole in avoiding the incidence of such deaths being caused by such dangers was much more apparent, covered ably by the press. This is an important feature of the public inquiry in increasing public awareness and can be seen in the debate in the UK Parliament on the death of 13 girls in a fire at the Grafton's department store in Glasgow on 4 May 1949, where:

> 'the transcript of the evidence at the inquiry is available, it will be carefully considered, and any salient points affecting fire prevention measures will be brought to the notice of lire authorities. The Government hope that one result of this tragic event will be a marked increase in the number of applications by the owners or occupiers of premises where there is any appreciable fire risk for advice, which is free, from the fire prevention officers of fire brigade.'[32]

3.46   This was not entirely new, as even in 19th century the coroner, through the use of press reporting, expressed his concerns over the number of domestic deaths of children in houses where fire guards were not being used. By 'choosing to report acts of everyday violence as news [...] the newspapers' narrative invoked wider concern of perceived disorder with working-class neighbourhoods and, in doing so, spelt out the case for regulation and reform', when eventually there was support to legislate in order to avoid such accidents.[33]

6.   FATAL ACCIDENTS AND SUDDEN DEATHS INQUIRY (SCOTLAND) ACT 1976

3.47   The Fatal Accidents and Sudden Deaths Inquiry (Scotland) Act 1976 (c.14) (the 1976 Act) substantially followed recommendations made by the Scottish Home and Health Department's Sheriff Court Report appointed by the Secretary of State for Scotland in 1967[34] (the Grant Committee). The 1976 Act repealed the 1895 Act, the 1906 Acts and the 1952 Act.

3.48   The 1976 Act was itself described as 'primarily a measure of law reform, consolidating and amending as it does the legislation governing public inquiries into

---

32   HL Deb Vol 163 cols 1120-1 (12 July 1949): *https://api.parliament.uk/historic-hansard/lords/1949/jul/12/glasgow-fire-tragedy#S5LV0163P0_19490712_HOL_19HL* (accessed on 21 February 2023).

33   Holmes, *Absent Fireguards And Burnt Children: Coroners And The Development Of Clause 15 of the Children Act 1908* (2012) Law, Crime and History, 1: *https://lawcrimehistory.org/journal/vol.1%20issue1%202012/Holmes.pdf* (accessed on 21 February 2023).

34   The Grant Committee, Command Paper No 3248.

deaths in Scotland and modernising the procedure to be followed at such inquiries'.[35] A number of factors lay behind the policy intention to review and to help inquiries to be conducted more effectively and more efficiently. The Grant Committee on the Sheriff Court, in its Report published in July 1967, had made several recommendations, though not all were included in the 1976 Act. The reform over the abolition of the jury was only one.

3.49   There was a feeling that the 1895 Act and the 1906 Act were felt to be 'for all genuine purposes, extinct and irrelevant'[36] apart from the technological and other changes that had occurred to society since then.

3.50   Over the intervening period, the work place had changed significantly. A considerable volume of legislation had come into force, examples of which included the Offices, Shops and Railway Premises Act 1963 and the Health and Safety at Work etc Act 1974. Any motivating factor that had existed in relation to the 1895 Act, that deaths in the work place might be hidden, had by now been largely addressed. Attempts to ensure improvements based on the grounds of public safety were therefore not so pertinent. The Committee rejected, after considerable debate, any dilution of the requirement to hold mandatory inquiries into work place accidents arising in the course of employment. Indeed, it sought to clarify that the scope of compulsory inquiries would expand to include not only industrial accidents as originally included but now would include inquiries into deaths resulting from accidents to those at work in offices, shops, schools and hospitals, as well as those in factories. There was in effect no basis on safety grounds to distinguish between employment in industrial or non-industrial premises.

3.51   Reform was also urgently needed in relation to the development of the North Sea for oil production. Powers to investigate lay with the Department of Energy's inspectors but such deaths might, in appropriate cases, give rise to civil or criminal liability. Even by the time the Bill was being debated, there had already been a number of deaths in oil-related work since North Sea oil rig building and maintenance had begun. There had been deaths as shown in this Table, of which[37] one had been fully investigated.

1973	1974	1975
3	9	8

35 Fatal Accidents and Sudden Deaths Inquiry (Scotland) Bill, HC Deb 2 March 1976 Vol 906 cc 1117–60, *https://api.parliament.uk/historic-hansard/commons/1976/mar/02/fatal-accidents-and-sudden-deaths* (accessed on 21 February 2023).
36 Fatal Accidents and Sudden Deaths Inquiry (Scotland) Bill, HC Deb 2 March 1976 Vol 906 cc 1117–60.
37 *Hansard*, Fatal Accidents and Sudden Deaths Inquiry (Scotland) Bill Lords, Vol 906 (2 March 1976) *https://hansard.parliament.uk/Commons/1976-03-02/debates/d4447ba4-decd-4dc4-94f6-bd040827a769/FatalAccidentsAnd Sudden Deaths Inquiry(Scotland) Bill Lords* (accessed on 21 February 2023).

3.52   The facts and circumstances of such deaths needed to be determined to the satisfaction of the public on a similar basis to those relating to industrial deaths or accidental deaths on land.[38] A short term fix had been put in place with The Continental Shelf (Jurisdiction) (Amendment) Order 1975[39] on 20 November 1975. This gave the sheriff jurisdiction to hold inquiries into Continental Shelf oil deaths, but only where the cause of death was clearly the act or omission of some person. This restriction was necessary to keep within the ambit of the Continental Shelf Act 1964, under which the 1975 Order was made. Few cases would allow the possibility of an accident to be ruled out before there had been an FAI. Where a death was accidental, no FAI could be held. Section 9 of the 1976 Act therefore extended the definition of 'Scotland' to include the continental shelf to allow FAIs to be conducted under Scots Law. The 1976 Act also allowed for inquiries to be instructed into deaths occurring up to three years earlier. This allowed for future inquiry into past deaths.

3.53   To provide flexibility, there was a need too to provide for powers enabling provisions to make procedural changes to FAIs without the time required to pass primary legislation.

3.54   There was no longer any provision to make a finding that someone was at fault, ie a negligence finding. As stated by the Lord Advocate, Mr Ronald King Murray:

> 'A FAI is not the place for accusation or condemnation. In such an inquiry there is no reason why the general rule of corroboration should be applied, because there is no accusation and no condemnation. Indeed, corroboration has already ceased to be essential in actions for damages in respect of death or personal injury, and it seems appropriate to relax the rule here too.'[40]

3.55   This is perhaps the most significant aspect for those studying the historical development of FAIs today. **Appendix 2** includes several earlier FAIs where in effect negligence findings were made on the basis of the evidence presented at the FAI. Reference is made to the boys' deaths at Balgowan Approved School and to the baby who died in the Forth ferry crossing.[41] Findings such as these today would not be possible.

---

38   Continental Shelf (Jurisdiction) (Amendment) Order 1975, which came into force on 20 November 1975 and gave the sheriff jurisdiction to hold inquiries into Continental Shelf oil deaths, but only where the cause of death was clearly the act or omission of some person. This restriction was necessary to keep within the limits of the parent Act, the Continental Shelf Act 1964, under which the Order was made. Such a restricted provision is, however, clearly only a partial remedy.
39   SI 1975/1708.
40   *Hansard*, HL Vol 906 col 1123 (2 March 1976).
41   Death of William Green Hogg and Angus McPherson, deaths of Alexander Cameron Boswell (11), George Samuel Murdoch Gibson (14), George Allan Penman (13), Harry Low (13), Thomas Thomson Bunt (14) and George Sinclair (13).

3.56   The provisions of the 1976 Act operated until it was repealed by the 2016 Act. A number of important FAIs were held under the 1976 Act, including the Lockerbie disaster.[42]

3.57   That FAI was held between 1 October 1990 and 13 February 1991 by Sheriff-Principal Mowat QC into the deaths of the passengers and crew, as well as the inhabitants of Lockerbie, on 21 December 1988 when Pan-Am flight 103 crashed as a result of an act of terrorism. The cause of death for all passengers and on the ground was due to:

> 'the detonation of an improvised explosive device located in luggage container AVE 4041 situated on the left side of the forward hold of … aircraft ….The detonation caused the nose and flight deck of the aircraft to become detached and the rest of the aircraft to descend out of control and to break up, eventually crashing into the ground at or near Lockerbie. The wing and centre fuselage section crashed in the Sherwood Crescent area of the town and caused the deaths [that referred to the residents in Lockerbie.] The deaths [that referred to the passengers and crew] resulted from injuries sustained either as a direct result of the explosion and the disintegration of the aircraft or from impact with the ground.'[43]

3.58   Paragraph [6] stated that the 'primary cause of … deaths was a criminal act of murder'.

3.59   The findings[44] went on to include that in 1988 there was a danger of an explosive device being concealed in an unaccompanied piece of baggage which was then loaded on to an aircraft. This baggage would be interlined at a particular airport from another airline with the person introducing it not checking in as a passenger at that airport. Passenger/baggage reconciliation was an important element in any system designed to prevent unaccompanied baggage being on an aircraft. A reasonable precaution considered ways in which positive passenger/baggage reconciliation procedures might be put in place and if these had been adopted as precautions these processes might have avoided the deaths. The effect of that disaster on air travel can be seen in the stringent processes now in place with regard to baggage checks.

3.60   The 1976 Act was not subject to substantial change from the time of its implementation until repealed. Section 12(4) of the Coroners and Justice Act 2009 extended the jurisdiction of the 1976 Act to FAIs to be held into the deaths of service personnel where the person's body was in Scotland or expected to be brought to the UK. It was felt that these deaths involving Scots persons should fall to be investigated under the FAI system.

---

42   *www.vetpath.co.uk/lockerbie/fai.pdf* (accessed on 25 November 2022).
43   Ibid at [4].
44   Ibid at [13]–[20].

7.   THE PASSAGE TO THE REFORM OF THE 1976 ACT

3.61   In March 2008, the then Cabinet Secretary for Justice, Kenny MacAskill MSP, announced that a major review of the operation of the FAI legislation was required. He appointed the Right Honourable Lord Cullen of Whitekirk KT[45] to lead the review. The remit was wide, outlining that it was:

> 'to review the operation of the Fatal Accidents and Sudden Deaths Inquiry (Scotland) Act 1976[46], which governs the system of judicial investigation of sudden or unexplained deaths in Scotland, so as to ensure that Scotland has an effective and practical system of public inquiry into deaths which is fit for the 21st century.'[47]

3.62   There were a number of reasons why reform of the FAI was being undertaken. The 1976 Act was over 30 years old (and 40 years old when the reforms actually took place). The system of FAIs had not kept up with other substantial reforms of the justice system which had been or were then under review, such as summary justice reform. The aims of these reforms included making the justice system faster, more efficient and visible. There had also been concerns expressed over the legal representation of bereaved families and the appropriate provision of legal aid, the legal status of the recommendations made by sheriffs at the conclusion of FAIs, delays in holding FAIs and the question of whether FAIs were the correct way in which to investigate deaths in hospitals and other healthcare situations.[48]

3.63   The report on the review was published by Lord Cullen on 3 November 2009[49] which concluded by making 36 recommendations for change. These recommendations covered a range of topics, aimed at the sheriff courts and sheriffs, COPFS and judicial training, the scope of mandatory fatal accident inquiries, decision making by COPFS, determinations and powers to commence fresh proceedings. These recommendations are outlined in full and discussed in **Chapter 13**. This allows an understanding of what the width and depth of these reforms undertaken by the 2016 Act set out to achieve.

3.64   The response from the Scottish Government to the review was not published until March 2012, where they accepted a number of these recommendations. Some

---

45   Judge in holding the inquiry into the shooting at Dunblane.
46   The scope included the 1976 Act and the Fatal Accidents and Sudden Deaths Procedure (Scotland) Rules 1977.
47   The announcement of the Review was followed by a public consultation exercise issued on 20 November 2008, *Review of Fatal Accident Inquiry Legislation: a consultation paper, www. webarchive.org.uk/wayback/archive/20150220123924/http://www.gov.scot/About/Review/fatal-accident-review/20094258/0* (accessed on 21 February 2023).
48   *Review of Fatal Accident Inquiry Legislation: The Report* (November 2009), para 1.2, *www.webarchive. org.uk/wayback/archive/20150219075856/http://www.gov.scot/Publications/2009/11/02113726/0* (accessed on 21 February 2023).
49   *Review of Fatal Accident Inquiry Legislation: The Report* (November 2009).

were to be implemented by rules to be made under powers provided in the Bill and others were to be put into effect by organisations such as COPFS and SCTS.

3.65 A Scottish Government consultation into 'Proposals to Reform Fatal Accident Inquiries Legislation' ran from July to September 2014, with the report on the consultation being published in November 2014.[50]

3.66 The introduction of the 2016 Bill then largely implemented the recommendations in the 2009 Review Report in so far as they had not been already implemented. COPFS had by that time already implemented a number of changes in its creation of the Scottish Fatalities Investigation Unit (SFIU) with its responsibility to oversee the progress of deaths investigation, both in mandatory and discretionary FAIs.

8. FURTHER REVIEW OF THE 2016 ACT

3.67 **Chapter 13** considers these recommendations in the light of an examination into the effectiveness of the operations of the FAI system today. Since the 2016 Act was passed, there has been no comprehensive review held of the operation of the 2016 Act. However, a thematic review of FAIs was conducted by the Inspectorate of Prosecution in Scotland.[51]

3.68 During the passage of the 2016 Bill, there had been criticisms made of the delays arising between the date of death and the start of FAIs. Causes for these delays were discussed which included the need to await the result of other investigations, such as health and safety considerations and/or considerations as to the holding of a prosecution, obtaining expert evidence, the complexity of deaths and the time in reporting of the death to COPFS. These factors are similar to those discussed under **Chapter 7** when considering delays in holding inquests in England and Wales.

3.69 That Report's aim was to obtain factual data on the causes of delay so that they could identify recurring themes and make recommendations to improve the efficiency and effectiveness of death investigations and the FAI process.[52] A number of recommendations were made, with a follow-up Report then published by Michelle McLeod, HM Chief Inspector, on 7 August 2019. She indicated that in:

---

50   Scottish Government, *Consultation on Proposals to Reform Fatal Accident Inquiries Legislation – Analysis of Consultation Responses* (21 November 2014), *www.gov.scot/publications/consultation-proposals-reform-fatal-accident-inquiries-legislation-analysis-consultation-responses/* (accessed on 21 February 2023).

51   Scottish Government, *Fatal Accident Inquiries: review* (18 August 2016), *www.gov.scot/publications/thematic-review-fatal-accident-inquiries/pages/1/* (accessed on 21 February 2023).

52   Scottish Government, *Fatal Accident Inquiries: review* (18 August 2016), para 14.

'almost three years since the thematic FAI report [had been] published, the lack of progress in many areas is disappointing. While there has been some improvement in the timelines for conducting FAIs, the time taken to conclude mandatory FAIs remains a concern as does their age profile with 20 inquiries more than 3 years old.'[53]

3.70   Plans were made to consider a follow-up report in 2020, but with Covid-19 that appears not to have been produced. That concern over delays in holding FAIs is a recurrent theme, as it impacts on all involved and affects the issue of public confidence in the system, which is the purpose of holding FAIs to identify the circumstances of the death and to avoid these circumstances repeating in subsequent years.

---

53   Scottish Government, *Fatal Accident Inquiries: follow up review* (7 August 2019), *www.gov.scot/ publications/follow-up-review-fatal-accident-inquiries/* (accessed on 21 February 2023).

Chapter 4

Inquiries into Fatal Accidents and Sudden Deaths etc. (Scotland) Act 2016

1. INTRODUCTION

4.01   This chapter outlines the background to the Inquiries into Fatal Accidents and Sudden Deaths etc. (Scotland) Act 2016 (asp 2) (the 2016 Act) and the scope of FAIs. The provisions of the 2016 Act are discussed in relation to the inquiries and the deaths covered in FAIs (ss 1–7 of the 2016 Act), provisions of information by COPFS (ss 8–9 of the 2016 Act), witnesses for precognition (s 10 of the 2016 Act), participants at the FAI (s 11 of the 2016 Act) and the location, jurisdiction and inquiries into multiple deaths (ss 12–14 of the 2016 Act).

2. GENERAL: INQUIRIES INTO FATAL ACCIDENTS AND SUDDEN DEATHS ETC (SCOTLAND) ACT 2016

4.02   The modernisation of the FAI system was reflected in the Scottish Government's objective in introducing the 2016 Bill 'to reform and modernise the law governing the holding of (FAIs) in Scotland'.[1] Since its commencement on 15 June 2017[2] the 2016 Act represents the law under which FAIs are held today. These processes relating to pre-inquiry, inquiry and post-inquiry will be examined in **Chapter 5** in detail.

4.03   The 2016 Act reiterated that FAIs were civil in process and not adversarial, and continued that at their conclusion, no criminal or civil findings could be made. It did not seek to change the format of the FAI developed from the 1976 Act. It continued to reflect the practices and jurisprudence which had evolved since the 1976 Act, with the removal of a jury in 1976 that had led to the judge (usually a sheriff) issuing a written determination at the conclusion of the FAI.

4.04   The policy objectives of the Bill[3] were:

- to build on the recommendations implemented by COPFS to make the system more efficient;
- to extend the categories of death in which it is mandatory to hold an FAI;
- to place a requirement on those to whom sheriffs direct recommendations at the conclusion of the inquiry to respond;
- to permit discretionary FAIs into deaths of Scots abroad where the body is repatriated to Scotland;
- to permit FAIs to be re-opened if new evidence arises or, if the evidence is so substantial, to permit a completely new inquiry to be held; and
- to provide flexibility for the locations and accommodation for FAIs.

4.05   An overview of the 2016 Act includes:

- **Scope of the FAI:** COPFS and the procurator fiscal continued to be responsible for investigating the death. FAIs were to consider what precautions, improvements or actions may be taken to prevent other deaths arising in similar circumstances. The FAI was not to consider any matters that lay outside the circumstances of the death. Setting out the limitations under the 2016 Act for the benefit of those attending the FAI[4] was considered to be good practice.

---

1   Policy Memorandum, Inquiries into Fatal Accidents and Sudden Deaths etc. (Scotland) Bill, para 2 *https://archive2021.parliament.scot/S4_Bills/Fatal%20Accidents%20(Scotland)%20Bill/b63s4-introd-pm.pdf* (accessed on 21 February 2023).

2   The Act received Royal Assent on 14 January 2016. Various provisions of the 2016 Act were enacted on 1 September 2016 and 1 December 2016 respectively by the Inquiries into Fatal Accidents and Sudden Deaths etc. (Scotland) Act 2016 (Commencement No.2, Transitional and Transitory Provision) Regulations 2016 (SSI 2016/370) and the Inquiries into Fatal Accidents and Sudden Deaths etc. (Scotland) Act 2016 (Commencement No. 3, Transitional and Saving Provisions) Regulations 2017 (SSI 2017/155) brought the remainder of the 2016 Act into effect on 17 June 2017 in so far as not earlier implemented.

3   Policy Memorandum, Inquiries into Fatal Accidents and Sudden Deaths etc. (Scotland) Bill, para 5.

4   *Dodds* 2009 GWD 27-425 Sh Ct (Tayside, Central and Fife).

- **Purpose:** The purpose of the FAI was not to find fault.[5] It seeks to examine the circumstances of the death but does not necessarily require 'that no stone is left unturned to ensure that every possible circumstance surrounding the death is aired in evidence'. It is the public interest that requires to be satisfied and not the bereaved families' own interests. There is an inevitable overlap between public interest and the family's interests in ascertaining what has happened.

- **Criticism:** From the prosecution's perspective, FAIs should not be the appropriate forum for criticising the decisions of the prosecuting authorities or the courts. In the FAI into the death of Mr Dekker,[6] it was determined that he was killed in a road traffic accident after his motor vehicle collided with a van that was travelling the wrong way in a one-way traffic system. At the FAI, the family asked the sheriff to make a number of recommendations. These recommendations clearly related to government policy suggesting that an FAI should be automatically held following any death in a road traffic accident. Road traffic legislation should be amended to increase the penalties where a death resulted from a road traffic accident and that the driver should be prosecuted for a road traffic offence. The sheriff could only make recommendations where these relate to the circumstances of death. None of these proposals contributed to the accident nor could they, had they been in place at the time of the accident, have resulted in the accident being avoided, and were well beyond the FAI's remit.

4.06   Looking at FAIs and where there may be consideration of decision making on the allocation of public resources, these would not tend to fall within the remit and be related to the circumstances of the death. An example of how examination of public decision making may feature can be seen in the public inquiry to be held into deaths in care homes in Scotland that related to Covid-19. That is being held under the Inquiries Act 2005 which provides for much wider terms of reference than is possible under the scope of the 2016 Act. This is discussed more fully in **Chapter 10**.

4.07   **Public accountability:** Courts are increasingly being asked to consider the challenges that arise in connection with allocation of healthcare resources, deference to the medical judgments, and patient treatment choice, along with a more informed public demanding increasing accountability.[7] The Emms case set this out:

'Doctors are not in the business of killing people. Sometimes things go wrong... because hospitals are institutions staffed by human beings, however well trained and competent the staff may be. If such mistakes are made, the person, or persons, responsible may be sued in a civil litigation. But such occurrences, however understandably distressing they may be to the relatives of the persons

---

5   *Black v Scott Lithgow Ltd* 1990 SC 322; [1990] 3 WLUK 393.
6   *Dekker* 2000 SCLR 1087 Sh Ct (South Strathclyde, Dumfries and Galloway).
7   Syrett, *Courts, Expertise and Resource Allocation: Is there a Judicial 'Legitimacy Problem'?* Public Health Ethics Vol 7, No 2 (July 2014), 112–122.

who die as a result, do not raise questions of public concern unless something has apparently gone quite seriously wrong, which is indicative of not just a one-off situation, or a single example of error of judgment, or carelessness, but is of such a nature that gives concern that the system and procedures in operation at the hospital were so deficient that there may have been a number of deaths attributable to them or, that if these deficiencies are not addressed, there may be more deaths in the future.'[8]

4.08   In Emms, the family had petitioned for a judicial review against the Lord Advocate's refusal to hold an FAI. They had claimed that there had been a systemic failure by the hospital employees which had caused or contributed to his death. The medical review conducted internally had concluded that there was no issue with the care or clinical decision making. An FAI would therefore achieve nothing more.

4.09   A number of discretionary FAIs have been held into medical or healthcare deaths, but it is important to remember that not every medical death will result in an FAI. FAIs are equally competent in relation to deaths in the private medical sector as well as within the NHS.[9] The FAI into the death of James McAlpine (aged 7) on 23 February 1985 in a private hospital concluded that the death might have been avoided if the parents had been more fully informed as to the nature of the procedure and its hazards and if the child had been more closely monitored post-operatively.[10]

4.10   **Professional conduct:** FAIs are also not the place for professional conduct inquires. These should lie within the forum of the respective professional bodies such as the General Medical Council (GMC). Frequently, potential disciplinary action will follow the outcome of an FAI. However, the FAI into the death of Gordon Greig[11] confirmed that an FAI should not be a general inquiry into 'the procedures, irregularities, acts, or omissions of an organisation'. This is important as it ties in with the need to understand the FAI's remit governed strictly in terms of the 2016 Act.

4.11   In Mr Grieg's death, the Greater Glasgow Health Board had decided that ECG equipment should have automatic software interpretation installed, along with sign off processes by a senior doctor on an ECG to ensure that any abnormality was detected. The question of training on reading of ECG results was an issue of medical training, but was not a change which would have avoided the death having occurred.

---

8   Emms at [27], pp 453.

9   Inquiry into the death of Norma Haq 2011 FAI 34, *www.scotcourts.gov.uk/search-judgments/judgment?id=4c5386a6-8980-69d2-b500-ff0000d74aa7* (accessed 21 February 2023) and FAI into death of James McAlpine, aged 7, on 23 February 1985.

10   Dyer, *Death from interventionist radiology: a cautionary tale* (1986) British Medical Journal Vol 293, 686–687, *https://europepmc.org/backend/ptpmcrender.fcgi?accid=PMC1341525&blobtype=pdf* (accessed on 21 February 2023).

11   Inquiry into the death of George Greig 2010 FAI 21: *www.scotcourts.gov.uk/search-judgments/judgment?id=fd9686a6-8980-69d2-b500-ff0000d74aa7* (accessed on 21 February 2023).

4.12 Where the determination errs, in any findings, challenges may be made to remedy by judicial review. There is limited scope as a finding in a determination can only be reduced where the sheriff failed to take into account a matter which they should have taken into account. The determination is competent, provided that the sheriff does not misdirect themselves or exceed the jurisdiction of the FAI.[12]

4.13 **The standard of proof:** This is the same as for any other civil process, namely on the balance of probabilities.

4.14 **Decision making to hold an FAI:** It is important that decisions are taken correctly and appropriately as to when an FAI is required. The judicial review of the determination issued in the death[13] of Robert Young Baird was unsuccessful where the determination sought to criticise the consultant. It argued that in the review that this should not have been the focus of an FAI which is a view with which one might tend to agree. However, it could not be reduced as it was based on facts from the FAI which the sheriff had made. However there is a view that the determination might have left the issues of competence which related to the internal (hospital) medical inquiries or professional competence questions to the GMC as the professional body best set up to ascertain such issues. Sheriffs can on occasion consider that the FAI is not one which should have been brought. The Global Santa Fe Drilling (North Sea) Ltd case was one where the FAI was felt by the sheriff not to have had merit.[14] At para 6, the Court states that:

> 'Solicitors acting for the owner of the rig had written to the Lord Advocate … questioning whether it was in the public interest to hold such an [FAI] inquiry as, it was suggested, the circumstances of the death had been established at the criminal trial. At a preliminary hearing … this concern was repeated by the solicitor for the interested companies. The procurator fiscal identified three topics which, he claimed, would be raised at the inquiry: the adequacy of the risk assessment; the systems put in place following the accident – to identify retrospectively defects in the system of working; and supervision and training. In the event, not all of these issues were raised at the inquiry. Where they were raised, the evidence in relation to them had been presented at the criminal trial.'[15]

4.15 In deciding similarly to hold an FAI, there is significant inevitable impact on all involved. The stress on all parties should not be underestimated. The family are of course mainly affected and should be supported by COPFS staff. Those who were involved or who may have witnessed the death are likely to be witnesses. Balance needs to be maintained, as outlined by the Sheriff Principal Sir Stephen Stewart

---

12 *Lothian Regional Council v Lord Advocate* 1993 SLT 432.
13 [2017] CSOH 32, *www.scotcourts.gov.uk/search-judgments/judgment?id=76d42ba7-8980-69d2-b500-ff0000d74aa7* (accessed on 21 February 2023).
14 *Global Santa Fe Drilling (North Sea) Ltd v Lord Advocate* 2009 SC 575.
15 *Global Santa Fe Drilling (North Sea) Ltd v Lord Advocate* 2009 SC 575.

Templeton Young, 3rd Baronet QC, in the FAI into the circumstances of the death of Mrs Eileen Peterson at Lerwick.[16] Notwithstanding the FAI, medical professionals whose actions are under scrutiny need to continue working and caring for patients. This subjects them to 'the strain inevitably associated with the prospect of having to give evidence at a [FAI] and perhaps being made the subject of any public criticism at the end…'.[17]

4.16　The impact too on the legal professionals should also be considered as outlined by the MSP Helen Eadie, who stated that:

'We must remember that any fatal accident inquiry has a profound impact on those who are involved in it, whether that person is an officer, a law servant, an MSP or a member of the public. For example, as a trade union official, my husband was involved in the inquiry into the Piper Alpha disaster and he cannot now speak of that disaster without a tear coming to his eye, because he is filled with the pain of other people.'[18]

4.17　**Expenses of holding a FAI:** The primary purpose of an FAI is to promote safety in the public interest by holding public inquiries into deaths.[19] They should therefore be 'expense neutral', as the public purse bears the costs incurred by COPFS and the procurator fiscal in representing the public in holding an FAI. COPFS Financial Strategy 2021–2024 indicates increasing resources to the SFIU.[20] Were cost to be a consideration in holding an FAI, one might suggest that few would fall to be instructed in the public interest.

4.18　Mention was made earlier of the Lockerbie FAI, which ran for 61 days and cost £3 million. Other long running FAIs have been held since, but it can be hard to calculate how long an FAI has taken from published resources in court. The medical FAI into the death of Sharman Weir was described then as the longest running medical FAI at 46 days of evidence and submissions.[21]

4.19　There is no mandatory form in the FAI determination of reporting the number of days in court from the date of the preliminary hearing to the conclusion of the evidence and the issue of the determination. Some sheriffs do include this information in the determination, so some information can be identified as to how many days an FAI took to hear evidence, but this does not really provide accuracy

---

16　10 July 2006.
17　Inquiry into the circumstances of the death of Mrs Eileen Peterson, para 9: *www.scotcourts.gov.uk/ search-judgments/judgment?id=da3d87a6-8980-69d2-b500-ff0000d74aa7* (accessed 21 February 2023).
18　Official Report on the Meeting of the Scottish Parliament on 27 March 2008 debate on Fatal Accident Inquiries, *https://archive2021.parliament.scot/parliamentarybusiness/report.aspx? r=4786&mode=pdf* (accessed 21 February 2023).
19　*Lord Advocate, Petitioner* 2007 SLT 849.
20　COPFS Financial Strategy 2021–2024.
21　Inquiry into the death of Sharman Weir, *www.scotcourts.gov.uk/search-judgments/judgment?id =13c286a6-8980-69d2-b500-ff0000d74aa7* (accessed 21 February 2023).

with regard to the costs of holding FAIs, as other factors such as expert witnesses' costs need to be factored in. **Chapter 12** discusses the question of the cost of FAIs in more detail.

4.20   Leaving aside the issue of costs falling to the State in holding an FAI, a sheriff can award expenses against a party to an FAI where the conduct of a party has been vexatious. In the FAI into a North Sea oil rig accident, just before the start of the FAI the procurator fiscal added an expert witness to the list of witnesses. This resulted in delays to allow the expert to produce a report and for all the parties to the FAI to consider the productions which had been lodged to support the expert witness. The expert gave evidence without having heard or seen transcripts of the evidence given at the earlier part of the inquiry where the evidence from the report contradicted or introduced matters extraneous to that earlier evidence.

4.21   The interested parties at the FAI moved successfully for expenses for their additional costs in relation to the FAI as a result of this late evidence. The sheriff noted that 'the purpose of a fatal accident inquiry was to ventilate the whole facts which led to the accident with a view to determining the cause of the accident and any failures which may have led to it; the nature and purpose of such an inquiry meant that it should be conducted as soon as possible after the accident and the evidence should be as full and detailed as possible'. The role of the Crown[22] was, so far as possible, 'to lead the whole evidence and canvass all relevant matters. The Crown might well enter upon a fatal accident inquiry with a particular view of the facts based on expert evidence; nevertheless it was not appropriate for the Crown to seek to tailor the evidence to its own view or to prevent evidence relevant to the aims of the inquiry being led.' Such a motion was held as competent, given that sheriffs have powers to award expenses in administrative or ministerial processes. This includes FAIs.[23]

3.   PRACTICAL APPLICATION OF THE 2016 ACT

4.22   **Responsibilities:** Under s 1(1) of the 2016 Act, COPFS remain responsible for (a) investigating the circumstances of the death, and (b) arranging for an FAI to be held.

4.23   The FAI will examine the circumstances of the death or the accident and is held in public. Witnesses will be called to the FAI and examined/cross-examined under oath. Evidence provided will be considered. Any party who has an interest in the circumstances of the death or accident is free to attend, given the public nature of the FAI.

---

22 *Meekison v Uniroyal Englebert Tyres Ltd* in which Sheriff Principal Nicholson overturned an award of expenses against the Scottish Courts Administration (SCA) on the ground that SCA was not a party to the proceedings.
23 *Global Santa Fe Drilling (North Sea) Ltd v Lord Advocate* 2009 SC 575.

4.24   The sheriff, being a sheriff of the sheriffdom in which the FAI is or is to be held,[24] is responsible for the conduct of the FAI.[25] The powers of the sheriff in relation to an FAI can also be exercised by a summary sheriff[26] and a sheriff principal.[27]

4.25   The sheriff is required to establish the circumstances of the death and to make mandatory findings as to the time, place and cause(s) of death or the accident. They can make any recommendations as to how the death might have been avoided. They can consider what precautions or improvements might be taken or made to prevent other deaths arising in similar circumstances in the future.

4.26   The purpose of the FAI under s 1(3) of the 2016 Act is to (a) establish the circumstances of the death and (b) consider what steps (if any) might be taken to prevent other deaths in similar circumstances.

4.27   The legislation continues to maintain the exclusion from establishing civil or criminal liability.[28] This will be discussed more fully in the section that deals with the content of the determination and recommendations. 'A determination is not the same as a judgment delivered at the end of a civil proof or a criminal trial. It has no consequences.'[29] When a determination is issued, any aspect of it can be ignored by the party and they can continue to maintain that the death was caused by something else. The findings, and recommendations where made, have no effect and no sanction can be brought by which to enforce any action on any party.

4.   INQUIRIES INTO DEATHS OCCURRING IN SCOTLAND

4.28   The 2016 Act continues the previous two categories of FAIs into deaths, namely mandatory and discretionary FAIs that were created by the 1895 and 1906 Acts and continued by the 1976 Act.

Mandatory deaths

4.29   The nature of mandatory FAIs were to be extended as the Bill's policy objective set out.[30] Section 2(1) (a) of the 2016 Act stated that FAIs are mandatory where the death of a person occurred in Scotland.

---

24   Section 1(5) (b) of the 2016 Act.
25   Section 3 of the 2016 Act.
26   Section 38 of the 2016 Act.
27   So far as necessary for the purposes, or in consequence, of the exercise by a member of the judiciary of a sheriffdom other than a sheriff of the jurisdiction and competence of a sheriff, references in any other enactment to a sheriff are to be read as including references to any of the members of the judiciary of a sheriffdom: s 134(2) of the Courts Reform (Scotland) Act 2014.
28   Section 1(4) of the 2016 Act.
29   FAI into the deaths of John Brian Hugh Barkley and others 2014 FAI 5.
30   Policy Memorandum, para 5.

4.30   Under s 2(1)(b) of the 2016 Act, that includes where the death of a person is as a result of an accident which occurred (a) in Scotland and (b) while the person was acting in the course of the person's employment or occupation.[31] This continues the scope of s 1(1)(a)(i) of the 1976 Act.

4.31   The reference to accident is not statutorily defined which is deliberate. The courts can seek to interpret the circumstances of the death as they arise in each case. The determinations in FAIs that are published have covered many varied causes of death, from food poisoning in a hotel at Loch Maree, suicides in prison, medical deaths from neglect, helicopter crashes and terrorist incidents. It is not possible therefore to define what an accident means. As a starting point, the dictionary defines an accident as:

> '[an] unfortunate incident that happens unexpectedly and unintentionally, typically resulting in damage or injury.'[32]

4.32   A further source to help to identify what an accident is could refer to how the Health and Safety approaches the issue. Under the Reporting of Injuries, Diseases and Dangerous Occurrences Regulations 2013 (RIDDOR),[33] duties were imposed on 'employers, the self-employed and people in control of work premises to report serious workplace *accidents* which are defined as separate, identifiable, unintended incident[s], which causes physical injury'.[34]

4.33   In the FAI into the death of Gerard McNally,[35] the word 'accident' was generally considered as meaning 'an unfortunate incident which happens unexpectedly and unintentionally, typically resulting in damage or injury'.

4.34   The category of deaths in the course of employment is, as was the case under the 1976 Act, intended to cover all deaths at , or in what occupation. It includes whether they are an employee, self-employed (which is commonly the case in farming accidents which make up a number of FAIs[36]) or as an employer.

4.35   Under s 2(4) of the 2016 Act, an FAI is held where the death occurred in Scotland and relates to the death of the person who was (a) in legal custody or (b) a child required to be kept or detained in secure accommodation.[37]

---

31   Section 2(3)(9a) and (b) of the 2016 Act.
32   *www.lexico.com/definition/accident* (accessed on 21 February 2023).
33   SI 2013/1471.
34   Health and Safety Executive, RIDDOR – Reporting of Injuries, Diseases and Dangerous Occurrences Regulations 2013, *www.hse.gov.uk/riddor/* (accessed on 21 February 2023).
35   [2012] 5 WLUK 820.
36   FAI into the death of Brian James MacIver 2015 FAI 26, *www.scotcourts.gov.uk/search-judgments/judgment?id=1facf5a6-8980-69d2-b500-ff0000d74aa7* (accessed on 21 February 2023). He died from head and chest injuries caused from falling from an agricultural shed when he was working on the roof. The FAI sought to outlined that more educational guidance should be provided in health and safety matters to the farming community.
37   Section 2(4) of the 2016 Act.

4.36   These provisions updated the 1976 Act and ensure that a mandatory FAI would be held where the death occurred in legal custody, irrespective of the location of the death. It is the status of the deceased person at the time that governs the holding of an FAI. It would therefore include deaths of person who were detained at their own homes as well as in the street or elsewhere. Section 2(5) of the 2016 Act defines 'legal custody'. This includes where the person is:

   (a) required to be imprisoned or detained in a penal institution;
   (b) in police custody within the terms of s 64 of the Criminal Justice (Scotland) Act 2016;
   (c) held in custody on court premises;
   (d) required to be detained in service custody premises.

4.37   Penal accommodation, secure accommodation and service custody premises are all similarly defined under s 2(7) of the 2016 Act.

4.38   For a child, it does not matter whether the death occurred in secure accommodation, a penal institution or service custody premises[38] as all these circumstances are included.

4.39   The term 'child' is not defined but is considered to be a person who has not yet reached the age of 18. The death of any child in any other form of residential care which was not mandatory could result in a decision to hold a discretionary FAI if the circumstances deemed it appropriate so to do. The death of a child arising in residential care as a result of natural causes would not be seen perhaps to amount to relevant circumstances unless there were questions over the medical care provided. These might be similar to those mooted in **Chapter 6** considering natural deaths in custody, which are of course the subject of a mandatory FAI as to the standard of care provided. A discretionary FAI relating to children was held into the circumstances of a fire that occurred at Seafield Residential School, Ardrossan in 1952, where six boys died who had gone there from care in Glasgow at East Park for a holiday.

4.40   Consideration was given to making it mandatory to hold an FAI into the death of anyone who was in compulsory detention by a public authority within the terms of the Human Rights Act 1998. This was not implemented as the Scottish Government considered that there were adequate resources already in place for investigations into mental health deaths. The types of inquiries that could already be held ranged from a medical internal adverse incident investigation and included independent investigations conducted by the Mental Welfare Commission Scotland.

4.41   These deaths are likely to be the subject of the independent investigation by the procurator fiscal in any event as they may well include, on occasion, suicides in a mental hospital. Adequate provision was in existence already as the Lord Advocate

---

38   Section 2(6) of the 2016 Act.

can exercise discretion in any relevant case rather than making this subject to a mandatory provision.[39]

4.42   In considering where an FAI is to be held, what can be seen from the SCTS website is that the majority of mandatory FAIs (from the publication of FAI determinations) result from deaths in prison. As is discussed in **Chapter 6**, an increasing number of these deaths are as a result of suicide, and a significant number will otherwise have resulted from natural causes.

4.43   The requirements of Art 2 of the ECHR were discussed earlier. There is a strong public interest in considering the circumstances of the deaths which have occurred in custody. These deaths, just as any other deaths that arise and are investigated with FAIs being held, must be subject to robust inquiry. Frequently these custody FAIs have been substantially completed by the use of joint agreements of evidence, though this practice is not always favourably received by the sheriffs. The implications of this practice in respect of the robustness of such FAI is considered in **Chapter 6**.

When an FAI may not be held

4.44   Section 3(1) of the 2016 Act provides that the Lord Advocate may decide not to hold an FAI into a death that was the result of an accident in terms of s 2(3), or resulted in custody in terms of s 2(4) of 2016 Act, if they are satisfied that the circumstances have been sufficiently established during the course of proceedings of a kind mentioned in subs (2) where these exceptions include:

4.45
   (a) criminal proceedings,
   (b) an inquiry under s 17(2) of the Gas Act 1965 (accidents);
   (c) an inquiry under s 14(2A) of the Health and Safety at Work etc. Act 1974 (power of the Health and Safety Executive to direct investigations and inquiries);
   (d) an inquiry under s 1 of the Inquiries Act 2005 (power to establish inquiry);
   (e) an inquiry under s 85(1) of the Energy Act 2013 (inquiries).

Criminal proceedings[40]

4.46   Criminal proceedings have not been further defined so this term has a very wide remit. This continues the practice, established under s 1(2) of the 1976 Act, where the Lord Advocate may decide not to hold an FAI where the circumstances of

---

39   Fatal Accidents and Sudden Deaths Inquiry (Scotland) Bill's Policy Memorandum, para 116.
40   Section 3(1) (a) of the 2016 Act.

a death have been sufficiently established in criminal proceedings. This exercise of the Lord Advocate's discretion would be justified if the circumstances of the death have already been sufficiently ascertained, as there would be no further purpose in holding another inquiry at public expense.

4.47 The Flying Phantom tug accident[41] resulted in the deaths of three men in the Clyde in December 2007. Prosecution under the Health and Safety at Work etc Act 1974 concluded in 2014 with a decision made thereafter not to proceed with an FAI. The delay of what appears to be seven years in concluding the prosecution may also have been a relevant factor in considering if there was then any purpose in holding an FAI.

4.48 These circumstances can also be seen to arise in the case where, in August 2022, the Lord Advocate held an FAI into the Cameron House fire in which two guests died in December 2017.[42] COPFS had conducted a successful prosecution in relation to the Cameron House hotel fire under the Health and Safety at Work etc. Act 1974.[43] The offences on which convictions resulted generally related to a failure to take fire safety measures necessary to ensure the safety of employees and guests.

4.49 The Lord Advocate had originally issued a decision not to hold an FAI, indicating that they were 'satisfied [that] the reasons for this tragedy have been established'. The families of the deceased men had successfully campaigned to have this decision overturned. The determination in the FAI now issued makes a number of recommendations including that:

> 'The Scottish Government should consider introducing for future conversions of historic buildings to be used as hotel accommodation a requirement to have active fire suppression systems installed. …
>
> The Scottish Government should constitute an expert working group to more fully explore the special risks which existing hotels and similar premises may pose through the presence of hidden cavities or voids, varying standards of 6 workmanship, age, and the variance from current standards and to consider revising the guidance provided by the Scottish Government and others.'

This identifies some areas in which the Sheriff considered that there were aspects or lessons to be learnt which had not been previously established in the course of the criminal proceedings. The circumstances of these deaths were that ashes from a fire had been put into a cupboard which contained kindling and newspapers which then went on fire, setting fire to the hotel from which the two men were unable to escape.

4.50 The FAI which is still to be conducted is to be held into the deaths of Lamara Bell and John Yuill who were two persons in an accident where their car went off on

---

41   BBC, *Clydeport fined £650,000 after Flying Phantom tug deaths* (29 September 2014), *www.bbc. co.uk/news/uk-scotland-glasgow-west-29410685* (accessed on 21 February 2023).
42   The determination has not yet been issued.
43   BBC, *Cameron House fined £500,000 over fatal hotel fire* (29 January 2021), *www.bbc.co.uk/news/ uk-scotland-glasgow-west-55855271* (accessed on 21 February 2023).

the M9 motorway. Though there was a report made to Police Scotland call handling about a car leaving the road, no investigation into this report was made for several days. When an investigation was conducted, both occupants of the car were found to be dead. This FAI follows the conclusion of the prosecution of Police Scotland,[44] where Police Scotland was fined £100,000 after admitting failings which 'materially contributed' to the deaths of the two in the car.

4.51   What may be concluded is that though the discretion on holding of an FAI exists within the statutory provisions, it is thought increasingly unlikely to be successfully exercised, given the families' demands to hold an FAI, notwithstanding that a criminal prosecution had been held. This may be the case where the criminal prosecution concludes with negotiated pleas, as in the case of with the Cameron House fire. The families may consider that the full circumstances of the death have not been reviewed in pleas conducted in private and consequently lack necessary transparency. They may also not have had their specific concerns or questions answered, having no place within the criminal and adversarial process.

4.52   Interestingly, with an increasingly global or international perspective, the term 'criminal proceedings' does not specify in what jurisdiction the criminal proceedings must be raised. Historically, it must have reflected the dual role of the COPFS, in investigating sudden deaths and prosecuting homicides. The Lord Advocate could however in theory decide to exercise their discretion not to hold an FAI, no matter where geographically the jurisdiction of criminal proceedings is located.

4.53   How the exercise of that discretion may develop in the future will depend on the circumstances of cases that arise. It is interesting to note that criminal jurisdiction was extended to Scotland in the case of Christopher Hughes, who was prosecuted for the murder of Martin Kok who was shot in Laren, in the Netherlands on 8 December 2016.[45] The recent Scottish High Court prosecution, as part of organised serious crime, took place in April 2022. That type of case may provide scope to see how their discretion in relation to other deaths that may arise abroad is exercised.

Other exemptions – industrial

4.54   Under s 3(2)(b)–(d) of the 2016 Act, three exceptions may be generally grouped together as these relate to industrial inquiries conducted in specific statutory circumstances:

---

44   The Scotsman, *Fatal accident inquiry to take place over M9 crash that led to death of Lamara Bell and John Yuill* (6 December 2021), *www.scotsman.com/news/crime/fatal-accident-inquiry-to-take-place-over-m9-crash-that-led-to-death-of-lamara-bell-and-john-yuill-3484448* (accessed on 21 February 2023).

45   BBC, *Martin Kok: Gangland figure guilty of murdering Dutch crime writer* (30 March 2022), *www.bbc.co.uk/news/uk-scotland-glasgow-west-60930678* (accessed on 21 February 2023).

1. An inquiry under s 17(2) of the Gas Act 1965: s 17(2) of the Gas Act 1965 outlines that 'the Minister may, where he thinks it expedient so to do, direct an inquiry to be held into any event notice of which is to be given under [section 17(1)] or any other event connected with the underground gas storage. Such inquiries shall be held in public.'[46]

2. An inquiry under s 14(2A) of the Health and Safety at Work etc Act 1974: under s14,[47] the Health & Safety Commission has the power to investigate 'any accident, occurrence, situation or other matter whatsoever which [the Executive[48]] thinks it necessary or expedient to investigate'. Section 14(2A) refers to the Executive, who may at any time, with the consent of the Secretary of State, direct an inquiry to be held into any matter to which this section applies.

   There may be an overlap with criminal proceedings, as seen in the example of the Cameron House fire above. There have been 17 fatal injuries to workers in Scotland reported in 2020–21, so this may provide a perspective on how many potential FAIs result from safety at work issues in each year.[49] Again, there may be a feeling that, given the need for transparency, families would seek out the holding of an FAI irrespective to give them their role at such an FAI.

3. An inquiry under s 85(1) of the Energy Act 2013: under s 85(1), the Office for Nuclear Regulation (ONR)[50]may, with the consent of the Secretary of State, direct an inquiry to be held into any matter if it considers the inquiry necessary or desirable for any of the ONR's purposes.

Other inquiries

An inquiry under Section 1 of the Inquiries Act 2005[51]

4.55 As discussed in **Chapter 10**, a death may well be made the subject of an inquiry instead of holding an FAI. A number of relevant inquiries into deaths in Scotland have been held under the 2005 Act. The shooting at the Dunblane primary school was an example of an inquiry, prior to the 2005 Act which was conducted by The Rt Hon the Lord Cullen of Whitekirk KT who went on to lead the review into

---

46 They are required to be held in accordance with Sch 5 to the Gas Act 1965, which sets out procedural requirements. An FAI was held into the gas explosion at Clarkston, Glasgow in 1971 and concluded before the conclusion to any Scottish Gas Board inquiry reported. See also Mawdsley, *The historical purpose and role of fatal accident inquiries* 2021 SLT 157–159.

47 Section 14 – Power of the Commission to direct investigations and inquiries.

48 Now the Health and Safety Executive as subject to transitional provisions as specified in SI 2008/960 Sch 2 paras 6 and 11 by Legislative Reform (Health and Safety Executive) Order 2008 (SI 2008/960) art 6(2) (1 April 2008: substitution has effect subject to transitional provisions as specified in SI 2008/960 Sch 2 paras 6 and 11).

49 HSE, Workplace health and safety statistics for Scotland, 2021: *www.hse.gov.uk/statistics/regions/scotland-statistics.pdf* (accessed on 21 February 2023).

50 Section 77 of the Energy Act 2013 defines the Office for Nuclear Regulation as the ONR.

51 Section 3(1) (d) of the 2016 Act.

the FAIs that resulted in the reforms which led to the 2016 Act.[52] In that case, an FAI was also held into the Dunblane shooting. It was a mandatory FAI as Gwen Mayor, the teacher who was killed, was acting in the course of her employment. Her family had requested that an FAI on 28 October 1996 was held as well as the holding of the public inquiry. The FAI followed the inquiry.

Deaths in Scotland during military service

4.56   There were only two categories of military service deaths that required mandatory FAIs to be held under s 7 of the 2016 Act. These arise where, under s 7(1)(a), the Lord Advocate is notified in relation to a death under s 12(4) or (5) of the 2009 Act (enacting the provisions of the 2009 Act which amended the 1976 Act – investigation of deaths of service personnel abroad).

4.57   Under s 7(1)(b), where the death is of a person who was at the time of death in circumstances analogous to legal custody,[53] or the Lord Advocate considers[54] that the death was (a) sudden, suspicious or unexplained or (b) occurred in circumstances giving rise to serious public concern.

4.58   Under Art 6 of the Inquiries into Fatal Accidents and Sudden Death etc. (Scotland) Act 2016, (Consequential Provisions and Modifications) Order 2016,[55] a further category of mandatory inquiry was added.

4.59   This now provides for an FAI where a death occurs in Scotland or the Scottish area of the continental shelf in the course of military service. For military service, the deceased person must be subject to service law by virtue of s 367 of the Armed Forces Act 2006 and was engaged in (a) active service, (b) activities carried on in preparation for, or directly in support of, active service, or (c) training carried out in order to improve or maintain the effectiveness of those engaged in active service.[56]

4.60   Similar provisions regarding exceptions operate in respect of exceptions under Art 3 of the 2016 Order. No FAI needs to be held in the circumstances in which it would otherwise be mandatory under s 2(4)(a) or s 2(5)(d) of the 2016 Act if the Lord Advocate is satisfied that the circumstances of the death have been sufficiently established. These circumstances relate to custody and would mean at the time of death, the person was required to be detained in service custody premises within the meaning given by s 300(7) of the Armed Forces Act 2006.

---

52   Scottish office, *Public inquiry into the shootings at Dunblane Primary School*, Independent Report, 16 October 1996, *www.gov.uk/government/publications/public-inquiry-into-the-shootings-at-dunblane-primary-school* (accessed on 21 February 2023).
53   Section 7(2) of the 2016 Act.
54   Section 7(3) of the 2016 Act.
55   SI 2016/1142.
56   Section 12(2) of the Coroners and Justice Act 2009.

4.61   The Lord Advocate may also decide that the circumstances of the death have been sufficiently established in the course of an inquiry under s 1 of the 2005 Act and an FAI is not to be held.

Discretionary inquiries

4.62   Under s 4(1) of the 2016 Act, an FAI will be held into the death of a person which occurred in Scotland if the Lord Advocate (a) considers that the death (i) was sudden, suspicious or unexplained or (ii) occurred in circumstances giving rise to serious public concern, and (b) decides it is in the public interest for the FAI to be held into the circumstances of the death.

4.63   This continues the wide exercise of the Lord Advocate's discretion to instruct the holding of an FAI in circumstances where otherwise an FAI is not mandatory. As under the 1976 Act, the death must be sudden, suspicious or unexplained or occurred in circumstances giving rise to serious public concern *and* where it is in the public interest (our emphasis). Both sections must be satisfied.

4.64   It may be difficult to imagine where a death might be sudden etc and give rise to serious public concern and that it was not in the public interest to hold an FAI. However, these provisions do provide a basis for not holding an FAI where a death has perhaps occurred as a result of a medical procedure where there has already been an internal hospital inquiry and all relevant changes have been made. There may be circumstances where nothing more may be considered that could be identified as a result of holding an FAI. It may be that much in that case would depend on the view of the family and how much they felt that they had to achieve and in seeking out what they considered was transparency of process in holding an FAI .

4.65   Public interest in the 2016 Act continues to be a term that is not defined. This provision replicates the discretion afforded to the Lord Advocate on making decisions on whether a prosecution in Scotland is to be initiated. This can similarly only be taken where the public interest is satisfied. It may be a term that cannot be well understood by the public but, assigning a normal meaning, the public interest is wider than the family interest, though there is an inevitable overlap.

4.66   Any relevant death, such as a sudden, unexplained and unexpected death, in theory, may give rise to a discretionary FAI, but not all deaths, as discussed in **Chapter 1**, give rise to public concern. The Lord Advocate decides and cannot be forced to undertake an FAI, though their decision not to do so may well be subject to challenge under a petition for judicial review. Where that review was decided against the Lord Advocate, it is likely that an FAI would then be instructed.

4.67   There is no test as to how the Lord Advocate is to exercise their discretion but the usual principles as to reasonableness as a test in judicial review would apply.

A standard of unreasonableness is used in assessing an application for judicial review of a public authority's decision. It is set out as if it is so unreasonable that no reasonable person acting reasonably could have made it.[57]

4.68   Exactly how often families do seek out an FAI where the Lord Advocate has declined to hold an FAI is not known. What limited information may be available would be determined from judicial reviews but only if that decision were then to be published: there have been relatively few. There may be several reasons, as it is costly to commence a judicial review and it is unlikely to be publicly funded through the provision of legal aid.

4.69   Understanding what the reasons commonly given for not holding an FAI would be useful too. Section 9 of the 2016 Act provides that COPFS, if requested, requires to give reasons for their refusal to hold an FAI. Such information may be able to be obtained. The 2016 Act deliberately did not create this as a statutory right, as it was considered when the Bill was being considered that this would inevitably impact on COPFS's staffing resources to handle such requests. Reasons can only be requested by certain categories of the deceased's family.

4.70   Some of the factors why a discretionary FAI would not be held are considered through the discussion on holding FAIs. However, it is important to stress that it is the balance of interests that need to be considered when deciding whether to hold an FAI. These include what can be achieved for the family as well as the public in the holding of an FAI.

4.71   Reference is made to the FAI into the death of Elizabeth Lowrie.[58] This discretionary FAI was held into the death of a woman in hospital. Sheriff Cubie usefully considered the scope and purpose of FAI[59] by considering the circumstances of the death. Though this was considered under the 1976 Act, this applies equally to the 2016 Act:

> 'The purpose of a fatal accident inquiry is to enlighten and inform those persons who have an interest in the circumstances of the death. It is to ensure that members of the deceased person's family are in possession, so far as possible, of the full facts surrounding the death. The broader function of such an inquiry can be additionally to ensure that the circumstances are fully examined and disclosed in the public domain.… Thus the objective of such a public enquiry must be to ensure where lessons can be learned and steps taken to avoid any future recurrence, that these are identified and brought to the attention of those who are in a position to implement them.'

4.72   He went on to outline that '…it is a legitimate aim of [a discretionary FAI] where there may be serious public concern, that wherever possible, that concern

---

57   *Associated Provincial Picture Houses Ltd v Wednesbury Corpn* (1948) 1 KB 223.
58   [2011] 10 WLUK 837.
59   Ibid, paras 4–11.

is assuaged and public confidence restored. This is particularly so where, as here, a public institution such as hospital is involved'. but he recognised that 'it would be inappropriate, in my view, for an FAI to be treated as if it were a public enquiry taking a nationwide approach and calling for far greater resources'.

4.73   The limitations of an FAI are therefore well articulated and need to be fully appreciated by all concerned.

4.74   An FAI needs to achieve 'something more than mere speculation that the death might have been avoided' in holding an inquiry. FAIs can be 'armed with the benefit of hindsight, [where] the evidence led at the Inquiry and the Determination of the Inquiry, [that] may be persuaded to take steps to prevent any recurrence of such a death in the future'. Recalling too that the determination in an FAI cannot be founded upon in any other processes which may follow, it is important to recognise as Sheriff Kearney stated:

> 'The availability of such evidence enables those legitimately interested parties, if so advised, to establish negligence or other culpability in the ordinary courts which, by their procedure of written pleadings which give advance notice of particular allegations, are well suited to dealing fairly and fully with such matters: hence, no doubt, the provision that the sheriff's determination in a fatal accident inquiry may not be founded upon in any such subsequent proceedings.'[60]

5.   INQUIRIES INTO DEATHS OCCURRING ABROAD

4.75   Sections 6 (General) and 7 (Service Personnel) of the 2016 Act deal with deaths abroad.

General

4.76   Under s 6(1) of the 2016 Act, an FAI can be held where:

(a) the death occurred outwith the UK which excludes deaths in England, Wales and Northern Ireland where these deaths continue to be subject to the system of coroners' inquests in those countries; and

(b) at the time of the death, the person was ordinarily resident in Scotland.

4.77   Under s 6(3) of the 2016 Act, the FAI can be held where the Lord Advocate considers that the death is (a) sudden, suspicious or unexplained or (b) occurred in circumstances giving rise to serious public concern. The Lord Advocate must also

---

60   *Foster* [2002] 2 WLUK 632; *Allen (FAI)* unreported 14 November 1985.

consider that the circumstances of the death have not been established in the course of an investigation by the appropriate authorities in the country where the death occurred. They must consider that there is a real prospect that those circumstances would be sufficiently established in holding an FAI in Scotland. Finally, the FAI will only be held if the Lord Advocate decides that it is in the public interest to investigate the circumstances of the death. An FAI into a death within this section will proceed in the same way as any other FAI under the 2016 Act.

4.78 However helpful potentially this section is in providing a legal framework and ability to investigate deaths that arise abroad, there is a need to remember that the bereaved family of the deceased person will have experienced a similar shock to any other such death that occurs in the UK.

4.79 Just how such deaths are to be investigated as well as the costs that such an investigation may entail, while not a specific resource issue for an FAI in considering whether an FAI should be held, must be an area of potential concern. An FAI cannot be held because the relatives of these families have had to deal with other foreign systems for investigation, compounded no doubt by potential language issues in ascertaining exactly what happened to their relative.

4.80 An example that admittedly precedes the 2016 Act was the unsuccessful judicial review petition made by Mohammed Al Fayed to hold an FAI to explore the cause of Dodie AlFayed's death along with Princess Diana in Paris.[61]

4.81 Perhaps the statutory provisions are best understood by having provided that opportunity to hold an FAI but not necessarily in providing a solution. The level of likely co-operation from the country where the death occurred is one of the matters which the Lord Advocate will have to consider in deciding whether to exercise their discretion.[62]

4.82 To date, no such FAI has been instructed, though several campaigns have been mounted to consider two separate deaths that have arisen abroad. Kirsty Maxwell died on a hen weekend when she fell from a balcony in Spain in April 2017. Craig Mallon died in Lloret de Mar in Spain in 2012 as a result of a punch where no criminal proceedings were subsequently taken.[63]

4.83 The concerns over both deaths were fully aired in a debate in the Scottish Parliament in 2018 but no further actions, including the question of post-mortems

---

61 *Al Fayed* 2004 SC 568.
62 Policy memorandum, para 141.
63 Justice abroad covered both cases: an organisation set up provide assistance to the victims of crime abroad and their families through conducting reviews of the evidence in cases in which they have been injured as well as using their expertise to investigate suspicious deaths abroad: *www.justiceabroad.co.uk/justiceabroad/about* (accessed on 21 February 2023).

being held in such cases and how to provide representation and support of the families, have resulted in any changes.[64][65]

4.84   **Service personnel:** An FAI is to be held into a death of service personnel if the Lord Advocate is notified by either the Secretary of State (where the person's body is within Scotland or is expected to be brought to the UK) or the Chief Coroner where the person's body is within England and Wales.[66] The death must be one where the service person was in custody, similar to the status of legal custody outlined at s 2(5) or of a civilian subject to service discipline who was accompanying service personnel who were engaged in active service.

4.85   The death must also have been sudden, suspicious or unexplained or occurred in circumstances that gave rise to serious public concern.[67] Under s 7(c)(i), the Lord Advocate decides that it is in the public interest for an FAI to be held into the circumstances of the death and (ii) does not reverse that decision.

4.86   The Lord Advocate is not required to hold an FAI if they consider that the circumstances of the death have been sufficiently established in the course of criminal proceedings.[68]

4.87   In appropriate cases, each military death where there are known links to Scotland will be the subject of discussion between the offices of the Secretary of State for Defence and the Lord Advocate. There is no domiciliary requirement set out under s 7. Where bereaved families indicate that that they wish the death to be considered at an FAI in Scotland, instead of at a coroner's inquest in England and Wales, it is expected that an FAI would be held.

4.88   The Lord Advocate will then decide in which sheriffdom the FAI should be held and would undertake the investigation towards that inquiry.

4.89   Exactly what is meant by reversal of the Lord Advocate's decision is curious as it is not clarified in either the 2016 Act or in the Explanatory Notes that accompany the Bill. This may envisage a case where the issue arising with the death has already been fully examined in an inquest in England and Wales, so little more would be achieved by holding an FAI in Scotland.

4.90   These provisions appear not to have been used to date to ascertain how they would operate in practice.

64   The Scottish Parliament, Meeting of the Parliament, 24 October 2018, *www.parliament.scot/ chamber-and-committees/official-report/what-was-said-in-parliament/meeting-of-parliament-24- 10-2018?meeting=11724&iob=106139* (accessed on 21 February 2023).
65   Scottish Government, *Victims Taskforce papers: January 2022* (8 February 2022), *www.gov.scot/ publications/victims-taskforce-papers-january-2022/* (accessed on 21 February 2023).
66   Section 12(4) and (5) the 2009 Act.
67   Section7(3) (a) and (b) of the 2016 Act.
68   Section 7(4) of the 2016 Act.

6. COMMUNICATIONS WITH COPFS

Family Liaison Charter

4.91   In the recommendations arising from Lord Cullen's Report, much was made of the need to achieve better liaison with the deceased's families. These changes did not require statutory intervention, with a number of changes introduced by COPFS through their systems. However, the requirements to prepare a Family Liaison Charter were then codified in the 2016 Act. This sets out basic requirements of the Family Liaison Charter.

4.92   It provides how the procurator fiscal will liaise with the family of the deceased.

4.93   It sets out (a) the information to be made available to the family and (b) the timescales for giving information.[69]

4.94   The most up to date published Charter is dated 2016,[70] whose date of publication was presumably in accordance with the timing of the commencement of the 2016 Act. It is described as 'The Family Liaison Charter – Charter to Bereaved Families: Access to Information and Liaison with the Procurator Fiscal' and was laid in the Scottish Parliament.

4.95   Interestingly, the 2016 Act does not require any revision, though power to revise from time to time is included. The Charter itself recognises that consultation under s 8(5)(a) was to be undertaken with various organisations but the discretion as to whom to consult lies with the Lord Advocate. There appears to have been no further revision despite the reference in the Charter to the Independent Inspector of the Prosecution Service in Scotland Report on Fatal Accident Inquiries published on 18 August 2016, where 'COPFS welcomes and accepts all the recommendations which the Inspector has made. COPFS will ensure those who have been previously consulted in the preparation of this Charter are further consulted on revisions that may be required to the Charter in light of those recommendations and will thereafter lay a revised Charter before the Scottish Parliament.'

4.96   It is not known if any such consultation has taken place, any revision undertaken or is in contemplation. Given the importance of good and effective communication with the families, keeping the Charter under review and ensuring that other organisations were consulted would be advisable.

---

69   Section 8(3) of the 2016 Act.
70   Crown Office & Procurator Fiscal Service, The Family Liaison Charter (1 September 2016), *www.copfs.gov.uk/publications/the-family-liaison-charter/* (accessed on 21 February 2023) – no subsequent revision have been published.

7.   REASONS WHERE AN FAI IS NOT TO BE HELD

4.97   Reference is made to the earlier discussions on the holding of judicial reviews. Judicial reviews of the Lord Advocate's decision can be instructed. By providing information as to why the Lord Advocate is not intending to hold an FAI, this promotes better transparency in relation to the decision-making process. Section 9 of the 2016 Act sets out to whom the Lord Advocate must give reasons in writing where an FAI is not to be held into the circumstances of the death. It applies to deaths arising in relation to both mandatory and discretionary FAIs, though less likely to be required in cases of mandatory FAIs as there will be fewer occasions, as set out in s 3 of the 2016 Act, where the Lord Advocate will decline to hold such an FAI.

4.98   The deceased's family must request the reasons. Reasons are not automatically supplied, said to be due to manpower issues for COPFS. These decisions may well be communicated in face-to-face meetings so some information will be made available in that way. However, how many deaths are investigated is set out in **Chapter 12** where the majority of these deaths would not normally require an FAI. It is to the discretionary category of deaths where figures cannot be ascertained – as discretionary FAIs will include a range of deaths being reported from many different sources such as medical, and road traffic where the figures cannot be identified.

4.99   The request for reasons only applies to specific categories of the deceased's family to limit the number of applications to being made by close family and to avoid what in effect is personal information being requested and made publicly available. The need to respect privacy is required against the need to provide justification for effective decision making.

4.100   These categories include:

- the spouse or civil partner at the time of the deceased's death;
- a person living with the deceased as if married to them at the time of their death; or
- their nearest known relative, if at the time of their death they did not have a spouse or civil partner and were not living with a person as if married to the person.[71]

4.101   It includes same sex couples living together.

4.102   The background to the procurator fiscal's decision needs to be fully understood. In investigating any death COPFS will be in touch with the deceased's family to explain the process and the result of their inquiries. The family will be asked their views as to whether an FAI should be held, which as indicated previously is only one factor in the consideration of COPFS and ultimately the Lord Advocate in deciding to hold an FAI.

---

71   Section 9(a), (b) and (c) of the 2016 Act.

4.103   By the time of the 2016 Bill, SFIU had already changed its processes to streamline and to promote consistency in the FAI process. They addressed the changes that had been proposed by Patricia Ferguson MSP[72] who lodged a proposed private member's bill on 2 June 2015, Inquiries into Deaths (Scotland) Bill.[73]

4.104   This Bill was intended to reform the FAI process. Though that Bill was subsequently withdrawn, consideration of a number of its recommendations had formed part of the discussions during the 2016 Bill's progress. She had proposed reforms to ensure families were kept informed as to what was happening and to enable them to be part of the FAI process. This was supported by Lord Cullen who recommended in circumstances where an FAI is discretionary and the Lord Advocate decides that no FAI should be held, written reasons for the decision should be provided to relatives of the deceased if requested by them.

4.105   Putting the bereaved families at the centre of the process may be seen too to form part of the Scottish Government's policy intentions of victim-centric justice.[74] It engages with the victim's families and focuses on their safety, rights, well-being, expressed needs and choices.

4.106   It must be recognised that there are difficult decisions to be taken. Families foster a mistaken belief that an FAI will allow the evidence to be explored that will support future civil action which is not a reason for holding an FAI. That is clearly not its purpose. FAIs are to be held in the public interest. The public interest may override that family's private interest on occasion but does not act as a precursor to the civil proceedings.

4.107   By providing this right to obtaining in a statutory form, the process is standardised. It provides the deceased's family with a clear and formal intimation process. They can thereafter seek a judicial review of the decision if required and not satisfied with the reasons. Whether it is successful, as a provision, depends on the family being aware of their right and exercising this. How that was to be achieved is not set out. The family need to know when and how they can exercise this right.

8.   THE PROCURATOR FISCALS' INVESTIGATION

4.108   Sections 10–14 of the 2016 Act deal with the preliminary matters leading up to the decision to be taken to hold an FAI and prior to pre-inquiry processes outlined in **Chapter 5**.

---

72   A Bill for an Act of the Scottish Parliament to re-enact, with amendments, the Fatal Accidents and Sudden Deaths Inquiry (Scotland) Act 1976.
73   The Scottish Parliament, *Inquiries into Deaths (Scotland) Bill, https://archive2021.parliament.scot/ parliamentarybusiness/Bills/89907.aspx* (accessed on 21 February 2023).
74   Scottish Government, *Improving victims' experiences of the justice system: consultation* (last updated 15 February 2023), *https://consult.gov.scot/justice/victimsconsultation/* (accessed on 21 February 2023).

4.109 **Witnesses:** Witnesses will be interviewed by COPFS as part of their investigations into the circumstances of the death. Section 10(1)(a) of the 2016 Act[75] provides that COPFS can cite persons to attend for precognition.

4.110 Precognition is a Scots law term meaning 'the preliminary examination of witnesses, especially to decide whether there is ground for a trial'.[76] Precognitions are by their very nature confidential as they are not the equivalent of a police statement. Interpretation of what is said is filtered through the person conducting the interview. Precognitions are important as they provide the basis on which the procurator fiscal and their staff will ascertain the relevant background information and assist in deciding whether an FAI should be held.

4.111 Those summoned for precognition to the COPFS will commonly include eyewitnesses, police, fire and other emergency service personnel, along with medical professionals. Expert evidence will be obtained from a wide range of persons. These experts will be asked to provide their opinion as to the cause or the circumstances of a death. In deaths that relate to medical practice, these experts will be asked to consider the circumstances of a death to ascertain if the practices were out of line with professional medical standards, whether these comprise of systemic failures, what lessons might be learnt and if more may be identified than may have been achieved from internal morbidity or adverse incident reviews. These will involve experts considering the medical records and statements from those involved in providing treatment, as well as the deceased families as to their issues or concerns over the medical care that was received. They are not however a precursor to a civil medical negligence case, so it is important given that where these are potentially discretionary FAIs, that they consider something more than merely a mistake having occurred

4.112 An example of a medical FAI was the FAI into Kirsty Thomson,[77] aged 13. The sheriff made no criticism of the standard of care which she received in hospital or at home. She had a very rare congenital condition which caused her bowel to obstruct. However, she had been discharged from hospital prematurely. Had her discharge been delayed, pending medical test results having been instructed having been interpreted, surgery may have avoided her death and which may have saved her life.

4.113 There is a two-stage process of citation for precognition. Where a witness who is cited by the procurator fiscal fails to attend for precognition without reasonable excuse or refuses to give information within their knowledge and that is relevant to the investigation, an application can be made to apply to the sheriff for an order requiring that witness to attend for precognition. Failure thereafter to comply with the order by attendance is enforced as a criminal offence under s10(5) and (6)[78] of the 2016 Act.

---

75   Restatement of the powers under s 2 of the 1976 Act.
76   *www.copfs.gov.uk/the-justice-process/precognition/* (accessed on 21 February 2023).
77   FAI into the death of Kirsty Rutherford Thompson 2011 FAI 35, *www.scotcourts.gov.uk/search-judgments/judgment?id=fd8786a6-8980-69d2-b500-ff0000d74aa7* (accessed on 21 February 2023).
78   On summary conviction, imprisonment for a term not exceeding 21 days or a fine not exceeding level 3 on the standard scale (£1000). Level 3 on the standard scale is set out in s 225(1) and (2) of the Criminal Procedure (Scotland) Act 1995.

9. PRELIMINARIES TO THE FAI

4.114 **Participants:** Section 11 of the 2016 Act updates the 1976 Act with regard to the parties who can participate in an FAI in addition to the procurator fiscal who leads the FAI. For relatives under s 11(1)(a)–(c) of the 2016 Act, it reflects the categories set out in s 9 of the 2016 Act to include those relatives who can request reasons for the refusal to hold an FAI.

4.115 At the time of the death of the deceased person, these include:

- the deceased's spouse or civil partner;
- a person living with the deceased as if married to the deceased; and
- the deceased's nearest relative if they did not have a spouse or civil partner and were not living with a person as if married to the person.

4.116 Where a mandatory FAI is to be held under s 2(3),[79] this includes a wide number of categories of specified officials who can participate. There is a catch all that allows the sheriff to include anyone where the sheriff is satisfied that they have an interest in the FAI so this would include specialist occupations in specific cases. The categories include:

- The employer if the deceased was acting in the course of that person's employment. The term 'employer' is undefined. It is unlikely that a dispute would arise but, presumably in the case of difficulty, this would consider the facts such as who was paying for their services, responsibility for National Insurance employer's payments, wearing a recognised uniform, providing equipment and issuing directions.
- An inspector appointed under s 19 of the Health and Safety at Work etc. Act 1974.[80]
- A trade union or staff association representative if the deceased person was a member of the trade union or staff association in connection with their employment or occupation at the time of their death.

4.117 Restrictions as to who can participate are necessary as FAI hearings can be time consuming. There is a need to maintain a focus on the issues that are relevant in the FAI and admit those who legitimately have an interest. The sheriff has been provided with that authority and discretion to decide, where necessary.

4.118 There may be obvious tensions within families where the deceased relationships or families may have been estranged. The sheriff can hear representations as to why there should be more than one party for the family in attendance. Just how many family members attend may also reflect whether they can obtain legal aid for professional representation.

---

79 Section 11(1) (d) of the 2016 Act.
80 Incorporates s 4(2) of the 1976 Act providing that, where the FAI involves a death at work, an inspector may be a participant if they wish.

4.119   There is no requirement for anyone attending the FAI to hold legal qualifications, but in practice, most parties will be legally represented. This does not require merely Scottish legal qualifications.

4.120   **Location of FAIs:** Section 12 of the 2016 Act sets out where FAIs may be held. Prior to Lord Cullen's Report, it was suggested that FAIs should not be held in courtrooms as they were a reminder of criminal proceedings, and provided a stressful environment for the families. These considerations may be compounded by the understanding that COPFS's main role is more commonly associated with criminal prosecutions.

4.121   Lord Cullen had recommended that FAIs should be undertaken in more suitable accommodation. If that were not possible, locations for FAIs should be chosen so that they had the least connection with a criminal court room. Options included looking to set up a dedicated FAI centre or the continuation of the use of ad hoc centres as required.

4.122   Part of the motivation was to avoid bereaved families having to travel considerable distances. This can be seen in contrast to the Cairngorm FAI, held some considerable distance from Edinburgh at Banff Sheriff Court, hardly the easiest location for the children's families who were based in Edinburgh to reach.

4.123   The size of the FAI will govern where it is held. FAIs have been held in buildings not used for court purposes previously, such as the Lockerbie FAI which was held at the Easterbrook Hall, Crichton Royal Hospital, Dumfries, the Clarkston Gas Explosion held at Paisley Town Hall and the Rosepark FAI held at the GLO Centre, Motherwell. The Lockerbie FAI was held at the Crichton Hospital, Dumfries close to Lockerbie, which was a much bigger venue than the local court which would not have been able to handle the number of witnesses, press and affected families. Where FAIs are held in local courts, this also impacts on the available space for conducting other court business which is a factor to consider in relation to the potential length of the FAI.

4.124   By retaining the use of courts and ad hoc centres, as seen with the Lockerbie FAI, this maintains flexibility in deciding where an FAI should be held. It also preserves local knowledge and a connection with the disaster where local residents were killed and in justice being seen to be administered.

4.125   No doubt costs would be considerable in setting up FAI centres that may then have been underused. During the Covid-19 pandemic,[81] FAIs were held remotely, which is a practice that is to continue if thought appropriate. The FAI into the death of Lee Tortolano[82] was one such FAI held 'in light of the Covid-19 constraints, the

---

81   Scottish Courts and Tribunals, *Access to remote Fatal Accident Inquiry hearings, hwww.scotcourts. gov.uk/the-courts/sheriff-court/preliminary-hearings-and-dates-of-inquiry/access-to-remote-fatal-accident-inquiry-hearings* (accessed on 21 February 2023).
82   [2020] FAI 39.

hearing was conducted remotely by teleconference'.[83] Just how much this will be utilised in the future is yet to be seen.

4.126 The SCTS has developed a purpose-built justice centre at Inverness, being described as the 'first in a new generation of Scottish courts – bringing together, in one location, the various organisations that support the justice system... The ambition articulated by SCTS was that the architecture should contribute to the reforms currently being instigated in the delivery of a contemporary justice system.'[84] This may provide the way forward for better facilities in which to hold FAIs, as there will be an increasing need to ensure that digitisation and IT support to examine what may comprise extensive documentary productions.

4.127 Regulations[85] may be made to designate places at which a sheriff court may be held. These are in addition to those places designated under the Courts Reform (Scotland) Act 2014 for the holding of sheriff courts that includes towns and cities where sheriff courts are held. Provisions for consultation are included. Such regulations if made require the consent of the Lord President and SCTS.

4.128   Jurisdiction in relation to FAIs: The requirement to ensure that there was a link between the location of the death and the local sheriff court district was removed by s 13(1) of the 2016 Act. The intention is still for the majority of FAIs to continue to be held in the same sheriffdom as the location of the death. This change from the 1976 Act was to provide greater flexibility. It was to avoid issues with court capacity, causing any delay in holding FAIs and to allow them to be held wherever there was court-capacity. Though delay in holding FAIs is a constant criticism, there appears no suggestion that this is caused in part by any issues in providing court estate. There may be other resource implications, such as the provision of court or COPFS staff, as there has always been provision to hold FAIs outside the court estate as discussed above.

4.129 The Lord Advocate can choose the sheriffdom in which the FAI is held after consultation with SCTS. This section deliberately does not state that the Lord Advocate can state the location ie the building where such an FAI would be held. It seems to be a matter in practice or administration for discussion among the Sheriff Principal, SCTS and COPFS, with the views of the participants presumably the relatives, being taken into account. The 2016 Act does not actually state any such requirement to obtain views from the relatives.

4.130 Under s 13(3) of the 2016 Act, a sheriff can transfer the FAI to another sheriffdom, but only after giving the procurator fiscal and the participants, the opportunity to make representations about the proposed transfer and with the Sheriff Principal's consent from each of the sheriffdoms – the one to which it is to be

---

83   Ibid, para [2].
84   *https://2021.scottishdesignawards.com/architecture-public-building/inverness-justice-centre/* (accessed on 21 February 2023).
85   Subject to the affirmative procedure.

transferred as well as the one in which the FAI was originally located.[86] Such an order can be made at the sheriff's own initiative or, on the application of the procurator fiscal or one of the other participants at the FAI.

4.131   When exactly these powers would be utilised is not clear. It would presumably only apply after the preliminary hearing had been held and not during the process of hearing evidence in the FAI. The transfer might be deemed to be expedient where the FAI proceedings are anticipated to be lengthier and more complex than initially expected. Then, for efficiency purposes, the FAI might be best held at some ad hoc location which may be situated in another sheriffdom.

4.132   Inquiries into multiple deaths: Section 14 of the 2016 Act[87] allows a single FAI to be held into multiple deaths if they are as a result of the same accident or occur in the same or similar circumstances. This provides a means to link up a number of deaths to explore possible systemic failures. Looking to **Chapter 6** on deaths in custody, there may be an opportunity to group suicides of young persons in prisons together to look at general causes and conditions, given a number of recent concerns which have been expressed publicly. The Covid-19 care home inquiry is not being conducted as an FAI but as an inquiry. The circumstances of the inquiry do demonstrate the need to look at the discharge of patients from hospital back to care homes at the start of Covid-19.

4.133   There are a number of past FAIs which have looked at the deaths arising in the same accident on the same date, such as the Dunblane primary school shooting of the children and their teacher. However, this provision extends to deaths that arise in similar circumstances, such as the FAI by Sheriff Principal Cox into the E. coli outbreak in Lanarkshire that was able to examine 21 deaths arising from those who had consumed contaminated meat in a variety of locations.[88]

---

86   Section 13(3) and (4) of the 2016 Act.
87   The 1976 Act only allowed FAIs into multiple deaths where they occurred in the same sheriffdom. There are numerous examples of FAIs into multiple deaths: Dunblane and Lockerbie are two such FAIs.
88   BBC, Health Sheriff criticises E. coli butcher (19 August 1998), *http://news.bbc.co.uk/1/hi/ health/154107.stm#:~:text=Twenty%2Done%20people%20died%20in,procedures%20and%20 deceived%20food%20inspectors* (accessed on 21 February 2023).

Chapter 5

Pre-Inquiry, Inquiry, Determinations and Further Inquiry Proceedings

1. INTRODUCTION

5.01   This chapter considers the course of an FAI through the pre-inquiry procedure, the FAI, and the findings made within the determination and any recommendations to be made. There is a concluding section which outlines the scope and arrangements in the case of any further inquiry proceedings that are to be held.

5.02   Before considering the procedure relating to an FAI, the background and role of the Rules applying in FAIs needs to be considered.

5.03   Section 36(1) of the 2016 Act[1] sets out the process to make provisions by way of an Act of Sederunt for (a) the practice and procedure to be followed in an FAI proceeding and (b) matters incidental or ancillary to an FAI. The Act of Sederunt (Fatal Accident Inquiry Rules) 2017[2] introduced the Rules which came into effect on the same date as many of the provisions of the 2016 Act.

5.04   The Rules have a significant role to play when setting up an FAI as well as providing the sheriff with the necessary discretion on how to run the FAI and admit evidence as they see fit. Lord Cullen's Review had recommended that there should

---

1   Repeals s 7 of the 1976 Act.
2   SSI 2017/103.

be a 'comprehensive self-contained set of rules for FAIs' which were key to the new system that was being introduced. The Scottish Civil Justice Council was responsible for drafting the Rules that then came into effect.

5.05 Producing an updated version of the Rules was important for several reasons. The rules of evidence and procedure for FAIs were not easily located as they had been previously contained within three documents, namely the Fatal Accidents and Sudden Deaths Inquiry (Scotland) Act 1976 (the 1976 Act), the 1977 Rules that had been since amended and the rules of civil cause in the sheriff court. The 2016 Act produced the framework for FAIs with the Rules setting out the necessary details. This also provided the flexibility for the Rules to be updated in the future and amended when required.

5.06 Sections of the 2016 Act need to read alongside the Rules. These include ss 15–21 which relate to certain aspects of the procedure and practice required to conduct and manage FAIs. The Rules also provide a number of styles and examples of the documents to be used in connection with holding an FAI. These include the Notices to be provided when calling for an FAI to be held; Sch 3 to the Rules provides examples under Form 3.1 where a mandatory FAI is to be held. Schedule 3 Form 3.2 provides the style where a discretionary FAI is to be held. Witness citations are found under Sch 3 Form 4.1A and a certificate can be found under Sch 3 Form 4.1B. A later section will deal with Sch 3 Form 6.1 which refers to the style of determination to be issued by a sheriff at the conclusion of the FAI.

5.07 The Rules aim to achieve greater efficiency to allow the FAI process to run smoothly and to reduce delays. They ensure consistency of practice in the conduct of FAIs across Scotland and reinforce the inquisitorial nature of the FAI with the sheriff in charge of the FAI management. The sheriff can therefore respond flexibly to the nature and complexity of the actual FAI before them.

5.08 Introducing a statutory basis for the practice that had grown up of holding preliminary hearings in FAIs was appropriate as it allows for the effective management of the FAI. It helps to identify the scope of the FAI which allows witnesses and issues to be identified in advance. It allows any difficulties to be discussed without the pressure of witnesses waiting to give evidence in court. Multiple preliminary hearings can be held in FAI cases of greater complexity.

5.09 The introduction of the Rules has been a helpful practice, though it appears commonly that few FAIs make reference to the Rules in the FAI determinations that are issued. The FAI into the death of Pawel Kocik,[3] does specify the operation of the 2016 Act and the Rules under the preliminary para [1]. One would anticipate that there should be reference made to the Rules where there had been a decision made that required specific reference to the Rules, such as in how evidence was to

---

3   [2022] FAI 35, *www.scotcourts.gov.uk/docs/default-source/cos-general-docs/pdf-docs-for-opinions/2022fai035.pdf?sfvrsn=e4c464f8_1* (accessed on 21 February 2023).

be gathered. The Rules are there to provide that flexibility of process. Just how much parties to the FAI are aware of the Rules and their limitations is not known.

5.10 Section 18 of the 2016 Act deals with agreement of evidence and should be read in conjunction with rr 4.10 and 4.11, what this envisages is that uncontentious evidence should be agreed to allow for the efficient and effective running of the FAI. That does not take away from the sheriff's overriding requirement of robust inquiry into the facts and circumstances of the death. The practice that has evolved of permitting a joint minute agreeing the whole facts and circumstances of the case does not appear to satisfy the requirements of an FAI; that practice runs far beyond the administrative management of the FAI, and the examples of the type of evidence to be agreed, while not prescriptive, are set out in r 4.11. These relate to evidence such as information relating to the details of the deceased person, their employment details, and the circumstances such as the discovery of the death which are unlikely to be contentious issues.

5.11 What is being agreed in practice by way of joint minute is not only the uncontentious factual evidence. It also consists of agreement of opinion evidence, examples of which include the Death in Prison Learning, Audit & Review (DIPLAR) processes (the joint SPS & NHS process for reviewing deaths in custody and provides a system for recording any learning and identified actions). The DIPLAR process is intended to enable areas for improvement and potential learning to be identified following a death in prison custody (including where the death occurs in hospital) in advance of an FAI.[4] Serious Adverse Event Reviews (SAER) are undertaken in hospital following adverse medical events. Both a DIPLAR or a SAER may feature as part of the evidence at an FAI. However both these documents go way beyond what is factual evidence and will include opinion evidence from the relevant organisations where the deaths arose, be it the hospital or the prison. Use of joint minutes as highlighted elsewhere have their purpose, but the practice has gone much further than was intended and should be addressed.

2. PRE-INQUIRY PROCEDURE

5.12 Once instructions to proceed with an FAI are received from the Lord Advocate, practical aspects are needed to initiate the holding of the FAI.

5.13 COPFS are required to give notice to the sheriff that an FAI is to be held. What is absent from these requirements is any specific time-periods with regard to the completion of a report by COPFS to the Lord Advocate, following the investigations into the circumstances of the death. There is also no time scale for an FAI to be initiated from the decision being made by the Lord Advocate. The FAI

---

4   Scottish Government, *Handling of Deaths in Prison* (7 November 2019), *www.gov.scot/news/handling-of-deaths-in-prison/* (accessed 21 February 2023).

will need to await its turn and whatever priority is then assigned to it by COPFS. What is difficult to quantify thereafter is exactly at what stage delays arise in the completing of FAIs. It is not possible to ascertain what delay may be attributed to any suggestion that there is an absence of actual court capacity or to other court timetabling issues.

5.14   The 2016 Act simplifies the process for making an FAI as there is no longer a need to make an application for an FAI to be held.[5] All that is now required is for the procurator fiscal to give notice to the sheriff under s 15(1) of the 2016 Act that an FAI is to be held. The sheriff is not required to determine on that application for an FAI. The sheriff either then proceeds to set the dates and places for the preliminary hearing and FAI to be held,[6] or proceeds only to set the date of the preliminary hearing where the sheriff does not consider it appropriate to fix the FAI date at the same time.[7] The sheriff will adopt that option where it is expected to be a lengthy or complex FAI and/or there are a number of preliminary matters still required to be dealt with.

5.15   Subsection (5) makes it clear that, in deciding the date for the holding of the FAI, the sheriff must have regard to the desirability of holding the inquiry as soon as is reasonably practicable. This means that the sheriff must bear in mind the need to hold the FAI soon. While the FAI need not be held immediately, the only practical aspects which may occasion a delay would tend to relate to the absence of available accommodation and/or the allocation of reasonable time for the participants to prepare or be ready for an FAI.

5.16   The statutory requirements[8] under the 2016 Act ensure that the notice should contain certain information which is set out in more detail under Pt 3 of the Rules. This includes a brief account of the circumstances of the death so far as known to the procurator fiscal and any other information required under the Rules.[9] That includes the identity of the deceased, and if the procurator fiscal considers that a preliminary hearing is unnecessary, the reasons for that view, and the nature of the FAI, whether it is being held as a mandatory or discretionary FAI. Where the FAI to be held is discretionary, it should specify how it satisfies the provisions of s 4(1)(a) and (b). Under section 4(1)(a) this should state that the Lord Advocate considers that the death (i) was sudden, suspicious or unexplained (whichever is relevant) or (ii) occurred in circumstances giving rise to serious public concern; and (b) has decided that it is in the public interest for an inquiry to be held into the circumstances of the death.. If the FAI is being held under s 6 or 7 (deaths abroad) respectively, it should specify how the relevant condition 6(3) is met. It is required

---

5   Section 1(3) of the 1976 Act.
6   Section 15(3) of the 2016 Act.
7   Section 15(4) of the 2016 Act.
8   Section 15(2) of the 2016 Act.
9   Under s 36(1) of the 2016 Act the Court of Session may make provisions about the practice and procedure to be followed in an FAI and any matter incidental or ancillary to an FAI.

to specify the identity of any person who the procurator fiscal considers may have an interest in the FAI.

5.17 Schedule 3 Form 3.1 of the Rules[10] outlines the style of Notice to be followed.

5.18 Rule 3.2 of the Rules requires that the sheriff must then make a 'first order'[11] initiating the FAI within 14 days of receipt of the first notice. If required, the sheriff can order the procurator fiscal to appear in chambers to discuss the first order. The guess would be if the sheriff has any questions, they would be likely to just pick up the phone for informal advice rather than demand an appearance.

5.19 The preliminary hearing should take place within 56 days of the date of the first order. If no preliminary hearing is to take place, the FAI should be held within 56 days of the notice. See the diagram below.

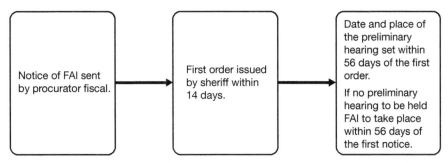

5.20 At the same time,[12] the sheriff will also grant warrant for the procurator fiscal and the participants in the FAI to cite persons to attend and to give evidence at the FAI. Such a right to cite witnesses does not arise unless or until the participants have been permitted to appear at the FAI. A participant need only cite witnesses if the participant is otherwise unable to ensure that witness's appearance. That is probably on the basis that most witnesses will be cited by the Crown and will appear.

5.21 The citation of witnesses is outlined in Pt 4, r 4.3, of the Rules which includes the form of citation under Sch 3 Form 4.1A. That requires citation to be effected at least seven days before the date fixed for the start of the FAI. Form 4.1B of the Rules provides the style of the certificate of citation to be lodged. Similar provisions as in criminal law exist where a witness who has been cited fails to answer the citation so that a warrant for apprehension can be granted by a sheriff and the sheriff can order a witness to make payment to a participant. The solicitor who cites a witness is liable for the fees and expenses.

---

10   Rule 1.4 of the Rules provides under Sch 3 the style of Forms to be used.
11   Rule 3.2 (2) of the Rules.
12   Section 15(3) of the 2016 Act.

5.22   For participants who are not legally represented, the participant must apply for caution to be fixed by the sheriff in such sum as the sheriff considers reasonable, having regard to the number of witnesses the participant proposes to cite and the period they may be required to attend. Before citing, the participant should find caution for such expenses which may reasonably be anticipated to be incurred by the witness in answering the citation.

5.23   Once the first order has been made, the participants can gather information for use in connection with the FAI as set out in Sch 5 to the Rules. The Rules set out how to deal with confidential material, how to obtain a warrant for production of original documents from public records, how to apply for commission and diligence, letters of request, information to be given on commission, interrogatories and taking of evidence in the EU.[13]

5.24   Once the notice is sent by COPFS to hold an FAI the process is set out clearly with timescales indicated – but of course any number of preliminary hearings can be held so in practice, notwithstanding the receipt of the notice to hold an FAI, there is no certainty as to how soon the FAI will start.

3.   PRELIMINARY HEARINGS

5.25   A significant informal practice began prior to the 2016 Act in holding preliminary hearings in advance of each FAI. This practice adopted the changes that had been made in criminal procedure to require preliminary or first diets to allow for the efficient and effective discharge of the court business. There were many advantages, such as resolving out the anticipated length of the FAI, issues with the availability and the number of witnesses. That practice has now been formalised by s 16(1) of the 2016 Act which requires that at least one preliminary hearing is to be held unless the requirement is dispensed with. These are proportionate and appropriate measures and allow the sheriff the flexibility to regulate the procedure to ensure that the FAI principles are satisfied. The FAI principles are set out under r 2.2 of the Rules.

5.26   Under r 2.2(1) and (2) of the Rules, an inquiry is to be inquisitorial, not adversarial, and for the FAI to be progressed as expeditiously and efficiently with as few delays as possible. All participants to the FAI are to be able to participate effectively in furthering the purpose of the FAI (r 2.(4)). The procedure at the FAI should be as flexible as appropriate and the manner in which information is presented is to be as efficient as possible, taking into account the nature and complexity of the FAI.

---

13   Despite the UK withdrawal these provisions seem still to refer to the UK as a Member State. Paragraph 12 of Sch 5 to the Rules.

5.27   Although holding a preliminary hearing will be appropriate in the vast majority of FAIs, there will be a small number where the issues are narrowly focused and where there has been appropriate engagement between the potential participants in advance. Section 16(2) allows the sheriff to dispense with the requirement, though the sheriff can subsequently make an order requiring an FAI to be held. The decisions as to whether or not to dispense with a preliminary hearing will remain one for the sheriff.

5.28   Paragraph 3.6 of the Rules sets out the purpose of the FAI. Under s 3.6.(1) of the Rules, a preliminary hearing ensures that the purpose of the FAI is achieved when the FAI actually takes place. It considers the scope of the FAI and identifies the issues which are in dispute, considers the information likely to be presented at the FAI and the manner in which it is to be presented.

5.29   Holding a preliminary hearing allows the sheriff to adopt a form of case management to ascertain how much evidence is likely to be heard, determine potential vulnerabilities and to ensure that the actual conduct and timescales for the FAI can be managed effectively. Any number of preliminary hearings in relation to any FAI may be held.[14] The FAI into the death of James Grahames[15] shows the holding of four preliminary hearings.[16] Exactly why there should be so many is unexplained. In issuing determinations, it would be useful if there was a standard provision whereby a sheriff was required to set out the full procedural history leading up to the FAI. This is commonly included in reported criminal cases and would show when the Notice to hold an FAI was first received, the preliminary hearing(s) and the number of days on which the FAI sat. This would be useful statistical information to help assess the efficiency of the FAI process.

5.30   Paragraph 3.7 of the Rules refers to the process to be adopted prior to the Preliminary Hearing. All of the participants must lodge, at least seven days before the first preliminary hearing, a brief notice outlining the matters considered to be likely in dispute at the FAI, a list of productions which might be used at the FAI and a note of their relevance to the purpose of the FAI, and the matters which the sheriff might be invited to address in the sheriff's determination.[17] The aspects to be discussed at the preliminary hearing are those set out under r 3.8 of the Rules. These are discussed below, along with the potential role of the agreement of evidence.

5.31   At the conclusion of the preliminary hearing, the sheriff must fix a date for another preliminary hearing or fix a date for the start of the FAI.[18] Where a further preliminary hearing is to be held, the sheriff must specify the reason for fixing another preliminary hearing and the matters which will fall to be considered at that preliminary hearing.[19]

---

14 Rule 3.6(2) of the Rules.
15 [2021] FAI 51.
16 3 February, 26 March, 28 April and 5 May 2021.
17 Rule 3.7 of the Rules.
18 Rule 3.8(3) of the Rules.
19 Rule 3.8(5) of the Rules.

5.32   After the sheriff has made an order fixing the date and place for the holding of a preliminary hearing and for the start of the FAI, the procurator fiscal must then notify potential participants and provide a public notice of the intention to hold an inquiry and its date and location. The diagram shows the possible process.

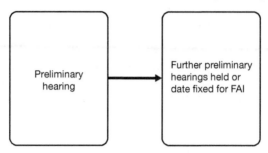

5.33   **Aspects to be covered at the preliminary hearing:** rule 3.8 of the Rules details these issues as:

- to identify any further persons who the sheriff is satisfied have an interest in the FAI;[20]
- to establish who is to participate in the FAI;
- to establish the nature and complexity of the FAI;
- to consider the likely length timetable and date for the start of the FAI;
- to establish any matters which are likely to be in dispute at the FAI;
- to establish the state of preparedness of the participants;
- to consider how much information should be presented to the FAI, including how information is to be gathered,[21] the timetable for lodging productions and witness lists,[22] arrangements for vulnerable witnesses,[23] how participants are progressing with discharging their duty to agree information,[24] whether notices to admit information are required,[25] whether witness statements,[26] video recordings[27] and how any expert witness should present information,[28] and how any other technology such as live links will be used;
- to consider any preliminary matter raised by a participant;
- to identify any legal aid application which have been or require to be made or renewed by participants.

---

20   Section 11(1) 9e) of the 2016 Act.
21   Rule 4.4.
22   Rules 4.6 and 4.7.
23   Rule 4.9 refers to Sch 6 which sets out in detail where a witness is vulnerable. The schedule incorporates the Vulnerable Witnesses (Scotland) Act 2004 and covers child witness notices and vulnerable witness application.
24   Rule 4.11.
25   Rule 4.12.
26   Rule 4.13.
27   Rule 4.14.
28   Rules 4.15–4.19.

5.34   The Rules are quite detailed. Reference is made in order to understand how broad and flexible the process of an FAI is, providing the sheriff with discretion on managing a range of topics, including at Pt 4 of the Rules under Information. These include the following.

5.35   **Evidence:** rule 4.1 provides that restrictions under the law of evidence do not apply to an FAI. Any rule of law or enactment that prevents evidence being led on the grounds of inadmissibility does not apply in an FAI. No rule of law restricts the manner in which the evidence must be presented. A sheriff can make an order so that information may be presented to the FAI in any manner and to allow the sheriff to reach conclusions based on that information. This removes any formal requirements about docqueting and best evidence for instance in relation to documentary evidence. Crucially it does not dispense with the need for a sheriff to ensure that robust inquiry is still made in relation to the circumstances of the death.

5.36   **Information management:** Powers are provided under r 4.2 so that the sheriff may make orders about the manner in which information is presented to the FAI or about how the sheriff will reach conclusions. The sheriff can by order restrict the information presented to particular issues or particular sources, determine the manner in which information is to be presented, whether by oral presentation, written statement, the production of documents or other item, live link video recording or otherwise. The sheriff can determine the manner in which they are to reach their conclusions.

5.37   **Productions:** Under r 4.6, productions intended to be used in the FAI must be lodged by the date ordered by the sheriff. However, where productions have not been lodged, there is in effect no bar to their production as they can be admitted in an FAI even if not lodged provided that leave of the sheriff is obtained.[29] Copy productions should be lodged with the sheriff court at least seven days prior to the start of the FAI.

5.38   **Witnesses:** Similarly, under r 4.7, a list of witnesses must be lodged with the sheriff by the date ordered by the sheriff. Additional unlisted witnesses can only be added with the leave of a sheriff.

5.39   **Agreement of evidence:** Section 18 of the 2016 Act sets out provisions where the procurator fiscal and any participant in the FAI intends to bring forward evidence at the FAI and which both or either of these parties consider are unlikely to be disputed at the FAI for agreement of evidence.[30]

5.40   Rule 4.10 supplements these provisions by setting out that agreement of evidence can be achieved by lodging joint minutes of agreement. This is a common practice, certainly in prison related deaths such as the FAI into the death of James

29   Rule 4.6(2).
30   Rule 18(2).

Grahames.[31] All evidence was agreed by joint minute, which certainly reduces the length of the FAI but has been open to criticism as it may limit the discretion exercised by a sheriff to examine witnesses on factual aspects relating to the FAI. This issue is discussed in **Chapter 7** where the family members may not be participants to the FAI. They cannot therefore have been asked to agree any evidence. Furthermore, the use of the joint minutes is much more extensive and being deployed for all factual information which is required for findings to be made by the sheriff in an FAI. This is surely not what was contemplated when these administrative provisions in the Rules were originally conceived. Discretion as to agreement to the joint minute lies in r 4.10(4); and where a participant is not legally represented, the joint minute must be approved by the sheriff.

5.41   All participants to the FAI must take reasonable steps to agree evidence as set out under r 4.11.[32] Rule 4.11(3) sets out that these should include what amounts to factual evidence such as:

- the name, age, address and occupation of the deceased;
- the location, date and time of the deceased's death;
- the circumstances in which the death was discovered;
- the identity of any person who witnessed the accident or discovered the deceased's body;
- the name of the doctor who pronounced the death of the deceased;
- any death under s 2(3) of the 2016 Act (in the course of employment), the name and address of the deceased's employer, the length and nature of employment, the deceased's employment duties at the time of death;
- any death under s 2(4)(a) of the 2016 Act (legal custody), the offence committed or alleged to be committed, the date of conviction or remand plus reasons for remand and the time spent in custody or reasons for the deceased to be in legal custody. A number of Covid-19 related deaths are still to be investigated;[33]
- any death in Scotland of service personnel,[34] the length of the period of service, the nature of service and the deceased's services at the time of death;
- any post mortem and/or toxicology report.

5.42   Crucially what it does not suggest is that they are used to agree the Death In Prison Learning And Review (DIPLAR) and Serious Adverse Event Reviews

---

31   2021   FAI   51,   *www.scotcourts.gov.uk/docs/default-source/cos-general-docs/pdf-docs-for-opinions/2021fai051.pdf?sfvrsn=745b 6d95_1* (accessed on 21 February 2023).

32   Section 257 of the Criminal Procedure (Scotland) Act 1995. If it is possible for the prosecutor and the accused to agree facts which are unlikely to be disputed by any of the other parties in criminal proceedings, where the standard of proof is higher than at an FAI, then there is no reason why this should not be possible in an FAI.

33   BBC, *Sixth prisoner death in Scotland linked to coronavirus* (15 May 2020), *www.bbc.co.uk/news/uk-scotland-52677858* (accessed on 21 February 2023).

34   Article 6 of the Inquiries into Fatal Accidents and Sudden Deaths etc. (Scotland) Act 2016 (Consequential Provisions and Modifications) Order 2016 (SI 2016/1142).

(SAERs), both of which will include opinion evidence based on factual information as produced by the prison or the hospital respectively. Though other evidence may well be agreed specific to the FAI as in any other court case, joint minutes should be used only where the evidence is uncontentious.

5.43 Rule 4.12 sets out the provisions where a sheriff orders notices to admit information. A participant may prepare a notice to admit information in a Form 4.12A where that process is being invoked.

5.44 Rule 4.13 sets out where the sheriff orders that a witness statement must be lodged. A 'witness statement' is defined under r 4.13(2) as a written statement containing information which a person could present orally at an FAI and signed by that person. The right to ask any questions of that witness to introduce, clarify or supplement the witness statement or ask questions relating to a new matter which have arisen since the witness statement was lodged are stated.

5.45 Other participants may question the witness. Rule 4.13(4) requires that a witness statement must be made available for inspection by the public during the FAI. What that means is curious. Is the public House in the court? Statements may contain personal information about the witness which should not be in the public domain, redaction may be required if such statements were to be made available for inspection by the public.

5.46 Rule 4.14 sets out the process where a witness is to present information at the FAI by video recording.

5.47 **Expert witnesses:** Rules 4.15–4.19 set out the process applying to expert witnesses.

5.48 Most FAIs can be expected to include evidence to be given by a range of expert witnesses that will likely include medical, technical and scientific evidence. The term 'expert' is not defined; it is understood to include those who have the relevant qualifications, competence, expertise and experience to speak to the 'relevant matters which are not within the knowledge of everyday life reasonably to be imputed to a jury or other finder of fact may be admissible'.[35]

5.49 The Rules echo much of the jurisprudence set out around the use of expert witnesses with regard to the mechanics of lodging reports which may be usefully summarised. The concern over the use of expert witnesses relates to multiple experts, experts exceeding their expertise or competence and the cost both to the public pocket as well as in court time.

5.50 There are many examples where expert evidence is regarded as having been sufficiently developed, examples of which include scientific (DNA) comparisons, forensic toxicology, reports and fingerprint evidence.

---

35 *Young v HMA* 2014 SLT 21 at [54].

5.51   The expert witness must be competent to speak to relevant matters from their expertise, otherwise that evidence will be inadmissible, irrespective of any objection taken from any participant to the FAI. The expert evidence must be relevant to the issues and based on a recognised and developed academic discipline. To be admissible, the evidence must have a sufficiently reliable foundation to be capable of assisting them in the proper determination of the issue before them.[36]

5.52   The judge at the FAI will treat the witness as any other witness and may accept the evidence, in whole or in part. There may be conflicting evidence[37] or they may not be satisfied by the evidence provided.

5.53   Helpful guidance may be found in *Kennedy v Cordia (Services) LLP*[38] where the Supreme Court set out some key questions when considering the provenance for expert evidence as to:

- whether the proposed skilled evidence will assist the court in its task;
- whether the witness has the necessary knowledge and experience;
- whether the witness is impartial in their presentation and assessment of the evidence; and
- whether there is a reliable body of knowledge or experience to underpin the expert's evidence.

5.54   This follows the general advice that 'if scientific, technical or other specialized knowledge will assist the trier of fact to understand the evidence or to determine a fact in issue, a witness qualified as an expert by knowledge, skill, experience, training, or education, may testify thereto in the form of an opinion or otherwise'.[39]

5.55   It is important to recognise the duty of an expert witness where they should be 'careful to recognise, however, the need to avoid supplanting the court's role as the ultimate decision-maker on matters that are central to the outcome of the case'.[40]

5.56   Any participant seeking to rely on an expert should remember that 'a party seeking to lead a witness with purported knowledge or experience outwith generally recognised fields would need to set up by investigation and evidence not only the qualifications and expertise of the individual skilled witness, but the methodology and validity of that field of knowledge or science'.[41]

5.57   Rules 4.18 and 4.19 both set out a process to use a single expert report and also the use of concurrent presentation of expert witnesses which replicates a process referred to as 'hot-tubbing'. This is a process whereby experts in any discipline give their evidence simultaneously.

---

36   Ibid at [55].
37   The FAI into Sharman Weir involved six medical experts in the field of preeclampsia deaths.
38   2016 SLT 209 at [44]; 2016 SCLR 203.
39   *Daubert v Merrell Dow Pharmaceuticals Inc* (1993) 509 US 579.
40   *Pora v The Queen* [2015] UKPC 9; [2016] 1 Cr App R 3 at [24].
41   Walker and Walker at para 16.3.5 refer to an obiter dictum in Lord Eassie's opinion in *Mearns v Smedvig Ltd* 1999 SC 243.

4. NOTICE OF THE FAI

5.58   Under s 17 of the 2016 Act, once the sheriff makes an order fixing the date and place for the holding of a preliminary hearing and the date of the FAI, the procurator fiscal must give notice in the style of Form 3.3A of the Sch 3 to the Rules, at least 42 days before the preliminary hearing or, where there is no preliminary hearing, the date fixed for the FAI. Rule 3.3 sets out the process in more detail.

5.59   That notice must be given to:

- The persons appearing to the procurator fiscal to be entitled to participate in the FAI. That includes the spouse or civil partner,[42] a person living with the deceased as if married at the time of their death,[43] their nearest known relative if at the time of their death they did not have a spouse or civil partner[44] and was not living with a person as if married to the person, and those falling into category under s 11(1)(d) of the 2016 Act as being an employer, inspector, trade union or staff representative.
- Any other person specified or in a category of persons specified under the Rules. Section 36 (2)(e) of the 2016 Act provides for provisions to be made for the representation of procurator fiscal and participants, including those participants in an FAI who are not solicitors or advocates or do not have the right to conduct litigation or a right of audience by virtue of s 27 of the Law Reform (Miscellaneous Provisions)(Scotland) Act 1990.
- These categories are reiterated to an extent in r 3.3(3) where it outlines notice to be served on a person named in the first order as a person whom the sheriff is satisfied has an interest in the FAI and in a category of death specified in column 1 any person specified in column 2. However additional categories have been added as follows:

Column 1 Circumstances of death	Column 2 Specified person
A death within s 2(3)[45] of the 2016 Act	The Health and Safety Executive[46]
A death within s 2(4)(b) of the 2016 Act[47]	The local authority or other provider of secure accommodation in whose care the child died, the Scottish Ministers and Social Care and Social Work Improvement Scotland

---

42   Section 11(1)(a) of the 2016 Act.
43   Section 11(1)(b) of the 2016 Act.
44   Section 11(1)(c) of the 2016 Act.
45   Death as a result of an accident which occurred while the person was acting in the course of the person's employment or occupation.
46   Repeats s 17(2)(a), (d) of the 2016 Act.
47   Death of a child required to be kept or detained in secure accommodation.

A death within s 2(5)(a) of the 2016 Act[48]	The Scottish Ministers or the Chief Constable of the relevant policy force[49]
A death within s 2(5)(b) of the 2016 Act[50]	The Chief Constable of the relevant police force[51]
A death within s 2(5)(c) of the 2016 Act[52]	The SCTS
A death within s 2(5)(d) of the 2016 Act[53]	The Secretary of State
A death within s 5[54] or s 6[55] or s 7 of the 2016 Act[56] or a death within Art 6 of the 2016 Order	The Secretary of State

5.60   Those supplied with a notice and who intend to participate must indicate that intention by lodging a notification in terms of Form 3.3B of Sch 3 at least 14 days before the start of the FAI.[57]

5.61   Public notice must also be given of the fact that an FAI is to be held and of the place and date of the preliminary hearing and the place and start date of the FAI. Rule 3.4(1) amplifies the provision by requiring that notice must be given in Form 3.4 of Sch 3. It must be given at least 42 days before the preliminary hearing or, if no preliminary hearing is to be held, the date fixed for the start of the FAI.[58]

5.62   SCTS must publish the notice on its website when it is received.[59] The only information which is conveyed shows the date of the preliminary hearing. A note of the preliminary hearing which was to be held on 30 December 2022 related to the deaths of three persons – only by further internet research is it possible to ascertain that this in fact related to the deaths of three babies.[60] Further research discloses that the preliminary hearing is a further preliminary hearing, since one was held on 5 September 2022, the FAI being justified on the basis that it is:

---

48   Death of a person required to be imprisoned or detained in a penal institution.
49   Presumably now there is only one police organisation, so namely Police Scotland.
50   Death in police custody.
51   See **fn 8** above.
52   Death in custody on court premises.
53   Death of a person detained in service custody premises.
54   Certain deaths and accidents to be treated as occurring in Scotland.
55   Inquiries into deaths occurring abroad: general.
56   Inquiries into deaths occurring abroad: service personnel.
57   Rule 3.3(4).
58   Rule 3.4(2).
59   Scottish Courts and Tribunals, *Fatal Accident Inquiry. Preliminary Hearings and Inquiry Dates*, *www.scotcourts.gov.uk/the-courts/sheriff-court/preliminary-hearings-and-dates-of-inquiry* (accessed on 21 February 2023).
60   Daily Record, *Law chiefs order probe into tragic deaths of three Scots babies* (29 July 2022), *www. dailyrecord.co.uk/news/scottish-news/scotland-baby-death-inquiry-ordered-27605084* (accessed on 21 February 2023).

'a discretionary inquiry under section 4(1)(a)(ii) and 4(1)(b) of the Inquiries into Fatal Accidents and Sudden Deaths etc. (Scotland) Act 2016, the Lord Advocate having considered that the deaths of Leo Lamont, Ellie McCormick, and Mirabelle Bosch occurred in circumstances giving rise to serious public concern and that it is in the public interest for a public inquiry to be held into the circumstances of the death.'[61]

5.63 A sheriff may order that the public notice is to be given by other methods. Wide discretion is afforded to COPFS on how it advertises the FAI, though the practice has been to publish a notice in newspapers. With the increasing use of social media, there could be opportunities to use other platforms to advertise the holding of an FAI.

5.64 Any other persons who wish to participate but have not been given notice may apply to the sheriff to participate under r 3.5(1). They need to set out in their application why their participation would further the purpose of the inquiry and must be made at least 14 days before the start of the FAI.

5.65 The diagram below shows the process leading up to the actual start of the FAI.

Procurator Fiscal sends notice to sheriff of FA under Rule 3.1
• Account of circumstances of the death, deceased identify, issues to be addressed at FAI, need for a preliminary hearing, mandatory or discretionary FAI identity of person who may have interest in the FAI
• If relevant how conditions met under section 6(3)(a) or section 7(1)(c)

↓

Sheriff makes first order and other participants become involved in FAI Rules 3.2-3.5
• within 14 days of notice being received preliminary hearing to be held within 56 days after first order or if no preliminary hearing FAI within 56 days of the first order
• Notice of FAI to be given to parties outlined in Rule 3.3 Public Notice of FAI to be given Notice to be given by any other person who wishes to participate in FAI

↓

Sheriff holds one of more preliminary hearings in terms of Rule 3.6-3.8 to make sure that the FAI is ready to start
• Rules 3.6-3.8 this covers purpose of the FAI and before the preliminary hearing and procedure at a preliminary hearing
• This also includes orders about the presentation of information and the participants will notify each other and the sheriff of the information they intend to present at the FAI Part 4 of the Rules

↓

Inquiry is held and sheriff presides procedure is determined by sheriff Part 5 of the Rules

↓

The sheriff produces a determination Part 6 of the Rules

---

61   Form 3.4, *https://scotcourts.gov.uk/docs/default-source/fatal-accident-inquiries/ham-b512-22-leo-lamont-ellie-mccormick-mirabelle-bosch.pdf?sfvrsn=bc98bfdd_2* (accessed on 21 February 2023).

5. FAI (THE INQUIRY)

5.66   Under s 19(1) of the 2016 Act, the sheriff has all the powers in connection with an FAI as they have in any civil proceedings. Schedule 3 Pt 5 r 5.1 of the Rules outline that the procedure at an FAI is to be as ordered by the sheriff.

5.67   Section 20(1) of the 2016 Act refers to the bringing forward of evidence at the FAI. In line with their role, the main obligation and responsibility lies with the procurator fiscal who must bring forward evidence relating to the circumstances of the death to which the FAI relates. A participant to the FAI may also bring forward evidence. Section 20(2) enables the sheriff to instruct the procurator fiscal or a participant in the FAI to lead evidence on any matter relating to the circumstances of the death. The sheriff is not, therefore, dependent upon the procurator fiscal, nor on the participants with regard to what evidence is led. Rule 2.2 sets out that an FAI is inquisitorial and not adversarial.

5.68   Evidence that has not been corroborated and hearsay evidence are both admissible in FAI proceedings (as set out in ss 1, 2 and 9(c) of the Civil Evidence (Scotland) Act 1988).[62] The evidential standard for facts to be proven for FAIs is the civil standard of proof on the balance of probabilities.

5.69   Judicial continuity is also provided for in r 2.5 so that the same sheriff is (a) to consider the first notice and make the first order, (b) preside at all preliminary hearings and (c) preside at the FAI. This is practical and makes sense to avoid unnecessary repetition.

5.70   The sheriff has to take into account the FAI principles when interpreting the Rules and making any orders. Participants[63] and representatives[64] must respect the FAI principles by taking into account the FAI principles when seeking any order and assisting the sheriff with their duty to take into account the interpretation of the Rules and any order that is made.[65]

5.71   Under r 2.6 the sheriff may make any order necessary to further the purpose of the FAI including:

(1) Any order made to assist the sheriff to identify which issues are in dispute such as an order:
- fixing a hearing and specifying a purpose for that hearing;
- requiring participants to disclose the existence and nature of information which they hold relating to the FAI;

---

62 Section 20(3) of the 2016 Act following s 4(7) of the 1976 Act.
63 Defined in r 1.2 which includes the procurator fiscal though within the 2016 Act participant as defined in s11(2)(b) of the 2016 Act does not include the procurator fiscal.
64 Undefined in the Rules except under r 2.4 where a participant except the procurator fiscal can appear on their participant's own behalf, may be presented by a solicitor an advocate or both or with the sheriff's permission be supported but does not say represented by a lay supporter.
65 Rule 2.3.

- requiring participants to lodge particular documents or other items or to lead particular witnesses;
- restricting participants to lodge particular documents or other items which a participant may present or witnesses a participant may lead;
- granting authority to recover documents or lead other items relating to the FAI.

(2) Any order made to allow the sheriff to manage time more efficiently such as an order imposing a time limit or any step to be taken by a participant or varying a deadline or time limit set out in the Rules.

(3) Any order dealing with a participant's non-compliance with a rule or order, such as an order requiring that a participant take a step as a consequence of not complying with a rule or order.

(4) Relieving the participant from the consequences of not complying with a rule or order imposing any condition on any relief from non-compliance.

5.72   The sheriff may make such orders for themselves or on the application of a participant which includes the procurator fiscal.

5.73   Section 20(5) of the 2016 Act contains the important provision that a person examined at the FAI is not granted immunity from prosecution. The safeguard is included under s 20(6) of the 2016 Act that any person at an FAI is not required to answer a question to show that person is guilty of an offence.[66] Rule 4.5 requires the sheriff to administer either an oath or affirmation to a witness prior to giving evidence.

5.74   An illustration of where there has been a warning given can be seen from the case where there was a subsequent criminal conviction for perjury.[67] The owner of a basement flat let to students, Mr Singh, was prosecuted where two students, Daniel Heron and James Fraser, had died as a result of a fire. An FAI held in 2000 focused on whether there had been a functioning smoke detector. Mr Singh gave evidence at the FAI that there was a smoke detector in the flat's hallway and another on top of the freezer in the kitchen. He had claimed that the smoke detector in the hallway was in working condition at the time of the fire which was incorrect. At the unsuccessful appeal of his conviction, Mr Singh claimed that he had not been legally represented, and had received no warning at the outset of the FAI that he could decline to answer questions that could be self-incriminatory.[68] There had been 'no irregularity or impropriety of any kind in the leading of the evidence … which would enable it to be said that any part of his evidence was incompetent'.[69]

---

66   These restate s 5 of the 1976 Act.
67   *Harpall Singh v Her Majesty's Advocate*, Appeal No XC140/02, 25 August 2004, *www.scotcourts. gov.uk/search-judgments/judgment?id=72aa87a6-8980-69d2-b500-ff0000d74aa7* (accessed on 21 February 2023).
68   The warning was set out then under s 5(2) of the 1976 Act.
69   Ibid.

5.75   There is a distinction between a warning given to a witness and the issue of whether a witness was in fact entitled to decline to answer a particular question. That FAI was decided under s 5(2) of the 1976 Act which did not require the giving of warning in advance to witnesses. It dealt with the issue of whether a witness could be compelled to answer a particular question, tending to show that he was guilty of some crime or offence. Providing a general warning might be good practice, but was not, in fact, required by law. However, perhaps going forward, where it is clear at the outset of a witness's evidence that they would be asked questions, the answers to which would tend to show that they were guilty of some particular crime or offence, a warning should be given.

5.76   The case is interesting too as the court went onto to examine the sentence and set out the importance of the evidence provided at an FAI:

'Fatal Accident Inquiries, in one of which [Mr Singh] has committed perjury, are of great public importance. Under our law they provide an opportunity for the court to investigate publicly and in a formal way the circumstances of a death. In order to make proper decisions in such [i]nquiries, sheriffs must have reliable information upon which to base them. Accordingly, it is of the greatest importance that witnesses called to give evidence at such Inquiries should provide reliable information. In this case, unfortunately, that did not happen. In addition to that particular consideration, perjury must always be seen as a serious crime, since it strikes at the fundamental basis of our system of justice and at the integrity and accuracy of the decisions reached in courts. It follows that when perjury is established, it must be dealt with seriously for the benefit of the courts and the public generally. Everyone should be made fully aware that, when an oath is taken in a court of law to tell the truth, that is what must be done.'[70]

5.77   Other FAIs have dealt with similar issues where a witness may be asked questions about their actions which could show that they were guilty of an offence. The problem is where they decline to answer a question that this does mean that the court may be unable to hear the full circumstances of the death.

5.78   This is illustrated in the FAI into the deaths of Mhairi Convy and Laura Stewart[71] who were both killed on 17 December 2010 when a car mounted a pavement in Glasgow. The Crown had dropped a criminal prosecution at an earlier stage against William Payne, the driver, where he had been accused of not having revealed that he suffered from blackouts earlier. At the FAI, he declined to answer questions regarding such matters related to his health.

---

70   Ibid.
71   BBC, *Inquiry into Mhairi Convy and Laura Stewart road deaths*, (20 November 2013), *www.bbc. co.uk/news/uk-scotland-glasgow-west-25023172* (accessed on 21 February 2023).

5.79 The Glasgow Bin Lorry related to the deaths of a number of pedestrians where a bin lorry went out of control. No criminal prosecution resulted against the driver of the bin lorry, Harry Clarke. Much discussion had followed the incident in connection with his pre-existing medical condition. In the FAI into the deaths of John Kerr Sweeney, Lorraine Sweeney, Erin Paula McQuade, Stephenie Catherine Tair, Gillian Margaret Ewing and Jacqueline Morton,[72] the driver had informed the court that he did not want to answer questions about his pre-existing medical condition. Key findings were made subsequently by the Sheriff J Beckett QC in his determination that showed the importance of this issue to the FAI. This is illustrated in the following section at paras 3.6– 3.8, where the sheriff set out in terms of s 6(1)(c) the reasonable precautions, if any, whereby the death and any accident resulting in the death might have been avoided. These included that:

'[3.6] For Mr Clarke to have provided true and accurate information about his medical history on BUPA medical questionnaires in December 2011.

[3.7] For Mr Clarke to have disclosed the incident of 7 April 2010 in DVLA form D47 and to Dr Willox in December 2011.

[3.8] For Mr Clarke, after fainting at the wheel of his bus on 7 April 2010, to have refrained from continuing to drive buses and to have refrained from seeking further employment as a group 2 driver in the absence of his having told the truth to doctors and without having acted upon the advice which would have been forthcoming, and thereafter without making his relevant medical history known to Glasgow City Council to the extent required in its recruitment, appointment and promotion processes.'

5.80 Section 21(1) of the 2016 Act provides that an FAI should be conducted in public, though s21(2) provides that the sheriff may order that the FAI, or part of it, may be held in private. The sheriff can make this order if the procurator fiscal or one of the participants applies for it, or may do so on their own initiative. Potential grounds which are unspecified could include those relating to national security, the protection of children or any other vulnerable person.

5.81 Under s 22 of the 2016 Act, a sheriff may prohibit the publication[73] of material that could identify a child[74] involved in an FAI. This includes but is not limited to their name, address, the name of the school or a picture of the child. Section 22(8) of the 2016 Act provides a definition of 'material' which is not limited but means 'anything capable of being read, looked at, watched, listened to either directly or after conversion from data stored in another form'.

---

72   [2015] FAI 31.
73   Section 22(8) provides publication means within a programme service defined by s 201 of the Broadcasting Act 1990 or cause to be published.
74   Being a person under 18.

5.82   The sheriff may make such an order on their own initiative or on the application of the procurator fiscal or a participant in the FAI. Failure to comply with the sheriff's order constitutes an offence with a Level 4 fine (£2,500)[75] on summary conviction. A defence is provided to show that they did not know or have reason to believe that the publication would identify the child in connection with the FAI. These publishing restrictions are extended by Order under s 104 of the Scotland Act 1998 and to refer to England and Wales and Northern Ireland.

5.83   Section 23 of the 2016 Act refers to offences by bodies corporate etc. This is where the publication offence under s 21(5) is committed by bodies such as companies, partnerships and unincorporated associations (eg a club). This allows for those who have an element of control over such bodies, such as a director or partner set out in subs 23(3) of the 2016 Act, to be held criminally liable and to be fined in certain circumstances.

5.84   Section 24 allows a sheriff to appoint an assessor to provide assistance to them in relation to the specific FAI based on the assessor's specialist knowledge or expertise.

5.85   Section 25 removes the right of the sheriff to make an award of expenses. The view was that the sheriff has extensive case management powers so any vexatious behaviour if it arises can be dealt with without the need to award expenses.

6. THE DETERMINATION

5.86   The most important aspect of the FAI is the determination which the sheriff is required to issue, following the conclusion of the hearing of the evidence in the FAI. The determination records the facts of the death along with the sheriff's analysis of the evidence led before the court. The facts will be identified by the sheriff on the balance of probabilities. The findings that are made cannot be relied on in any civil or criminal proceedings.

5.87   Lord Cullen's Review proposed that there should be a timescale imposed on the issue of a determination in an FAI by a sheriff, after all the evidence had been completed. However, that was not accepted so that s 26 of the 2016 Act merely requires that the sheriff is to issue the determination 'as soon as possible' after the evidence and the submissions have concluded.

5.88   It is understandable why there should be no specific publication timescales imposed for the issue of any FAI determination. It is impossible to ascertain how long it will take a sheriff to issue their determination. Clearly, some FAIs are very complex, running to a requirement to issue many pages of a determination, reflective of days of hearing evidence and various parties' submissions. Other FAIs are of

---

75   Criminal Procedure (Scotland) Act 1995, s 225(1).

course very short, much of the evidence, if not all, having been agreed by means of a joint minute. Given the difference and also that sheriffs will be undertaking other work would mean that the imposition of any arbitrary timescale would be unrealistic – however what is lost is any effective monitoring of how long in practice this takes.

5.89   Though, as has been reflected elsewhere, delays are a source of major criticism in FAIs, there is no evidence to show that that there are long delays by sheriffs in issuing the determination from an FAI. This would be easier to track were all determinations produced in a similar style to include a note as to all dates of any prior proceedings held, such as the date of the Notice received to hold an FAI, the dates of the preliminary hearing(s) and the dates on which evidence was heard.

5.90   The question of 'issue' of the determination should be read as separate from the publication required by SCTS[76] under s 27 of the 2016 Act. Section 27(1) now makes it mandatory for SCTS to publish the determination resulting from each FAI. Though the manner of publication is for SCTS, this represents a significant change as previously only those determinations which a sheriff considered should have been published, were published. This, as discussed in **Chapter 12**, makes it difficult to have sight of earlier determinations as the practices were inconsistent as to what may have been published. An FoI request made to SCTS[77] dated 16 November 2022 for a previously unpublished determination in the FAI of Stephen Miller who died on 12 July 1999 by then Sheriff Craig AL Scott dated 31 January 2003 was successfully obtained. Stephen Miller had died of a massive pulmonary thromboembolism, chronic pulmonary thromboembolism and pulmonary embolism. Under s 6(1)(e) of the 1976 Act tranexamic acid should not be prescribed to any patient unless and until a proper diagnosis has been made.

5.91   Now, all determinations in every FAI, certainly since the 2016 Act commenced, require publication, though how quickly after their issue (the date by the sheriff) appears is quite arbitrary since there are no set timescales for publication either after issue. The FAI into the death of Christopher Moses was dated 18 August 2022 but was not published until 23 December 2022.[78]

5.92   In practice, SCTS now publish these electronically on their website. These are published in chronological order – so only the last 50 determinations show at any one time. Though the intention was that FAIs should be fully searchable, there is a need to know in advance salient facts such as the deceased's name, the sheriff court and/or the sheriff to make it possible to locate any specific determination outside the last 50 that are published.

76   Section 27(1) of the 2016 Act.
77   FOI 2022-238, 16 November 2022. SCTS Publication Scheme 2019 (updated February 2019), *www.scotcourts.gov.uk/docs/default-source/default-document-library/publication-scheme-2019. pdf?sfvrsn=52ac0bd2_2* (accessed 21 February 2023).
78   [2022]   FAI   39,   *www.scotcourts.gov.uk/docs/default-source/cos-general-docs/pdf-docs-for-opinions/2022fai039.pdf?sfvrsn=4ae672b_1* (accessed 21 February 2023).

5.93   Why only 50 appear in chronological order remains unclear. The SCTS has the discretion to publish 'in such manner as it considers appropriate'.[79] One would have expected a fully searchable database to comply with the spirit of of the 2016 Act's intentions. Searching using "unlimited" now advances search capacity.

5.94   The information on the SCTS website is shown as follows:

Case Title	Date of determination	Date of publication	Judge	Responses
Determination under [the 2016 Act] into the death of Richard Farquhar[80]	8/6/2022	22/6/2022	Sheriff Andrew McIntyre	N/A

5.95   When the determination is published on the SCTS website, this may be the first time that the public, other than those participants that were directly involved in the FAI, may have sight of and examine the determination.

5.96   There are requirements on SCTS under s 27(1)(b) of the 2016 Act to provide a copy of the determination to certain specific parties who were those most directly affected and have been involved in the FAI. These include the Lord Advocate (in effect, COPFS), each participant in the FAI, each person being one to whom a recommendation is addressed in the determination, and any other person whom the sheriff considers has an interest in the recommendation(s) made in the determination.

5.97   As the names of the parties to whom the determination is sent are not published, and where recommendations cover medical training issues, it would be useful to know if these are routinely sent to the GMC as the regulator of medical professionals and/or the relevant medical training providers, such as the universities.

5.98   SCTS is required on request to give to office-holders in the Scottish administration – the Scottish Government, a Minister of the Crown, the UK government, or the Health and Safety Executive – a copy of the determination, along with any original notice given under s 15(1) of the 2016 Act,[81] any transcript of the evidence at the FAI and any report or documentary production used in the FAI.

5.99   From a practical perspective, when the determination is ready to be published, the press will receive an embargoed copy so that reports in the press tend to appear contemporaneously with the publication of the determination on the SCTS website. Certainly, that is a practice which is adopted in respect of major or significant FAIs.

---

79   Section 27(1) of the 2016 Act.
80   Determination under the Inquiries into Fatal Accidents and Sudden Deaths etc (Scotland) Act 2016 into the death of Richard Farquhar, *www.scotcourts.gov.uk/search-judgments/judgment?id=f754c44c-f2b7-428d-8326-16bc7bab4ee3* (accessed on 21 February 2023).
81   Notice initiating the FAI.

5.100   Determinations are very much items of public interest. They will end up being reported by the press, who are the representatives of the public interest inherent in and establishing the purpose of the FAI with the societal benefit justifying the holding of such inquiries. Press publication also supports the transparency required in having a robust deaths inquiry system and for the families and indeed the public to ascertain that lessons have been learnt.

5.101   In issuing a determination, issues regarding sensitivity are reserved to the sheriff under s 27(5) of the 2016 Act. A sheriff may decide that part of the determination is not to be given to a person to whom either a recommendation in the determination has been addressed and any other person who the sheriff considers has an interest in the recommendation. This must be a rare occurrence. However, there may be cases where persons should not receive all the details, such as those involving children where their identities may be required to be withheld.

5.102   Subsection (5) provides that the sheriff may decide that part of the determination may be dealt with by means of redacting (editing for publication), rather than the determination not being published. The sheriff has the right to withhold any part of the determination from publication.[82]

5.103   The determination to be issued must set out (a) in relation to the death to which the FAI relates, the sheriff's findings as to the circumstances outlined below and (b) such recommendations as the sheriff considers appropriate.[83] There are two stages.

5.104   Schedule 3 Pt 6 of the Rules at r 6.1 sets out that the determination under s 26 of the 2016 Act is to be in Form 6.1. While most FAI determinations correspond broadly to that style, some do not, such as the FAI into the death of Ian Alexander Jolly.[84] This adherence to the style seems important as the determination is in effect the document which concludes the FAI process. Its contents are significant as discussed in respect of the public interest and should be relied on to demonstrate that the FAI process has been achieved satisfactorily and in a robust manner.

What the determination must include

5.105   The determination must include the circumstances of the death as outlined under s 26(2) of the 2016 Act. That will require:

- when and where the death occurred;
- when and where any accident resulting in the death occurred.

5.106   These will tend to be the least contentious issues on the basis that the death will have already been formally certified and registered. That is followed by:

---

82   Section 27(5)(b) of the 2016 Act.
83   Section 26(1) of the 2016 Act.
84   [2020] FAI 35.

- the cause or causes of the death;
- the cause or causes of any accident resulting in the death.

5.107   These will rely on the evidence provided from the postmortem examination which tends then to be replicated in the determination.

5.108   Following the issue of the determination, post-FAI the procurator fiscal is required to give information to the Registrar General of Births, Deaths and Marriages as to the name and last known address of the deceased and the date, place and the cause of death.[85] If there has been any change in the cause of death from the cause as originally set out under the death certification, then there will be rectification made of the cause of death with the National Records of Scotland.[86]

What the determination may include

5.109   Thereafter the following aspects to be included in the determination may prove much more contentious and depend on the facts and circumstances established in each case. However, in many FAIs, there will be no findings made with regard to:

- Any precautions which could reasonably have been taken and had they been taken might realistically have resulted in the death being avoided (s 26(2)(e) (i) and (ii) of the 2016 Act).

These changes seek to clarify the original wording under s 6(1)(c) of the 1976 Act. The word 'reasonable' in relation to precautions has now been inserted to show how the death or accident might have been avoided. The precautions that the sheriff identifies relate to the death in the FAI and might not be the same as those recommended to prevent other deaths in the future under s 26(4)(a) of the 2016 Act.

The FAI into the death of Philip Reid[87] provides a good example of a sheriff making findings regarding precautions, and of defects in the system of working. Recommendations were made in terms of s 26(1)(b) of the 2016 Act.

Philip Reid died in the course of his employment when working on a farm where a wall fell on him when undertaking demolition works. His cause of death as to when and where the accident resulting in his death occurred were uncontentious.

In terms of s 26(2)(e) of the 2016 Act, the sheriff found that precautions could reasonably have taken which had they been taken, might realistically have resulted in the death, or any accident resulting in the death, being avoided. Had an exclusion zone been established when demolition work was being carried out, this

---

85   Section 27(6)(a) and (b) of the 2016 Act.
86   See **Chapter 1**.
87   Under the Inquiries into Fatal Accidents and Sudden Deaths etc (Scotland) Act 2016 into the death of Philip Reid, *www.scotcourts.gov.uk/search-judgments/judgment?id=2adb1d47-5cea-400f-83af-5afad419d1f4* (accessed on 21 February 2023).

would have identified an area of danger arising from anyone being struck by falling debris. It would have helped to prevent anyone from unnecessarily entering that exclusion zone. The exclusion zone could have been created using fencing, or post and tape, or similar, or have been agreed in advance by all involved in the work, by reference to a particular identifiable physical area or features.

- Any defects in any system of working which contributed to the death or any accident resulting in the death (s 26(2)(f) of the 2016 Act).

The FAI into Joyce Gardiner is also an example of an FAI where the sheriff found that no precautions could reasonably have been taken under s 26(2)(e), there were no defects in any system of working contributing to the death under s 26(2)(f) or any other facts which were relevant to the circumstances of the death under s 26(2)(f).

This was a mandatory FAI [88]due to the nature of her employment status. Her death had been caused as a result of a road traffic accident. Her vehicle was found to have stopped suddenly on the A90 dual carriageway and then was struck to the rear by another vehicle.[89] There was no explanation found as to why she had stopped suddenly, meaning that no subsequent findings could be made.

In contrast, back to the FAI into the death of Philip Reid,[90] a defect in the system of working was identified in terms of s 26(2)(f) of the 2016 Act with regard to the failure to discuss, assess, create and observe an exclusion zone which then contributed to the death of Mr Reid.

- Section 26(2)(g) of the 2016 Act allows the sheriff to specify any other facts which are relevant to the circumstances of the case. This permits the sheriff a wide discretion.

5.110 Section 26(3) of the Act, as far as identifying any precautions under s 26(2)(e) or defects under s 26(2)(f) are concerned, states that it does not matter whether it was foreseeable before the death or accident that the death or accident might occur if: (a) the precautions were not taken; or (b) as the case may be, as a result of the defects. This ensures that a sheriff can consider the matters that have taken with the benefit of applying hindsight.

5.111 This practice of the application of the benefit of hindsight was set out by Sheriff Reith in the FAI into the death of Sharman Weir as follows:

'In my opinion a Fatal Accident Inquiry is very much an exercise in applying the wisdom of hindsight. It is for the Sheriff to identify the reasonable precautions, if any, whereby the death might have been avoided. The Sheriff is required to proceed on the basis of the evidence adduced without regard to any question of the state of knowledge at the time of the death. The statutory provisions [under

---

88   Section 2(3) of the 2016 Act.
89   [022]   FAI   12,   *www.scotcourts.gov.uk/docs/default-source/cos-general-docs/pdf-docs-for-opinions/2022fai012.pdf?sfvrsn=647d 26c1_1* (accessed on 21 February 2023).
90   Ibid.

the 1976 Act] are concerned with the existence of reasonable precautions at the time of the death and are not concerned with whether they could or should have been recognised. They do not relate to the question of foreseeability of risk at the time of the death which would be a concept relevant in the context of a fault-finding exercise, which this is not. The statutory provisions are widely drawn and are intended to permit retrospective consideration of matters with the benefit of hindsight and on the basis of the information and evidence available at the time of the Inquiry. There is no question of the reasonableness of any precaution depending upon the foreseeability of risk. In my opinion, the reference to reasonableness relates to the question of availability and suitability or practicability of the precautions concerned.'[91]

5.112   The findings made in a number of mandatory FAI determinations are outlined under **Appendix 2, Part D** for full reference.

Recommendations

5.113   One of the significant changes that took place with the 2016 Act was that the sheriff may make recommendations under s 26(1)(b) of the 2016 Act, which relate as specified to:

- the taking of reasonable precautions;
- the making of improvements to any system of working;
- the introduction of a system of working;
- the taking of other steps which might realistically prevent other deaths in similar circumstances.[92]

5.114   The purpose in making recommendations reflect the holding of an FAI is that they then reflect lessons learnt. They are intended to prevent deaths arising in similar circumstances in the future. The 2016 Act created a framework to look ahead and highlight systems that were not working effectively. Recommendations, where they are made, are made on the balance of probabilities – so that there must be 'a real or likely possibility that the matters recommended may prevent other deaths in similar circumstances, rather than a remote chance that a similar death in the future might be prevented'.[93]

5.115   The sheriffs can direct recommendations to specific bodies or individuals. As outlined above, they have the power to direct the delivery of the FAI determination to

---

91   Inquiry into the death of Sharman Weir, *www.scotcourts.gov.uk/search-judgments/judgment? id=13c286a6-8980-69d2-b500-ff0000d74aa7* (accessed on 21 February 2023).
92   Section 26(4) of the 2016 Act.
93   Inquiries into Fatal Accidents and Sudden Deaths etc. (Scotland) Bill, Explanatory Notes, *https:// archive2021.parliament.scot/S4_Bills/Fatal%20Accidents%20(Scotland)%20Bill/b63s4-introd-en. pdf* (accessed on 21 February 2023)..

participants at the FAI and to any relevant body concerned with safety in the relevant industry or activity in relation to which the accident took place.

5.116   In the FAI into the death of Philip Reid, the sheriff made a recommendation under s 26(1)(b) of the 2016 Act as the taking of any other steps, which might realistically prevent other deaths occurring in similar circumstances. As the organisation responsible for safety in the farming industry, he made a recommendation to the Health and Safety Executive[94]. They should ensure that sufficient information is available and communicated effectively, so that those involved in construction and demolition works in relation to agricultural premises are aware of their duties to take account of health and safety risks in terms of relevant regulations and industry standards, including the requirement to assess and identify exclusion zones.

Where recommendations are made

5.117   The effect of making recommendations and their status through the inclusion of compellability was a matter of considerable discussion during the 2016 Bill's passage. A number of commentators thought that where recommendations were made that they should become legally binding on the parties to whom they were made. Previously, there had been considerable concerns[95] about the system of FAIs and the status of findings by sheriffs at the conclusion of the FAI under the 1976 Act. This need to review the making of recommendations was one of the main features of the 2016 Act reforms.

5.118   These concerns about recommendations were summed up by Norman Dunning, the then Chief Executive of Enable, who stated that:

'Given all that I have said about the conduct of fatal accident inquiries, it seems incredible that the outcome has no legal force. A sheriff reaches a determination, but it is no more than a recommendation to an individual or a public body. Such recommendations can be ignored.'[96]

5.119   Concerns expressed by the other side reflected the ability to enforce compellability and interference with the premise that the determination may not be founded upon in judicial proceedings of any nature. Recall the fact that no finding can be made with regard to either civil or criminal liability. However, it is difficult to understand the exact concerns as the evidential status of recommendations that are

94   *www.hse.gov.uk/* (accessed on 21 February 2023).
95   Scottish Parliament debate on 27 March 2008, .Official report available at *www.parliament. scot/chamber-and-committees/official-report/search-what-was-said-in-parliament/chamber-and-committees/official-report/what-was-said-in-parliament/meeting-of-parliament-27-03-2008?meeting=4786&iob=39999* (accessed on 21 February 2023).
96   Public Petitions Committee, 29 September 2004, *https://archive2021.parliament.scot/ parliamentarybusiness/report.aspx?r=3051&mode=pdf* (accessed on 21 February 2023).

made is clearcut. The determination (and the recommendations) cannot and do not determine the rights and obligations of anyone.

5.120   Section 28 of the 2016 Act replicates the spirit, if not entirely the practice, adopted in England and Wales. This is set out in more detail in Sch 5 to the Coroners and Justice Act 2009 and discussed at **Chapter 7**. Some comparison with the process in Scotland can be outlined as follows:

1.   Recommendations from coroners' inquests as in Scotland are also not legally enforceable.

2.   Recommendations are made if, in the opinion of the coroner, action should be taken to prevent the occurrence or continuation of such circumstances creating a risk of other deaths, or to eliminate or reduce the risk of death created by such circumstances, the coroner *must report* the matter to the person who seems to have the power to take appropriate action (our emphasis).

     The scope to make recommendations seems wider than in Scotland, since it looks at mitigating the risk rather than the cause.

3.   Where a recommendation is made, that person *must make* a written response to the coroner, but they are not obliged to comply with the coroner's recommendation and may simply explain why they have not complied (our emphasis).

     In Scotland, under s 28(1) of the 2016 Act, it is only those persons to whom a recommendation is made that must respond and only if they were a participant to the FAI (s 28(1)(a)). In any other case where a recommendation is made, the person to whom it is directed may make a response. This has a much weaker effect than the coroner system.

4.   Any response too must set out details of what they have done or propose to do in the light of the recommendations or if they do not intend to do anything in response to the recommendation.

     This does not require any continued judicial involvement to gauge the effectiveness of the response or even if it fully relates to the recommendation. This was a specific policy intention set out in para 191 of the Bill's Policy Memorandum that 'the sheriff would thus not be tasked with ensuring compliance with the recommendation – indeed, the sheriff would have no further involvement in the procedure once they have written the determination'. This lack of any shrieval continuity seems to impact significantly on making recommendations effective. Responses become what seems purely to be an administrative process, which does not appear to send out the right message to the parties to whom any recommendations may be made if there is not judicial scrutiny.

     What also should be noted is that each individual determination needs to be read to ascertain if there are any recommendations made – all that is recorded is where a response has been received. Where an FAI includes a determination with a recommendation, since this is not noted, the response records N/A. In the FAI into the death of Pawel Kocik[97] there were recommendations, though only recently made, which may require a response in due course. This can only be ascertained by looking at the determination issued from the FAI. Furthermore, this system presents a challenge in checking with any accuracy the Report to Scottish Ministers made under s 29 of the 2016 Act as to the number of recommendations that have been made in FAIs. Responses do not equal the number of recommendations that have been made.

5. The response to the recommendations is then passed to the Chief Coroner's Office, which can choose to publish a summary or the complete response if it decides to release the response, and/or send the response to any body that may have an interest in the response.

In Scotland, all that is set out is an eight-week[98] requirement to respond which echoes the 56-day practice for responses applying in England and Wales. However, it is the party who makes the response who can request that it is withheld in part or in full. SCTS has the full power to decide on that publication in that event. There is no mention of shrieval input in making that decision, in contrast to the coroner who has a significant overseeing and continuing role now, as discussed in **Chapter 7**, who is also now required to be legally qualified.

5.121   By contrast with the coroner,[99] there is a requirement to report to prevent future deaths. The coroner[100] has a duty to make reports to a person, organisation, local authority or government department or agency where they believe that action should be taken to prevent future deaths (PFD Report). These reports must be sent to the Chief Coroner and mostly they are published on the judiciary website. The Chief Coroner has a policy on the publication and redaction of reports and responses.[101] This includes an obligation to make such reports during the inquest proceedings. Where a coroner becomes concerned about circumstances that create a risk of future deaths, the coroner must make a PFD report to the person or organisation that the coroner believes should take preventative action. Regulations 28 and 29 of the Coroners (Investigations) Regulations 2013 set out the processes for PFD reports and are discussed in more detail in **Chapter 7**.

---

97   [2022] FAI 35.
98   Section 28(3) of the 2016 Act.
99   Courts and tribunals Judiciary, Reports to Prevent Future Deaths, *www.judiciary.uk/courts-and-tribunals/coroners-courts/reports-to-prevent-future-deaths/* (accessed on 21 February 2023).
100 Coroners and Justice Act 2009, Sch 5, para 7.
101 Chief Coroner, *Prevention of Future Deaths Reports. Publication Policy, www.judiciary.uk/wp-content/uploads/2021/11/PFD-publication-policy-9-11-21.pdf* (accessed on 21 February 2023).

5.122   The publication of all PFD Reports can be seen on the Courts and Tribunals Judiciary website.[102] An example of one such report into the death of George Dimond is included in **Appendix 1 Part D**.[103] The detail of the Report can be seen, as well as the searchable capacity of the webpage to look for recommendations being made in specific categories of cases such as medical or health & safety cases.

In Scotland, where there has been no response within eight weeks, a notice to that effect is published. The practice as to recording that notice is inconsistent, as it is recorded as either as no response or alternatively, that response was received. This is discussed below. The SCTS webpage reflects the public record of any follow up to recommendations.[104] Since the SCTS website only shows the last 50 determinations, there is no complete register to go back to identify in which cases recommendations have been made following the issue of the determination in the FAI. Though there was a suggestion in the Bill's Policy Memorandum that sheriffs make such recommendations in around a third of all FAIs,[105] this is certainly not borne out statistically from a recent examination of the SCTS's last 50 FAIs or as outlined below in the Report published under s 29 of the 2016 Act. The publication of the last 50 determinations issued from 3 August 2021–28 October 2022 have been analysed as follows.

5.123   There were four FAIs marked with responses which does not of course necessarily reflect the number of FAIs in which recommendations have been made. The FAI into the death of Pawel Kocik is discussed in **Appendix 1**.

5.124   These four FAIs have been analysed further.

5.125   In the FAI into Philip Reid,[106] the recommendation was directed at the Health and Safety Executive and a response was received from them.

5.126   In the FAI into the deaths of Przenyslaw Krawczyk and Duncan MacDougall,[107] the sheriff did not direct the recommendation to any party. 'The Sheriff, having considered the information presented at the inquiry, made the following recommendation in terms of 26(1)(b) of the Act: 1 that stability awareness training be made mandatory for masters of fishing vessels of between 7 and 16 metres in length.'

---

102   *www.judiciary.uk/?s=&pfd_report_type=&post_type=pfd&order=relevance* (accessed on 21 February 2023).
103   Courts and Tribunals Judiciary, *Keith Dimond: Prevention of future deaths report* (28 October 2022), *www.judiciary.uk/prevention-of-future-death-reports/keith-dimond-prevention-of-future-deaths-report/* (accessed on 21 February 2023).
104   Paragraph 192 of the Bill's Policy Memorandum.
105   Inquiries into Fatal Accidents and Sudden Deaths etc. (Scotland) Bill. Policy Memorandum, *https://archive2021.parliament.scot/S4_Bills/Fatal%20Accidents%20(Scotland)%20Bill/b63s4-introd-pm.pdf* (accessed on 21 February 2023).
106   [2021] FAI 43.
107   [2021] FAI 58.

5.127   Though the recommendation was not directed to anyone specific, a response was noted from the Maritime and Coastguard Agency[108] that they were 'currently working on an update to the relevant Regulations relating to fishing vessel training and certification. Whilst there is no fixed date as yet for any new regulation, the intention is to consult later this year [2022]'.

5.128   In the FAI into the death of the baby, Leylan Forte,[109] the sheriff did make a recommendation under s 26(4)(d) that:

5.129   GP practices making greater use of Key Information Summaries on Emergency Care Summaries where appropriate to improve information sharing between GP practices and NHS 24 might realistically prevent other deaths in similar circumstances. There was no response from the GP surgery on SCTS website. This illustrates the problem, as GP training and their requirements would lie with the relevant training providers or the GP college requirements. Whether they would have seen or become aware of that recommendation is not known.

5.130   Though the SCTS website disclosed a response, it records that a response was not received from the GP practice. It is assumed that the GP practice was a party to the FAI where they were required to give a response under s 28(1) of the 2016 Act. There is no sanction or follow up where that section appears not to have been complied with which demonstrates the lack of effect that results from the 2016 Act. With continuing shrieval import, this could be managed much more effectively.

5.131   In the FAI into the death of George Steen Docherty Gibson Bartlett,[110] detailed recommendations were made to prevent deaths in the 'circumstances in which members of staff on offshore installations require to carry out work or other activities on or in relation to lifeboats, and involving the attachment of pendants, of a similar nature to those used on the Harding Platform at the time of this fatal accident'.

5.132   These were directed at 'operators of offshore installations whose procedures prohibit the operation of lifeboat release gear during any type of work or other activity in relation to lifeboats amend any applicable template work control certificate or equivalent document so that it states that prohibition clearly and prominently'. These seem not to be directed to anyone specific, though presumably at the FAI evidence was led about such practices with the relevant operators being present. While not mentioned, it is queried whether the Health and Safety Executive had a role in such matters.

---

108 *www.scotcourts.gov.uk/docs/default-source/cos-general-docs/pdf-docs-for-opinions/ res_2022lfai58.pdf?sfvrsn =51438d45_1* (accessed on 21 February 2023).
109 [2022] FAI 2, *www.scotcourts.gov.uk/search-judgments/judgment?id=5fc272d8-c908-41ac-bc6b-22e05a989a7e* . (accessed on 21 February 2023).
110 [2022] FAI 17.

5.133   In any event there was no response within the relevant period since the FAI was published on 11 April 2022. There is no requirement for follow up on what seem extensive and detailed FAI recommendations.

5.134   Presumably the practical assessment is that where there is no response, the lack of response could be used or known about publicly. In effect, how practical or significant this process is remains uncertain, given the lack of join up or searchability of the organisations to whom such recommendations have been directed.

5.135   In conclusion, the system for making recommendations seems weak and lacks any measurable effect including continued monitoring. It requires the sheriffs to make a recommendation which do not frequently happen and the reasons for this might be worth researching. Where recommendations are made, they need to be made to the right person or body. That means the person to whom there exists the authority or the appropriate powers to effect a change.

5.136   Given the number of FAIs which relate to prison deaths, there appear to have been no responses published from SPS, which may relate to the fact that no FAIs with recommendations involving deaths in custody appear to have been made. Given, as discussed in **Chapter 6**, the majority of FAIs are conducted into such deaths involving deaths in custody, it is worth observing that fact.

5.137   Where recommendations were made, and there is no response, all that happens is for SCTS to publish notice of that fact.[111] Similarly, there is no assessment made of the response where it is received to ascertain if it complies with what was required. There is public notice, but that too is hard to identify given that only the last 50 FAIs chronologically can be easily tracked. It is difficult in the absence of detailed information to effectively search for responses, though s 29 of the 2016 Act does require the submission of relevant information to appear in the report required from Scottish Ministers under s 29 of the 2016 Act. It does not then go on to require identification in which cases recommendations have been made.

Publication of the report

5.138   Section 29 sets out the reporting of recommendations requirements touched on above.

5.139   Scottish Ministers must publish a report setting out the number of FAIs that ended in the financial year and the number in which recommendations requiring a response were made, the total number of recommendations made, the number of such recommendations in relation to which a response was received by SCTS under s 28(1) of the 2016 Act, and the number of such recommendations in relation to

---

111   Section 28(7) of the 2016 Act.

which a notice was published under s 28(7) of the 2016 Act where no response was given within the eight-week period.

Analysis of reports

5.140

Year	Number of FAIs ended during the financial year	Number in which recommendations requiring a response was made	The total number of such recommendations	Number of such recommendations in relation to which a response was received by SCTS under s 28(1) of the 2016 Act	Number in such recommendations in relation to which a notice was published under s 28(7) of the 2016 Act
15 June 2017– 31 March 2018	12	1	2	2	0
1 April 2018– 31 March 2019	32	0	0	0	0
1 April 2019– 31 March 2020	54	5	27	27	0
1 April 2020– 31 March 2021	61	8	18	17	1

5.141 The report from 1 April 2021–31 March 2022 seems not yet to be publicly available. Notwithstanding, the number of recommendations made is very small, which reflect the analysis of the published determinations set out above.

Miscellaneous or subsequent provisions post the FAI

Further proceedings

5.142 Sections 30–35 of the 2016 Act govern the holding of further FAI proceedings. This could arise where an FAI might be reopened and continued into any death or a new FAI held.[112] Schedule 3 Pt 7 of the Rules also applies as to the Forms of Notice required (Form 7.1).

---

112 Section 30(5) of the 2016 Act.

5.143   For this circumstance to arise, there needs to be new evidence in relation to the circumstances of the death. The Lord Advocate needs to consider that it is likely that a finding or recommendation set out in the determination would have been materially different had that evidence been before the original FAI. They must decide that it is in the public interest for further proceedings to be held into the circumstances of the death. This has some similarity to the policy intentions lying behind the implementation of the Double Jeopardy (Scotland) Act 2011 where circumstances are found to exist in which a person who was convicted or acquitted of an offence may be prosecuted anew.

5.144   New evidence is defined as evidence which was not available and could not with the exercise of reasonable diligence have been made available at the FAI.

5.145   References to an 'inquiry' in s 30 of the 2016 Act (further inquiry proceedings) include reference to any inquiry held under the 1976 Act.[113]

5.146   The 2016 Act grants appropriate powers if the FAI is being reopened or a new FAI is being held that includes:

- citing of persons for precognition under s 31 of the 2016 Act;
- how to initiate further proceedings under s 32 of the 2016 Act.

5.147   Sections 15–18 of the 2016 Act relate to the notification. The need to hold preliminary hearings in such cases apply equally to any such reopened or new FAI. It is assumed that the need to reopen an FAI or hold a new FAI would be rarely, if ever, exercised.

5.148   Under s 32(4) of the 2016 Act, once a notice under s 32(1) is given, a date will be fixed for a hearing to be held to hear from the procurator fiscal and participants in the FAI as to whether the further proceedings should be reopened and continued or a fresh FAI held.

5.149   Section 33 governs the process that operates in a reopened FAI. After further proceedings have been initiated, the sheriff will set aside the original determination, either by reopening or continuing the FAI or requiring a fresh FAI to be held. The sheriff will only hold a fresh FAI if they consider it is in the public interest to do so. SCTS are required to publish a notice stating that the determination has been set aside.

5.150   Notice must be given in connection with the reopened FAI to anyone who was a participant in the original FAI or to whom a recommendation in the original determination was made.[114]

---

113 The Inquiries into Fatal Accidents and Sudden Deaths etc. (Scotland) Act 2016 (Commencement No. 3, Transitional and Saving Provisions) Regulations 2017 (SSI 207/155).
114 Section 33(3) of the 2016 Act.

5.151 Evidence can only be brought forward at the reopened FAI if it relates to a matter to which the new evidence relates. The sheriff may require evidence to be brought forward about any other matter relating to the circumstances of the death, on the application of the procurator fiscal or a participant in the FAI.[115]

5.152 Section 34 of the 2016 Act applies where a new FAI is held. Similar notice provisions operate as in s 32.

5.153 Section 35 governs the issue of a new determination. The sheriff can make a determination (after the earlier determination has been set aside) at the conclusion of a re-opened or fresh FAI even if the only change to the original determination is to record the new evidence led at that FAI. There are provisions for resolving any differences in the issue of the new determination.

---

115 Section 33(6) of the 2016 Act.

Chapter 6

Deaths in Custody

1. INTRODUCTION

6.01   There has already been discussion of deaths that have occurred in custody, when explaining the mandatory nature of such FAIs held under the Inquiries into Fatal Accidents and Sudden Deaths etc. (Scotland) Act 2016 (asp 2) (the 2016 Act). All deaths affect the deceased's survivors and unexplained deaths need to be investigated. This applies equally where the person who dies is in the custody of the police or the prison service, where such cases justify greater scrutiny to ensure transparency of process.

6.02   Before the commencement of the 2016 Act, and certainly in the years between 1895 and 1976, FAIs tended to be more focused on accidental deaths such as those occurring in the course of common forms of industrial employment such as in collieries, fishing or in fires. That may reflect the prevailing societal concerns over improving health and safety practices concurrently post-World War 2 with the rise and strength of the trade union- movement.

6.03   Today, there is increasing interest and awareness in considering a range of issues relating to deaths arising when the person who died was in custody. Certainly, the Scottish Government's recent policy development focuses on young persons within the criminal justice system in relation to exploring options of punishment other than custody.[1] More generally, their interest extends to considering the mental health of prisoners and that relationship with custodial deaths that go on to result from suicides.

6.04   In Carmichael's seminal book on FAIs, he discussed '[s]ome interesting [i]nquiries'[2] in which only one is attributed to a death in custody. In the nearly 50 years since that book's original publication, it is recognised that there is an increasing need now to examine the practice of investigation into such deaths from a public interest perspective, not least as the death rates of those in custody are rising. The majority of FAIs being undertaken today, looking at the published determinations, arise from deaths in custody. This is not too surprising, given their mandatory nature under the 2016 Act and that COPFS appear to have prioritised holding FAIs into this specific category of deaths. These factors justify a closer examination of FAIs looking at this category of deaths, especially in relation to some of the issues of concern already highlighted within the current FAI practices in Scotland.

2.   WHY ARE CUSTODY INVESTIGATIONS IMPORTANT?

6.05   **Chapter 3** considered the early historical role of the procurator fiscal in relation to deaths arising in custody. The procurator fiscal was integral when investigating deaths in custody, as they were responsible for the Crown's role in instigating the original criminal prosecution. Thereafter, the procurator fiscal was required to follow up on conviction in any cases where the then mandatory imposition of the death penalty, where the capital sentence on a murder conviction, was imposed. They were required to certify that due legal process of carrying out the sentence had been satisfactorily undertaken.

6.06   **Chapter 2** looked at Scotland's responsibilities to respect Art 2 of the ECHR, which is highly pertinent in understanding the State's role in relation to death investigations. However, when people are deprived of their liberty, responsibility for their welfare and their health rests with those detaining them, effectively, the State. An independent investigation into their death in custody is required to be conducted, irrespective of the cause of death, so, this will ensue whether it was sudden, unexplained, suspicious, natural or otherwise. Even a natural cause of death could reflect unlawful killing, neglect, ill-treatment, inadequate conditions within the custody facilities, or failures in the medical attention administered during custody.

6.07   Deaths in custody involve the State as the detaining authority, be it usually the police or prison service. Transparency in ensuring the independence of process

---

1   This accords with the Scottish Government policy with regard to young persons who should not be sentenced to custody if other non-custodial options exist. The Scottish Sentencing Council Guidelines reflect this policy: Sentencing Young People, *www.scottishsentencingcouncil.org.uk/ sentencing-guidelines/approved-guidelines/* (accessed on 25 November 2022).

2   Carmichael, *Sudden Deaths and Fatal Accident* Inquiries (Thomson W Green, 2005), Ch 9.

in investigating such deaths is essential, as well as being robust in order to negate any potential challenge as to a conflict of interest. In addition to Art 2 ECHR considerations, such deaths may well have implications under Art 3 of the ECHR – where no one shall be subjected to torture or to inhuman or degrading treatment or punishment. The UK, in effect Scottish Ministers, was found wanting for prison slopping out processes. These processes described as the process 'where in-cell sanitation[was] not available an electronic system is available for night time needs. This provides for electronic unlocking of cells to access communal facilities in response to the pressing of the cellular call button.'[3]

6.08   This system was approved as part of the ending of 'slopping out', where an 'age-old practice [referred to as] of "slopping out" and … considered by penal reform groups as the "single most degrading element of imprisonment this century".'[4]

6.09   Indeed these instances were held to have amounted to degrading treatment under Art 3 of the ECHR.[5]

6.10   As a starting point, for practices relating to deaths in custody, reference may be made to the International Committee of the Red Cross who have produced guidelines for investigating deaths in custody.[6] They acknowledge that there is 'no one internationally accepted document that offers practical guidance to detaining authorities and humanitarian workers on the standards and procedures to be followed when a death occurs in custody'. Under Annex 1 of their Report 'all deaths in custody must be investigated promptly by an independent and impartial body, regardless of whether the relatives of the deceased request it'. That need to investigate sits outside the wishes of the family and fully within the scope of fulfilling Art 2 ECHR requirements.

6.11   In Scotland, as has been already discussed, that responsibility to investigate such deaths is discharged by COPFS, undertaking its functions to investigate the circumstances of the death under the 2016 Act. In England and Wales, that responsibility as set out under the 2009 Act is carried out by the coroner and under the inquest system. That system involves mandatory use of a jury, with the appointment of lay persons, in such inquests when the deceased 'died while in custody or otherwise in state detention'.

---

3   Independent Monitoring Boards, *'Slopping out': A Report on the lack of in-cell sanitation in Her Majesty's Prisons in England and Wales* (August 2010), *www.justice.gov.uk/downloads/prison-probation-inspection-monitoring/In-Cell_Sanitation_Report_V2_Aug_10.pdf* (accessed on 21 February 2023).
4   Independent Monitoring Boards, *'Slopping out': A Report on the lack of in-cell sanitation in Her Majesty's Prisons in England and Wales* (August 2010), *www.justice.gov.uk/downloads/prison-probation-inspection-monitoring/In-Cell_Sanitation_Report_V2_Aug_10.pdf* (accessed on 21 February 2023).
5   *Robert Napier v the Scottish Ministers*, 2005 CSIH 16, *www.scotcourts.gov.uk/search-judgments/judgment?id=6b2c87a6-8980-69d2-b500-ff0000d74aa7* (accessed on 21 February 2023).
6   ICRC, *Guidelines for Investigating Deaths in Custody* (October 2013), *www.icrc.org/en/doc/assets/files/publications/icrc-002-4126.pdf* (accessed on 21 February 2023).

6.12   The Red Cross guidelines[7] go on to set out the standards for the investigation. It should be thorough. There is a need to obtain and preserve the physical/documentary evidence to identify who the relevant witnesses are and to record their evidence. The deceased needs to be correctly identified. The cause of death must be determined, along with establishing the manner, place and time of death. The process being undertaken should be 'prompt, impartial and [achieve an] effective investigation'. Importantly, investigations should consider 'any pattern or practice that may have caused it'.

6.13   Considering the Red Cross standards, does the FAI system meet these standards or not? By applying that criteria, it is questionable whether it successfully achieves these standards as fully as it could.

3.   ISSUES WITH CUSTODY DEATH INVESTIGATIONS

6.14   A number of factors have already been discussed in relation to the FAI system. These are relevant when evaluating how successfully the FAI system operates in relation to deaths in custody.

6.15   Is the FAI carried out promptly? The delays in holding mandatory FAIs from the date of the death are as significant in relation to deaths in custodial cases as with other categories of deaths. As such FAIs are mandatory; there is certainty at the outset that an FAI needs to be held. It is important that these FAIs take a priority because the State is involved. The need to avoid delay therefore is important as opportunities to consider lessons learnt inevitably diminish over time. The circumstances of such deaths may therefore be repeated if problems are not satisfactorily addressed. Many deaths in custody may well relate to similar issues, irrespective of which prison in Scotland such deaths have occured.

The public inquiry into Sheku Bayoh's death, which is currently ongoing, commenced seven years and seven days after he had died in police custody. It was also two years after COPFS, through the then Lord Advocate, had advised the Bayoh family that no police officer would face charges for his death. There is always a need to remember the priority assigned to the completion of criminal investigations and whether charges are going to result. However, there is a need to recognise that there is a significant impact on all those involved, especially and including the family, so that such delays should be kept to the minimum. The evidence of the delays can be seen in concerns expressed in the press such as '"Staggering" fatal accident inquiry delays of up to eight years revealed'.

6.16   These concerns with delay are echoed in two FAIs yet to be held. These relate to the deaths of Linda Allan and William Lindsay in June and October 2018 respectively. Ms Allan was sentenced to 16 months in custody, following her conviction

---

7   They were aimed at humanitarian workers, detaining authorities and other stakeholders.

for a drink-driving incident where a teenager had been injured in an accident. Her family had expressed concerns to the prison authorities prior to her death about her mental state and with her being the subject of bullying within the prison. William Lindsay died in custody when he was 16 and on remand at the Polmont Young Offenders' Institution. His death took place within 48 hours of his arrival there. In September 2021, COPFS have brought no charges against SPS though there was an indication suggested that 'there was credible and reliable evidence of a breach of the Health and Safety Act by the Scottish Prison Service that materially contributed to the deaths of Katie Allan and William Lindsay, yet Crown Immunity means there can be no prosecution of the Scottish Ministers …'.[8] Common factors exist in that both these deaths involve the issue of mental health and young persons within the prison environment.

6.17   When these kind of delays in holding FAIs are considered, they can be contrasted with the coronial system in England and Wales. There is a monitoring requirement for reporting on delays in holding inquests. In Scotland, there are no targets for these FAIs to be completed. There is no need too for any reporting accountability as to why such FAIs have not yet been carried out.

6.18   Bringing in that sort of monitoring existing in England and Wales might help in keeping families advised and also looking at the need to identify lessons to be learnt as soon as possible.

6.19   **Scope of deaths in custody:** deaths in custody include prison deaths, but these are not the only source of deaths falling within this mandatory category of FAIs.

6.20   Deaths occurring within police custody[9] also need to be included. However, unlike the SPS who publish the statistics on the number of prison deaths, in Scotland there is no similar source from Police Scotland for the provision of information as to those deaths in custody. However, England and Wales routinely include that type of information under the report issued by the Independent Office for Police Conduct (IPOC) on 'Deaths during or following police conduct'.[10] In providing this information, they differentiate among categories of deaths which adds clarity to understanding the range of deaths that may arise.

---

8   Aamer Anwar & Co, Press Release, *4 years since the suicides of William Lindsay & Katie Allan* (27 October 2022), *https://aameranwar.co.uk/news/press-release-27th-october-2022-4-years-since-the-suicides-of-william-lindsay-katie-allan/* (accessed on 21 February 2023).

9   In terms of European jurisprudence, there can be a debate about what being in custody means. For practical purposes, this means not being free to leave. Useful guidance may be found in the criminal context in *Ambrose v Harris* [2011] UKSC 43 at [71]: "The feature of this case …, although G had not yet been formally arrested and or taken into police custody, there was a significant curtailment of his freedom of action. He was detained and he had been handcuffed. He was, in effect, in police custody from that moment onwards.'

10   *https://www.policeconduct.gov.uk/deaths_during_or_following_police_contact_statistics_england_and_wales-202122* (accessed on 25 November 2022).

6.21   There are five categories defining what a death in custody or a death following contact with the police, which include[11] road traffic fatalities, fatal shootings, deaths in or following police custody, apparent suicides following police custody and other deaths following police contact that are subject to that independent investigation. These categories have been set out under **Appendix 1 Part E** in much greater detail as they provide a useful reference point to learn from the scope of these deaths as well as making any comparison. Further information is included in the Report as to gender, age and ethnicity which could be useful to be aware of and when considering any equality and diversity implications.

6.22   Box A[12] of that report sets out the number of incidents by the type of death within the financial years 2010/11 to 2020/21, where the following table sets out a snapshot of the figures for illustrative purposes from 2010/2011 and 2020/21:

Category	Type of Incident	2010/11	2020/21
1	Road traffic incident	24	20
2	Fatal shootings	2	1
3	Deaths in or following police custody	21	19
4	Apparent suicides following custody	46	54
5	Other deaths following police contact	37	91

6.23   In comparison to Scotland, information is limited to those deaths that occurred in a custody facility, or when a person has been arrested/detained by police. Deaths following police contact include those where the person at or before the time of death had contact (directly or indirectly) with the police, acting in the course of their duty and there is an indication that the contact may have caused (directly or indirectly) or contributed to the death of the person.

6.24   What 'in custody' means for these purposes is presumably that the deceased was no longer free to go about their business. This seems a quite restricted definition. Ensuring that the specification of deaths in police custody is the same as it appears in the English reporting system would be a better approach. This would produce a greater degree of certainty as to which deaths require investigation. **Appendix 2** includes the FAI into the death of Shania Collins which resulted when in police custody.

6.25   In practice, the distinction between England and Scotland practices may make little difference, though road traffic fatalities involving the police in Scotland may not result in a mandatory FAI being held. For any such road traffic death to require an FAI, the Lord Advocate would need to exercise their discretion, such as in the FAI to be held into the deaths of John Yuill and Lamara Bell from July 2015. This was a road traffic death where there was no contact from the police in following up

---

11   College of Policing, Deaths in Custody (23 October 2013, last updated 1 July 2020), *www.college. police.uk/app/detention-and-custody/deaths-custody* (accessed on 21 February 2023).

12   *https://www.policeconduct.gov.uk/deaths_during_or_following_police_contact_statistics_england_ and_wales_202122* (accessed on 25 November 2022).

on the report of a car going off the road. The circumstances of that case resulted in successful criminal proceedings held against Police Scotland and a fine for breaches of the Health and Safety Act 1974. The conviction having taken place has meant that the relevant FAI can now be held.[13]

6.26   There is also a clear difference too as the deaths of serving police officers and their staff will be investigated by way of a mandatory FAI as these will have taken place within the course of employment. Deaths of civilians on their own would, unless arising under the ambit of their employment, not themselves justify an FAI. Discretion in such cases to hold an FAI lies with the Lord Advocate. In England, there is no discretion as an inquest must be held.

4.   NUMBER OF DEATHS IN CUSTODY

6.27   **Police:** A Freedom of Information request[14, 15] provides an indication as to the number of the deaths arising in Scotland through contact by the police. There were 115 deaths (26 custody and 89 following police contact) arising in the period from 1 April 2014[16] to 17 March 2021. As no information is included as to deceased's names, it is not possible to check how many of these FAIs have since been completed, with the determinations subsequently issued. It should be noted that as well as these deaths requiring a mandatory FAI, these deaths are investigated under the auspices of the Police Investigations and Review Commissioner as required by Police Scotland, namely '[a]ll deaths following police contact must therefore be immediately referred to COPFS SFIU to ensure that an independent investigation is commenced at the earliest opportunity'.[17] That, though independent, is not the same as holding an FAI.

6.28   Going forward, consideration might be given to a clearer categorisation of the types of deaths, including what falls under those occurring within police custody. That will ensure that the holding of such FAIs is mandatory in order to satisfy the State's requirements under Art 2 of the ECHR.

6.29   **Prison:** Turning to the number of deaths in prison, that information is available on a quarterly basis. The following table shows the number of deaths arising from 1 January 2018 to 23 June 2022.

---

13   The Guardian, *Police Scotland apologises for failings that contributed to car crash death* (8 September 2021), *www.theguardian.com/uk-news/2021/sep/07/police-scotland-admits-failings-that-contributed-to-car-crash-death* (accessed on 21 February 2023).

14   *www.scotland.police.uk/spa-media/eqfpnpwb/21-0659-response.pdf* (accessed on 25 November 2022): this no longer seems to be available.

15   The information is supplied by the police's Professional Standards Department, but the national database did not operate until 1 April 2014. Prior to this there were eight legacy forces.

16   Information does not exist prior to this date as under the separate Scottish police forces, there was no means to systematically access the legacy forces records.

17   Police Scotland, *Death or Serious Injury in Police Custody National Guidance*, 2 June 2021.

Table of deaths

6.30

Year	Deaths in custody	Status – Prisoner/Other
2018	32	23/9
2019	37	31/6
2020	34	26/8 (5 Covid-19 related)
2021	53	41/12 (5 Covid-19 related)
2022 (statistics only available to 23/6/2022)	22	16/6

6.31   There are of course a wide range of reasons why prisoners die in prison. The categorisation adopted in the 'Report on Nothing to see here'[18] has been followed as it is a useful way to classify and consider what categories arise and for these purposes these are taken to comprise natural deaths, drugs deaths and self-inflicted deaths.

Natural causes

6.32   Natural causes, of course, of necessity, includes a broad category of many pre-existing conditions, such as cancer or heart disease. From the SPS statistics, deaths from these conditions appear to comprise the majority of natural deaths that occur in prison. These may be explained as the result of poor health, experienced by the prisoners. However, questions arise as to whether the death rate for other sections of the public would be broadly similar, though a possible explanation may lie in relation to alcohol and substance abuse playing an underlying role in such deaths.

6.33   At any FAI, the crucial issue should be whether all medical attention provided to the deceased prisoner was undertaken appropriately and timeously. Importantly, there should have been no discrimination as a result of their having been detained in prison. That may well require the commission of an expert and independent medical report to establish that medical attention was administered and what was provided was satisfactory.

6.34   In the FAI into the death of John Thomas Forsyth Hughes,[19] a natural death where no other findings were made, a joint minute was produced with no evidence being led at the FAI. Does this satisfy the requirement of the holding of a robust inquiry? At para [15], it states that:

---

18   Armstrong et al, *Nothing to see here? Statistical briefing on 15 years of FAIs into deaths in custody* (October 2021), *www.sccjr.ac.uk/wp-content/uploads/2021/10/Nothing-to-See-Here-Statistical-Briefing.pdf* (accessed on 21 February 2023).
19   [2019] FAI 31.

'Mr Hughes' death was due to natural causes as indicated in the post mortem report. *No information available to the court suggests that his being in custody at the time contributed to his passing.* He did seek medical intervention regularly for the discomfort being caused by his persistent cough. *The Crown raised no concerns that the treatment he received in this regard* was in any way impacted as a consequence of his being in custody and thus required examination by the inquiry.' (emphasis added)

6.35   This section illustrates some of the difficulties. The court should be in a place to answer that the medical care given to the deceased was adequate and their being in custody did not contribute to their death. It is not for the Crown to raise concerns. Another way to consider this issue is to consider had the death not occurred in custody, would a post mortem examination have been instructed? If so, would the procurator fiscal have accepted the cause of the death without further investigation? Probably, yes but that would usually depend on a report from Police Scotland confirming that there were no suspicious or unusual circumstances or indeed any concerns expressed by the deceased's family. The family were not represented at this FAI. How therefore should the FAI system replicate and provide assurance for custody deaths that indeed there were no issues arising from the deceased's incarceration and the provision of medical treatment to them?

Drug deaths

6.36   Prisoners are on occasion able to access illicit drugs in prisons. The cause of death may be clear, but challenges can be found in identifying the exact cause of death even after a forensic post-mortem examination. This can mean a finding of the death is made as being unascertained in an FAI. The FAI into the death of Tammi Bruce was one such death[20] That remained unascertained even after the FAI had been held.

6.37   Where such a death is due to consumption of drugs that needs to be recorded as the cause of death.

6.38   However, FAIs should not be about right and wrong, as accords with the statutory requirement that findings are not made as to any civil or criminal liability. Any sense of judgement on the actions taken by the deceased therefore should be avoided. In the FAI into the death of Steven Gunn,[21] at para [1.5], it states that 'in terms of section 26(2)(e) of the Act, there were, on the available evidence, no precautions which (i) could reasonably have been taken, and (ii) had they been taken, might realistically have resulted in the death, or the accident resulting in the death, being avoided, *other than Mr Gunn refraining from consuming said unprescribed drugs.*' (emphasis added)

---

20   [2020] FAI 12 at [4].
21   [2022] FAI 28.

6.39   Though inevitably true that had the deceased not taken drugs, they may not have died, this is perhaps in a similar category as stating in an accident had the car not been driven in a careless fashion, the accident would not have occurred. It seems to add nothing to the determination and indeed, may not be seen of comfort to the deceased's family. As was stated in the *Report on Nothing to see here,*[22] this 'moral tone in FAIs ... ...appear inconsistent with Scotland's public health approach to addiction'.[23]

6.40   The issue of drugs in prison is of a wider societal concern. As the sheriff in the FAI into the death of Mark Allan[24] indicated at para [11], she was not content:

'with the terms of the joint minute and that I required evidence of the protocols and procedures which were in place at the time of the deceased's death in relation to the prevention of the introduction of drugs into the prison estate and also the measures which ought to have been taken to search prisoners and their cells for banned substances and items.'

6.41   She sought to focus the FAI on the need 'to examine is whether the policies, which were not in fact being criticised, were properly followed and applied in this particular case'.[25] This chapter returns to the need to look at the systems, including drug searches and monitoring, in place within prisons to learn lessons and avoid similar deaths occurring.

Self-inflicted deaths

6.42   These comprise a range of deaths. Though the cause of death may be clear, as a suicide, that does not exclude the need for a robust investigation to be completed into the death, as there are management strategies in place in prison to look at reducing the risk of suicide in prison. This is similar to the point regarding the monitoring of drug deaths in prison made above. Various reports have been commissioned and have focused on the deaths in custody and suicides which are discussed below. Turning back to the SPS's statistics on deaths in prison, though the prisoner's names are provided, changes have been made to the recording of the cause of death over the past four years so that they now record only the medical cause of death, such as hanging rather than suicide.

6.43   To complete any comparison, given the change in referencing, the FAI determination itself would establish whether suicide was established as the cause of death. Where an FAI has been held and the determination subsequently published,

---

22   Armstrong et al, *Nothing to see here? Statistical briefing on 15 years of FAIs into deaths in custody* (October 2021), *www.sccjr.ac.uk/wp-content/uploads/2021/10/Nothing-to-See-Here-Statistical-Briefing.pdf* (accessed on 21 February 2023).
23   *A Defective System: Case analysis of 15 years of FAIs after deaths in prison*, October 2021.
24   [2020] FAI 8.
25   [2020] FAI 8 at [13].

this can be completed. However, it would be helpful if the cause of death was subsequently cross referenced and updated in the SPS records, as this would provide a check as well as a reference to when FAIs were completed. It would help establish how many deaths were indeed through suicide. This is not a practice routinely undertaken.

6.44   The terminology regarding the status of the prisoner too has varied on occasion from 'untried', 'remand', and 'recall', without any explanation as to what this means or why this was changed. Why this matters is of course where decisions as to remanding in custody may be questioned whether the deceased should have been in prison in the first place. This is particularly pertinent when looking to consideration of the timing of Covid-19 and its cause of death in prison deaths as many more prisoners were held on remand for longer.

6.45   **Covid deaths:** Covid-19 has been recorded as a cause of death in approximately 12 deaths, though none of the relevant FAIs have been completed to date. Looking at how Covid-19[26] was managed within prison, and within SPS as a whole, as well as avoiding the incidence of suicides, reflects the need to look at these deaths in a systematic manner. Emergency Covid-19 legislation meant that there were delays in court process with the suspension of statutory time limits on certain trials taking place, meaning more were held in remand for longer. How SPS managed those on remand within the prison to avoid exposure to Covid-19 is relevant in examining lessons to be learnt. Holding FAIs into such deaths in due course will be mandatory. Crucially, the public Covid-19 inquiry by the Scottish Government does not include such deaths within its remit. Provision exists under s 14 of the 2016 Act for the Lord Advocate to exercise their discretion to conduct such an inquiry into all these Covid-19 prison deaths. No such decision to do so has yet been taken.

6.46   The number of suicides in prison would also appear to potentially vindicate the requirements of s 14(1)(b) of the 2016 Act occurring 'otherwise in the same or similar circumstances'. A similar view could be taken in relation to the Covid-19 deaths.

5.   THE ROLE OF THE FAI

6.47   FAIs are conducted under the auspices of an independent sheriff. By considering the role and effect of the judicial inquiry, this helps consider how robust and effective these FAIs are and what they can achieve.

6.48   A practice has developed, especially with FAIs, into deaths in prison where evidence is frequently presented by means of joint minutes. Joint minutes are found commonly in criminal proceedings to allow the parties, the accused and the Crown to

---

26   The public inquiry into the Covid-19 pandemic does not include such deaths with its scope.

agree non-contentious evidence and avoid witnesses coming to court unnecessarily. The circumstances in an FAI do not replicate that adversarial criminal process.

6.49   Joint minutes may have their place in ensuring efficient court process in that they seek to agree evidence without the need for witnesses to attend the FAI. They may be useful where the evidence is not contentious and is substantially factual. There are however limits to the use of such joint minutes and even where they are to be used, other witnesses such as experts may still be required to give opinion evidence in person. The joint minutes are agreed by the parties to the FAI but frequently they do not include the deceased or their representatives so they may well be unaware of their terms.

6.50   It is not possible to ascertain from the published determinations whether such joint minutes are indeed read out in open court so that the deceased's relatives can hear the evidence.

6.51   A significant number of FAIs conclude on the basis of the joint minutes where there seems no significant inquiry into the evidence they provide, which in effect has led to the findings made by the sheriff in the determination. The practice as to the use of joint minutes needs to be reviewed – and indeed a consistent practice identified – if they are to be used as well as providing training as to what should be their limited purpose in a FAI.

6.52   Alternatively, use could be made of expert affidavits in terms of r 10 of the Rules which still simplifies the process. Affidavits are sworn statements, usually in the presence of a notary public or commissioner for oaths, who must also sign the affidavit. These could be used to confirm, for instance that, based on that undisputed factual information, the system of medical treatment in relation to management of ongoing physical or mental conditions was adequate and appropriate. Significantly, it has not disadvantaged the prisoner on account of their liberty being restricted. This statement does not seem to be routinely included.

6.53   Joint minutes are drawn up by COPFS. However, that is not the only responsibility which COPFS has. Their role in the FAI is central in presenting evidence. They also make submissions at the conclusion of the evidence along with any other parties to the FAI. However, and this is important, their role in representing the public interest should reflect the evidence which has been led. There may be some issues about what their role is where the family is not represented at the FAI. The family may well have a separate interest from that of COPFS in the role of the State.

6.54   Arguably, part of the practice in not providing legal aid to the family is that their interests are already represented in the public interest factor of ascertaining the circumstances as to the deceased's death. There may well be an overlap of interests, but this omits the fact that there may be issues relevant to the family that are not covered or included from a public interest perspective. These could include the deceased's state of mind at the time of their death or the operation of the visiting policy. Covid-19 involved lots of lock downs with prisoners restricted through the risk of infection from visitors; this may well have had implications for their mental health. These issues may not directly relate to the cause of death but are factors which the family may want explored. Given a public inquiry represents an intrusion into very personal circumstances of a family's grief, the family may have issues that they perceive are relevant to the death to be explored, even if they are excluded ultimately by the sheriff in making the actual findings in the determination. Achieving that balance satisfactorily in the judge issuing the determination is a matter for their legal judgment.

6.55 In many of the FAIs into custody deaths, the deceased's family are neither represented nor a party to the FAI. What then results is that they in particular do not have the opportunity to scrutinise or indeed question the evidence that is led. Why they are not represented may be down to personal factors or indeed, relate to the absence of automatic legal aid by way of advice and assistance.

6.56 The percentage of families represented at an FAI into custody deaths seems low. The Report *Nothing to See Here?*[27] outlined that families were only present in 31% of FAIs (this presumably means in attendance in court as compared to observing within the court.) Only 16% had legal representation. They indicated that only 17% gave evidence at the hearings. Again, whether this means giving evidence refers to evidence in person, as it is possible that their evidence can be agreed by joint minute to save them from any further upset by appearing in court. Their evidence may well be uncontentious. It is not possible to make any conclusion other than this illustrates an area for future research to see why these figures are so low and any relationship with the current legal aid provision. The practice too of the use of joint minutes and submissions from the Crown tends to invite only the making of formal findings. Does that fully address the family or public interest in the death investigation?

6.57 Acceptance of joint minutes has been subject to criticism on occasion by the sheriffs. In the FAI into the death of Darren Kerr Smith,[28] Sheriff Lindsay Foulis outlined that:

> 'the role of the sheriff at an inquiry is different from that played in adversarial proceedings. This is made clear by reference to the provisions of section 20(2) of the 2016 Act. It accordingly appeared to me that the parties entering a joint minute and intimating to me that this dealt with the matters which were to be the subject matter of the inquiry did not constrain me from seeking certain information to ensure that there were not matters upon which I should consider evidence in an appropriate form to be presented to me.'[29]

6.58 The sheriff required the Crown to lodge a list of their proposed witnesses, accompanied by a synopsis of the subject matter of the evidence from each witness.

---

27 Armstrong et al, *Nothing to see here? Statistical briefing on 15 years of FAIs into deaths in custody* (October 2021), *www.sccjr.ac.uk/wp-content/uploads/2021/10/Nothing-to-See-Here-Statistical-Briefing.pdf* (accessed on 21 February 2023).
28 [2018] FAI 40.
29 [2018] FAI 40 at [5].

Affidavits were then required from witnesses who appeared to him to have 'something material to impart'. These focused on three issues including the respective benefits of providing manual as opposed to automatic defibrillators in prison, the respective difference in their cost and the reasons why two nurses did not respond to an alarm. Though, ultimately, this evidence did not affect his FAI findings, it did ensure that a robust examination of the circumstances of the death took place. However, at para [6], there was surprise from parties to the FAI when the sheriff indicated that he was not content to proceed on the basis of the joint minute. This perhaps promotes the need for better understanding of the respective roles of the parties to the FAI and more scrutiny of the appropriateness of using joint minutes and agreement of evidence.

6.59 This issue of shrieval discretion in hearing evidence is important to remember. Court resources are finite in time and costs so unnecessary, inquiry or leading of evidence should be avoided, though not at the expense of failing to ensure an effective and thorough FAI is undertaken.

6.60 The FAI into the death of Ian Alexander Jolly[30] illustrates this potential dilemma where the determination proceeded on the basis of 'the hearing of unchallenged evidence'. Just because the evidence is not challenged by the parties at the FAI does not reduce the need for the sheriff to undertake a robust inquiry. There need to be no gaps in the evidence, especially it is submitted where the FAI has had no family representation.

6.61 The FAI into the death of John Hanley Harrison[31] also illustrates this point as that was another inquiry proceeding by way of a joint minute. The sheriff's determination, at para [22], states that 'in light of the evidence before the Inquiry and the submissions made, I am satisfied that the medical care provided to Mr Harrison within both hospital and prison as is relevant to the remit of this Inquiry, was entirely appropriate'.[32]

6.62 While this may be correct, the determination lists various documents but crucially does not refer to any SPS Death in Prison Learning Audit and Review (DIPLAR), nor whether the delay in taking the deceased to hospital from the time when he became unwell mattered. Did that have any effect on his death? Was the medical care given at the prison and in hospital satisfactory? These seem to be potential gaps in the determination. It seems that there would be merit in ensuring judicial training reflects an understanding of the DIPLAR process – it is an internal SPS investigation but does not discharge the sheriff from ensuring that the determination covers the essential questions. That is to ensure that the death of the deceased in custody was not as a result of any inadequate medical attention.

---

30   [2020] FAI 35.
31   [2022] FAI 31.
32   [2022] FAI 31.

6.63   There is an absence in the determinations issued in prison deaths in identifying or making any recommendations, though there are as identified in **Chapter 5** few recommendations made generally in relation to FAIs. Quite why this should be the case is not clear, though recommendations do not require to be implemented, so lack any robust mechanism to ensure that such matters have been resolved. However, identification of any reasonable precautions or system defects should be made where possible and pertinent.

6.64   Part of the reluctance to make any findings may indeed be the acceptance within an FAI that internal reviews were conducted under the DIPLAR system and have identified all necessary issues with all systems thereafter having since improved. DIPLARs are an important process and have the advantage of being conducted in a timely fashion, soon after the event, but they are internal to SPS process. They do not necessarily have the robustness of an external independent inquiry such as within an FAI, though of course they are important.

6.65   Notwithstanding any recommendations from a DIPLAR and its implementation, recommendations under s 26 of the 2016 Act could still be made so that other prisons can learn if appropriate from the circumstances of that death. Is there an aspect for SPS in administering palliative care, or ensuring dignity in death with prisoners suffering from terminal conditions?

6.66   The FAI into Andrew Croall Hutchison[33] made no findings as to any defects or precautions to be taken following his death. Similarly, no recommendations were identified or made. However, a DIPLAR (prison) and an Adverse Event Review (medical) were both undertaken. These disclosed learning points albeit that they were said to have been remedied by the time of the FAI as their recommendations had since been implemented.

6.67   For the prison, through the DIPLAR, it highlighted that the Risk Management Team NHS representative should discuss any patient due for discharge who has complex health care needs with the relevant SPS clinical staff. With patients being discharged from hospital following an episode of care, a timely discharge letter/plan should be sought. Direct contact between the prison and hospital should establish care and treatment needs.[34] Paragraph [27] notes that these recommendations had been completed but does not state how these systematic changes were made and how to avoid such deaths in the future. Is there a possible wider application from such finding on the discharge of patients for both the NHS and SPS?

6.68   In this death, no post-operative discharge information was made available and could not be immediately obtained as the unit was closed. Though this was remedied in this case, what changes were required to be made to the system? Did they go wider than merely dealing with the circumstances of this death?

---

33   [2022] FAI 33.
34   Paragraph [27] notes that these recommendations have been made.

6.69   Overall, by accepting the internal reviews, verbatim, valuable as they are, there is perhaps a suggestion that the organisations have "marked their own homework", vindicated by no further inquiry or recommendations being made in court. This has and must give rise to some concerns over the effectiveness or indeed the purpose of undertaking such FAIs. If the reviews have been conducted satisfactorily, why use further public resources to rubber-stamp these findings within the FAI process?

6.70   Again, looking to the English and Welsh coronial system, they have powers to make Recommendation 28 Reports where their scope, as discussed in **Chapter 7** seems much broader. The narrow focus of causation and use of joint minutes may on occasion restrict more robust and thorough inquiries being made in Scotland.

6. THE ROLE OF THE FAI AND AN INQUIRY

6.71   When considering the scope of the current public inquiry into the death of Sheku Bayoh in May 2015 when in police custody,[35] the narrowness of the FAI process can be seen. This inquiry is being conducted by Lord Bracadale[36] as a public inquiry under the Inquiries Act 2005. That allows any causal link to be established as to the allegations of possible racism that may have been operating within the police at that time. Its Terms of Reference focus on the immediate circumstances leading to the death of Mr Bayoh, how the police dealt with the aftermath of his death, the subsequent investigation undertaken into the death and whether race was a factor. They have also produced FAQs which is a practice to consider extending more widely possibly in relation to the conduct of FAIs.[37] These FAQs provide practical answers to key questions such as what is a public inquiry, the key stages in the inquiry, and outlines the respective roles in the inquiry. It is suggested that production of these would assist the public and the families navigate the FAI process.

---

35 Now set up as a death in public inquiry under Lord Bracadale. Evidence is due to resume in November 2022. It will examine *inter alia* the post-incident management conducted by Police Scotland, the cause of death, the investigation conducted by the PIRC and the Lord Advocate and the issue of race. The Terms of Reference are set out at *www.shekubayohinquiry.scot/sites/default/files/2020-11/Inquiry%20terms%20of%20reference.pdf* (accessed on 21 February 2023).

36 Public Inquiry into the death of Sheku Bayoh – Terms of Reference, *www.shekubayohinquiry.scot/sites/default/files/2020-11/Inquiry%20terms%20of%20reference.pdf* (accessed on 21 February 2023).

37 Sheku Bayoh Inquiry – Frequently Asked Questions, *www.shekubayohinquiry.scot/faq* (accessed on 21 February 2023).

7. CURRENT POSITION ON DEATHS IN CUSTODY

6.72   As discussed above, the number of deaths in prison is increasing.[38] There are various explanations to put forward for this, including that the prison population is getting older.[39] That observation is not unique to Scotland, being driven partly due to an increase in the number of older adults being sentenced for sexual offences, and specifically, for historical sexual offending. Increases too in the length of sentences being imposed means that more people will grow old and die in prison from natural causes. These deaths albeit natural still require an FAI.[40]

6.73   The projection is that the older prisoner population will continue to increase so that the requirement for more such FAIs to be completed will continue to increase. This will need resources factored in to complete these FAIs. These prisoners will require greater medical attention for diseases and disability in order to satisfy their health and social care requirements.[41] Such deaths when they arise will still require thorough investigation.[42]

6.74   Various reports now evidence that growing interest and concerns over the deaths arising in custody. These consider different aspects in looking at how best lessons are to be learnt from these prison deaths, though there is some overlap as well as similarity in the recommendations that they make.

6.75   In May 2019, the HM Inspectorate of Prisons for Scotland undertook the *Report on an Expert Review of the Provision of Mental Health Services, For Young People Entering and in Custody at HMP YOI Polmont*.[43] Its background was that '[e]very death of a young person is a tragedy, for them, their families and their friends, but also for Scottish society that has lost the opportunity of their talent and potential

38   Daily Record, *Deaths in Scots prisons are on the rise as shock figures confirm 'worst fears' of grieving families* (22 January 2022), *www.dailyrecord.co.uk/news/politics/deaths-scots-prisons-rise-shock-26017387* (accessed on 21 February 2023).

39   House of Commons Justice Committee, *Ageing Prison Population*, Fifth Report of Session 2019–21, HC 304, *https://committees.parliament.uk/publications/2149/documents/19996/default/* (accessed on 21 February 2023).

40   The FAI into the death of Angus Sinclair was one where the deceased was sentenced to a minimum term of 40 years in respect of his conviction for the girls in the Worlds End Murders: [2020] FAI 14. He had longstanding health issues – but where the sheriff notes at para [0] that '[t]here is no criticism directed to the care of the deceased within the prison'. As evidence was agreed by joint minute it is unknown whether that is a factual recording evidence from external evidence.

41   House of Commons Justice Committee, *Ageing Prison Population*, Fifth Report of Session 2019–21, HC 304, *https://committees.parliament.uk/publications/2149/documents/19996/default/* (accessed on 21 February 2023).

42   Armstrong et al, *Nothing to see here? Statistical briefing on 15 years of FAIs into deaths in custody* (October 2021), *www.sccjr.ac.uk/wp-content/uploads/2021/10/Nothing-to-See-Here-Statistical-Briefing.pdf* (accessed on 21 February 2023).

43   HMIPS, *Report on an expert review of the provision of mental health services, for young people entering and in custody at HMP Yoi Polmont* (May 2019), *www.prisonsinspectoratescotland.gov.uk/sites/default/files/publication_files/Report%20on%20Expert%20Review%20of%20Provision%20of%20Mental%20Health%20Services%20at%20HMP%20YOI%20Polmont%20-%20Final%20Version.pdf* (accessed on 21 February 2023).

contribution'. Though the focus was on young persons, similar points apply to any person entering custody as the issues, examined, included:

- information provided to SPS prior to entering custody;
- reception, screening and assessment arrangements;
- health and wellbeing culture linked to ongoing support and supervision;
- treatment and interventions during their time in custody;
- arrangements by SPS for their return to the community.

6.76   The recommendations identified that there was a lack of proactive attention to the needs, risks and vulnerabilities of those on remand and in their early days of custody. Of significance, it highlighted that there should be enhanced and more consistent DIPLAR processes, as flagged above, undertaken by SPS to maximise learning from previous incidents. The follow up from the report can be tracked through the report by Scottish Government to the Scottish Parliament.[44]

6.77   In October 2021, *A Defective System-Case analysis of 15 years of [FAIs] after deaths in prison* was published. That briefing presented information from a review of 15 years of FAIs, covering 196 deaths in custody (mainly within prison) in Scotland between 2005–2019.[45] It was mostly focused on the family's position. It recognised that:

> 'every death in custody has a profound impact – for the family of the person who has died, for the prisoners who cared for or were near to them at death, and for the staff responding to and dealing with mortal emergencies. Each one raises questions about the quality of care and accountability of the state on whom those in custody depend.'

6.78   That review also looked at the need to consider:

> '[t]he effectiveness of holding such an inquiry after such a delay …, evidenced … where no recommendations are made, not because there were no defects or precautions that could have been taken, but because the necessary changes have already been made by those involved. This does not even begin to take into account the distress which in many cases will be occasioned to families in re-opening the circumstances around the painful loss of a loved one so long after the event.'

6.79   In November 2019, the then Justice Secretary Humza Yousif MSP requested Her Majesty's Chief Inspector of Prisons for Scotland (HMCIPS) review the

---

44   The Scottish Parliament, *Expert review of Mental Health support for Young People entering and Custody,* correspondence at 30 June 2022, *www.parliament.scot/chamber-and-committees/committees/current-and-previous-committees/session-6-health-social-care-and-sport-committee/correspondence/2022/expert-review-of-mental-health-support-for-young-people-entering-and-in-custody* (accessed on 21 February 2023).

45   Barkas et al, A Defective System. Case analysis of 15 years of Fatal Accident Inquiries after deaths in prison (October 2021), *www.sccjr.ac.uk/wp-content/uploads/2021/10/A-Defective-System.pdf* (accessed on 21 February 2023).

response to deaths in prisons. That Independent Review of the Response to Deaths in Prison Custody[46] adopted a human rights approach with the report being published in November 2021. It made a number of recommendations including that:

- An independent body should carry out an investigation into every death in prison custody stating that this would complement the current inquiry processes. This was said to bring Scotland in line with England, Wales and Northern Ireland.

  Exactly what 'independent' means in this context is unclear. One could reflect on the context of Art 6 of the ECHR, where it states that 'In the determination of [their] civil rights and obligations …, everyone is entitled to a fair and public hearing within a reasonable time by an independent and impartial tribunal established by law'.

  COPFS are indeed independent in conducting any FAI in the public interest, though ultimately the judge is responsible for making the relevant findings. By suggesting that the FAI should be carried out by 'a body wholly independent of the Scottish Ministers, the SPS or the private prison operator, and the NHS, it is not clear what the role of the Crown would be under that model'.[47]

- For families or next of kin, investigations into prisoners' deaths must be completed within a matter of months.

  That may not be possible where there is complexity in investigating some deaths. Introducing a method of recording the progress of such investigations publicly however would seem to be good practice. It would provide a much more rigorous means of scrutiny.

- The investigation process must involve the families or the next of kin of those who have died in prison custody.

  That does occur though many families do not take a formal part in the procedure. Understanding the reasons why this may be the case is important. There may be a need to look at an automatic grant of legal aid or some alternative State funded resource to help in achieving their representation.

  The purpose of the investigation should be to establish the circumstances surrounding the death, examine whether any operational methods, policy, practice or management arrangements would help prevent a recurrence, examine relevant health issues and assess clinical care, provide explanations and insight for bereaved relatives, and help fulfil the procedural requirements of Art 2 of the ECHR. All investigations must result in a written outcome.

---

46   HMIPS, *Independent Review of the Response to Deaths in Prison Custody* (November 2021), *www. prisonsinspectoratescotland.gov.uk/sites/default/files/publication_files/Independent%20Review%20 of%20the%20Response%20to%20Deaths%20in%20Prison%20Custody%20p6%20%281%29%20 WEB%20PDF.pdf* (accessed on 21 February 2023).

47   HMIPS, *Independent Review of the Response to Deaths in Prison Custody* (November 2021), *www. prisonsinspectoratescotland.gov.uk/sites/default/files/publication_files/Independent%20Review%20 of%20the%20Response%20to%20Deaths%20in%20Prison%20Custody%20p6%20%281%29%20 WEB%20PDF.pdf* (accessed on 21 February 2023).

These recommendations seem entirely in line with the observations made above about looking at systems and how best to consider what lessons can be learnt.

- The independent investigatory body must have unfettered access to all relevant material, including all data from SPS, access to premises for the purpose of conducting interviews with employees, people held in detention and others, and the right to carry out such interviews for the purpose of the investigation. Corresponding duties should be placed on SPS and other relevant institutions requiring the completion, retention and production of relevant information in their possession.

Full powers exist for COPFS at present to instruct such inquiries. It is the use of joint minutes that might provide a basis of why all materials may not be before the FAI effectively in each case.

- Access to full non-means-tested legal aid funding for specialist representation throughout the processes of investigation following a death in custody should be provided, including at the FAI. This seems to be appropriate.

8. CONCLUSION

6.80 There are long delays in FAIs into deaths in custody being carried out, with a significant backlog due still to be heard against a background of rising concerns about the nature of these deaths of those in custody. The Independent Report[48] concluded that from the 'evidence ... heard from bereaved families that existing practice fails to provide them with choice and control – two pillars of trauma-informed practice. At every step of the journey currently, there is a noticeable lack of family engagement.' Families need to be engaged and supported to command respect and ensure trust in the FAI process.

6.81 Similarly, the independent report concluded that there seemed to be a lack of clarity in leading in respect of the various organisations tasked with investigating a death and where any criminal proceedings might be in contemplation. Should the other organisations await the outcome of the criminal investigation by COPFS and/ or Police Scotland before undertaking their own?

6.82 Paragraph 159 of the report[49] recognised that it was important that the gathering of evidence in criminal proceedings was not prejudiced. The factual evidence will be the same, but complications may well arise where it is the organisation itself which is at the core of the investigations, such as Police Scotland

---

48 Scottish Government, News, *Death in Custody Review* (30 November 2021), *www.gov.scot/news/ death-in-custody-review/* (accessed on 21 February 2023).

49 Ibid.

or SPS. These have been seen recently in both the FAI into the deaths on the M9[50] where Police Scotland were prosecuted and the suicides in prison where no criminal proceedings can be taken against SPS due to Crown immunity.[51] Delays are also not good for anyone as recognised in discussions on delays in FAIs, partly because of strain but also to refer to their memory of events. It must be possible to agree at the outset a potential timescale for concluding investigations with provision made for undertaking regular reviews.

6.83 There appears to be a lack of join-up of relevant information from the provision of statistics of the number of deaths in prison to the issue of the actual determinations. Why are the SPS death statistics not regularly updated with information about whether an FAI has been completed or noting when it is being scheduled? When the FAI is completed, and the determination issued, the cause of death and other information should be cross referenced. Why are statistics not routinely provided on the number of deaths in police custody? Only by joining up the information from death within the relevant organisation to the issue of the determination can meaningful references be undertaken to allow trends and systemic issues, to be identified and to make recommendations seeking to promote good practice.

6.84 There needs to be a robust approach taken to the use of joint minutes to identify where they can be used to good effect and without any reduction in the quality of the evidence or robust nature of the FAI.

6.85 The promotion of better understanding of the roles adopted in an FAI is required to understand what the Crown can and indeed should present by evidence. The need is for the independent reviewer as in the judges undertaking their role to ensure that they demand robust and thorough scrutiny of the evidence.

6.86 In general, the FAI system seems neither to be ill-equipped nor resourced to ensure that FAIs into deaths in custody are completed in a manner that fully satisfies the guidelines discussed by the International Red Cross. Whether or how the Scottish Government will implement any of the report of their recommendations remains to be seen.

---

50 Central FM, *Fatal accident inquiry after M9 crash deaths* (26 October 2022), *www.centralfm.co.uk/news/local-news/fatal-accident-inquiry-after-m9-crash-deaths/* (accessed on 21 February 2023).
51 BBC, *Families' anger as no prosecution over young prisoner suicides* (27 October 2022), *www.bbc.co.uk/news/uk-scotland-63416035* (accessed on 21 February 2023).

Chapter 7

Sudden Death Investigations in England and Wales

1. BACKGROUND

7.01   Early chapters of this book have fully described the procedure in Scotland for investigating sudden, unexpected, suspicious and unexpected deaths. The purpose of the system is to satisfy the public interest in investigating deaths, by exploring lessons to be learnt by holding FAIs. Sudden deaths and the role of the procurator fiscal have always been popular in providing the fictional background to television programmes and books.[1] That has helped to increase some of the public awareness of the FAI role and their scope, though it inaccurately reports on occasion by depicting the English system. Having a basic knowledge of the differences between the systems in England and Wales and Scotland is useful.

---

1   See BBC *Sutherland's Law* which depicted a procurator fiscal in Oban – books include Quintin Jardine, Val McDermid and James Robertson.

7.02   The Scottish system is unique in its process as is the role of the procurator fiscal. However, there is merit in understanding how other countries need and put in place a system to investigate sudden deaths.

7.03   This chapter focuses on an analysis of the system in England and Wales. As with Scotland, not all deaths are reported. The advice for deaths in England and Wales indicates that about half of all the deaths are not reported to the Coroner as a Medical Certificate of Cause of Death is available. Where it is not available the death is reportable. Other similar criteria exist such as: deaths related to medical treatment, surgery or anaesthetic, possible suicide, suspicious circumstances or history of violence asbestos related deaths and custody or those detained under the Mental Health Act even if due to natural causes.[2]

England and Wales has a coroner and inquest system, which undertakes a broadly similar role to an FAI in relation to their investigations into deaths. There are further reasons to consider their system in some depth as there is an inevitable overlap of interests in relation to deaths in the UK. These derive from common institutions such as the NHS and the Health and Safety Executive, of course, though always respecting the nature of the respective devolved responsibilities. Their system in relation to deaths in England and Wales is governed by the Coroners and Justice Act 2009 (the 2009 Act).

7.04   Legislation passed in the UK Parliament may on occasion apply to both, though in a more limited application to Scotland. The 2009 Act applies to Scotland in relation to death investigations and inquiries into service personnel deaths.[3] It is not the only legislation to apply where interests in certain deaths are relevant to both countries.

7.05   The Northern Ireland Troubles (Legacy and Reconciliation) Bill, currently before the UK Parliament, in Pt 2 seeks to introduce a new Sch A1 into the Inquiries into Fatal Accidents and Sudden Deaths etc. (Scotland) Act 2016 (asp 2) (the 2016 Act). That section will govern inquiries and investigations into Troubles-related deaths. The purpose of the Bill itself is to address 'the legacy of the Northern Ireland Troubles' by promoting reconciliation by establishing an Independent Commission for Reconciliation and Information Recovery, and 'limiting … inquests ….'. A request for the review of a death in Scotland caused directly by conduct forming part of the Troubles may be made by:

- the sheriff in Scotland who was responsible for conducting an inquiry into that death, or was responsible for conducting an inquiry into that death which has been discontinued in accordance with para 1(3) of Sch A1 to the 2016 Act; or

---

2   For more information the Manchester Coroner's Office provides a good source of public information
     https://www.manchester.gov.uk/info/626/coroners/5532/when_death_occurs.
3   These provisions are now included in the 2016 Act.

- the procurator fiscal in Scotland who was responsible for conducting an investigation into that death, or was responsible for conducting an investigation into that death which has been discontinued in accordance with para 1(4)(b) of Sch A1 to the 2016 Act; or
- the Lord Advocate, if the Lord Advocate is prohibited by para 3(a) of Sch A1 to the 2016 Act from exercising functions so as to cause an inquiry to be held into the death.

7.06   An overlap of the two jurisdictions' processes may be seen too from the inquiries into the two deaths that took place in the Cameron House fire. An inquest in England has already been held into the deaths which have now been the subject of an FAI in Scotland.[4] On similar lines, a petition brought for an FAI to be held into Dodi Al-Fayed's death in Paris was unsuccessful.[5] The inquest into his death along with Princess Diana was heard in London, as the coroner has authority as the Lord Advocate has in Scotland and can hold inquiries into deaths abroad.

7.07   A number of other countries adopt a form of the coroners' system, largely based on the English model. That framework into investigating deaths therefore has widespread influence and is highly developed. The coronial system does have similarities to the Scottish system. There are a number of its practices, such as the imposition of timescales on completion of inquests, the requirements for coronial training, the specialism of judicial roles and the issue of Regulation 28 Reports[6] in making recommendations, that might be reforms worthy of consideration in addressing some of the criticisms discussed regarding the FAI system in Scotland.

2.   INTRODUCTION TO THE CORONIAL SYSTEM

7.08   Both the coronial and FAI systems have evolved quite separately. The main legislation governing the coronial system is now set out in Pt 1 of the Coroners and Justice Act 2009. That 2009 Act reformed the law in relation to coroners, the certification and the registration of deaths. It replaced the prior framework for the investigation of certain deaths by coroners, originating under the Coroners Act 1988. The 1988 Act had achieved similar reforms of the processes of investigation into deaths as had the 1976 Act; it sought similarly to consolidate the earlier coroner legislation that had dated back to the early 1900s.

---

4   Cameron House fire inquest: *www.judiciary.uk/wp-content/uploads/2021/04/Richard-Dyson-and-Simon-Midgley-2021-0108-Redacted.pdf* (accessed on 21 February 2023).
5   Mohamed Moneim Ali Fayed for judicial review of a decision of the Lord Advocate to refuse to instruct a public inquiry into the death of Emad al Fayed, P905/03, *www.scotcourts.gov.uk/search-judgments/judgment?id=978487a6-8980-69d2-b500-ff0000d74aa7* (accessed on 21 February 2023).
6   The Coroners and Justice Act 2009 allows a coroner to issue a Regulation 28 Report to an individual, organisations, local authorities or government departments and their agencies where the coroner believes that action should be taken to prevent further deaths.

7.09 The 2009 Act made significant changes to the deaths system; these changes focused on the pre-inquest processes (reflecting similar processes to the procurator fiscal's prior investigations into certain categories of sudden death). Much of that work relating to sudden death investigations is inevitably not that visible to the public. By reforming these processes, this has helped with transparency for the public – much needed after the perceived weaknesses in the system. They were, in part, a response to what had happened in the Shipman case, by improving the certification of deaths processes.[7] It is vital to ascertain whether the death at the initial stage is one which falls under the coroner's jurisdiction and then requires further 'public' investigation.

7.10 Other 2009 Act reforms reflected on the experience of the inquest into Princess Diana's death in Paris. Section 46 of the 2009 Act therefore abolished the Office of Coroner of the Queen's household. Previously, that Office's function had been to investigate the death of anyone whose body was lying 'within the limits of any of the Queen's palaces; or within the limits of any other house where Her Majesty is then residing'.

7.11 The antiquity of that provision was exposed by that inquest, where the coroner, Baroness Butler Sloss, responsible for the inquest as the then Depute Coroner to the Royal Household, decided to sit alone. Her decision was reviewed by the High Court, with the subsequent inquest then heard by a jury.[8] She stepped down in favour of a High Court judge, Lord Justice Scott Baker, as the inquest judge, citing her lack of jury experience. The public interest and speculation about Princess Diana's death had required to be satisfied in that need to hold an inquest with a jury.

3. THE 2009 ACT

7.12 The 2009 Act commenced on 25 July 2013 along with the sets of rules and regulations, referred to as the Coroners (Inquests) Rules 2013[9] and the Coroners (Investigations) Regulations 2013. Both of these seek to supplement the 2009 Act, by regulating the practice and procedure. When seeking guidance, on operations, there are a number of further publications that set out detailed processes and procedures. These are comprehensive.

7.13 Reference to these further publications can be found under the Chief Coroner's Guidance, Advice and Law Sheets.[10] These are numbered sequentially. A recent example has reflected the recent Covid-19 pandemic with the issue of

---

7   *Death Certification* and *Investigation and the Shipman Inquiry*, both published in 2003 (*www. archive2.offcial-documents.co.uk/document/cm58/5831/5831.pdf* and *www.archive2.official-documents.co.uk/document/cm58/5831/5831.pdf*, respectively).

8   A prior French investigation had been held but its report was not published. The inquest into her death opened in January 2004 under Michael Burgess the Coroner to the Royal Household.

9   Made under the powers set out in s 45 of the 2009 Act.

10   Chief Coroner's Guidance, Advice and Law Sheets, *www.judiciary.uk/related-offices-and-bodies/office-chief-coroner/guidance-law-sheets/coroners-guidance/* (accessed on 21 February 2023).

Guidance No 34.[11] It noted there that the pandemic had had a significant impact on the functioning of the coronial service with restrictions requiring its working practices to be changed. Notwithstanding the return to previous practices, the Judicial Review and Courts Act 2022 has sought to retain some of the practices developed to allow matters to be dealt with remotely. Further, Guidance No 39[12] dealing with recovery directly from the pandemic has now been issued.

7.14   There is also a Coroners Benchbook,[13] though it is currently under review with a new version due to be re-published. These make up the detailed guidance to coroners on various matters relating to the 2009 Act. They also include commentary on the law, and developing jurisprudence in what is referred to as Law Sheets,[14] with examples such as where important cases have been decided with relevant principles of law involved. One such example is the Law Sheet Number 5 which 'set[s] out for coroners the main headlines from the authorities on the exercise of the coroner's discretion..... [and] consider generally the ambit, limits and possible challenge to its exercise'.[15]

7.15   That guidance assists coroners with their law and duties, as well as providing commentary and advice on relevant policy and practice. None of these practices currently exist in Scotland though the Judicial Institute for Scotland, responsible for judicial training, does issue both a Bench book for juries and Practice Notes on occasion to judges. Extending these practices into the issuing of guidance that was publicly available would help in promoting consistency of practice as well as transparency of the FAI process in Scotland.[16]

7.16   Since the commencement of the 2009 Act, there has been scrutiny into how well that system is working. The Chief Coroner's combined Annual Reports 2018–2019 and 2019–2020 included a review of the operation of the Coroner Service, reflective of the work being undertaken by coroners and their staff during the Covid-19 pandemic, progress in promoting consistency in coroner practices, guidance for coroners and the training that has been facilitated for coroners, as well as making recommendations to improve coroner services. A Justice Committee

---

11   Chief Coroner, Guidance No 34, Covid-19, *www.judiciary.uk/wp-content/uploads/2022/07/ Guidance-No-34-Chief-Coroners-Guidance-for-coroners-on-Covid-19-PDF-opens-in-a-new-tab. pdf* (accessed on 21 February 2023).

12   Chief Coroner, Guidance No 39, Recovery from the Covid-19 pandemic, *www.judiciary.uk/wp-content/uploads/2021/05/GUIDANCE-No-39-Covid-recovery-20-05-2021-002.pdf* (accessed on 21 February 2023).

13   This Bench Book (PDF) is currently under review and not all of the information contained within should be treated as current. It may not reflect current case law. A new version will be published presently: *www.judiciary.uk/courts-and-tribunals/coroners-courts/coroners-legislation-guidance-and-advice/coroners-guidance/*   (accessed on 21 February 2023).

14   This refers to Chief Coroner's Guidance, Advice and Law Sheets available at https://www.judiciary. uk/courts-and-tribunals/coroners-courts/coroners-legislation-guidance-and-advice/coroners-guidance/   (accessed 31/8/2023).

15   Chief Coroner's Law Sheet No 5 (18 January 2016), *www.judiciary.uk/guidance-and-resources/ chief-coroners-law-sheet-no-5/*   (accessed on 21 February 2023).

16   Judiciary of Scotland, Judicial Institute Publications, *https://judiciary.scot/home/media-information/ publications/judicial-institute-publications*   (accessed on 21 February 2023).

Report[17] by the UK Parliament into the coroners' system followed, that concluded by making a number of recommendations.

7.17 The UK government[18] has accepted some of the recommendations in their response, as well as further reforms having now been included in chapter 4 of the Judicial Review and Courts Act 2022. These measures may be seen in Section 40 which refers to the power to hold non-contentious hearings in writing, section 41 which refers to the use of audio or video links and s. 42 which refers to the suspension of requirement for jury at inquest where Covid-19 is suspected[19]

7.18 As has been discussed in the **Chapter 6** on deaths in custody, Scotland has also undertaken some reports into considering the effectiveness of the FAI system. In 2019 the Inspectorate of Prosecution in Scotland published a follow-up report on FAIs. That report examined issues raised in the FAI report published by the inspectorate in August 2016. It noted that '[g]iven the number of recommendations that remain in progress and the continuing concerns regarding delays in dealing with mandatory FAIs and the new recommendations made in this report, the Inspectorate plans to re-visit the investigation of FAIs in a further follow-up report next year.' That next year was 2020 and in January 2023, no subsequent report has yet been published.[20]

4. THE ADMINISTRATION OF THE CORONER'S OFFICE

7.19 The Chief Coroner[21] heads the coroner system adopting a similar position to that of the Lord Advocate. They have overall responsibility and national leadership for coroners in England and Wales.[22] Coroners however are appointed by the local authority with the Chief Coroner and the Lord Chancellor required to give consent to each proposed appointment.[23]

7.20 Coroners, as sheriffs, are independent judicial officers. They were previously either doctors or lawyers, charged with the responsibility for investigating the cause of deaths. Going forward, now all new appointments require all coroners (of whichever rank) appointed to be lawyers. They remain judicial appointments.

---

17 *https://publications.parliament.uk/pa/cm5802/cmselect/cmjust/68/6802.htm* (accessed on 21 February 2023).
18 *The Coroner Service: Government Response to the Committee's First Report Third Special Report of Session 2021–22*, 10 September 2021.
19 All measures commenced on 28 June 2022.
20 Scottish Government, News, *Inspectorate of prosecution publishes follow-up report on Fatal Accident Inquiries* (7 August 2019), *www.gov.scot/news/inspectorate-of-prosecution-publishes-followup-report-on-fatal-accident-inquiries/* (accessed on 21 February 2023).
21 First appointment was made in September 2012.
22 With the issue of guidance as outlined above.
23 Schedule 3 para 2(5) of the 2009 Act.

7.21   There are around 98 coroners in England and Wales that cover approximately 109 coroner areas,[24] which generally reflect the local authority boundaries. As with COPFS, through the operation of procurator fiscals, coroners employ officers and staff to assist with their investigations.

5.   PROCESS UNDER THE CORONER

7.22   **Where a death occurs in England and Wales:** 'An 11-year-old girl has died after getting into difficulty at a water sports and activity park':[25] this BBC News report states that the death is unascertained with the police confirming that an investigation is under way. This death will inevitably be required to be reported and be subject to investigation by the senior coroner. The contrast with Scotland is that the press report would be likely to conclude in Scotland with 'a report [that] will be sent to the Procurator Fiscal'.

7.23   **Certification of death:** The Notification of Death Regulations 2019 outlines the categories of deaths that need to be reported to the coroner. All deaths will be reported to the coroner in writing though this will now tend to be completed by means of e-reporting.[26]

7.24   A doctor can only complete a medical certificate of the cause of death form (MCCD) if the patient has died from a natural cause and the doctor is able to state the cause of death to the best of their medical knowledge and belief. Certainty is not required with the standard of proof being on the basis of more likely than not.[27] The doctor needs to have attended a patient for their last illness and either that attendance was within the last 14 days (though this can be extended at the coroner's discretion; they extend routinely to three months and, exceptionally, to six months) or the doctor has seen the patient after the death. The coroner has indicated a doctor should not write the MCCD unless they have attended upon the deceased for their last illness. As highlighted above, these are all safeguards emanating from the investigations into the Shipman case.

24   Coroners and Justice Act 2009 (Coroner Areas and Assistant Coroners) Transitional Order 2013 (SI 2013/1625).
25   BBC, *Girl dies after going missing at Windsor water park* (7 August 2022), *www.bbc.co.uk/news/ uk-england-berkshire-62453312* (accessed on 21 February 2023).
26   In exceptional circumstances, an oral report can be made: s 4(2) of the Notification of Death Regulations 2019.
27   This is deliberate avoidance of the more commonly acknowledged term in civil proceedings of the 'balance of probabilities'. A lecture by the Chief Coroner noted that an inquest is not a trial and the use of language was not as accurate as it should be, and picked up on the Guidance No 17 para 37 notes that uses the term level of certainty in that 'The *level of certainty* required when reaching conclusions at an inquest (whether those conclusions are short-form or narrative) is *the same as* the civil standard of proof, namely the balance of probabilities'. Chief Coroner – Leeming Lecture 2022 (22 July 2022), *www.judiciary.uk/publications/chief-coroner-leeming-lecture-2022/* (accessed on 21 February 2023).

7.25   Once a death has been reported to the coroner, the Registrar for Deaths cannot go ahead with the registration until the coroner has decided whether any further investigation into the death is necessary. Where no further investigation is necessary, the registration of the death can be completed there and then.

7.26   Under reg 2 of the Notification of Death Regulations 2019, a registered medical practitioner must notify the relevant senior coroner of a person's death if (a) the registered medical practitioner comes to know of the death on or after 1 October 2019 and (b) at least one of the circumstances described in reg 3(1) applies. These circumstances include where the registered medical practitioner suspects certain circumstances apply. These appear generally to follow those categories of deaths to be reported in Scotland. These circumstances include under reg 3(1)(a):

(i)   poisoning, including by an otherwise benign substance;

(ii)   exposure to or contact with a toxic substance;

(iii)   the use of a medicinal product, controlled drug or psychoactive substance;

(iv)   violence;

(v)   trauma or injury;

(vi)   self-harm;

(vii)   neglect, including self-neglect;

(viii) the person undergoing a treatment or procedure of a medical or similar nature; or

(ix)   an injury or disease attributable to any employment held by the person during the person's lifetime.

7.27   This also includes deaths falling under:

- Regulation 3(1)(b) where the registered medical practitioner suspects that the person's death was unnatural but does not fall within any of the circumstances listed in reg 3(1)(a).
- Regulation 3(1)(c) where the registered medical practitioner is an attending medical practitioner required to sign a certificate of cause of death in relation to the deceased person; but despite taking reasonable steps to determine the cause of death, considers that the cause of death is unknown.
- Regulation 3(1)(d) where the registered medical practitioner suspects that the person died while in custody or otherwise in state detention.[28]
- Regulation 3(1)(e) where the registered medical practitioner reasonably believes that there is no attending medical practitioner required to sign a certificate of cause of death in relation to the deceased person.
- Regulation 3(1)(f) where the registered medical practitioner reasonably believes that (i) an attending medical practitioner is required to sign a certificate of cause of death in relation to the deceased person; but (ii) the

---

28   "State detention" is defined under s 48 of the 2009 Act.

attending medical practitioner is not available within a reasonable time of the person's death to sign the certificate of cause of death.

- Regulation 3(1)(g) where the registered medical practitioner, after taking reasonable steps to ascertain the identity of the deceased person, is unable to do so.

7.28 Regulation 4(3) and (4) set out the information that a medical practitioner must, in so far as it is known to them, provide to a senior coroner when making a death notification. If this information is not known to the medical practitioner, they are not required to provide this information as part of their notification. The medical practitioner is required to give the coroner the name of the next of kin or, where there is none, the person responsible for the body of deceased.[29] The medical practitioner needs to indicate why the death is being notified. Though there is no prescribed form, they are also required to provide further information that they consider is relevant for the coroner.[30]

7.29 When a death is notified, a coroner's investigation may not be necessary if the senior coroner is satisfied that they do not need to open an investigation. They may issue a 100A form,[31] or refer the case back to the medical practitioner, who can then issue an MCCD. This might include where the deceased was receiving palliative care at home, which was recorded, but the medical practitioner was unavailable at the time of notification.

7.30 Where a death is reported to the coroner, the coroner has three choices:

- The medical practitioner is given permission to issue an MCCD and the coroner takes no further action.
- A post mortem examination is instructed which leads to a finding of natural death. The case is closed or opened for investigation as more information is required and an inquest is opened.
- They can open an inquest without a post mortem examination.

7.31 This replicates a similar process to the procurator fiscal and Scotland. The Royal College of Pathologists has a useful diagram clearly setting out this process.[32]

---

29 Regulation 4(3)(c): where there is no identifiable person who may be responsible for the body, the local authority is responsible for the disposal of the body.
30 Regulation 4(3)(d).
31 This is a form from the coroner informing the registrar that they are aware of the death but no further investigation is necessary and permission has been given to the doctor to issue the medical certificate.
32 Scottish Government, News, *Inspectorate of prosecution publishes follow-up report on Fatal Accident Inquiries* (7 August 2019), *www.gov.scot/news/inspectorate-of-prosecution-publishes-followup-report-on-fatal-accident-inquiries/* (accessed on 21 February 2023).

6. CORONER'S INVESTIGATION

7.32   Under s 1(1) of the 2009 Act, when the coroner[33] is made aware that the body of a deceased person is within their area, they, as soon as practicable, should conduct an investigation in the circumstances outlined above. The coroner should have reason to believe that (a) a death has occurred in or near the coroner's area, (b) the circumstances of the death are such that there should be an investigation into it, and (c) the duty to conduct an investigation into the death does not arise because of the destruction, loss or absence of the body.

7.33   When a report is received, the Chief Coroner may direct a senior coroner to conduct an investigation into the death. Where a direction is given, the investigation into the death should be undertaken as soon as practicable.

7.34   The coroner for one geographical district is no longer restricted to conducting that investigation and may relocate it if it is in the interests of the bereaved family.[34] When coroners investigate the causes and circumstances of a death, the purpose of that investigation is directed at:

- who the deceased was;
- how, when and where the deceased came by their death; and
- the particulars (if any) required by the Births, Registration and Deaths Act 1953[35] to be registered concerning the death.[36]

7.35   Up to this stage, the system replicates that in Scotland. However, there is an accountability thereafter as far as monitoring the investigation process is concerned. During an investigation, the Chief Coroner may at any time require information from a coroner in relation to a particular investigation or investigations that have or are being conducted by that coroner.[37] The Chief Coroner can 'take over an investigation at any stage' where the coroner's investigation has not been completed or discontinued *within a year* from the day in which the coroner is made aware of the deceased's death[38] (our emphasis). Where that year is exceeded, the coroner is required to notify the Chief Coroner of that fact as soon as possible. The Chief Coroner has a statutory duty to report to the Lord Chancellor on investigations lasting more than 12 months, beginning with the day on which the coroner was made aware that the person's body was within the coroner's area.[39]

---

33 The 2009 Act refers to senior coroner but for ease the chapter refers to coroner. Senior coroner is appointed by the relevant authority for each coroner area (the 'senior coroner'): Sch 3 para 1(1) of the 2009 Act.
34 The Coroners (Investigations) Regulations 2013, para 18.
35 1953 Chapter 20 1 and 2 Eliz 2.
36 Section 5(1) of the 2009 Act.
37 The Coroners (Investigations) Regulations 2013, para 25(1).
38 The Coroners (Investigations) Regulations 2013, 26(1).
39 Section 16 of the 2009 Act.

7.36   Intervention is not necessarily going to take place in every case, but where cases involve consideration as to possible criminal proceedings, the Crown Prosecution Service (CPS) may be contacted by the Chief Coroner, or the coroner handling the case, for a progress report. There is no statutory requirement for the CPS to act, but they should consider assisting the coroner to progress the case.

7.37   The Chief Coroner is required to write an annual report for the Lord Chancellor. This includes a number of matters including[40] a summary for the year of the number and length of (i) investigations in respect of which notification of delay in investigation was given and (ii) investigations that were not concluded or discontinued by the end of the year, as well as the reasons for the length of those investigations and the measures taken with a view to keeping them from being unnecessarily lengthy.

7.38   The latest published reports by His Honour Judge Mark Lucraft QC were combined for 2018–2019 and 2019–2020.[41] Annex B of the reports show the numbers of cases taking over 12 months. In 2019, there were 2,278 cases out of 29,100 in England and Wales not completed within 12 months of being reported to the coroner.[42]

7.39   Coroners are not required publicly to provide reasons for delay in completing an investigation. However paras 22–25 of the annual reports[43] indicated some reasons for delays which generally reflect those that would apply to the delays in death investigations in Scotland. Generally, the death investigations affected through delay were those where:

- There is an investigation or possible prosecution by external authorities such as the Health and Safety Executive or in cases involving the Prisons and Probation Ombudsman inquiries, the Independent Office of Police Complaints inquiries or investigations by one of the specialist accident investigation bodies. These include homicide offences.[44] The investigation may well be suspended or adjourned under s 11 of the 2009 Act. The inquest will be adjourned until such time as the court proceedings are concluded. Though perhaps inevitable, as discussed earlier, investigations where the death occurs during the State's detention through the prison service or the police would tend to merit a degree of prioritisation.

- the death has occurred abroad: these investigations are inevitably lengthy as information is required from abroad. That can take time to achieve, plus

---

40   Section 26 of the 2009 Act.
41   MoJ, Chief Coroner's Combined Annual Report 2018 to 2019 and 2019 to 2020 (5 November 2020), *www.gov.uk/government/publications/chief-coroners-combined-annual-report-2018-to-2019-and-2019-to-2020* (accessed on 21 February 2023).
42   There are no complete figures for 2019-2020. No further reports have yet been published.
43   Report of the Chief Coroner to the Lord Chancellor, Sixth annual report: 2018–2019, Seventh annual report: 2019–2020, *https://assets.publishing.service.gov.uk/government/uploads/system/uploads/attachment_data/file/932518/chief-coroner_s-annual-report-1920.pdf* (accessed on 21 February 2023).
44   Schedule 1 and s 6 of the 2009 Act.

the issues of obtaining relevant translation of documents where these are required.

- these are complex cases which have legal issues, or have difficult medical issues which require the obtaining of specialist reports.

7.40 The implication of any scarcity of coroner resources have been identified as an issue too. This was relevant during and as a result of the impact of Covid-19 no doubt on staffing and the effect of the necessity to work at home will have had significant implications. This too has formed the basis of similar issues in Scotland with observations at the time of the HM Inspectorate report that the 'reasons for delays include overstretched workloads and inefficient collaboration with other agencies'.[45] These difficulties were no doubt compounded by communication issues over Covid-19.

7.41 There is assurance that the Chief Coroner monitors these figures and discusses them with senior coroners in an effort to understand the reasons for delay and to address any practice or resourcing issues. The Ministry of Justice publishes statistics annually on deaths reported to coroners, including the number of inquests and post mortems held, and the inquest conclusions that are recorded.[46] Though some reporting of statistical information can be found in the COPFS annual report, and SCTS's published determinations, there is no true comparison to be made with the detailed categorisation of information that is published in England and Wales. If there was a requirement in Scotland for similar information to be published in a consistent manner collated across the organisations, this would allow enhanced transparency as well as a meaningful comparison to be undertaken and analysed. **Chapter 12** looks at the absence of information, such as collating the time from the date of death until an FAI is held and the determination published.

7.42 The categories are outlined in the table below:

Headlines	Narrative
Increase in the number of deaths reported to the Coroner in 2021	195,200 deaths
Number of reported deaths to the coroner	33%
Deaths in state detention	580[47]
Post-mortem examinations were carried out on	43% of all deaths reported in 2021 – a 7% rise
2% more inquests were held	32,800 inquests held

---

45   Scottish Legal News, *Crown office 'simply incapable' of handling fatal accident inquiries* (8 August 2019), *www.scottishlegal.com/articles/crown-office-simply-incapable-of-handling-fatal-accident-inquiries* (accessed on 21 February 2023).

46   Coroners and burial statistics (25 July 2013, updated 14 May 2015), *www.gov.uk/government/collections/coroners-and-burials-statistics* (accessed on 21 February 2023).

47   Reflecting an increase consistent too with SPS statistics in Scotland. It explains that these are 'up from 562 in 2020, the increase was driven by a 17% rise in deaths in prison custody'.

Headlines	Narrative
Inquest conclusions up 4%	The largest rise seen in accident/ misadventure, suicide and unclassified conclusions
Average time taken to complete an inquest rose by four weeks	The estimated average time taken to process an inquest increased from 27 weeks in 2020 to 31 weeks in 2021
Prevention of Future Deaths reports[48]	440 Prevention of Future Deaths reports

7.43   Similar criminal offences exist in that it is a common law offence to obstruct a coroner, by disposing of a body before a coroner can openly inquire into the circumstances of a death or acting to prevent an inquest.

7.   CONSIDERATIONS UNDER ARTICLE 2 OF THE ECHR

7.44   Should Art 2 of the ECHR affect the scope or conclusion of the inquest and the directions given to the jury? Issues involving Art 2 considerations arise in relation to deaths in custody and those where the police may be involved in the detentions. Section 5(2) of the 2009 Act seeks to avoid a breach of any Convention rights (within the meaning of the Human Rights Act 1998) as it is 'to be read as including the purpose of ascertaining in what circumstances the deceased came by his or her death'. Identification of the concerns about such deaths can be seen, for instance, through the rising number of suicides in prison. Deaths during detention (in cases of mental health and involving the police) were noted to have increased by 18% in the Coroners Statistics 2020: England and Wales to 562 deaths.[49] Such deaths are investigated by the Prison and Probation Ombudsman and thereafter by the coroner.

7.45   In a relevant death, the coroner will consider if it is in effect an Art 2 ECHR inquest. The High Court has indicated that not all deaths in custody should automatically be treated as Art 2 ECHR inquests.[50] Where the coroner's decision recorded a natural death from cancer, this was subject to judicial review from the family who sought to widen the scope and for an inquest to be held. The coroner had determined that Art 2 of the ECHR did not impose any obligation for any further investigation. His investigations concluded that the treatment provided had been acceptable. In similar cases, 'in the context of a natural death in custody, the responsibility of the state for the purposes of the duty to protect life will arise only if there has been a failure to provide timely and appropriate medical care to a detainee obviously in need of it.'

---

48   Regulation 28 Reports discussed at para **7.13**.
49   MoJ, Coroners Statistics 2020: England and Wales, 4. Deaths in State Detention (13 May 2001), *www.gov.uk/government/statistics/coroners-statistics-2020/coroners-statistics-2020-england-and-wales#deaths-in-state-detention* (accessed on 21 February 2023).
50   *Tyrrell v HM Senior Coroner County Durham and Darlington* [2016] EWHC 1892 (Admin).

7.46   This decision was felt to have an important effect as there is an increasingly elderly prison population where there is a greater likelihood that more deaths are going to result from natural causes. It is not suggested that the procedural requirements of Art 2 should only be triggered where deaths in custody result from violence, unnatural deaths such as suicides or where there are questions as to the death which may indicate that this death was not from natural causes.[51] It should be a key factor in the holding of any relevant inquest or mandatory FAI into deaths in custody to ensure that any medical treatment provided to the deceased in custody met the standards of timely and appropriate medical care and did not discriminate as a result of their being in custody.[52]

7.47   The decision in this inquest affects the inquest's conclusion, the implications of which are then discussed in the relevant Chief Coroner's Guidance. The conclusion can still be in a narrative form but the coroner must record 'in what circumstances' the deceased came by their death. These may include the 'causes of death, defects in the system which contributed to death and any other factors relevant to the circumstances of the death'.[53] That Guidance states that 'a conclusion in an Article 2 [ECHR] case may be a "judgmental conclusion of a factual nature [on the core factual issues], directly relating to the circumstances of death", without infringing either section 5(3) of the 2009 Act (limiting opinion) and section 10(2) of the 2009 Act (avoiding questions of civil or criminal liability).'

7.48   Paragraph 52 of the Guidance indicates that judgmental words can include 'inadequate', 'inappropriate', 'insufficient', 'lacking', 'unsuitable', 'unsatisfactory', and 'failure', though civil liability such as 'negligence', 'breach of duty', 'breach of Article 2' and 'careless' are not permitted as they may breach s 10(2) of the 2009 Act and purport to imply finding as to civil liability arising from the death.

7.49   The Supreme Court decision in the appeal case of *Rabone*[54] considered the positive duty imposed by Art 2 of the ECHR on the State to take preventative operational measures to safeguard an individual's life in certain circumstances. That duty is owed to all citizens but is of greater relevance to those described as being the most vulnerable as a result of their physical or mental condition[55] and for whom the State has assumed responsibility, including immigrants and military conscripts. At para [33], it stated that '…But the Strasbourg jurisprudence shows that there is such a duty to protect persons from a real and immediate risk of suicide at least where they

---

51   Exchange Chambers, *Louis Browne acts for Ministry of Justice Article 2 ECHR Judicial Review* (27 July 2016), *www.exchangechambers.co.uk/louis-browne-acts-ministry-justice-article-2-echr-judicial-review/* (accessed on 21 February 2023).

52   See **Chapter 6** where these issues are discussed in relation to satisfying the requirement of the FAI investigations in Scotland as to deaths in custody and adequate provision of medical care to prisoners.

53   *R (Middleton) v HM Coroner for West Somerset* [2004] 2 AC 182.

54   Death by suicide of a mental health patient who was discharged from hospital. *Rabone v Pennine Care NHS Foundation Trust* [2012] UKSC 2; [2012] 2 A.C. 72; [2012] H.R.L.R. 10.

55   Ibid at [22], [33].

are under the control of the state.' That assumption of responsibility was outlined by Lord Rodger in *Mitchell v Glasgow City Council*:[56]

> 'The obligation of the United Kingdom under Article 2 goes wider, however, In particular, where a state has assumed responsibility for an individual, whether by taking him into custody, by imprisoning him, detaining him under mental health legislation, or conscripting him into the armed forces, the state assumes responsibility for that individual's safety. So in these circumstances police authorities, prison authorities, health authorities and the armed forces are all subject to positive obligations to protect the lives of those in their care.'

8. POST MORTEM EXAMINATIONS

7.50 Post mortems into deaths in suspicious circumstances in Scotland require two doctors because of the longstanding evidential requirements of corroboration. Similarly, where criminal charges are being considered for a homicide offence[57] in England and Wales, a further or second post mortem may be instructed. The coroner will liaise with the bereaved relatives regarding the release of the body, and with the police and CPS, where needed, if criminal proceedings are being considered. The Chief Coroner has issued guidance where second post mortem examinations are to be undertaken.[58]

7.51 While a coroner has legal control over the body of a deceased person, the coroner decides whether to instruct a first or subsequent post mortem examination. There is no automatic right to a second post mortem examination. The Guidance indicates the coroner will scrutinise each case on its merits. Where a second post mortem examination is arranged by a coroner, it should be undertaken as quickly as possible, and usually within days of the first and before the expiry of 28 days from the date of death.

7.52 The timing of the holding of post mortems was seen to be a contentious point in Scotland. Not only are all suspicious deaths subject to a second post mortem instructed by the Crown, there may well be a third post mortem instructed by the defence. This causes potential delay– and also, upset to the family who naturally want the body of their deceased released for funeral arrangements, as well as not being subject to such invasive processes. There are no time periods imposed in Scotland though attempts have been made to introduce them.[59]

---

56   [2009] AC 874 at [66].
57   Coroners and Justice Act 2009 Sch 1, para 1(6).
58   Guidance No 32, Post-Mortem Examinations Including Second Post-Mortem Examinations.
59   Post Mortem Examinations (Defence Time Limit) Scotland Bill, *www.parliament.scot/bills-and-laws/bills/post-mortem-examinations-defence-time-limit-scotland-bill* (accessed on 21 February 2023).

7.53   Where there is a suspicion that a criminal act led to the cause of death, the coroner will open an inquest and must adjourn it until the outcome of any criminal proceedings is finalised.[60]

9.   WHEN AN INQUEST IS HELD

7.54   The coroner will hold an inquest in terms of s 6 of the 2009 Act. An inquest is generally held if it was not possible to find out the cause of death from the post mortem examination, or the death is found to be unnatural. An inquest is a legal inquiry into the cause and circumstances of a death. They are limited, fact-finding inquiries, held in a public court. The coroner establishes who died and how, when and where the death occurred. A coroner will consider both oral and written evidence during the course of an inquest. Inquests are held with or without juries.

7.55   Under r 8 of the Coroners (Inquest) Rules 2013, coroners are required to complete an inquest within six months of the date on which the coroner is made aware of the death, or as soon as is reasonably practicable. If the death occurred in prison or custody, or if it resulted from an accident at work, there will usually be a jury at the inquest.

7.56   An inquest will be held by a coroner if the circumstances of the death fall under those offences listed in para 1(6) of Sch 1 to the 2009 Act. These include:

- homicide offences including murder, manslaughter, corporate manslaughter or infanticide, and offences under the Road Traffic Act 1988 where death results;[61]
- an offence under s 2 of the Suicide Act 1961[62] (criminal liability for complicity in another's suicide);
- an offence under s 5 of the Domestic Violence, Crime and Victims Act 2004 (of causing or allowing the death of a child or vulnerable adult);
- 'related offence' meaning an offence (including a service offence) that involves the death of the deceased, but is not a homicide offence or the service equivalent of a homicide offence,[63] or involves the death of a person other than the deceased (whether or not it is a homicide offence or the service equivalent of a homicide offence) and is committed in circumstances connected with the death of the deceased.

---

60   Paragraph 1 of Sch 1 to the CJA 2009.
61   In Scotland deaths under similar provisions would be unlikely to trigger an FAI unless they occurred in the course of employment. Though not a road traffic offence, see the FAI into the death of Joyce Gardiner [2022] FAI 12.
62   This Act does not apply in Scotland. See Chalmers, J, *Clarifying the law on assisted suicide? Ross v Lord Advocate* (2017) Edinburgh Law Review 21(1), 93–98.
63   Section 42 of the Armed Forces Act 2006 (or s 70 of the Army Act 1955 (3 & 4 Eliz 2 c 18), s 70 of the Air Force Act 1955 (3 & 4 Eliz 2 c 19) or s 42 of the Naval Discipline Act 1957) corresponding to a homicide offence.

10.   PRE-INQUEST REVIEW (PIR) HEARING

7.57   Under r 6 of the Coroners (Inquests) Rules 2013, a coroner can hold a Pre-Inquest Review Hearing (PIR) at any time during the course of an investigation and before an inquest starts.[64] These are held in more complex cases and recorded to decide what issues should be identified as providing provide the focus of the inquest. These are similar to the holding of preliminary hearings that are held in Scotland.[65]

7.58   The guidance sets out that there should be an agenda for these hearings which include consideration as to the identity of interested persons, the scope of the inquest, whether Art 2 of the ECHR is engaged as discussed above, if a jury is required, any matters meriting further investigation, the provisional list of witnesses, disclosure, the jury bundle, any dates for another PIR hearing, the date and length of inquest and the venue for hearings.[66]

7.59   The 'interested person' is defined under s 47(2) (a) of the 2009 Act as being:

'(a) a spouse, civil partner,[67] partner, parent, child, brother, sister, grandparent, grandchild, child of a brother or sister, stepfather, stepmother, half-brother or half-sister;

(b) a personal representative of the deceased;

(c) a medical examiner exercising functions in relation to the death of the deceased;

(d) a beneficiary under a policy of insurance issued on the life of the deceased;

(e) the insurer who issued such a policy of insurance;

(f) a person who may by any act or omission have caused or contributed to the death of the deceased, or whose employee or agent may have done so;

(g) in a case where the death may have been caused by (i) an injury received in the course of an employment or (ii) a disease prescribed under section 108 of the Social Security Contributions and Benefits Act 1992 (c. 4) (benefit in respect of prescribed industrial diseases, etc), a representative of a trade union of which the deceased was a member at the time of death;

(h) a person appointed by, or representative of, an enforcing authority;

(i) [where the death is a homicide or related offence other than a service offence],[68] a chief constable;

(j) [equivalent to (i) for service offences][69], a Provost Marshal of a service police force or of the tri-service serious crime unit;

---

64   Guidance No 22 Pre-Inquest Review Hearings.
65   Section 16 of the 2016 Act.
66   Paragraph 7 of Guidance No 22 Pre-Inquest Hearings.
67   Section 47(7) of the 2009 Act a person is the partner of a deceased person if the two of them (whether of different sexes or the same sex) were living as partners in an enduring relationship at the time of the deceased person's death.
68   Section 47(3) of the 2009 Act.
69   Section 47(4) of the 2009 Act.

(k) [where the death is or has been the subject of an investigation managed or carried out][70] by the Director General of the Independent Office for Police Conduct;

(l) a person appointed by a Government department to attend or follow an inquest into the death or to assist in, or provide evidence for the purposes of, an investigation into the death under this Part;

(m) any other person who the senior coroner thinks has a sufficient interest.'

7.60   The requirement to observe appropriate dealings with interested parties such as the police is also outlined in *Brown*.[71] Coroners are not to be 'too familiar or close to [them] and not to encourage the same … even though the coroner may know [them] well in the course of coroner work. …Even first names may not look good to an outsider particularly to somebody of the older generation…' This highlights the standard ethical considerations of ensuring that proceedings are fair and unbiased. It is interesting that it is set out in writing – as the police will give evidence in Scotland before sheriffs frequently in criminal and other cases. Normal court etiquette and professional ethical responsibilities would expect this standard, failing which complaints or appeals are likely to be expected.

7.61   A PIR is normally held in public, except where the 'interests of justice or national security' are invoked under r 11(5) of the Coroners (Inquests) Rules 2013. A PIR was held into the three terrorist deaths that arose at Fishmongers' Hall and London Bridge in November 2019.[72] The coroner however is under no obligation to hold an inquest solely in the public interest.

7.62   A discussion which may feature at a PIR is whether the inquest should be held with a jury or not. The inquest into the deaths of the 11 men who died at the Shoreham air-show on 22 August 2015 discussed this.[73]

7.63   The original inquest opened on 2 September 2015 at Horsham, West Sussex. The inquest was adjourned to allow the criminal prosecution to take place of the pilot that resulted in a not guilty verdict. On the inquest's resumption, the senior coroner, Penelope Schofield[74] determined that she would sit without a jury, having heard submissions from the interested parties. These submissions had been mixed

---

70   Section 47(5) of the 2009 Act.

71   *Brown v HM Coroner for Norfolk* [2014] EWHC 187 (Admin).

72   *https://fishmongershallinquests.independent.gov.uk/wp-content/uploads/2020/10/FHI-PIR-16-October-2020.pdf* (accessed on 25 November 2022).

73   The inquest has now concluded in December 2022 where the Coroner ruled that they were unlawfully killed. The coroner stated that the 11 lives had been 'cruelly lost' and that it was clear that the aircraft's pilot should have abandoned a manoeuvre he was undertaking: The Guardian, *Shoreham airshow victims were unlawfully killed, coroner rules* (21 December 2022),*www.theguardian.com/uk-news/2022/dec/20/shoreham-airshow-victims-were-unlawfully-killed-coroner-rules* (accessed on 21 February 2023).

74   *www.westsussex.gov.uk/media/14348/shoreham_jury_ruling_2020.pdf* (accessed on 21 February 2023).

in their views. They tended to reflect the need for transparency and independence so that the public could see all necessary measures had been taken to improve safety at air shows. This reflected the need to determine lessons learnt for the future and safety of air shows and the public. The Flying Display director opposed this, indicating complexity of evidence, presumably citing the public as in the jury's difficulty in potentially understanding technical evidence, but also the length of time and the cost for such an inquest to be held.[75]

7.64   Section 7 of the 2009 Act includes a presumption that an inquest will be held without a jury unless the circumstances under s 7(2) apply. Had criminal proceedings not been instigated, an inquest with a jury would have been required under s 7(2)(c) as the circumstances gave rise to a notifiable accident.[76] However s 7(3) of the 2009 Act permits discretion exercised by the senior coroner having considered (i) the wishes of the family,[77] (ii) submissions made on behalf of any other interested persons, (iii) whether the facts were covered by the mandatory provisions, (iv) the circumstances of the death, and (v) any uncertainties in the medical evidence. A coroner could provide explanations which could be open to public scrutiny in a way that the jury could not do.

7.65   The contrast of juries and inquests with Scotland is obvious. Scotland abolished the use of juries in FAIs, following the 1976 Act. That change introduced by the 1976 Act meant that FAIs would be held by a sheriff sitting alone instead of a sheriff sitting with a jury of seven people. 'This should effect a considerable saving of time and expense.' It would seek to avoid 'the use of juries in such inquiries [that] had ceased to be useful, with the jury merely rubber-stamping a verdict dictated by the sheriff'.[78] The perspective that juries made of lay members may bring is of course a focus on the English coronial system by ensuring that lay representation and effecting public scrutiny. There is currently no discussion of bringing back such a jury system within the criticism being made of FAIs in Scotland. A contrast may be made perhaps in discussing the suggestions that the jury would be removed in the criminal prosecution of certain offences justified on the basis that there is evidence of jurors misunderstanding key issues.[79] That

---

75   These were not considered relevant as administrative costs and inconvenience were not relevant factors.

76   Schedule 1 para 11(3) of the 2009 Act applies so that an inquest plus a jury is no longer mandatory in such cases.

77   *R (Paul) v Deputy Coroner of the Queen's Household and the Assistant Deputy Coroner for Surrey* [2008] QB 172; [2007] Inquest LR 259.

78   *Hansard*, Fatal Accidents and Sudden Deaths Inquiry (Scotland) Bill Lords Vol 906, *https:// hansard.parliament.uk/Commons/1976-03-02/debates/d4447ba4-decd-4dc4-94f6-bd040827a769/ FatalAccidents AndSuddenDeathsInquiry(Scotland)BillLords* (accessed on 21 February 2023).

79   Scottish Government, Publication – Consultation paper, Improving victims' experiences of the justice system: consultation (12 May 2022), *www.gov.scot/publications/improving-victims-experiences-justice-system/pages/11/* (accessed on 21 February 2023).

criticism appears to echo the issues for not having the inquest held with a jury and discussed in the Horsham air show inquiry. However, would there be scope to introduce a jury FAI system where there were significant issues of public concern? That might be a way forward if the criticism were directed at any determinations not being fair or impartial. Though determinations do not follow a consistent style, and lack detail and may indeed empathy, at times, any criticism has not focused on the need fundamentally to change the system back to a jury and FAI. Costs in so doing would inevitably focus as a considerable constraint.

11. DOES THE INQUEST REQUIRE A JURY?

7.66   The coroner will often sit alone to hear an inquest, but in the circumstances outlined under s 7 of the 2009 Act, a jury is required. These circumstances include where the death:

- occurred in prison or similar place of detention or in police custody, or resulted from an injury caused by a police officer(s) in the purported execution of their duty.

7.67   Other circumstances include where deaths were:

- caused by an accident, poisoning or disease reportable to the relevant government department or inspector appointed under s 19 of the Health and Safety at Work etc Act 1974;
- in circumstances where the continuance or reoccurrence of these circumstances is prejudicial to public health;
- was unnatural, sudden or unexpected or in other suspicious circumstances.

7.68   The Attorney General can exercise their public interest function independent of the government, to apply[80] to the High Court to hold an inquest. This may arise where a coroner has refused or neglected to hold an inquest where one should have been held or where an inquest has been held and it is in the interests of justice that another inquest should be held.[81] The Attorney General made such a request in connection with the victims of the Hillsborough football stadium but not with regard to an inquest into the death of Dr David Kelly, the government scientist. An inquest was opened in his case but never resumed with the suicide verdict delivered by the report on the Hutton inquiry.[82]

---

80   Or a third party with the Attorney General's consent.
81   Section 13 of the Coroners Act 1988 amended by the Coroners and Justice Act 2009 (Consequential Provisions) Order 2013.
82   Lord Hutton, Report of the Inquiry into the Circumstances Surrounding the Death of Dr David Kelly CMG.

12.DETERMINATION FROM INQUESTS

7.69   Under s 9C of the 2009 Act,[83] the preference is that the jury verdict should be unanimous. A majority verdict can be recorded either if one or two of the jury do not agree or the senior coroner thinks it reasonable after the jurors have deliberated for a period of time. Alternatively, the jury can be discharged, and another jury brought in.

7.70   In making a determination, the senior coroner or the jury must (a) make a determination as to the questions mentioned and (b) if particulars are required by the 1953 Act to be registered concerning the death, make a finding as to those particulars. Section 10 (2) of the 2009 Act requires that no determination of any question of criminal liability on the part of a named person, or civil liability can be made. This reflects fully a similar position in Scotland with an FAI.

7.71   Under s 9C of the 2009 Act, known as a r 23 inquest or documentary hearing,[84] inquests without a jury can be conducted at a hearing or if the senior coroner decides a hearing is unnecessary, in writing. That cannot be decided unless (a) they have invited representations from each interested persons known to the coroner, (b) no interested person has represented on reasonable grounds that a hearing should take place, (c) it appears to the coroner that there is no real prospect of disagreement among interested persons as to the determinations or findings that the inquest could or should make, and (d) it appears to the coroner that no public interest would be served by a hearing. These changes reflect inquests undertaken during the pandemic and these measures have been retained to help the efficient and effective administration. Directions allow remote observation of in-person and hybrid hearings which enables more participants to attend inquest hearings remotely.[85] These mirror similar provisions that were introduced in Scotland as a result of the pandemic to allow remote hearing to be held. These provisions still continue in effect with their use most interestingly, referred in a recent FAI at paragraph [1] to being a 'formal' hearing FAI.[86] Presumably this is meant to be an FAI where '[t]he evidence before me took the form of witness statements, documentary productions and a Crown notice to admit on the basis of which I find the following matters established.'

7.72   **Inquest conclusions:** Section 10 of the 2009 Act requires the coroner (or the jury if there is one) to make a 'determination' of the matters to be ascertained by the investigation and to make 'findings' for registration of death purposes. The s 10 'determination' and 'findings' must be recorded on the Record of Inquest. The

---

83   Judicial Review and Courts Act 2022 , ss 40(2), 51(3).
84   Chief Coroner's Guidance No 29 Inquests in Writing and Rule 23 Evidence (28 June 2022), *www.judiciary.uk/guidance-and-resources/chief-coroners-guidance-no-29-inquests-in-writing-and-rule-23-evidence/* (accessed on 21 February 2023).
85   Under s 85A of the Courts Act 2003 inserted by s 198 of the Police, Crime, Sentencing and Courts Act 2022 and implemented by the Remote Observation and Recording (Courts and Tribunals) Regulations 2022, courts and tribunals including the coroners courts.
86   FAI into the death of Steven John Redpath [2023] FAI 2.

Record of Inquest should be available for public inspection at the coroner's office on request. The signatures of jurors should be redacted as should the address of the deceased, if required. Redaction otherwise is only undertaken where the public interest requires it.

7.73   At the end of the evidence and additional to determining the medical cause of death, the coroner will:

- Make findings of fact based upon the evidence heard. If a coroner acts on their own, they should state the key findings of fact orally in open court. Where there is a jury, the jury need to be directed to make findings of fact based upon the evidence. These are not recorded in public unless they are part of a narrative conclusion.
- record 'how' the deceased came by their death. This includes a description of the death such as 'by hanging from an exposed beam using a ligature made from a bedsheet' (with the conclusion of 'suicide' entered). It includes the date and place of death where this is known and, where necessary, any further words which briefly explain how the deceased came by their death. It should not include an opinion other than on matters which are the subject of statutory determination.[87]
- The conclusion should be recorded on the Record of Inquest.

7.74   Conclusions[88] can be in either a short form or narrative style. In more complex cases, the coroner will invite submissions from interested persons in relation to the type of conclusion. Where there is a jury, they will outline the short-form conclusions that the coroner is considering leaving to the jury, what written directions will be given to the jury (including in what order the jury should consider the conclusions), and what questions (if any) may be asked of them. The coroner can rule on any of these submissions.

7.75   A short-form conclusion is simple, accessible and clear, in the style provided in the Notes to Form 2 of the Schedule to the 2013 Rules. These include, among others, accident or misadventure, lawful /unlawful killing,[89] road traffic collisions and open. As an 'alternative' to a short-form conclusion, the coroner (or the jury, if so directed by the coroner) may record a 'brief narrative conclusion'.

7.76   An open conclusion is the conclusion used when another short-form conclusion has not been proved. Where an open conclusion is left to a jury with one

---

87   It must not determine any question of criminal liability on the part of a named person or civil liability.

88   Chief Coroner, Guidance No 17, Conclusions: Short-form and Narrative, *www.judiciary.uk/wp-content/uploads/2021/09/GUIDANCE-No-17-CONCLUSIONS-7-September-2021.pdf* (accessed on 21 February 2023).

89   The conclusion of unlawful killing is restricted to the criminal offences of murder, manslaughter (including corporate manslaughter) and infanticide. Cases where driving causes death may, therefore, only be regarded as unlawful killing for inquest purposes if they satisfy the ingredients for manslaughter (gross negligence manslaughter) or where a vehicle is used as a weapon of assault and deliberately driven at a person who dies (murder or manslaughter depending on the intent).

or more other short-form conclusions, the coroner should tell them (a) not to use the conclusion because they disagree amongst themselves on the other short-form conclusion(s) and (b) if they do come to an open conclusion, not to consider that they will be criticised for it or that they have failed in their duty in any way.

7.77 An open conclusion, once entered and recorded, may not be revisited without the intervention of the High Court. In some cases, a narrative conclusion will be preferable to an open conclusion. A narrative will give the coroner (or jury) the opportunity to state what findings are made and what are not. The detailed nature of the directions given to the jury can be seen at the inquest into the deaths of Fishmongers Hall.[90]

7.78 **Appendix 1** refers to the coronial process.

13. PREVENT FUTURE DEATH (PFD) REPORTS (REGULATION 28 REPORTS)

7.79 The coroner is under a duty to make a report to prevent other deaths under para 7(1) of Sch 5 to the 2009 Act.[91] The senior coroner conducting the investigation into the death determines anything revealed by the investigation that gives rise to a concern where circumstances creating a risk of other deaths will occur, or will continue to exist, in the future. The coroner must report the matter to a person who the coroner believes may have power to take where action should be taken to prevent the occurrence or continuation of such circumstances, or to eliminate or reduce the risk of death created by such circumstances. This is similar to the powers of a sheriff under s 26 of the 2016 Act to consider making recommendations. There is a requirement too to publish such recommendations when made in FAIs in Scotland. Similarly the Chief Coroner's office publishes the PFD reports.[92] Under para 7(2) of Sch 5 to the 2009 Act, a person to whom the senior coroner makes a report must give them a written response. The UK Parliament Justice Committee considered that the information being published was the minimum and was difficult to search and analyse. They recommended that the Ministry of Justice should provide funding so that PFD reports and responses to them were freely available online and that the information was well-organised and easily searchable.[93] These mirror observations

---

90 *https://fishmongershallinquests.independent.gov.uk/wp-content/uploads/2021/06/Saskia-Jones-and-Jack-Merritt-Inquests-Jury-Legal-Directions-2.pdf* (accessed on 25 November 2022).
91 Paragraphs 28 and 29 of the Coroners (Investigations) Regulations 2013 (SI 2013/1629).
92 Courts and Tribunals Judiciary, *Coroner training overview, www.judiciary.uk/publication-jurisdiction/coroner/* (accessed on 21 February 2023).
93 The Coroner Service Report. *https://publications.parliament.uk/pa/cm5802/cmselect/cmjust/68/6802.htm* (accessed on 21 February 2023). On 27 May 2021 the Justice Committee published its First Report of Session 2021–22, The Coroner Service (HC 68), the Government's Response was received on 27 July 2021.

made in relation to public searchability and access to SCTS's publication of FAIs in Scotland.

7.80 A copy of the PFD Report must be sent to the Chief Coroner and to every interested person who in the coroner's opinion should receive a copy. If it involves a deceased person believed to be under 18, a copy is sent to the appropriate Local Safeguarding Children Board. A copy of the report will also be sent to any other person who the coroner believes may find it useful or of interest.

7.81 Under reg 29(3), a response must contain details of any action that has been taken or which it is proposed will be taken by the person giving the response or any other person whether in response to the report or otherwise. It should set out a timetable of the action taken or proposed to be taken or an explanation as to why no action is proposed. Under reg 29(4), the response must be provided to the coroner who made the report within 56 days, though this period can be extended. Copies of all responses will be sent to the Lord Chancellor, who may publish the response or a summary of it, unless the coroner has exercised their power to request a restriction to the publication to the Chief Coroner.[94]

7.82 In response to the Justice Committee recommendations,[95] the number of PFD reports issued by coroners is now included in their annual statistics as outlined above. It was seen for the first time in the reports made in 2019/2020 and 2020/2021.[96]

7.83 There were 440 PFD Reports made in 2021. These included reports made to the Department of Health and Social Care, NHS England and HM Prison and Probation Service. The reports covered:

- community healthcare;
- care home health related deaths;
- hospital death (clinical procedures and medical management);
- mental health related deaths.

7.84 The Chief Coroner has issued guidance[97] on PFD Reports which was last revised in November 2020. It stresses some key features in the context of lessons to be learnt from the death in seeking out changes to avoid future deaths occurring. As para 4 indicates, the role of the PFD should be 'to improve public health, welfare and safety' and should be 'clear, brief, focused, meaningful and, wherever possible, designed to have practical effect'.

94 Paragraph 29(10) of the Coroners (Investigations) Regulations 2013 (SI 2013/1629).
95 MoJ, National Statistics, *Coroners Statistics 2021: England and Wales* (12 May 2022), *www.gov.uk/ government/statistics/coroners-statistics-2021/coroners-statistics-2021-england-and-wales#fn:18* (accessed on 21 February 2023).
96 MoJ, National Statistics, *Coroners Statistics 2021: England and Wales* (12 May 2022), *www. gov.uk/government/statistics/coroners-statistics-2021/coroners-statistics-2021-england-and-wales#prevention-of-future-death-reports* (accessed on 21 February 2023).
97 Chief Coroner, Revised Guidance No 5. Report to prevent future deaths, *www.judiciary.uk/wp-content/uploads/2020/11/GUIDANCE-No.-5-REPORTS-TO-PREVENT-FUTURE-DEATHS.pdf* (accessed on 21 February 2023).

7.85   Where a potential PFD recipient has already implemented appropriate action to address the risk of future fatalities, such as in cases of medical deaths, the coroner need not make a report. Their decision will be made on a case-by-case basis, though a PFD report to a relevant national organisation to highlight the issues more widely may still be appropriate. By contrast, recommendations are infrequently made in FAIs. They seem not to be made where circumstances would seem to justify their use about raising awareness of the systemic nature of a death. These circumstances may well arise in relation to medical deaths and prison deaths which might be of general application respectively to the Heath Service or to SPS.

7.86   Why might this be helpful? Actions to improve systems may not yet have been fully implemented and may still be ongoing. Factors that merit robust examination include the nature of the commitment of the organisation involved in the death to take action, to ensure that they seekout any evidence in support of the recommendations, and the coroner's assessment of the organisation's understanding of, and commitment to addressing, the area of concern.

7.87   The coroner should not detail what action should be taken and should only raise issues as outlined by Hallett LJ.[98] 'However, it is neither necessary, nor appropriate, for a coroner making a report under rule 43[99] to identify what any necessary remedial action may comprise. As is apparent from the final words of rule 43(1), the coroner's function is to identify points of concern, not to prescribe solutions.' The language in such reports should be moderate, avoiding emotive concepts.

7.88   As with FAIs, there is an absence of any powers of enforcement in relation to any recommendations that are made by the coroner. This was seen in the inquest into the Lakahal House deaths in 2013 which arose in a high-rise flat fire. The Regulation 28 Report outlined to the Secretary of State that there should be a review of the stay put policies during a fire.[100] These recommendations were not followed which were then seen to be relevant to the circumstances of the Grenfell fire in 2017.

7.89   Examples of Recommendation 28 Reports are provided in **Appendix 1 Part G**. These include the death of Ella Roberta Adoo Kissi-Debrah, Billy Longshaw and Molly Russell.

14.   PROCESS AT AN INQUEST

7.90   Coroners have the power to call witnesses to appear at an inquest, and to determine the evidence that is to be heard. There is a general duty of every citizen

---

98   7/7 Bombings Inquests, p 15.
99   Prior to para 7 of Schedule 5 to the 2009 Act
100 Belfast Telegraph, *'Stay put' advice exceptions left out of fire guidance, Grenfell inquiry hears* (9 March 2022) *www.belfasttelegraph.co.uk/news/uk/stay-put-advice-exceptions-left-out-of-fire-guidance-grenfell-inquiry-hears-41429173.html* (accessed on 21 February 2023).

to attend an inquest if they are in possession of any information or evidence that details how a person came to their death. Notification to appear as a witness will generally be informal, but a coroner can, if required, issue a summons for attendance or to produce documents. The contrast with the FAI is that the witnesses there are called by the parties seeking to obtain their evidence. The majority of witnesses will therefore lie with the Crown to call. On occasion, they may well facilitate other parties by calling witnesses whose testimony is required by other parties. The sheriff can request them to do so as well.

7.91   Once sworn in, a witness may refuse to answer any questions put to them on the grounds of self-incrimination.[101] Again, this is similar to the position in Scotland.

7.92   All inquests are held in public (except where the 'interests of justice or national security' apply). Coroners can hold sections of inquests privately[102] although this will only apply to a specific part of the hearing.[103]

7.93   Coroners can impose reporting restrictions to avoid any prejudice to the administration of justice.

15. MISCELLANEOUS

7.94   There are a couple of processes within the coroner system which are worth highlighting when illustrating the differences between the two countries. The incorporation of such provisions might usefully be considered in Scotland.

7.95   **Pen portrait:** The Chief Coroner's Guidance Note No 41[104] sets out the process for bringing a pen portrait of the deceased to the attention of the inquest, reflecting a practice that has been developed even in short inquests. Though an FAI may have evidence led by the family at the start of the process as to what they would like the FAI to achieve, there has not been a general practice of leading evidence about the person who has died. At the discretion of the coroner, they permit the family to bring material to the inquest as to what the deceased did, including their interests, hobbies and 'details of their wider circle of family and friends', including providing family photographs. That allows the press at the outset of the inquest to report on the person who has died. In the Manchester arena bombing, the tributes to those who died at the concert were screened on YouTube[105] That has helped to

---

101 Rule 22 of the Coroners (Inquests) Rules 2013 (SI 2013/1616).
102 Rule 11 of the Coroners (Inquest) Rules 2013 (SI 2013/1616).
103 Sections 6–11 of the Justice and Security Act 2013 (c.18).
104 Courts and Tribunals Judiciary, Chief Coroner's Guidance No 41 Use of 'Pen Portrait' Material (5 July 2021), *www.judiciary.uk/guidance-and-resources/chief-coroners-guidance-no-41-use-of-pen-portrait-material1/* (accessed on 21 February 2023).
105 BBC, Manchester Arena Inquiry: Relatives present 'pen portraits' for second day (15 September 2020), *www.bbc.co.uk/news/uk-england-manchester-54164952*; ITV News, Manchester Arena Inquiry: Victims' 'pen porraits' heard in court, *www.youtube.com/watch?v=3eZd48ikqvY* (accessed on 21 February 2023).

'humanise the process, give dignity to the bereaved and – importantly – be one part of honouring the duty to keep the family at the heart of the inquest process'.[106]

7.96   Disclosure: This is the subject of specific guidance issued by the Chief Coroner under Guidance Note No 44.[107] The sheriff can require evidence to be brought forward in an FAI, though this is relatively unusual given that the sheriff will rely on the evidence led by the Crown and the parties to the FAI. There are no disclosure requirements formalised, though gathering of evidence is set out under Sch 5 to the FAI Rules. Looking to the practice in England and Wales, the function of the coroner fully reflects the inquisitorial nature of the inquest as 'marshalling evidence is a judicial function' but the 'evidence needs to be relevant, reasonable, sufficient, and proportionate to the scope of the inquest'.[108] There is no requirement on any party to abduce evidence, with the exception of the Crown, that they may have obtained which may be held back for the purpose of any subsequent civil processes. There might be a review of the FAI Rules to understand how the implications of disclosure affect the roles of the various parties to the FAI.

7.97   Training: The topic of training of the parties, including the judiciary, to undertake FAIs has been the subject of observations. The Chief Coroner's Guidance No 20[109] outlines the key skills for assistant coroners which would be those that require to be utilised too by COPFS and sheriffs. This illustrates how the coronial system differs. This is illustrated by roles undertaken by the assistant coroner[110] that can be divided into two sections, including those of:

Knowing when a doctor can provide an MCCD
Knowing when a death needs referral to the coroner
Triaging deaths; deciding which require investigation and which can be signed as Form As
Understanding the difference between preliminary inquiries and investigation
Authorising post mortems, histology, toxicology
Authorising forensic post-mortems
Approval of organ or tissue donation
Considering COD following post-mortems; approving Form Bs; discontinuance
Deaths overseas
Issuing disposal certificates

106 Wakeman, H, *Use of Pen Portrait Materials at Inquests*, TGC Inquests & Inquiries, Issue II, November 2021, 12: *https://tgchambers.com/wp-content/uploads/2021/11/TGC-Inquests_ Newsletter_IssueII_v2.pdf* (accessed on 21 February 2023).
107 Chief Coroner, Guidance No 44 Disclosure, *www.judiciary.uk/wp-content/uploads/2022/09/ GUIDANCE-No-44-DISCLOSURE-final.pdf* (accessed on 21 February 2023).
108 Ibid.
109 Courts and Tribunals Judiciary, Chief Coroner's Guidance No 20 Key Skills for Assistant Coroners (15 April 2019), *www.judiciary.uk/guidance-and-resources/chief-coroners-guidance-no-20-key- skills-for-assistant-coroners/* (accessed on 21 February 2023).
110 Ibid.

7.98   Those other functions would include those that are clearly judicial in nature:

Opening inquests and fixing dates for future hearings
Provision of disclosure
Knowing when and how to hold a PIR hearing
Conducting straight-forward inquests; R23 inquests
Completing Records of Inquest
Transfers between coroner areas
Out of England orders

7.99   **Faith requirements:** The Chief Coroner's Guidance Note No 28 provides guidance as to how coroners should handle urgent decisions where there are features of a particular death justifying it being handled as urgent. Similar problems can arise in Scotland where the body of the deceased is required to be released to allow certain faith requirements to be observed timeously.

7.100   In *R (Adath Yisroel Burial Society) v Senior Coroner for Inner North London*,[111] it held that a coroner could not lawfully exclude religious reasons for seeking expedition of decisions made by that coroner, including the coroner's decision whether to release a body for burial. However, not all cases are required to be treated in a strictly chronological sequence as the coroner has discretion to assign which cases have priority. This is very much reflective of the discretion afforded to the Lord Advocate with their exercise too of a 'margin of judgment'.

7.101   Decisions about enquiries to be made (including post mortem examinations), or about concluding investigations and releasing bodies for burial, are judicial decisions in England and Wales but in Scotland are decisions for the procurator fiscal to take in each case. While decision making can be subject to judicial review, the guess is that it is unlikely to arise as by the time of a court hearing the circumstances would have already been resolved.

7.102   Two key factors were stressed: that a coroner should be open to representations that a particular case should be treated as a matter of urgency (whether for religious or other reasons) and that proper respect should be given to representations based on religious belief.

7.103   Though these circumstances have not directly arisen in Scotland, a statement of practice would set out transparency and allow for consistency of process.

---

111   [2018] EWHC 969 (Admin) at [160].

Chapter 8

Sudden Death Investigations Abroad – Process and Practice

1. INTRODUCTION

8.01   The focus of this book is on the sudden death inquiry and investigation system that exists in Scotland. **Chapter 7** considered the coronial and inquest system which is established and operates in England and Wales. However, no detailed examination of the topic of sudden death investigations would be complete without a basic comparison in understanding how other countries deal with their processes and investigations into sudden deaths. This chapter considers:

- What happens when there are deaths of UK nationals abroad (looking separately at Scotland and England and Wales).
- A brief overview of the sudden death procedures in various countries.

8.02   Northern Ireland and Ireland follow the coronial system of England and Wales. These countries, along with other common law countries, adopt the coronial (English) system. These include Australia, Canada and the USA.

8.03   To provide a contrast, the civil law jurisdictions in Europe of Germany and France are both examined. There are historic reasons why these systems have all developed separately in the way that they have, and broadly, which reflects their culture and traditions.

8.04   The common law countries, including Scotland, generally investigate sudden deaths fully even where there is no suspicion that any crime has been committed. Civil law countries, largely, investigate sudden deaths to ascertain or indeed exclude that these have been caused as the result of a crime. The actual inquiry, in common law countries whether an inquest or an FAI, are generally carried out in public (closed courts are seen as the exception). With investigations in civil law countries the inquiry is held in private, resulting in the issue of a much-contracted form of death certificate. Information as to the cause and circumstances of a death are seen there to be about maintaining privacy, rather than a matter of public record.

8.05   Of course, there is a balance to be struck between the invasive processes involved in a post mortem examination and inquest or an FAI, where both require a very high degree of public scrutiny of the circumstances of the death when compared to the private interest of relatives in the deceased person's death. The focus of the common law system is the interest in learning lessons from a death which overrides the confidentiality vested and maintained in the civil law system.

8.06   The investigation into death system of FAIs in Scotland under COPFS and the procurator fiscal is unique. It is commonly described as a mixed system, incorporating practices from both the civilian and common law systems. Its aims in investigating sudden deaths and lessons learnt to echo the public interest similar to those of the English and Welsh coronial practice. The finding and publication of a determination in an FAI is a factual process, similar to the English inquest and its conclusion. However, in Scotland, the determinations that are publicly issued are much longer and more detailed than those issued in England and Wales – though they may vary in consistency and in information that is provided. Arguably, recommendations where issued in Scotland may lack the force at times of the comparative Regulation 28 reports made in England.[1]

8.07   There are other examples of mixed systems, such as Malta and the Channel Islands.

8.08   The coronial process reflects the background to the system which developed from 1194, when the Office of Coroner[2] was established, and related to a form of collecting medieval taxes. It is now a system of an independent judicial officer investigating sudden, violent or unnatural death. Historically, investigations into deaths resulted where persons were found guilty of murder. In these circumstances, their estates fell to be forfeited to the Crown (this practice still exists for both England and Wales in recovery of treasure[3] and in Scotland with COPFS being responsible for *ultimus haeres*[4]).

---

1   The Money Laundering, Terrorist Financing and Transfer of Funds (Information on the Payer) Regulations 2017 (SI 2017/692), *www.legislation.gov.uk/uksi/2017/692/regulation/28/made* (accessed on 21 February 2023)
2   *www.justice.ie/en/JELR/ReviewCoronerService.pdf/Files/ReviewCoronerService.pdf* (accessed on 21 February 2023).
3   Coroners Act 1988 (c.13), s 30.
4   King's and Lord Treasurer's Remembrancer, *www.kltr.gov.uk/* (accessed on 21 February 2023).

8.09   The coroner system has adapted over the years from when the Births and Deaths Registration Act 1836 was passed, which represented the start of requiring the formal certification of deaths. This was promoted by the need to record accurate statistics of the actual numbers of deaths arising at that time from epidemics such as cholera. There are obvious similarities in the purpose with the emergency legislation passed to ascertain and ensure the accurate reporting of deaths that occurred from the Covid-19 pandemic which simplified processes to allow for the numbers who had died.

8.10   From a historical perspective, as a result of the English systems being embedded, many of the original British colonies have adopted investigation into sudden deaths that are similar to the coronial system. What is in common with Europe and the UK is how death investigations interact with the obligations set out under Art 2 of the ECHR.

2.   SCOTLAND AND ENGLAND AND WALES WHERE DEATHS OF NATIONALS OCCUR ABROAD

8.11   **General:** The Scottish Government advises if the death happens outside Scotland, the death can be arranged as a local burial or cremation in that country, or the body brought back to Scotland. This choice applies equally to England and Wales.

8.12   A death certificate or the equivalent is required. Permission is required from the appropriate authorities to move the body out of the country where the death occurred. For more information, Healthcare Improvement Scotland is responsible for the Death Certification Review Service[5] which was discussed in **Chapter 1** which outlined the process to be followed where deaths occurred abroad and were required to be reported to the Scottish authorities.

8.13   If someone dies in England or Wales, permission from a coroner is required to move the body for a funeral outside that country. There is a need to apply at least four days before the body is to be moved.[6] Advice is then provided on the formal processes if a death arises abroad. It outlines that contact should be made with the Tell Us Once[7] service in order to report a death to most government organisations at one time. The Tell Us Once service operates if the person who died normally lived in England, Scotland or Wales and was abroad temporarily (for example, on holiday or a business trip).[8]

---

5   Healthcare Improvement Scotland, *Death Certification in Scotland*, *www.
    healthcareimprovementscotland.org/our_work/governance_and_assurance/death_certification.
    aspx* (accessed on 21 February 2023).
6   *www.mygov.scot/death-abroad* (accessed on 21 February 2023).
7   Gov.uk, *Tell Us Once*, *www.gov.uk/after-a-death/organisations-you-need-to-contact-and-tell-us-
    once* (accessed on 21 February 2023).
8   Gov.uk, *What to do if someone dies abroad*, *www.gov.uk/after-a-death/death-abroad* (accessed on
    21 February 2023).

8.14   **Scotland:** where a death of a person ordinarily resident in Scotland arises outside the UK, under s 6 of the Inquiries into Fatal Accidents and Sudden Deaths etc. (Scotland) Act 2016 (asp 2) (the 2016 Act) the Lord Advocate can hold an inquiry into the death if it was sudden, suspicious, unexplained or occurred in circumstances giving rise to serious public concern. Under s 6(3)(b)–(d) of the 2016 Act, the Lord Advocate needs to consider that the circumstances of the death have not been sufficiently established in the course of an investigation in relation to the death, and there is a real prospect that these circumstances would be sufficiently established in holding an FAI. Furthermore, it needs to be in the public interest for an inquiry to be held into the circumstances of the death.

8.15   Since the 2016 Act commenced, no FAI has yet been instructed into any such death, though there are several ongoing campaigns, including those relating to the deaths of Kirsty Maxwell and Craig Mallon depicted in a BBC documentary *Killed Abroad*, to do so. What is clear from the 2016 Act is that there is no intention to duplicate the investigation process where such deaths of nationals arise in England and Wales, since s 6(1)(a) refers specifically to deaths outside the UK. That process remains with the coroner.

8.16   In the case of *R v West Yorkshire Coroner, ex parte Smith*[9] the applicant challenged the refusal of the coroner to hold an inquest into the death of his daughter in Rhodesia. It held that coroners in England and Wales are under a duty to investigate a death which occurred overseas if both the body is returned to the coroner's district and the circumstances are such that an investigation would have been conducted if the death had occurred in England and Wales. These provisions are much wider than the equivalent Scottish measures.

8.17   Coroners in England and Wales are under a duty to investigate deaths that occur overseas where the body is repatriated and the circumstances require.[10] These deaths include those that were as the result of violence or were unnatural, or where the cause of death is unknown, or where the person died in prison, police custody or another form of state detention. The coroner may seek to instruct a post mortem report in addition to any such report which may have been produced abroad.

8.18   Coroners have statutory powers, in addition to their common law powers, to compel evidence to be given in connection with such an inquest. Such witnesses may well choose in any event to participate in the inquest. However as these powers do not reach beyond the England and Wales's jurisdiction, there may be difficulties in effecting these where the evidence or witnesses in question are located overseas.

8.19   The coroner has the power to summon witnesses and to compel the production of evidence for the purposes of an investigation (para 1(2) of Sch 5 to the 2019 Act) or an inquest (para 1(1) of Sch 5 to the 2019 Act) by way of written notice.

---

9   [1983] QB 335.
10   Coroners and Justice Act 2009 (c.25), s 1.

Attendance can also be facilitated by r 17 of The Coroners (Inquests) Rules 2013,[11] which permits the coroner to direct that a witness may give evidence via video link where appropriate. If an overseas witness cannot or will not attend the inquest (either in person or via video-link), the coroner may be able to use r 23 of the 2013 Rules to admit evidence by way of written statements. Rule 23 can only be relied upon where all reasonable steps have been taken to try and secure the attendance of relevant witnesses. This would be in order to ensure the sufficiency of evidence in relation to the inquest.

8.20   Requests for information from foreign authorities can be directed to the Foreign, Commonwealth & Development Office Consular Directorate's Coroners' Liaison Officer in terms of the Murder, Manslaughter and Infanticide of British Nationals Abroad Memorandum of Understanding between the Foreign, Commonwealth & Development Office and National Police Chief's Council and the Chief Coroner of England and Wales.[12]

8.21   Since the coroner's powers are limited, they cannot compel either the disclosure of documentation or witnesses. In the death of Shafi,[13] it was recognised that 'there is only so much that a coroner can do to obtain evidence from a foreign state, however friendly'.[14] '[E]xperience shows that there must come a time when coroners have to be realistic and when no useful purpose would be served in deferring the hearing of the inquest further. At that stage, the coroner must proceed with the inquest on the basis of the material (even if limited) before him, so long as he is satisfied that it would be in the interests of justice to do so.'[15] In Shafi,[16] a challenge had been made regarding the coroner's approach in obtaining CCTV material that had not been forthcoming from Dubai.

8.22   Looking to the outcome of the inquest into a death abroad, the coroner can still issue Prevention of Further Death (PFD) reports. The Shepherd inquest[17] involved the death of two children from carbon monoxide poisoning in a hotel in Corfu. The Greek hotel group was an interested party in the proceedings, so that the PFD report was addressed to them together with the British tour operator, the travel industry bodies and government departments. The matters of concern outlined in the report were, however, focused primarily on actions that could be taken by the British recipients to ensure health and safety standards were upheld overseas.

---

11   SI 2013/1616.
12   *Murder Manslaughter and Infanticide of British Nationals Abroad*, *www.judiciary.uk/wp-content/ uploads/2021/07/MoU-with-the-Foreign-Commonwealth-and-Development-Office-and-National-Police-Chiefs-Council.pdf* (accessed on 21 February 2023).
13   *Dorish Shafi v HM Coroner for East London* [2015] EWHC 2106 (Admin).
14   Ibid at [26].
15   Ibid at [30].
16   Ibid.
17   Inquests touching the deaths of Christianne Shepherd and Robert Shepherd *www.judiciary.uk/wp-content/uploads/2015/10/Shepherd-2015-0338.pdf* (accessed on 21 February 2023).

8.23 38 holiday makers were killed when a gunman opened up with an assault rifle in Sousse, Tunisia on 26 June 2015. An inquest was held into the death of the 30 British nationals, of whom four were Scottish. There was no point in holding a separate FAI into their deaths – and this incident preceded changes brought in the 2016 Act that would have allowed an FAI to be held where the death occurred abroad.[18] The interest in learning from the deaths was the same which related to the tourists having travelled to Tunisia when the Foreign Office was warning against travel there.

8.24 The Coroner may therefore hold an inquest into a death of an English national in Scotland. The Cameron House fire involving Simon Midgely and Richard Dyson illustrates the operation of these provisions. Following the inquest, Kevin McLoughlin, Senior Coroner for the coroner area of West Yorkshire, sent a Regulation 28 Report to the UK Government. This confirmed that on 29 December 2017, he had commenced an investigation into their deaths. The inquest's conclusion, reached on 14 April 2021, was that they had been unlawfully killed as a result of (a) inhalation of smoke and fire gases and (b) hotel fire. The coroner went on to outline concerns that revealed matters which could cause future deaths unless action was taken (the basis of Regulation 28 Reports). These concerns included that:

> 'Every hotel should have a readily accessible an accurate list of the guests and staff members in an establishment on a particular night. In an emergency, it is imperative that the Fire and Rescue Service are provided with accurate information speedily in case anyone remains trapped in a building. It is a situation in which every second occurs.
>
> It is foreseeable that in the stressful atmosphere of an emergency, people may hesitate or make mistakes. In this case, forgetting to take the guest list as the building was evacuated. In consequence, although the Fire and Rescue Service had arrived at the hotel at 6.51am, it was not until sometime after 8am that it was established that two guests were missing. Critical time was lost before rescue efforts began to find them. The precise times cannot be provided as the Procurator Fiscal was not willing to disclose copies of the witness statements or reports on the grounds that they were confidential.
>
> To avoid needless impediments to rescue efforts, it would be prudent for hotels to have an electronic system such as SharePoint which would enable the emergency services to gain prompt access to such vital information.'[19]

---

18   Regulation 28 report to prevent future deaths, *www.judiciary.uk/wp-content/uploads/2017/07/Sousse-Inquest-2017-0206.pdf* (accessed on 21 February 2023).

19   The FAI into the deaths of Simon Midgely and Richard Dyson [2023] FAI 1 has now concluded in Scotland with the issue of the determination, In making his findings, the sheriff reflected a concern over the available information regarding the guests in the hotel at section F7 in terms of s 26(2)(g) of the 2016 Act (any other facts relevant to the circumstances of the deaths) that '(a) Due to the delay in obtaining a guest list there was a delay in carrying out an accurate roll call'.

8.25   Interestingly, though the Regulation 28 Report was not directed to the Scottish Government, (and they were a copy recipient), the response was sent by Ash Denholm MSP Minister for Community Safety, dated 11 June 2021. She recognised that there was a need for 'learning from incidents and investigations, including your report, albeit Regulation 28 of the Coroners (Investigations) Regulations 2013 does not extend to Scotland (the coroner system only applying in England and Wales)'. What the original response perhaps illustrates is some tension in how these systems in Scotland and England and Wales cross border inter-relate.

8.26   The Scottish Government's Fire Safety Guidance for existing premises with sleeping accommodation was published in 2018. It recommended that the premises management should have an emergency fire action plan in place, specific to the premises, that should include procedures for checking whether the premises have been evacuated, and for meeting the Scottish Fire and Rescue Service and passing on details of the incident, including whether all persons are accounted for. Reference was then made to actions being taken to strengthen fire safety in the hotel accommodation sector, including refreshing wider prevention and protection awareness and disseminating key points from the investigation internally. It also included working with the hotel sector to ensure that lessons are learned and engaging with duty holders to ensure they are aware of their fire safety responsibilities and the potential consequences of failing to address any shortcomings.

8.27   It also mentioned preparing a public education campaign on fire action plans and escape routes. Time will tell how the recommendations which went further than only the guests list will be responded to. These included that 'owners or operators of hotels or similar sleeping accommodation in Scotland should ensure that clear and robust arrangements are in place for promptly ensuring all persons are accounted for in the event of evacuation of such accommodation in the event of a fire, such arrangements, where possible, to address foreseeable contingencies such as difficulties in accessing guest lists, or inclement weather' and '[t]he Scottish Government should consider introducing for future conversions of historic buildings to be used as hotel accommodation a requirement to have active fire suppression systems installed'.[20]

8.28   The coroner in England and Wales has held inquests into deaths of their nationals abroad, such as Lady Diana's death in Paris.[21]

3.   DEATH INVESTIGATIONS ABROAD

8.29   These have been categorised into three headings which include examples from the coronial system, the civil law system, and mixed systems, which have a

---

20   [2023] FAI 1.
21   Following the inquest, the jury decided on 7 April 2008 that Diana had been unlawfully killed by the 'grossly negligent driving of the following vehicles [the paparazzi] and of the Mercedes driver Henri Paul'.

number of similarities to those practices in Scotland. There is not the opportunity to discuss any of the systems in each country in detail. If this is required, as a starting point, a reference should be made to the comprehensive handbook on inquests *Jervis on Coroners*, 14th edn,[22] at Pt V1 on the International Dimension.

Coronial system

Ireland

8.30   The statutory office of coroner in Ireland was created by the Coroners (Ireland) Act 1846 which, as in Scotland with the 1895 Act, sought to consolidate the existing law and practices. It set out the basis of the modern system of administration and outlined the role of the coroner and their duties. The Coroners (Ireland) Act 1881 followed, requiring coroners to be qualified medical practitioners, barristers or solicitors, removing any property qualification.

8.31   The current law is now governed by the Coroners Act 1962, as amended by the Coroners (Amendment) Act 2019. The 2019 Act followed the implementation of recommendations from the Working Party Review into the Coroner Service Report.[23] In effect, they sought similarly to Scotland with the introduction of the 2016 Act to bring in changes to strengthen and modernise the 'powers of coroners, clarifying and broadening the scope of enquiries at inquest and modernisation of the 1962 Act [that] will reassure the next of kin of deceased persons'.[24]

8.32   The current coroner, as an independent office holder, acts in a judicial capacity, investigating sudden and unexplained deaths, performing these quite separate from the medical profession, the Gardaí, the State or any parties with an interest in the outcome of these death investigations. Their role is similar to that in England and Wales and Scotland where they cannot attribute civil or criminal responsibility. The focus is an investigation in the public interest in order to obtain societal benefit. It states that 'the coroner service is a public service for the living, which, in recognising the core value of each human life, provides a forensic and medicolegal investigation of sudden death having due regard to public safety and health epidemiology issues'.[25]

8.33   Inquests are not limited merely to establishing the medical cause of death, but may also seek to establish the circumstances in which the death occurred.[26] As

---

22   Professor Paul Matthews, *Jervis on Coroners* (14th edn, Sweet and Marshall, 2019).
23   Review of the Coroner Service Report of the Working Group.
24   Review of the Coroner Service Report of the Working Group: *www.justice.ie/en/JELR/Pages/ Minister%20Flanagan%20announces%20further%20commencement%20of%20provisions%20 of%20the%20Coroners%20(Amendment)%20Act%202019* (accessed on 21 February 2023).
25   *The Coroner's Inquest: Patient Safety Issues, https://assets.gov.ie/11475/ c66915bc31784b9fb0c5f54377cb6f0a.pdf* (accessed on 21 February 2023).
26   Review of the Coroner Service Report of the Working Group.

outlined in the Review,[27] 'in essence, this reflects not only the reassurance given to society by such independent action but also mirrors the great value placed on life itself by our Constitution. In other words, society is demanding that no death be left un-investigated unless there is a clear and certifiable reason for that death.'

8.34   The administrative responsibilities are undertaken by the Department of Justice, Equality and Law Reform, who is responsible for the legislation and policy, the Department of the Environment and Local Government who is responsible for coroners' appointment, salaries and fees and the Department of Health and Children who pay for the relevant pathology services and post mortem facilities.

8.35   The number of deaths in 2018 is outlined the table below:

Number of deaths	Deaths reported to the coroner	Post mortem examination undertaken	Inquests conducted
31,116	17,528 (56% of all deaths)	5,467	2,092

8.36   The categories of deaths to be investigated include sudden, unnatural, violent or unexplained deaths (where a doctor cannot sign a Death Notification Form), deaths where the doctor has not attended to the deceased in the last month and deaths in a number of other categories, including Covid-19 related deaths.[28]

8.37   Ireland is, of course, a member of the European Union (EU) where the s 36 of the 2019 Act reforms sought to strengthen their law which permits the discretion to the coroner to seek High Court directions on law; the purpose of which was partly to allow for 'interpretation of the European Convention of Human Rights on a new or difficult issue'. Other reforms included:

- clarifying that the purpose of the inquest goes beyond establishing the medical cause of death, to establishing the circumstances in which death took place;
- express requirements for mandatory reporting and inquest in all maternal and late maternal deaths;
- express requirements for mandatory reporting and inquest of a death comprising those in State custody or detention;
- mandatory reporting to a coroner of all stillbirths, intrapartum deaths and infant deaths, and to enquire into a stillbirth where there is cause for concern;
- creation of an offence for a responsible person not to report a mandatory reportable death to the coroner;
- specific provisions on notice of an inquest to be provided to family members of the deceased person.

27   Review of the Coroner Service Report of the Working Group.
28   Gov.ie, *Report a death to the Coroner* (12 August 2021, updated 9 December 2021), *www.gov.ie/en/ service/e6ab3-report-a-death-to-the-coroner/* (accessed on 21 February 2023).

8.38   Under s 40 of the 1962 Act, an inquest must be held with a jury consisting of between 6–12 members in relation to homicide, deaths in prison, a notifiable accident, poisoning or disease, and deaths in circumstances prejudicial to public health or safety. Since the 2019 Act in road traffic cases, a jury is no longer required and is otherwise optional. *Jervis on Coroners*[29] suggests that there is no prescribed list of 'verdicts' in Ireland though the verdicts can include accidental death, misadventure, suicide, natural causes, unlawful killing and an open verdict. These are substantially similar to those verdicts available in England and Wales, with the exception of a finding of a lack of care/neglect.

8.39   Applications for legal aid can be made under s 60 of the 1962 Act which will be granted in certain specific cases. There is no constitutional right to legal aid.[30] Categories where legal aid may be granted include where the deceased was, at the time of their death or immediately before their death in custody,[31] a child in care, was a maternal death or a late maternal death. This also applies where the coroner is of the opinion that the death of the deceased occurred in circumstances the continuance or possible recurrence of which would be prejudicial to the health or safety of the public or any section of the public, such that there is a significant public interest in the family member of the deceased person being granted legal aid or legal advice, or both, for the purposes of the inquest.

8.40   The coroners' decisions may be subject to judicial review as in Morris v Dublin City Coroner.[32] It upheld that the coroner, in observing the requirements of natural justice and fair procedures, was entitled to conduct the inquest in the manner which they thought best adapted to serve the grounds of public interest. Here, that was justified by preserving the anonymity of the gardaí giving evidence included the screening of the gardai witnesses from the public.

8.41   As inquests are public enquiries, the post mortem report and any depositions taken at the inquest can be obtained along with a copy of the verdict. This was a source of criticism in the Death Investigation, Coroners' Inquests and the Rights of the Bereaved, A Research Report for the Irish Council on Civil Liberties.[33] These were not routinely being published where a recommendation stated that 'a redesigned web-site should publish full and thorough information'. The coroner retains their own case records with them being transferred to the County Registrar when they leave their role.

---

29   14th edn, Sweet & Maxwell, 2019.
30   *Magee v Farrell* [2009] I.E.S.C. 60.
31   In the custody of the Garda Síochána, in custody in a prison, in service custody, they were involuntarily detained under Pt 2 of the Mental Health Act 2001 or they were detained in a designated centre within the meaning of s 3 of the Criminal Law (Insanity) Act 2006 or was a person to whom s 20 of that Act refers.
32   [2000] IESC 24.
33   Irish Council for Civil Liberties, *Death Investigation, Coroners' Inquests and the Rights of the Bereaved* (April 2021), *www.iccl.ie/wp-content/uploads/2021/04/ICCL-Death-Investigations-Coroners-Inquests-the-Rights-of-the-Bereaved.pdf* (accessed on 21 February 2023).

Northern Ireland[34]

8.42   The coroner system is currently regulated by the Coroners Act (Northern Ireland) 1959, The Coroners (Practice and Procedure) Rules (Northern Ireland) 1963 and The Coroners (Practice and Procedure) (Amendment) Rules (Northern Ireland) 1980. Information on the processes and procedures are published and can be found on the government website at Judiciary NI.[35]

8.43   Coroners are all now solicitors or barristers, similar to the requirements in England and Wales who have been phasing out coroners coming from medical practice. Appointments are now made through the judicial appointments process rather than by the Lord Chancellor. Along with the coroners work under the Coroner Service, coroners' liaison officers[36] liaise with the bereaved by contacting the family and supplying information for the family about the preliminary cause of death.

8.44   Not all sudden deaths must be reported to the coroner. Doctors can certify the medical cause of death with the Registrar of Births, Deaths and Marriages, registering the death in the usual way. Where a doctor has not seen and treated the deceased for the condition from which they died within 28 days of death, or the death occurred in any of the circumstances detailed below, then the death should be reported to the coroner.[37] A number of categories of deaths are therefore reportable, broadly mirroring those categories operating in Scotland and England and Wales.

8.45   A coroner will hold an inquest into certain types of deaths. They have a discretion whether to hold this with a jury.[38] This choice arises where it appears that there is reason to suspect that the death occurred in prison, or that the death was caused by an accident, poisoning or disease, or where the death occurred in circumstances the continuance or possible recurrence of which is prejudicial to the health or safety of the public. Otherwise, in other deaths, the coroner has a discretion[39] whether to hold an inquest or not with their decisions being subject to judicial review. Juries in homicide and road traffic cases are no longer mandatory since the 1980 Rules were passed. If the coroner does not hold an inquest, s 14 of the 1959 Act empowers the Attorney General to direct a coroner to hold an inquest where the Attorney General has reason to believe that a death has occurred in circumstances which make the holding of an inquest advisable.

---

34   Coroners Service for Northern Ireland, *www.justice-ni.gov.uk/articles/coroners-service-northern-ireland* (accessed on 21 February 2023).
35   *www.judiciaryni.uk/legacy-inquests-general#toc-0* (accessed on 21 February 2023).
36   NI direct government services, *Coroners, post mortems and* inquests, *www.nidirect.gov.uk/articles/coroners-post-mortems-and-inquests#:~:text=Coroners%20Liaison%20Officers%20are%20people,mortem%20examination%20has%20been%20ordered* (accessed on 21 February 2023).
37   Department of Justice, *Coroners Service for Northern Ireland, www.justice-ni.gov.uk/articles/coroners-service-northern-ireland* (accessed on 21 February 2023).
38   Section 18 of the 1959 Act.
39   Section 13 of the 1959 Act.

8.46   Under r 22(1) of the 1963 Rules, the coroner or the jury, after hearing the evidence, shall give a verdict in writing. This is a statement of the matters set out in r 15 setting out who the deceased was, how, when and where they came by their death, and the particulars required for the formal registration of death. There is no provision for a coroner to accept a majority verdict and all members of the jury must agree upon their verdict. Where there is a failure to reach a unanimous verdict, the jury will be discharged.

8.47   Most specific verdicts were abolished by 1980 Rules which have been replaced by findings. Inquests can only return factual fundings and the jury cannot make any recommendations, though they can record a rider if in the opinion of the coroner it may prevent the recurrence of fatalities.[40] Questions of any finding of criminal or civil liability are forbidden. There is also no verdict or finding of 'unlawful killing' which is perhaps a consideration in relation to the Troubles.[41]

8.48   Unlike the position in England and Wales and Scotland, the deceased person may include a foetus in utero, which is then considered to be capable of being born alive.[42]

8.49   An inquest is to be held into the death in 2020 of Noah Donohoe, a 14-year-old boy in 2020. There have been a number of issues in this inquest, including a debate as to holding the inquest before a jury which is the family's preference.[43] A issue of a public immunity notice with regard to disclosure of the information relating to reference numbers, the grading of intelligence, information relating to police sources, and details of Police Service of Northern Ireland investigative methodologies has been upheld. This reflects the view that information can be withheld from inquests where it is considered to create a risk to the public interest. The coroner confirmed that 'nothing has been redacted which shows that any third party was involved in Noah Donohoe's death, nor that would suggest there has been any cover-up in the course of the investigation'.[44]

Australia

8.50   Each Australian state and territory has its own coroner system, but where there are smaller territories, they link in with another state's coroner system. Each state or territory has its own constitution as well as their own statutes and common

---

40   Coroners (Practice and Procedure) Rules (Northern Ireland) 1963, r23(2).
41   *Re Jordan's Application* [2002] NIQB 7.
42   Section 18(1) of the 1959 Act.
43   Belfast Live, *Noah Donohoe: Details of how inquest jury system works* (8 October 2022), *www. belfastlive.co.uk/news/belfast-news/noah-donohoe-details-how-inquest-25209435* (accessed on 21 February 2023).
44   The Irish News, *Redacted material in Noah case contains no information on possible third party involvement, cover-up: judge, www.irishnews.com/news/northernirelandnews/2022/09/09/ news/redacted_material_in_noah_case_contains_no_information_on_possible_third_party_ involvement_cover-up_judge-2822346/* (accessed on 21 February 2023).

law practices. However, most have similar functions in relation to investigations into deaths. These determine the identity of the deceased, when and where they died, the cause of death and how it occurred.[45] In that, they adopt a substantially similar system to that of the common law system in English and Wales.

8.51   All State coroners are required to have formal qualifications in law.

8.52   The coroner will generally investigate all unexpected, unnatural or violent deaths (including homicides and suicides). This includes deaths where the identity of the deceased is not known, or when the cause of death is not known, or a death where a person was in care or custody.

8.53   A unique feature of their system is the creation of a national computer database (National Coroners Information System (NCIS)). This comprises a national database of coronial information on every death reported by a coroner in Australia from July 2000 (in Queensland from July 2001).[46] This provides information for coroners, their staff, public sector agencies, researchers and other agencies in obtaining data to advise on preventable death and injury.

8.54   In Queensland, the processes follow the English and Wales procedures in holding of an inquest, including pre-inquest hearings, but these inquests are not heard in front of a jury. The indication is that there are few coronial investigations that proceed to inquest. Inquests must be heard where the death occurred in custody, or where the death occurred while the person was in care and there are issues about the care, or the death occurred as a result of police operations, unless the coroner considers an inquest is not required. The Attorney General or State Coroner can direct that an inquest be held. A coroner may also hold an inquest if the death is in the public interest to do so. This may exist where there is significant doubt about the cause and circumstances of death, or they believe an inquest may prevent future deaths occurring or uncover systemic issues that affect public health and safety.

8.55   A family is also able to request that an inquest is held by outlining why one should be held and the public interest. The coroner must make the decision within six months. The coroner must give written reasons for their decision.[47] Such decisions about whether to hold an inquest are subject to review, though such powers may vary from state to state.

8.56   The coroner cannot determine any question of civil liability or to suggest that any person is guilty of any offence. There are differences in process where there are criminal charges in consideration.

---

45   Western Australian Coroners Act 1996 permits the coroner may comment and make recommendations about public health or safety or the administration of justice aimed at preventing similar deaths from happening in the future.
46   New Zealand from July 2007.
47   Queensland Courts, Inquests, *https://www.courts.qld.gov.au/courts/coroners-court/coroners-process/inquests#:~:text=An%20inquest%20is%20a%20court,and%20there%20is%20no%20jury* (accessed on 21 February 2023).

8.57   Representation at the inquest is interesting as the coroner has a lawyer known as the 'counsel assisting' who ensures all relevant information is presented to the coroner. They are independent and do not act for the family. They can explain the process, the issues and the witnesses to be examined and any matters the family would like the coroner to consider.[48] Some of these practices appear to echo the role of the procurator fiscal. The family or individuals involved in an inquest can seek independent legal advice in what is described as a 'Coronial Assistance Legal Service that provides advice about any aspect of the coronial process and associated issues'.[49]

Canada

8.58   Death investigations are the responsibility of each Canadian province or territory where the death occurs. There is no overarching legislation. There are two systems in existence – the coronial system based on the English and Welsh model and a chief medical examiner, following the American practices. As an example, both Quebec and Ontario have coronial systems. Alberta, Manitoba, Newfoundland and Labrador have medical examiners. British Columbia has a coroner system that includes medical, legal and lay members as jurors.

8.59   All provinces and territories have a common goal to investigate certain deaths. The aim is to establish the identity of the deceased and to establish the cause and the manner of their death. Most include a means of having a public hearing such as holding an inquest or public inquiry. They go on to develop recommendations to avoid the recurrence of other deaths but without making any findings of fault. To that extent, this process is very similar to the systems in England, Wales and Scotland.

8.60   Looking to Ontario, the Office of the Chief Coroner and the Ontario Forensic Pathology Service undertake the death investigations. The coroner or forensic pathologist require to ascertain the identity of the deceased, the date of death, the location of death, the medical cause of death and by what means the death arose, to establish whether it was as a result of natural causes, accident, homicide, suicide or remains undetermined. In Ontario, the Coroners Act 1972 is the main legislative authority.

8.61   Deaths that are required to be reported are those which occur suddenly and unexpectedly, at a construction or mining site, those while in police custody or while a person is incarcerated in a correctional facility or involve the use of force by a police

48   Queensland Courts, Inquests, *www.courts.qld.gov.au/courts/coroners-court/coroners-process/inquests#:~:text=An%20inquest%20is%20a%20court,and%20there%20is%20no%20jury* (accessed on 21 February 2023).

49   *www.courts.qld.gov.au/courts/coroners-court/coroners-process/inquests#:~:text=An%20inquest%20is%20a%20court,and%20there%20is%20no%20jury* (accessed on 21 February 2023).

officer, special constable, auxiliary member of a police force or First Nations constable or those which appear to be the result of an accident, suicide or homicide.[50]

8.62   Mandatory inquests are held when a death occurs at a construction site, mine, pit or quarry, where a person is in custody or is being detained (unless, in some circumstances, a death investigation determines the death occurred from natural causes in which case, the inquest is discretionary), or it occurs due to an injury sustained or other event that occurred in custody, or when the use of force of a police officer, special constable, auxiliary member of a police force or First Nations Constable is the cause of death, it involves a death of a child which is the result of a criminal act of a person who has custody of the child, if certain circumstances are met or the death occurs while being physically restrained and detained in a psychiatric facility, hospital or secure treatment program.

Discretionary inquests are held where there is enough information from a death investigation to support an inquest. It is then considered that is desirable for the public to have an open and full hearing of the circumstance of a death, and a jury could make useful recommendations to prevent further deaths. An inquest may be held upon request if a relative of the deceased submits a request in writing to the investigating coroner. The Regional Supervising Coroners Management Team determine whether an inquest should be conducted.

8.63   The verdict in an inquest does not need to be unanimous and can be reached by majority. Juries may make recommendations based on the evidence presented to them, but this is not a requirement. Inquest juries are not allowed to make any finding of legal responsibility, express any conclusion of law and therefore not to assign blame, free someone from blame or state or imply any judgment.

8.64   After each inquest, the coroner sends the verdict and recommendations to the Chief Coroner. They are sent to agencies, government, industry and public safety officials who are either expected or invited to respond. Verdicts and recommendations of inquests are published each year in the Review the Office of the Chief Coroner's 2022 inquests' verdicts and recommendations.[51]

8.65   The verdict in an inquest involving three murders that must have related to domestic violence has been included at **Appendix 1 Part H**. This verdict makes an interesting comparison to the UK practices as the inquest involves murders which would not normally be expected to form the basis of an FAI in Scotland, though to do so would not be incompetent and theoretically possible . The jury recommendations are wider and perhaps replicate what would be anticipated to appear in report in a public inquiry in England, Scotland or Wales rather than in an inquest or FAI.

---

50   Ontario, *Death Investigations, www.ontario.ca/page/death-investigations* (accessed on 21 February 2023)

51   Ontario, *2022 coroner's inquests' verdicts and recommendations, www.ontario.ca/page/2022-coroners-inquests-verdicts-and-recommendations* (accessed on 21 February 2023).

8.66 On 22 September 2015,[52] Carol Culleton, Anastasia Kuzyk and Nathalie Warmerdam were all murdered by the same man with a known history of violence against women (intimate partner violence). The coroner's inquest focused on the gaps in the criminal justice system about the interactions between one of the victims and her killer in the months before her death. The inquest heard from experts recommending changes to policies and protocols to better protect and support survivors of intimate partner violence in rural communities in the future. The inquest concluded making a number of recommendations that were sent to a number of parties, including the Government of Ontario. These covered a range of topics and specification outlining the need for undertaking a comprehensive reform of domestic violence, including legislative reforms, the formation of support groups, funding provisions, training for all involved and the management of risk. Recommendations were made to other groups, including the Chief Firearms Officer, the Office of the Chief Coroner and the Information and Privacy Commissioner of Ontario. Finally, it called upon the parties to the inquest to meet in a year's time to review the progress made in relation to the recommendations. Clearly, a lay jury could not make those kind of detailed recommendations, so presumably these were discussed prior to and then included within the submissions invited from the parties to the inquest.

8.67 There are approximately 27,000 death investigations per year and 100 inquests held each year in Ontario.

8.68 Ontario, through its Chief Coroner, has set up a number of advisory committees to provide expert assessment and advice to coroners in some specialised areas of medicine. The four existing committees include at present the Anaesthetic Advisory Committee, the Paediatric Review Committee, the Geriatric and Long Term Care Review Committee, and the Obstetrical Care Review Committee.

8.69 There may be reimbursement of the costs of legal representation for an inquest for parents or spouses of the deceased, if the deceased was a victim of crime and if standing was granted by the coroner at the inquest. The deceased is a victim of crime where there are reasonable grounds to believe that the death was the direct result of conduct by another person that is prohibited under the Criminal Code of Canada.[53]

United States of America (US)

8.70 There is not one unified system of death investigation in the USA. There are coroner-only systems where each county is served by a coroner, while others have a medical examiner systems which are administered by state agencies and some

---

52 CBC News, *Police didn't know killer stalked murder victim, triple homicide inquest hears*, www.cbc.ca/news/canada/ottawa/coroners-inquest-intimate-partner-violence-renfrew-county-1.6490696 (accessed on 21 February 2023).
53 Ontario, *Coroner's inquests*, www.ontario.ca/page/coroners-inquests (accessed on 21 February 2023).

have mixed systems referred to as a hybrid system. These involve referral (where a coroner refers cases to a medical examiner for an autopsy).

8.71 There has been a move towards replacing coroners who need not always have had legal or medical qualification by medical examiners who are professionally qualified.[54] Over time, there have been changes in systems that have been adopted. Since 2000 six counties in the US have converted to a medical examiner system, but no states have converted since 1996. One county has reverted to a sheriff-coroner system.[55]

8.72 Over half of the US population is covered by coroners, with the other half under the charge of medical examiners.

8.73 The role of coroners and medical examiners within the US is to conduct death investigations in sudden and unexplained deaths or those which involve external causes such as injury and poisoning.

8.74 There is a National Association of Medical Examiners (NAME) founded in 1966. NAME is a national professional organisation of physician medical examiners, medicolegal death investigators and death investigation system administrators. They undertake the official duties of the medico-legal investigation of deaths of public interest in the US. That now includes physician medical examiners and coroners, medical death investigators and medico-legal system administrators from throughout the US and other countries. Their members provide expertise to medico-legal death investigation to ensure the effective functioning of the civil and criminal justice systems.[56]

Civil law systems

Germany

8.75 Each individual German state has its own laws on what happens in the case of sudden death. Some indicate that cremation or burial must take place within 96 hours.

8.76 In Germany, physicians are required to report deaths that are unnatural or where the death is unexplained, the body is unidentified and any factor or condition requiring reporting under the Infection Protection Act.[57] The police should inform the public prosecution office or local court of such deaths without delay.[58] Suicides,

---

54 Hanzlick and Combs, 1998.
55 R Hanzlick, *The conversion of coroner systems to medical examiner systems in the United States: a lull in the action* (2007) Am J Forensic Med Pathol, Dec;28(4):279-83.
56 National Association of Medical Examiners, *www.thename.org/about-name* (accessed on 21 February 2023).
57 Gesetz zur Verhütung und Bekämpfung von Infektionskrankheitenbeim Menschen.
58 Strafprozessordnung (Criminal Procedure Code) s 159.

accidents, homicides and deaths occurring during medical treatment are all treated as unnatural deaths. Where the death is reported, the written permission of the public prosecution office in Germany shall be required for burial. This has echoes of the Scottish FAI system where, similarly the procurator fiscal needs to discharge the body in deaths reported to them before the funeral arrangements can take place.

8.77 Following an external examination of the body, if a post mortem examination is required, it is carried out by two physicians. One will be a court physician or the head of a public forensic or pathology institute or a physician of the institute authorised to do so and having specialist knowledge of forensic medicine. The post mortem cannot be performed by the physician who treated the deceased person during the illness which preceded their death. That physician however can be asked to attend to provide information regarding the deceased's medical history. The public prosecution office may attend the autopsy. Upon application by the public prosecution office, the autopsy shall be carried out in the judge's presence.[59] A written report is thereafter made to the state prosecutor. Every death is reported to the local standesbeamter (civil status registry officer).

8.78 As a result, the number of reportable deaths in Germany are low and much lower than in other European countries. Reportable deaths are understood to account for approximately 5–10% of all deaths. This has been described as a 'frighteningly low [autopsy rate] compared to other European countries' concluding that 'the low medicolegal autopsy rate is responsible for the high number of undetected non-natural or violent deaths'.[60]

8.79 Registrars issue the death certificate (sterbeurkunde) in German. German death certificates (todesbescheinigung) do not give the cause of death on the grounds of patient medical confidentiality. They give only the date and the time of death. A non-confidential part of the death certificate can be issued by the physician who confirmed the death. That specifies whether the deceased died of a natural cause or whether there were unusual circumstances.

France

8.80 France adopts a civil investigation approach to death investigations. Deaths that are as a result of violence (but not suicide), arise when the deceased person is in custody or their interaction with police actions or in large scale disasters are required to be reported to the public prosecutor (Procureur de la République). There is an overlap of interest in deaths arising abroad that also fall to be investigated within the UK jurisdiction. An inquest was held into the death of Nick Alexander, who was working as a merchandise manager for Eagles of Death Metal at the Parisian theatre, Bataclan, in November 2015, when a number of people were killed in a terrorist

59   Strafprozessordnung (Criminal Procedure Code) s 87(2).
60   May 2002 DMW Deutsche Medizinische Wochenschrift 127(15):791-5.

attack. The Senior Coroner for Essex, Caroline Beasley-Murray, recorded a verdict of unlawful killing in relation to his death at an inquest in Chelmsford. The cause of death was given as gunshot wounds to the abdomen and chest.[61]

8.81   Post mortems will then be undertaken where the deaths occurred on public highways, whether accidental or not, the death is considered to be criminal or suspicious, or relates to an unidentified body, or 'a body transported with public health measures'.[62] The Legal Medical Institute (Institut Medico Legal (IML)) undertake those examinations where cultural or religious sensitivities may not always be taken into account. The body may not leave the IML until the burial permit has been issued by the investigating magistrate.

8.82   Only medical staff and the police and/or the magistrate in charge of the investigation can attend these post mortems. After the post mortem, the medical examiner will write a report and give it to the magistrate. The responsibility for issuing the death certificate and burial permit lies with the Public Prosecutor (Procureur de la République) at the local high court (Tribunal de Grande Instance). The family can obtain the conclusions of this report by contacting the magistrate directly. The medical examiner is not authorised to provide this information.

8.83   The death certificate (*acte de décès*) that is issued is in two parts. For the family, it provides information on where and when death took place but does not indicate the cause of death. In the second part seen by government officials, it includes the cause of death, including an opinion whether the death occurred through violence, crime or accident.

8.84   There is no automatic judicial inquiry, unless there is a criminal trial or the refusal to prosecute is challenged, such as in the case of the death of Diana, Princess of Wales.[63]

8.85   Where a judicial inquiry (enquête judiciaire) follows a death, it is conducted by an investigating magistrate (juge d'instruction.) The juge d'instruction in carrying out his functions may delegate some information-gathering functions to the police officer and to experts.

61   The Guardian, *Inquest hears of Briton's final moments in Bataclan attack* (19 May 2016), *www.theguardian.com/world/2016/may/19/inquest-hears-of-britons-nick-alexander-final-moments-in-bataclan-attack* (accessed on 21 February 2023).

62   Forensic Institute. Information for Families, *www.prefecturedepolice.interieur.gouv.fr/sites/default/files/Documents/PLQ-IML%20Anglais.pdf* (accessed on 21 February 2023).

63   Al Fayed – France (No 38501/02).
      A judicial investigation was opened on 2 September 1997, where ten press photographers were investigated for unintentionally causing death and injury and failing to assist a person in danger. He applied to join as a civil party and the investigation should consider invasion of privacy allegations. On 3 September 1999, a no case to answer was established. The complaint of invasion of privacy *was* referred with the Court of Cassation finally dismissing an appeal from the applicant in the context of the proceedings on the charges of unintentionally causing death and injury and failing to assist a person in danger. Subsequently compensation was paid for the French delays in process.

8.86 That approach is focused on establishing whether there was any criminality involved in the death, rather than an investigation into the full circumstances of the death. The deceased's family was not originally considered to be a party to the proceedings until the decision in *Slimani v France*.[64] The deceased's family can now lodge a criminal complaint for homicide with the juge d'instruction and seek leave to join the proceedings as a partie civile under the Code de Procédure Pénale art 85, where: "Any person who claims to be injured by a crime or misdemeanor may file a complaint as a civil party before the competent investigating judge…".

8.87 In Slimani, the applicant's partner, a foreign national, had a longstanding psychiatric condition, and died from acute pulmonary oedema during his time in police detention in the Marseille-Arenc Detention Centre. He was under medication which was not administered appropriately during his detention. The judicial authorities investigated to establish the cause of death. As his death was found not to be the result of criminal action, no further action was taken. However, the applicant was not provided with access to the investigation file and was not informed of its outcome as there was no inherent right of access.

8.88 Where a prisoner dies in suspicious circumstances, Art 2 of the ECHR places on the authorities an obligation to carry out an effective official investigation to establish the cause of death and to identify and deal with any responsible parties. The investigation was an official investigation requiring the automatic inclusion of the applicant who should not have been required to lodge a criminal complaint. The national investigation had not been 'effective' for the purposes of the Convention.[65]

8.89 The deceased's family can make a 'plainte contre X'[66] a criminal complaint against an unknown person. *Bone v France*[67] illustrated this practice though it was unsuccessful where a 14-year-old boy attempted to alight on the track-side rather than on the appropriate platform as the train approached a station. He was struck and killed by another train. A complaint was lodged by his family against a person(s) unknown, alleging manslaughter, and applying to join as a civil party. Article 2 ECHR could not guarantee everyone an absolute level of safety in all everyday activities and the State could not be expected to assume an obligation to protect a careless traveller. His reckless conduct had been the cause of his accidental death.

64   App No 57671/00 (ECtHR, Second Section, Judgment 27 July 2004).
65   *Slimani v France*, 57671/00, Council of Europe: European Court of Human Rights, 27 July 2004: *www.refworld.org/cases,ECHR,42d264864.html* (accessed on 21 February 2023).
66   *www.demarches.interieur.gouv.fr/particuliers/porter-plainte#:~:text=Si%20la%20victime%20 ne%20conna%C3%AEt,pr%C3%A9judice%20(dommages%2Dint%C3%A9r%C3%AAts)* (accessed on 21 February 2023).
67   ECtHR, Judgment 1 March 2005 (railway passenger who got out of the train on the wrong side and was killed by a passing train). *Bone v France* (dec), no 69869/01.

Mixed systems

Malta

8.90   Under Malta's Criminal Code Art 551(1), in cases of sudden, violent or suspicious death or where the cause of death is unknown, a report shall be made by the Executive Police to a magistrate. The magistrate shall hold an inquest on the body for the purpose of ascertaining the cause of death and shall take all such evidence as may be possible for them to process. Thereafter, the magistrate shall draw up and sign a written report of proceedings (procès-verbal) as to the cause of death.

8.91   Inquests will be held where a person dies while they are imprisoned or detained in any place of confinement under the Prisons Act,[68] or while they are in police custody. Similar provisions operate where a person dies in Mount Carmel Hospital while they are kept there under an order of a court[69] or for the purpose of being examined by experts to advise on any plea of insanity.

8.92   Where the death is sudden or of unknown cause, the magistrate may, instead of holding an inquest, appoint a senior police officer (assisted by a photographer or other expert) to establish the facts and to give evidence on the facts, by producing all photographs taken and other articles or documents relevant to the investigation.[70]

The Channel Islands

8.93   Both the Bailiwicks of Jersey and Guernsey have independent legal systems though they are dependencies of the British Crown. They operate inquest systems similar to that of England and Wales. Jersey has specific legislation relating to inquests with the Inquests and Post-Mortem Examinations (Jersey) Law 1995.

8.94   Under Art 2(1) of the 1995 Act, where a person has reason to believe that a person has died, they are required to notify a police officer of the facts and circumstances of the death where the death has occurred:

(a) as a result of violence or misadventure;

(b) as a result of negligence or misconduct or malpractice on the part of others;

(c) from any cause other than natural illness or disease for which the deceased person had been seen and treated by a registered medical practitioner; or

(d) under such circumstances as may require investigation.

8.95   The police are then required to notify as soon as reasonably practicable thereafter, the Viscount, who is responsible for carrying out the duties of a coroner,[71] of the facts and circumstances regarding the death.

---

68   Article 551(2).
69   Sub article (3) of article 525 or to article 623(1).
70   Criminal Code art 551(4), referring to art 546(3).
71   Gov.je, *About the Viscount's department, www.gov.je/Government/NonexecLegal/Viscount/Pages/ WhoWeAre.aspx* (accessed on 21 February 2023).

8.96   Under Art 3(a), where a dead body has been found in a public place, there is reason to believe that a deceased person died in any of the above circumstances in police custody or in prison or a legal place of detention and where a person dies while (a) a patient in an approved establishment within the meaning of the Mental Health (Jersey) Law 2016 or (b) a child in a children's home in terms of the Children (Jersey) Law 2002 or a home consisting of a care home service defined in the Regulation of Care (Jersey) Law 2014,[72] the body comes under the jurisdiction of the Viscount. The Viscount issues instructions and instructs such investigation to enable them to determine whether or not an inquest should be held.[73]

8.97   Under Art 4, the Viscount may hold an inquest (a) where a dead body has been found in a public place (b) where (i) the body of the deceased has been removed into Jersey, (ii) the Viscount has reason to believe that the death occurred in Jersey but the body of the deceased has been destroyed or cannot for any reason be found or recovered, and the Viscount has reason to believe that the deceased died in any of the circumstances mentioned outlined above or where the Viscount has any reason to believe that the deceased died suddenly and unexpectedly or in suspicious circumstances.

8.98   Under Article 5, the Viscount shall hold an inquest as outlined under Art 4 unless a certificate is given under Art 64 of the Marriage and Civil Status (Jersey) Law 2001 by a registered medical practitioner or the Viscount is satisfied that there is no ground for holding an inquest. The Viscount may summon a jury (of 12 persons) for any inquest.[74] The test is whether the Viscount considers it to be in the public interest.

8.99   In *Re Cotter*,[75] the deceased died of septicaemia and peritonitis due to a perforated duodenal ulcer in circumstances apparently requiring investigation. An inquest was ordered under the 1995 Act, but the Viscount[76] decided to hear evidence themselves and not to summon a jury. The parents submitted that it was a serious situation as a recurrence of the circumstances of the death would endanger other people. The appeal was dismissed, the question of public interest was held as a matter for the Viscount.

8.100   The jury gives a finding in writing, stating who the deceased was, and how, when and where they came by their death, and also as to the registration particulars but may not make any finding of legal responsibility.[77]

---

72   Paragraph 1(2) of Schedule 1 of the Regulation of Care (Jersey) Law 2014.
73   Inquests and Post-Mortem Examinations (Jersey) Law 1995 art 2(3) and art 2(4).
74   Inquests and Post-Mortem Examinations (Jersey) Law 1995 art 7(1).
75   1997 JLR 12, CA.
76   Article 7(1), where this was considered in his discretion to be 'in the public interest'.
77   Inquests and Post-Mortem Examinations (Jersey) Law 1995 art 14(1).

8.101   The inquest into the 10 deaths which occurred as a result of the gas explosion in Jersey on 15 December 2022 opened on Friday 30 December 2022 and was adjourned as the police investigation continues.[78]

8.102   In Guernsey, the Magistrate's Court can hold inquests into the cause of death.[79] The States of Deliberation allow them to make any further provision for the holding of an inquests.[80]

8.103   Information is provided on how an inquest will proceed with it presided over by a Magistrate and to be held as soon as is practicable after all enquiries have been completed. It is a public inquiry with the Magistrate able to examine the witnesses under oath.

8.104   The Magistrate will return a verdict which is a short statement. A number of verdicts can be given including natural causes, industrial disease, dependence on drugs/non-dependent abuse of drugs, want of attention at birth, suicide/killed themselves (whilst the balance of their mind was disturbed), accident or misadventure, disaster which is the subject of a public inquiry, attempted or self-induced abortion, unlawful killing and an open verdict, stillbirth, and a narrative verdict.

78   ITV News, *Inquests adjourned for ten victims of Jersey explosion* (30 December 2022), *www.itv. com/news/channel/2022-12-29/inquests-open-for-ten-victims-of-jersey-explosion* (accessed on 21 February 2023).
79   Magistrate's Court (Guernsey) Law 2008 s 21.
80   Magistrate's Court (Guernsey) Law 2008 s 22.

Chapter 9

Family Representation and Legal Aid Funding at the FAI

1. INTRODUCTION

9.01 This chapter focuses on the availability and the provision of legal aid to support the deceased person's family in connection with the FAI process from the time of the death to the FAI's conclusion. Before assessing what may be potentially available from the state by way of legal funding, there is a need to understand why the deceased person's family might require legal advice in connection with the FAI process. An understanding of the background as to the provision of legal aid funding in Scotland is also relevant.

2. THE ROLE OF THE DECEASED PERSON'S FAMILY

9.02 Earlier chapters have considered the interests of the family in relation to an FAI. It is worth stressing some of these points again to understand their importance and the potential need for legal advice and representation.

9.03 The deceased's family will have been involved from the death with all the practical implications and formalities of the death itself, leading up to the certification of the death. In most deaths that are reported to the procurator fiscal, the deceased's body should be cleared or released to the family relatively soon after the death has occurred. This will follow the preliminary processes, including the reporting of the death and the completion of any post mortem examination.

9.04   There may be delays in the release of the deceased's body in the circumstances where the death was the result of any potential criminal action, such as a murder. In that case, the deceased's body will remain the property of the Crown (as a potential production) who are responsible for investigating the death. Delays arise inevitably where no accused is identified as being potentially responsible for causing the death. The Crown will be reluctant in these circumstances to release the body until the defence solicitors, who will not have been identified at that time, are given an opportunity to instruct a defence post mortem examination. These issues of delay and distress being caused to the family were the subject of the private member's bill introduced by Gil Paterson MSP in January 2019.[1] He had proposed that there should be 'the right of defence counsel for a person accused of homicide to instruct a post-mortem examination of the alleged victim subject to an extendable time-limit in order to minimise delays and uncertainty for victims' families'.[2] No changes have been made since to the timescales in post-mortems to date.

9.05   In most cases, however, this problem of delay in effecting the release of the deceased's body is not a significant issue. The deceased's family will be permitted to make funeral arrangements following the release of the body as they wish, though instructions can be given were cremation to be excluded, but that is however unlikely. Where the death is one that may lead to an FAI, or the circumstances are still being investigated, COPFS will continue their investigation work after the body has been released.

9.06   Historically, the interests of the family in the outcome of these investigations were relevant but did not sway a decision taken by COPFS as to whether to hold an FAI or not. It is an important factor, but only one of a number to be considered when looking to the potential of holding a discretionary FAI. Decisions as to holding any FAI will focus on what is the societal interest and the outcome of any lessons to be learnt.

9.07   Mandatory FAIs will normally be held, regardless of the families' wishes, though as discussed below, COPFS should keep in touch as their investigations continue so that the family are aware of what is going on and is likely to take place.

9.08   The families' interests in the death were traditionally seen as part of the role being undertaken by the procurator fiscal who was acting in the public interest. That limited role taken by the relatives in an FAI can be seen from a study of the FAI held into the deaths of six boys at Balgowan Approved School, Dundee, in 1947. The boys had escaped from what was then a List D school or approved school and were poisoned on an RNLI launch where they had taken refuge for the night. They had

---

1   Proposed Post-Mortem Examinations (Defence Time-Limit) (Scotland) Bill.
2   The Scottish Parliament, Propsoed Post-Mortem Examinations (Defence Time-Limit) (Scotland) Bill (8 January 20189), *www.parliament.scot/bills-and-laws/proposals-for-bills/proposed-post-mortem-examinations-defence-time-limit-scotland-bill* (accessed on 21 February 2023).

tampered with a fire extinguisher which emitted methyl-bromide and the fumes had thereafter poisoned a number of them.

9.09 The transcript of evidence from the FAI records that the fathers were witnesses at the FAI but only for the purpose of establishing the identity of their sons and who their mothers were. The only other information sought at the FAI was that they were told that their son had died or on a rare occasion, they had managed to arrive at the hospital before their son died. There was no invitation to them at the FAI to express any concern that the parents might have as to the circumstances of their sons' deaths that were being investigated during the FAI process. The view which prevailed was that the FAI was being held in the public interest which encompassed any of the families' interests. Increasingly this is considered not to be the right position. The interests of the families in such deaths are much more clearly considered and included in an FAI held today. This is usually achieved by them giving evidence at the outset as to their concerns and interest in what the FAI establishes.

9.10 The potential conflict of interest between the interests of the deceased's relatives and the state may be apparent, certainly, when considering a death arising from the circumstances of the deceased having been in State custody or, at the time, detained by the police. The family may well feel that their interests do not coincide with the Crown even though the COPFS role, as discussed earlier, is independent and is one of acting in the public interest. The public interest should therefore include the families' concerns.

9.11 Such deaths arising in custody or prison, of course, would result in a mandatory FAI being held under s 2 of the Inquiries into Fatal Accidents and Sudden Deaths etc. (Scotland) Act 2016 (asp 2) (the 2016 Act).

9.12 However, it is suggested that the deceased's family interests should lie at the centre of the FAI system. Their private grief in the death of their deceased relative has become a matter of public interest, played out as seen at the time of the big disasters in what can amount to highly intrusive publicity. The family have a right to be involved at every stage of the proceedings from the death to the FAI itself and if required or desired, to give evidence at the FAI.

9.13 It is important to understand what information is made available to the families when they become involved in death investigations and FAIs.

9.14 Earlier chapters have referred to the COPFS's *The Family Liaison Charter*[3] that required to be produced by COPFS in terms of s 8 of the 2016 Act. That sets out that 'this charter for bereaved families sets [the] standards for the communication

---

3   Crown Office & Procurator Fiscal Service, *The Family Liaison Charter* (September 2016), *www. copfs.gov.uk/resources/publications/the-family-liaison-charter/* (accessed on 21 February 2023). Published in 2016; it seems not to have been updated since though it references that 'COPFS will ensure those who have been previously consulted in the preparation of this Charter are further consulted on revisions that may be required to the Charter in light of those recommendations and will thereafter lay a revised Charter before the Scottish Parliament'.

that COPFS will have with them'. The Charter also refers to two other specialist information documents relating to:

- deaths which are the result[4] of a murder or culpable homicide produced by the Scottish Government;[5] and
- deaths on roads in Scotland[6] (it goes further by specifically referring to the process whereby a relative may become involved in a FAI 'by asking witnesses questions, or instructing a solicitor to do this for them'. It states that 'Legal aid may be available to fund the cost of representation'.).

9.15   The charter also refers to the COPFS's *Information for bereaved relatives: The role of the Procurator Fiscal in the investigation of deaths*[7] which was produced in 2017. The aims of that booklet are to 'to help relatives understand the role of the Procurator Fiscal in certain deaths, and to explain what the Procurator Fiscal will do'.[8]

9.16   This document does outline briefly the process of certification of deaths and FAIs but no reference is made to any need or the provision of information that the family might require to seek legal advice or assistance. It includes reference to some organisations who may support families in connection with certain types of deaths.

9.17   What remains unclear is when and who are responsible for providing this leaflet to the deceased person's family. Additionally, there is now a guide for bereaved family members which was updated at 20 September 2022[9] which seems to contain more general advice. However, there is not one web portal with all up-to-date information and advice being made available to the families to answer their questions.

9.18   This can be contrasted with information available from the England and Wales Coroner's system and the Ministry of Justice as *A Guide to Coroner Services for Bereaved People* (2020)[10] and in particular, looking to Section 4 therein which

4   The Scottish Government, *Information for bereaved family and friends following murder or culpable homicide* (2013), *www.gov.scot/binaries/content/documents/govscot/publications/advice-and-guidance/2013/03/information-bereaved-families-friends-following-murder-culpable-homicide/documents/information-bereaved-family-friends-following-murder-culpable-homicide/information-bereaved-family-friends-following-murder-culpable-homicide/govscot%3Adocument/00416423.pdf.* (accessed 21 February 2023).
5   It makes no reference to any FAI process, though it is competent in a murder/culpable homicide case to hold an FAI as well.
6   *Information and advice for bereaved families and friends following a death on the road in Scotland*, Brake the Road Safety Charity, published in 2020–2021: *www.brake.org.uk/how-we-help/get-help-if-a-crash-victim/information-and-advice-after-road-death-or-serious-injury/guide-for-bereaved-families-and-friends-following-death-on-the-road-in-scotland-2020-2021* (accessed on 21 February 2023).
7   The Crown Office & Procurator Fiscal Service, *Information for bereaved relatives. The role of the Procurator Fiscal in the investigation of deaths, www.sudiscotland.org.uk/wp-content/uploads/2020/06/October-2017-Information-for-nearest-relatives.pdf* (accessed on 21 February 2023).
8   Ibid.
9   Crown Office & Procurator Fiscal Service, *Guide for bereaved family members* (9 February 2023), *www.copfs.gov.uk/services/bereavement-support/guide-for-bereaved-family-members/* (accessed on 21 February 2023).
10   MoJ, A Guide to Coroner Services for Bereaved People (2020) *https://assets.publishing.service.gov.uk/government/uploads/system/uploads/attachment_data/file/859076/guide-to-coroner-services-bereaved-people-jan-2020.pdf* (accessed on 21 February 2023).

covers 'Legal Advice – there is going to be an inquest- will I need a lawyer'. The key points from the guide are set out at the outset as:

- You do not need to have a lawyer to attend or participate in an inquest. The coroner will help you understand what is happening at the inquest and why.
- You may want to consider getting legal help for an inquest hearing if other interested persons are represented, for example if the state or a public body has legal representation at the inquest.
- Depending on your financial circumstances, you may have a right to financial support from the government to pay for legal help to prepare for the inquest, or legal representation at the inquest.
- Public funding ('legal aid') to have a lawyer represent you at an inquest hearing is only available in certain circumstances.

9.19   These principles could easily be incorporated in information provided in Scotland for the deceased's families so that they are aware of the position and of the relevance of legal advice and funding at the outset.

9.20   Looking to the Charter though, it is useful as it helps to identify where the interests of the deceased person's family may arise which can be outlined as follows:

- the initial stages (1–3) which relate to the death and certification processes;
- the further investigations/possible criminal investigations (4–5); and
- the FAI (6).

9.21   However, the focus of the Charter is about COPFS and what they will do which is set out under the 'Summary of our Commitments'. It is worth looking at the Summary of the Commitments below to show where the deceased family may consider that legal advice/assistance might be sought.

Stage	Actions from COPFS	Legal advice/assistance required
Initial	- To advise the bereaved family whether a post mortem examination is necessary and when this is likely to take place. - Once the cause of death is confirmed the family can proceed with funeral arrangements. - If the Final Post Mortem Report is not going to be available within 12 weeks, provide an update on the expected timescales.	The family in a homicide is likely to be in touch with a solicitor so legal advice and assistance may be required.
Investigations	Contact the family no later than 12 weeks after the death to advise on investigations. A personal meeting will be offered at this time which will take place within 14 days unless the family indicate they do not wish a personal meeting.	The family may wish legal advice and assistance and may wish the solicitor to attend this meeting.

Stage	Actions from COPFS	Legal advice/assistance required
Investigations – *contd*	Ongoing requirements for updates.	In potential civil cases the family may well want to receive updates in case civil action is being pursued though sisted until the outcome of the FAI investigation process.
Criminal	To advise the bereaved family within 14 days of Crown counsel's decision on whether or not there should be criminal proceedings in relation to the death.	The family may well be in touch with lawyers for advice and assistance on the decision.
Fatal Accident Inquiry	To inform the bereaved family when a report is to be submitted for Crown Counsel's instructions on whether or not there should be an FAI and will take into account their views in reaching a decision and in how they communicate that decision.	The family may well be in touch with lawyers for advice and assistance.
	If Crown Counsel decide that there should not be an FAI, a meeting will be offered with the family within 14 days of notifying them of that decision, to explain the reasons for this decision.	The family may well want to discuss that decision and to consider the possibility of a judicial review of the decision following receipt of the reasons.
	Where Crown Counsel decide that an FAI should be held the procurator fiscal will explain to the family about what happens next and will meet with the family to discuss this process if the family wishes.	The family may well be instructing solicitors to appear on their behalf at the FAI – so require advice and representation.
	The procurator fiscal will also make an application to the court within two months of that decision being made in order that the FAI will take place as soon as possible.	The Charter does not continue but the family will be entitled to be present and represented at the FAI. They are likely to be witnesses.

9.22   As the table illustrates, the deceased person's family do need to understand how deaths are reported, the role of COPFS and the relationship within the FAI system. However, the Charter may be seen to have quite a narrow focus in not reaching out to indicate or indeed suggest how advice might support the deceased's family at such an important time.

9.23   In conclusion, since the families' interests are crucial to the death investigation process, they need to understand what the FAI system aims to achieve in comparison to their own personal interests relating to the circumstances of the death. Having a central information webpage process under the control of Scottish

Government that referenced from the initial stage (the death) to the conclusion of the FAI, would help in ensuring and achieving transparency of process, the clarity of relevant timescales and permit the family to understand what the FAI system is designed to achieve.

9.24 This should also highlight the possibility of requiring legal representation. Information should be about what the family might need to know in relation to the circumstances of the death and why the death occurred. They will wish to know that there is some learning to be gained and that other deaths will not occur in similar circumstances. Where there are any criminal proceedings, they wish to know that these proceedings are being or will be raised. What they need to understand is that the FAI system does not replicate the criminal or civil court processes in determining any questions of liability. By setting out clearly that relevant information in one place, it is much easier to meet their expectations within the constraints of the current system. This sort of information process may sit best with Scottish Government though responsibility for providing the relevant up to date information rests with both COPFS and SCTS.

9.25 Since SCTS provides other information and are responsible for the publication of the determination at the conclusion of the FAI, there may also be an opportunity to provide a factsheet in relation to the FAI, similar to that produced in respect of the inquest system – *Inquests- A Factsheet for Families*.[11] What this leaflet ensures is that it provides information to allow the families to understand the process and where there is a need for possible legal representation. It covers the background and why an inquest is being carried out, along with an explanation as to what the possible verdicts are. It includes:

1. Preamble:
    What is an inquest, when is an inquest necessary, conclusions and prevention of future deaths. (These are easily replicated from an FAI perspective. That sets out the expectation of the FAI as to what it is not.)
2. Inquest:
    What happens at the inquest, giving evidence at the inquest, inquest step by step, asking questions at the inquest.
3. Legal Representation.
4. Miscellaneous:
    This includes practicalities, criminal prosecution, useful contacts and post mortem/autopsy.

9.26 It is also interesting to note the families' experiences outlined in connection with the *Independent Review of Responses to Deaths in Prison Custody: Responses*

---

11   The Coroners' Courts Support Service, *Inquests – A Factsheet for Families, https:// coronerscourtssupportservice.org.uk/wp-content/uploads/2018/11/CCSS-EL_Inquest_Factsheet_ Final29317221_3.pdf* (accessed on 21 February 2023).

from the Families, published in November 2021.[12] From evidence provided in connection with that report, families appear to have been aware of the possibility of obtaining legal representation. They seem not to have necessarily thereafter applied for it. The reasoning outlined was that 'they didn't think they needed it or that they couldn't afford it' or "[o]ne mum spoke about her efforts to get a lawyer but said that no one would take the case, telling her that this would be a waste of time as an "open and shut" case (a drug-related death).'[13] The difficulty of finding a lawyer to take on the case may be the result of current issues with the availability of civil legal aid lawyers in Scotland. What is true is that most of the FAIs into prison deaths do not have any family representation for whatever reason.

9.27 Further research into why that is the case would help identify whether (a) there is any problem in public awareness that there is a possibility of receiving legal aid and the likelihood of receiving it, (b) any perception that there is a need for their family interests to be represented at an FAI and (c) to dispel any misunderstanding that their relative's death is not deserving of legal aid. Though the deceased family may represent themselves and the rest of the family at an FAI, there is an acknowledgement that families may well find attendance at an FAI distressing, leaving aside the potentially daunting thought of appearing in a court. When families are at a vulnerable time, they face the need to complete the necessary legal aid funding application. They may emotionally be unable to cope and therefore not take forward any application.

9.28 Equally, the family may decide not to be represented at an FAI. Even were there to be an extension of the access to legal aid without any financial eligibility considerations, it is far from automatic that a deceased family would necessarily seek representation at an FAI.

3. WHAT IS LEGAL AID

9.29 Legal aid is the assistance that is provided where someone cannot afford to pay their own legal costs. In order to apply for legal aid, there is a need to find a solicitor who undertakes legal aid work which may continue to be problematic.[14]

---

12 *Independent Review of the Response to Deaths in Prison Custody: Responses from Families* (November 2021), *www.prisonsinspectoratescotland.gov.uk/sites/default/files/publication_files/ Independent%20Review%20of%20the%20Response%20to%20Deaths%20in%20Prison%20 Custody%20-%20Family%20Paper.pdf* (accessed on 21 February 2023).
13 *Independent Review of the Response to Deaths in Prison Custody: Responses from Families* (November 2021), *www.prisonsinspectoratescotland.gov.uk/sites/default/files/publication_files/ Independent%20Review%20of%20the%20Response%20to%20Deaths%20in%20Prison%20 Custody%20-%20Family%20Paper.pdf* (accessed on 21 February 2023).
14 Law Society of Scotland, *Legal aid crisis hitting Scotland's most deprived families* (20 October 2022), *www.lawscot.org.uk/news-and-events/law-society-news/legal-aid-crisis-hitting-scotlands-most-deprived-families/* (accessed on 21 February 2023).

9.30   Apart from legal aid funding, it is of course open to any deceased person's family to instruct and pay for a solicitor privately. Legal aid if granted will cover advice and assistance[15] which includes the costs of obtaining legal advice from a solicitor, such as information on the rights and options outlined above or just with assistance with understanding the processes.

9.31   It should be noted that referring to legal aid in this context is separate from any entitlement to legal aid needed to raise any personal injury action that lies outside the scope of the FAI and is a separate matter.

9.32   In addition to publicly available legal aid, there may well be funding opportunities provided from union representation, charities or third sector organisations such as Action on Asbestos,[16] or the deceased's own house or personal insurance policies. The majority of interested parties at an FAI will fund representation themselves – and those such as medical professionals will have professional representation through their specialist union representation such as the Medical Dental Defence Union Scotland (MDDUS).[17] Where there is an FAI instructed, a solicitor can potentially obtain legal aid to represent someone in court in an FAI.

4.   THE LEGAL AID PROCESS

9.33   The administration of legal aid is Scotland is funded by the Scottish Legal Aid Board (SLAB)[18] who are an executive non-departmental public body of the Scottish Government, responsible for managing legal aid. SLAB was established in April 1987, under the Legal Aid Act 1986, taking over functions on legal aid previously exercised by the Law Society of Scotland.

9.34   As far as FAIs are concerned, SLAB advise that they prioritise applications for representation at FAIs. Civil legal aid may be available for an FAI and an application for legal aid should be submitted as soon as possible after the First Notice of the FAI is received.[19] There is no mention within such as notice of the possibility of obtaining advice and assistance. Where a death has occurred, any civil legal aid application or application for legal advice can be made and that will be dealt with under the usual criteria. This may well take place in advance of any knowledge that an FAI, where it is potentially discretionary, is to be held. Prison deaths are of course a category of deaths, as are deaths in custody, that it will be obvious from the start

---

15   Access to public services in Scotland, *www.mygov.scot* (accessed on 21 February 2023). The eligibility of legal aid is not discussed.
16   Action on Asbestos: Industrial Injury and Disease, *www.clydesideactiononasbestos.org.uk/* (accessed on 21 February 2023).
17   MDDUS, *www.mddus.com* (accessed on 21 February 2023).
18   Scottish Legal Aid Board, *www.slab.org.uk/* (accessed on 21 February 2023).
19   Section 15 of the 2016 Act.

that an FAI will need to be held. These are the ones where the families may benefit from obtaining advice at the outset, and to start from the time of the death having occurred.

9.35   Civil legal aid is not available automatically for an FAI. Any application can be made by a family member for their own representation to participate in FAIs. That is subject to the application of the usual statutory tests of civil legal aid for all civil legal aid actions which are required to consider probable cause, reasonableness and financial eligibility.

9.36   The applicant, namely the family member, must show why they require representation and that its grant is reasonable. That will cover why separate representation in the FAI from the interests of the state through COPFS is desirable with its public interest remit. They need to state why it is required, outlining the issues, presumably any factual or evidential matters, in dispute and being of concern to the family. There is no difference to the assessment of the application whether it is made in connection with a mandatory or discretionary FAI. There is however a view expressed that there may be more latitude exercised by the SLAB when determining applications that are made in respect of mandatory inquiries. This may follow the trend that these are the type of FAIs where the interests of COPFS and the deceased's family may not be seen to coincide.

9.37   For deaths in prison and police custody (and presumably similar mandatory FAIs, though their website does not state that), the test for legal aid to be applied is statutory under probable cause. The family member must fall within the category of 'persons entitled to be represented' at the FAI as a relative of the deceased or as a potential defender (their terminology, but presumably relates to a party who may be liable to carry some responsibility for the circumstances of the death but cannot of course be found liable in the FAI under civil or criminal law). Under the statutory test of reasonableness, where the relative is of a person who died in prison or police custody, SLAB consider the application favourably (subject to there not being more than one request from a family member) as indicated above. SLAB seem to advocate some support for the family's position that 'it is appropriate for relatives to have their own independent representation at the inquiry to determine the facts'. That also supports Lord Cullen's recommendation in his Review at para 10.23 that:

> 'In regard to legal aid, relatives of the deceased should not have to justify the reasonableness of the granting of legal aid for their representation at the FAI and the Scottish Ministers should consider increasing the limit for legal aid in FAIs and the extent to which legal aid is available within that limit. Legal aid should, as a matter of course, be granted in any case where the participation of the relatives is necessary in order to comply with article 2 of the ECHR.'[20]

---

20   Review of Fatal Accident Inquiry Legislation, *www.webarchive.org.uk/wayback/archive/ 20150220033359/http://www.gov.scot/Publications/2009/11/02113726/11* (accessed on 21 February 2023).

9.38   This proposal for civil legal aid without any restriction in what might be defined as Art 2 ECHR deaths has not been implemented by the Scottish Government. The criteria for assessing such applications has not been reviewed since the regulations were made under the Legal Aid (Scotland) Act 1986. Notwithstanding, there have been review questions included within the Scottish Government's consultation into legal aid[21] which concluded in September 2019.

9.39   For all other deaths, SLAB state that probable cause can be established if the deceased's relative falls within the category of persons entitled to be notified of an FAI. Under the statutory test of reasonableness, SLAB considers to meet the test of reasonableness that there is a need to show:

- why the client needs separate legal representation at the FAI, in addition to the role of COPFS acting in the public interest;
- any potential areas of dispute with COPFS in relation to the approach taken to the FAI or the evidence to be led;
- any areas of concern in relation to any other party involved in the FAI that might result in the need for representation;
- any areas of FAI that the client wants to pursue which will not be addressed by COPFS or should be pursued in a different way;
- why they consider these different areas of inquiry are appropriate and reasonable to be taken forward at the FAI; and
- any other relevant factors.

9.40   SLAB specifically state that they will not consider the test of reasonableness to be met where the process is being used to obtain representation to identify and gather information that might support a reparation claim. (SLAB also refers to the circumstances where the client requires representation to protect their legal position against self-incrimination or avoiding any further proceedings.)

9.41   Some of the issues that arise with regard to the grant of legal aid were demonstrated in the FAI into the Clutha helicopter crash.[22]

9.42   On 29 November 2013, a police helicopter operated by Bond Air Services for Police Scotland crashed into the Clutha, a public house in central Glasgow. The crash killed all three crew members on board and seven of those clients in the bar at the time. The Clutha FAI was mandatory[23] in respect of those who were killed in the helicopter but not for the clients in the bar. Some families were partially granted legal aid while others sought to make up the shortfall by means of charity funding.[24]

21 Scottish Government, *Legal aid reform: consultation analysis* (16 June 2020), *www.gov.scot/ publications/legal-aid-reform-scotland-consultation-response/* (accessed on 21 February 2023).
22 [2019] FAI 46: *www.scotcourts.gov.uk/docs/default-source/cos-general-docs/pdf-docs-for-opinions/ 2019fai46.pdf?sfvrsn=0* (accessed on 21 February 2023).
23 [2019] FAI 46: *www.scotcourts.gov.uk/docs/default-source/cos-general-docs/pdf-docs-for-opinions/ 2019fai46.pdf* (accessed on 21 February 2023).
24 BBC, Court told Clutha families will need charity cash for FAI (11 January 2019), *www.bbc.co.uk/ news/uk-scotland-glasgow-west-46834743* (accessed on 21 February 2023).

9.43   This was felt to be unfair as the interests of all families did not necessarily coincide when considering the pilot's interest as having been in charge and responsible for flying the helicopter, in contrast to those who had been killed on the ground. The issue arose as to why some should benefit from State funding and others be denied, especially in what was described as 'a substantial inquiry attracting considerable public interest'.[25]

9.44   To illustrate the extent of the respective interests which highlight the discrepancies when reflecting on legal aid considerations, the parties actually in attendance at the Clutha FAI are worth examination. This helps to understand its length and complexity and understand the respective different interests. This is of course not unique in relation to FAIs of this type. All would have had different interests in identifying the cause of the accident – whether it was pilot error, mechanical failure or any other factor.

9.45   Clutha FAI representation in attendance included:

- The procurator fiscal in representing the public interest in the FAI.
- The families of six of the persons who died were represented at the FAI.[26] The fiancée of pilot of Captain Traill was also represented.[27] The families of the four other people who died did not participate in the FAI.[28]
- Airbus Helicopters Deutschland GmBH, the manufacturer of G-SPAO.
- Babcock Mission Critical Services Onshore Limited, the operators of G-SPAO and the employer of Captain Traill.
- Safran Helicopter Engines, the manufacturer of G-SPAO's engines.
- With a wider perspective or overview, the Department for Transport and the Air Accidents Investigation Branch, Police Scotland, the employer of Constable Collins and Constable Nelis and for whom G-SPAO was operating.
- British Airline Pilots' Association along with the European Aviation Safety Agency attended.

9.46   The Ministry of Justice in England and Wales have conducted a similar exercise that resulted in the publication of the *Final Report: Review of legal aid for inquests*.[29] Though that report deals with the English system of a coroner, its findings are relevant to the FAI system too in that it stresses that the purpose in holding an inquest is about seeking 'to establish who the deceased was and how, when and

---

25   [2019] FAI 46 at [22] : *www.scotcourts.gov.uk/docs/default-source/cos-general-docs/pdf-docs-for-opinions/2019fai46.pdf?sfvrsn=c99c15d2_0* (accessed on 21 February 2023).
26   These included families of Gary Louis Arthur, Robert James Jenkins, John McGarrigle, James Diver, Samuel Bell McGhee and Mark Edward O'Prey.
27   She could not apply for legal funding until her finances 'run out' but that she cannot apply for legal aid until that has happened as her salary was 'significant'.
28   Constable Collins, Joseph Robert Cusker, Colin Gibson and Constable Nelis.
29   Ministry of Justice, *Final Report: Review of legal aid for inquests*, February 2019, CP 39: *https://assets.publishing.service.gov.uk/government/uploads/system/uploads/attachment_data/file/777034/review-of-legal-aid-for-inquests.pdf* (accessed on 21 February 2023).

where they came by their death'. What is common to both systems is the search to find out what happened.

9.47   This is important not only for the deceased relatives but also the public interest in establishing lessons to be learned to prevent other similar deaths arising in the future. Public interest as the focus for holding such FAIs may be relevant to considering when and how to provide legal aid.

9.48   Under the current arrangements, SLAB has no flexibility to decide whether to disapply or disregard the statutory requirements that operate to assess an applicant's finances. Application of the criteria as with Clutha FAI may mean some families receive legal aid while others do not and are represented in the same inquiry. What that means for the public is a perception that the grant of legal aid in connection with FAIs is random. These discrepancies with funding remain embedded within the current legal aid system. The funding approach remains somewhat piecemeal and would benefit from a significant overhaul with a view to achieving consistency.

5.   LEGAL AID AND REPRESENTATION AT AN FAI

9.49   Exactly who should be given legal aid in estranged families is also a matter on which views need to be considered more fully. This is not necessarily automatic or an easy decision to make. Under s 11 of the 2016 Act, the persons who may participate in the FAI include:

- the spouse or civil partner at the time of the death;
- a person living with A as if married to A at the time of A's death;
- A's nearest known relative if, at the time of A's death, A did not have a spouse or civil partner, and was not living with a person as if married to the person;
- where the death is within s 2(3) A's employer, if A was acting in the course of the person's employment, an inspector appointed under s 19 of the Health and Safety at Work etc. Act 1974 (appointment of inspectors);
- a trade union, or similar body, representing the interests of workers in connection with the employment or occupation concerned, if A was at the time of A's death a member of the trade union or body, and any other person who the sheriff is satisfied has an interest in the inquiry.

9.50   Challenges can and do arise as seen in Mitchell, Applicant.[30] An application to participate in an FAI was made by the half-sister of the helicopter pilot in the crash at the Clutha public house in Glasgow. The pilot's fiancée had already indicated her intention to attend and to participate.

---

30   [2018] 9 WLUK 253; 2018 G.W.D. 31-386.

9.51   The court held that there was no reason to grant the half-sister's rights to participate since she had not seen her brother, the pilot since 1991. Though she had an interest in the FAI, by virtue of being a family member, intimation was limited to only one individual in terms of s 11(1)(a)–(c).[31] There was no basis on which her participation 'would further the purpose of the inquiry, namely, to establish the circumstances of the death, and to consider what steps, if any, might be taken to prevent other deaths in similar circumstances'.

6.   LEGAL AID FUNDING – FUNDING OF FAIS

9.52   The cost of legal aid to fund FAIs will vary each year as there are differences in the numbers of FAIs that are held, as well as inevitably the complexity and length of the actual FAIs. This is discussed in **Chapter 11**. A number of FAIs may not involve any applications being made for legal aid. Accordingly, discerning any trends in how much and when legal aid will be granted is challenging. The accounting periods for payment of legal aid made, including any interim payments, differ too as the length of FAIs can span different financial years. Exact identification of funding costs will depend when the FAI completed. (Families on an income over £27,000[32] are required to fund the costs themselves.)

9.53   The table below shows the total expenditure on civil legal aid on FAIs.

Year	Amount (total) spent on civil legal aid (£)	Number of applications granted for FAIs	Amount spent on civil advice and assistance (£)
2020–2021	369,000	9	2,000
2019–2020	762,000	10	8,000
2018–2019	213,000	19	9,000

9.54   All the expenditure figures have been rounded to the nearest thousand pounds and are inclusive of VAT.[33]

7.   LEGAL AID FUNDING IN CONTRAST WITH INQUIRIES

9.55   Legal aid may be provided in relation to public inquiries in order to fund legal representation in certain circumstances. Alternatively this can be funded

---

31   Section 11(1)(a)–(c) of the 2016 Act.
32   Scottish Legal Aid Board, *Civil legal aid: how we calculate income and what's included*, *www. slab.org.uk/guidance/civil-legal-aid-how-we-calculate-income-and-whats-included/* (accessed on 21 February 2023).
33   Scottish Legal Aid Board, FOI Response Issued (17 February 2022), *www.slab.org.uk/app/ uploads/2022/09/Query-regarding-civil-legal-aid-expenditure-applications-granted-for-FAIs.pdf* (accessed on 21 February 2023).

privately or the costs may be recovered if there is a civil claim (such as a personal injury or medical negligence claim) as part of the costs of the case.

9.56　Funding differs, depending on the actual inquiry. Where core participant status is granted in the inquiry, in the majority of cases, funding will be granted by the inquiry which will pay for reasonable legal provisions. It is not means-tested and is paid on a monthly basis (unlike legal aid funding which is usually paid at the conclusion of the case). It is usually paid by whichever Government Minister's department has called for the inquiry.

9.57　The power of a Chairman of the inquiry to make an award of public funding is restricted to payments of compensation for loss of time, expenses properly incurred in attendance at the inquiry, and to fees for legal representation where a person is providing evidence, or is a person who, in the opinion of the Chairman, has a particular interest in the proceedings or outcome of the inquiry that justifies such an award. The Chairman is required to act with fairness and must avoid any unnecessary costs, whether to public funds, witnesses or others.[34] Retrospective awards are forbidden. Consideration as to the 2005 Act and the 2007 Rules is in part to avoid multiple representations of persons who have had similar interests. Rule 18 requires the Chairman to take into account the financial resources of an applicant together with the public interest when considering making an award pursuant to an application under s 40 of the 2005 Act.

9.58　The issue of legal representation was a focus in the ICL Inquiry[35] Explosion at Grovepark Mills, Maryhill Glasgow on 11 May 2004.[36] This was first inquiry to be held under the 2005 Act which introduced a new framework for public inquiries to increase the efficiency of the process. The Chairman, Lord Gill, indicated that 'the essence of this approach is that inquiries will be *inquisitorial* processes … rather than the *adversarial, litigation-based* processes typical of major inquiries in the past …. In this new approach, there is no reason to fear that the truth-finding process will be compromised.' The underlining is our emphasis but is curious given the purpose of an FAI is equally an inquisitorial and not an adversarial process.

9.59　In relation to public inquiries at an earlier stage in 1990, the then Attorney General said '[i]n general, the Government accept the need to pay out of public finds the reasonable costs of any necessary party to the Inquiry who would be prejudiced in seeking representation were he in any doubt about funds becoming available'.[37] Issues arose over possible disparities from the relatives so that the Chairman determined that those core participants who were next of kin (or were injured survivors) to

---

34　Section 17 of the 2005 Act.
35　*The ICL Inquiry*, HC 838, *https://assets.publishing.service.gov.uk/government/uploads/system/ uploads/attachment_data/file/229279/0838.pdf* (accessed on 21 February 2023).
36　This was an inquiry conducted under s 26 of the 2005 Act presented to both the House of Commons and the House of Lords.
37　*The ICL Inquiry*, HC 838, *https://assets.publishing.service.gov.uk/government/uploads/system/ uploads/attachment_data/file/229279/0838.pdf* (accessed on 21 February 2023).

have single legal representation so that all interests were represented by one firm of solicitors.[38]

8. CONCLUSION

9.60 Legal aid remains an issue in connection with FAIs and has presented a similar problem in England and Wales in relation to the funding of inquests. There have been calls to establish a level playing field for all. Bereaved families should be provided with automatic non-means tested funding for their legal representation following deaths where the State has had a hand, such as deaths in custody or prison. The issues are ones of equality of arms since the bodies and representatives of the State, such as Police Scotland or SPS, have unlimited access to public funding and relevant experts. Though the determination in an FAI does not involve any criminal or civil liability, it may still have implications for future civil settlements. Access to justice is also affected as all parties may not have the same access to legal advice and representation.

9.61 In December 2021, the UK Government announced the removal of the means test for Art 2 inquests (Exceptional Case Funding)[39].[40] Perhaps the Scottish Government may seek to provide similar funding for such FAIs in the future.

---

38 Section 40 of the 2005 Act.
39 The inquest group have produced a timeline showing their campaign on this topic over a number of years: MoJ and Legal Aid Agency, *Exceptional Case Funding for representation at inquests* (3 October 2022), *www.gov.uk/government/publications/exceptional-case-funding-for-representation-at-inquests* (accessed on 21 February 2023).
40 Dame Elish Angiolini's *Report of the independent review of deaths and serious incidents in police custody*, where it called for the introduction of non-means tested legal aid for bereaved families where someone has died in the care of the state: 'In order to facilitate their effective participation in the whole process there should be access for the immediate family to free, non-means tested legal advice, assistance and representation from the earliest point following the death and throughout the preinquest hearings and Inquest hearing.' *https://assets.publishing.service.gov.uk/government/uploads/system/uploads/attachment_data/file/655401/Report_of_Angiolini_Review_ISBN_Accessible.pdf* (accessed on 21 February 2023).

Chapter 10

Inquires under the Inquires Act 2005

1. INTRODUCTION

10.01   In **Chapter 2** when discussing the Art 2 ECHR requirements, it was noted that compliance by the State with its Art 2 obligations can also be achieved by means of an inquiry held under the Inquiries Act 2005 set up by a government minister rather than by means of an FAI.[1] Inquiries may be set up, involving those who have died in Scotland, though the scope of holding investigations under the Inquiries Act 2005 is not restricted merely to those inquiries related to deaths.[2] In order to understand the difference between inquiries and FAI, there is a need to look further at how and why inquiries are set up.

2. FRAMEWORK OF AN INQUIRY

10.02   Section 1(1) of the Inquiries Act 2005 provides the power under a minister whether UK or a minister of the devolved administrations to hold an inquiry where (a) particular events have caused, or are capable of causing, public concern or (b) there is public concern that particular events may have occurred.

---

1   *Kennedy v Lord Advocate* [2008] SLT 195: *https://scotcourts.gov.uk* (accessed on 21 February 2023).
2   Edinburgh Tram Inquiry is one such example where it does not relate to a death.

10.03   Section 28 of the Inquiries Act 2005 specifically refers to Scotland. It ensures that the terms of reference of any inquiry, being the responsibility of Scottish ministers, should not require it to determine any fact or make any recommendation that is not wholly or primarily concerned with a Scottish matter[3] (s 28(2)).

10.04   The 2005 Act sets out a basic procedural framework and is supplemented by the Inquiry Rules 2006. These Rules are made under s 41 of the 2005 Act. The Rules set out matters of evidence and procedure, retention of documents given to or created by the inquiry, and any awards under s 40.[4] They have powers to require a person to give evidence, provide written statements and to produce documents. They provide the detail of the processes in a similar manner to the relationship between the FAI Rules and the Inquiries into Fatal Accidents and Sudden Deaths etc. (Scotland) Act 2016 (asp 2) (the 2016 Act).

10.05   The inquiry itself will set out how evidence should be taken and provided. The Chair of an inquiry may require a person to attend to give evidence before the inquiry, produce any documents in their custody or under their control and that relate to a matter in question at the inquiry, or to produce any other thing in their custody or control for inspection, examination or testing. The Chair may also require a person to provide evidence by way of a written statement.

10.06   Factors which will be taken into account when considering whether the evidence should be given by way of witness statement or orally will include the nature of the subject matter and the importance of the evidence to the inquiry. Where witness statements are to be used, they may be produced by an investigator commissioned by the inquiry to take a statement from the witness, or a formal request to produce a witness statement within a set timescale. Witnesses may also be asked to give evidence orally. This makes the process flexible and easier to manage.

10.07   Under s 35 of the 2005 Act, enforcement provisions by way of sanctions can be applied by way of a criminal offences, where, without reasonable excuse, there is a failure to give evidence at the inquiry, provide a witness statement or to produce documents.

10.08   Many of these evidential procedures echo the powers in the Rules to the 2016 Act. However, these are not limited by the requirements of causation where there is a need to ensure and provide the link between the death and the circumstances and findings made by the sheriff. In an inquiry, other matters can be explored, such as in the Dunblane Inquiry where the inquiry looked at many aspects of future gun

---

3   Under s 28(5), 'Scottish matter' means a matter that relates to Scotland and is not a reserved matter (within the meaning of the Scotland Act 1998).
4   Provision as to how and by whom the amount of awards is to be assessed, including provision allowing the assessment to be undertaken by the inquiry panel or by such other person as the panel may nominate and make provision for review of an assessment at the instance of a person dissatisfied with it.

control.[5] Chapters 7–9 of that inquiry refer respectively to the control of firearms and ammunition, the certification system relating to section 1 firearms and the availability of section 1 firearms. These would have been outside the remit of the FAI under the then 1976 legislation.

10.09 It is the duty of the Minister (or the Chairman if s 25(2) applies[6]) who commissioned the Report to arrange to publish this.[7] The report should be published in full,[8] though subs (4)[9] allows for material in the report to be withheld from publication. That will be justified where that is required by any statutory provision, any retained enforceable EU obligation, the rule of law or where it is considered to be necessary in the public interest. Discretion is provided therefore to withhold aspects of the inquiry's report were it considered necessary. There is of course a balance to be respected.

10.10 Regard is required in particular to matters such as the extent to which withholding material might inhibit the allaying of public concern, any risk of harm or damage that could be avoided or reduced by withholding any material and any conditions as to confidentiality, subject to which a person acquired information that they have given to the inquiry.

10.11 The Litvinenko Inquiry considered the circumstances of the death of Mr Litvinenko who was poisoned on 1 November 2006 and later died in hospital on 23 November 2006. He was the victim of lethal polonium-210-induced acute radiation syndrome. This inquiry illustrated clearly the wider remit of the purpose of an inquiry in contrast to an inquest. The inquest had run into difficulties with an inquiry then replacing it.[10] The inquest's problem had centred on the existence of sensitive government documents that were relevant to the investigation regarding the possible Russian State's responsibility for Mr Litvinenko's death.[11] These would not have been able to be explored in the context of the narrower focus of an inquest. The report which was published included a number of closed appendices, no doubt justified on the grounds of national security. However, the inquiry had been able to consider the possible involvement – though then did not issue any conclusions in the public domain.

---

5   Scottish Office, Public inquiry into the shootings at Dunblane Primary School 16 October 1996), *www.gov.uk/government/publications/public-inquiry-into-the-shootings-at-dunblane-primary-school* (accessed on 21 February 2023).

6   This applies where applies (a) the Minister notifies the chairman before the setting-up date that the chairman is to have responsibility for arranging publication, or (b) at any time after that date the chairman, on being invited to do so by the Minister, accepts responsibility for arranging publication.

7   Inquiries Act 2005, s 25(1).

8   Inquiries Act 2005, s 25(3).

9   Inquiries Act 2005, s 25(4)

10   The Manchester arena bombing to was held as a public inquiry rather than an inquest for similar reasons.

11   Paragraphs 2.3 and 2.4 of the Report into the death of Alexander Litvinenko presented to Parliament pursuant to Section 26 of the Inquiries Act 2005, 21 January 2016.

3. INQUIRIES IN SCOTLAND

10.12   A number of inquiries have been undertaken in Scotland. Prior to the 2005 Act, one example was in relation to Piper Alpha[12] disaster where the explosion on an offshore oil rig occurred on 6 January 1988. The inquiry was conducted by Lord Cullen. **Appendix 2** outlines the background and nature of that inquiry. Instructing an inquiry in these circumstances provided the opportunity for greater examination of the subject matter and especially as there was a need to consider reserved matters, within the meaning of the Scotland Act 1998. That allowed that inquiry to be a 'joint inquiry'.[13] Section 32 of the 2005 Act stated that a 'joint inquiry' is one where two or more Ministers are responsible. Section 33(1) of the 2005 Act refers to a joint inquiry for which the Ministers responsible are not all United Kingdom Ministers and are not all Northern Ireland Ministers.

10.13   The ICL Factory Inquiry[14] was held after the 2005 Act came into force. The holding of an Inquiry was, announced on 1 October 2007 jointly by the then Lord Advocate, the Rt Hon Eilish Angiolini QC, and the then Secretary of State for Work and Pensions, the Rt Hon Peter Hain MP. This inquiry was the first example of a joint inquiry across respective interests of England and Scotland held under the 2005 Act.[15] The inquiry was a joint inquiry since health and safety matters were not within the competence of the Scottish ministers. The inquiry was also required to consider matters relating to Scotland that were not reserved.

10.14   It was held under the chairmanship of Lord Gill, the then Lord President. He described this as the 2005 Act having allowed for:

'a new framework for public inquiries that will greatly increase the efficiency with which they are conducted without compromising the thoroughness of the process. The essence of this approach is that inquiries will be inquisitorial processes, in which the relevant questions will be determined by the inquiry, rather than the adversarial, litigation-based processes typical of major inquiries in the past in which the inquiry agenda has been set by the participants themselves. In this new approach, there is no reason to fear that the truth-finding process will be compromised.'[16]

---

12   Department of Energy, *The Public Inquiry into the Piper Alpha disaster*, Cm 1310, *www.hse.gov.uk/offshore/piper-alpha-public-inquiry-volume1.pdf* (accessed on 21 February 2023).
13   Inquiries Act 2005, ss 32 and 33.
14   The ICL Inquiry Report Explosion at Grovepark Mills, Maryhill, Glasgow 11 May 2004, Presented to the House of Commons and the Scottish Parliament under S26 Inquiries Act 2005, Presented to the House of Lords by Command of Her Majesty.
15   *The ICL Inquiry*, HC 838, *https://assets.publishing.service.gov.uk/government/uploads/system/uploads/attachment_data/file/229279/0838.pdf* (accessed on 21 February 2023).
16   *The ICL Inquiry*, HC 838, Introduction, *https://assets.publishing.service.gov.uk/government/uploads/system/uploads/attachment_data/file/229279/0838.pdf* (accessed on 21 February 2023).

10.15 The background of the inquiry is set out in Appendix 4 of the report. Its terms of reference were to inquire into the circumstances leading up to the incident on 11 May 2004 at the premises occupied by the ICL group of companies, Grovepark Mills, Maryhill, Glasgow. These were to:

- consider the safety and related issues, including the regulation of the activities at Grovepark Mills;
- make recommendations in the light of the lessons identified from the causation and circumstances leading up to the incident; and
- report as soon as practicable.

10.16 Strictly speaking the time scales of reporting timeously should have been implicit in undertaking any inquiry into deaths. As has been observed, no timescales to regulate the time taken from the date of death to the holding of an FAI were included within the 2016 Act. This has continued to cause concerns about the delays in holding, let alone in concluding, FAIs.

4. WHY SHOULD A PUBLIC INQUIRY BE HELD INSTEAD OF AN FAI?

10.17 The focus here is on inquiries taking place on a statutory footing, though an inquiry can be held on a non-statutory basis. Non-statutory inquiries rely on the co-operation of the relevant organisations and individuals, and the potential reputational damage should a person or organisation refuse to co-operate. Inquiries held under the 2005 Act have greater powers to compel witnesses to give evidence or to produce documents. These inquiries also tend to be held where there are a large number of victims, which was of course the case with Piper Alpha.

10.18 The goals of a public inquiry are set by the government, usually taking into account the questions and concerns of the interested parties, including individual members of the public and organisations. They are usually held when there is public concern that something has happened requiring an open, fair and thorough investigation by a body independent from the problem. Public inquiries are not necessarily held in public, nor will the report of the inquiry necessarily be available for public view.

10.19 Public inquiries may be held in relation to events that suggest a breakdown in the rule of law, or where there has been a shocking crime, or those which have caused deaths in cases such as the death of Victoria Adjo Climbié, where the Inquiry Report[17] published in January 2003 found that she had been murdered by her great aunt, and her aunt's boyfriend. Lord Laming conducted the inquiry, which took evidence from authorities representing social services, health, housing as well as the

---

17 *The Victoria Climbié Inquiry,* Cm 5730, *https://assets.publishing.service.gov.uk/government/uploads/system/uploads/attachment_data/file/273183/5730.pdf* (accessed on 21 February 2023).

police. The Laming Report made a number of significant recommendations which were set out in Chapter 18 which included social care, healthcare recommendations and the police.

10.20   An inquiry can make recommendations to the Government so that:

'With the support of the Prime Minister, a ministerial Children and Families Board should be established at the heart of government. The Board should be chaired by a minister of Cabinet rank and should have ministerial representation from government departments concerned with the welfare of children and families.'[18]

10.21   A public inquiry usually has a much broader remit than an inquest or an FAI. It will typically involve looking at a much wider range of evidence. It is therefore common for these proceedings to take much longer, often stretching over several years. One other way in which public inquiries differ from inquests or FAIs is that they do have the power to assign blame, which to an extent is seen in the Laming Report where it had powers to recommend significant changes in practice to be brought in from government and extending beyond that death itself.

10.22   The terms of reference can sometimes be subject to public consultation which provides an opportunity for organisations and other interested parties to have their say on the proposed breadth and scope of the inquiry. That process engenders the potential for greater public support for the inquiry. The inquiry may still present conflicting aims and objectives, and challenges with regard to procedural issues which may have the capacity to delay the inquiry.

10.23   Public inquiries are an inquisitorial rather than an adversarial process, and are not able to make decisions about a person's or organisation's civil or criminal liability. The inquiry's recommendations are not legally binding as it is up to the government or any other relevant bodies to take forward or implement any recommendations.

10.24   Inquiries may be held on occasion to respond to political pressure. An Institute for Government Report *Public Inquiries: How can they lead to change published in December 2017*[19] made a number of criticisms that the recommendations in inquiries lacked effect. There was no requirement for a statutory follow-up process regarding the recommendations resulting from the inquiry, at either ministerial or any other level. It was rare for government departments[20] to follow up inquiry recommendations so failures in process found by an Inquiry were not necessarily addressed.

---

18   *The Victoria Climbié Inquiry* , Cm 5730.
19   Institute for Government, *How public inquiries can lead to change* (12 December 2017), h*www. instituteforgovernment.org.uk/publications/how-public-inquiries-can-lead-change* (accessed on 21 February 2023).
20   Only six have been fully followed-up by select committees to see what government did as a result of the inquiry.

10.25 The leadership role under s 3 of the 2005 Act is seen as crucial. The 2005 Act sets out options for chairing, though subject to consultation with the Prime Minister before appointing the chair.[21] The majority of chairs are judges, providing for consultation requirements under s 10 of the 2005 Act with the relevant head of the judiciary for certain sitting judges. There is also the option for the appointment of the chair or a chair and other panel with issues as to requirements as to suitability and impartiality addressed under ss 8 and 9 of the 2005 Act. It can, unlike the FAI process, be the target of the media discussion, as was the case with the Grenfell Tower Inquiry.

10.26 When retired Court of Appeal judge Sir Martin Moore-Bick[22] was chosen to lead the Grenfell public inquiry, there was criticism from campaigners after he said the scope of his investigation would be 'limited to the problems surrounding the start of the fire and its rapid development'.[23] They objected to his appointment because he was a commercial judge and in an earlier case had decided that the council should rehouse a tenant 50 miles away, though his decision in that case was later overturned.[24] Inquiries just as FAIs must be conducted with transparency and with the judge acting independently. The only recusal of a judge should be where there is any conflict of interest, just as in any civil or criminal case. Inquiries require public confidence in the judicial appointment that is made- which may on occasion present a challenge when emotions may be running high. This was certainly the case in Grenfell with the horrific circumstances of these multiple deaths.

10.27 Inquiries, as seen with FAIs too, are criticised for taking too long to publish any findings, with one in seven inquiries taking five years or longer to release their final report.[25] What was concluded was that the government should systematically explain how it is responding to inquiry recommendations, use select committees to examine annual progress updates from government on the state of implementation from inquiries, publish interim reports and involve expert witnesses in developing the recommendations of inquiries. The introduction for timescales and update inquiry reports echoes that need for reports of progress and in accounting for delays in inquests and FAIs. Bringing in that enhanced monitoring would seem an improvement in relation to the holding of all death inquiries, whether a FAI, inquest or inquiry.

---

21 2018 Ministerial Code.
22 BBC, *Grenfell Tower: Retired judge to lead disaster inquiry*, www.bbc.co.uk/news/uk-40438701 (accessed on 21 February 2023).
23 Politics Home, *Labour MP calls for Grenfell inquiry judge to be removed from his post*, www.politicshome.com/news/article/labour-mp-calls-for-grenfell-inquiry-judge-to-be-removed-from-his-post (accessed on 21 February 2023).
24 The Guardian, Grenfell Tower inquiry judge has controversial history in housing cases (29 June 2017), www.theguardian.com/uk-news/2017/jun/28/grenfell-tower-inquiry-judge-retired-martin-moore-bick (accessed on 21 February 2023).
25 Institute for Government, *How public inquiries can lead to change* (12 December 2017), www.instituteforgovernment.org.uk/publications/how-public-inquiries-can-lead-change (accessed on 21 February 2023).

10.28   Inquiries are criticised for their expense as well as delay. There have been delays due to staff turnover, such as the Independent Inquiry into Child Sexual Abuse, which was by the end of 2017 on its fourth chair. One further well-known example was the Bloody Sunday Inquiry which cost £210.6 million.[26]

10.29   Between 1990 and 2017, the UK and devolved nations spent at least £630 million on public inquiries[27] but the costs may be higher, since not all inquiries publish their costs while other inquiries are still continuing. The costs are incurred through the cost of counsel including those directly assisting the inquiry, and office space as a number are held outside the court estate. **Chapter 12** considers the difficulties in quantifying the costs in FAIs.

5.   NUMBER OF INQUIRIES HELD

10.30   To provide a perspective, on numbers, between 1990 and 2017, there have been 46 inquiries held with 2,791 recommendations made. Outstanding Scottish inquiries currently include the Edinburgh Tram Inquiry under Lord Hardie which commenced on 5 June 2014[28] and the Scottish Child Abuse Inquiry under Lady Smith which commenced 17 December 2014.

10.31   Of relevance to discussions on death investigations, the holding of a public inquiry into the death of Sheku Bayoh was announced on 20 May 2020 under the chair, Lord Bracadale.[29] The terms of reference have been agreed which include the purpose of the inquiry as:

- Establishing the circumstances surrounding the death of Sheku Bayoh in police custody on 3 May 2015 and making recommendations to prevent deaths in similar circumstances (as would have been required under the 2016 Act).
- Assessing and establishing aspects of the case that could not be captured, or fully captured through the FAI process, namely (a) the post incident management process and subsequent investigation and make any recommendations for the future in relation to these, and (b) the extent (if any) to which the events leading up to and following Mr Bayoh's death, in particular the actions of the officers involved, were affected by his actual or perceived race and to make recommendations to address any findings in that regard.[30]

---

26   In 2017 prices.
27   In 2017 prices.
28   £12.111 million as at 21 December 2021: https://www.gov.scot/publications/foi-202100256857/.
29   With the preliminary hearing held on 18 November 2021.
30   Public Inquiry into the Death of Sheku Bayoh – Terms of Reference, *www.shekubayohinquiry.scot/sites/default/files/2020-11/Inquiry%20terms%20of%20reference.pdf* (accessed on 21 February 2023).

10.32 It can be seen and is acknowledged just how much wider the remit of that inquiry is compared to that the FAI.

10.33 Of further note relating to the examination of deaths are the two Covid -19 inquiries which are being held under

- Coronavirus (UK) Act 2020[31] (on 12 May 2021) that is to examine the extension process for the legislation and evidence that the government should produce to justify such an extension.
- Coronavirus (Scotland) Act 2020 (on 24 August 2021)[32] which is to look at examining how the authorities responded to the Covid-19 pandemic. Originally this inquiry was set up under Lady Poole but she resigned in October and has been replaced by Lord Brailsford.[33]

10.34 The Terms of Reference have been set which include inquiry into care and nursing homes: the transfer of residents to or from homes, treatment and care of residents, restrictions on visiting, infection prevention and control and inspections. (These investigations cover the period between 1 January 2020 and 31 December 2022 though in accordance with the 2005 Act, it can consider only 'Scottish matters'.[34]) The inquiry respects the independent role of the Lord Advocate in relation to the prosecution of crime and the investigation of deaths in Scotland and must make reasonable efforts to minimise duplication of investigation, evidence gathering and reporting with any other public inquiry established under the 2005 Act.

10.35 Related to this inquiry is the investigation under Operation Koper, which was investigating Covid-19 linked deaths in Scotland, a number of which include those relating to care home residents. The Operation is investigating deaths in at least 474 separate Scottish care homes. Just how much the inquiry will cover deaths from Covid-19 outside of care homes is unknown or what FAI or further inquiries may be held.

---

31 UK Parliament, *Coronavirus Act 2020 Two years on*, *https://committees.parliament.uk/work/1718/ coronavirus-act-2020-two-years-on/* (accessed on 21 February 2023).

32 House of Commons Library, Statutory public inquiries: the Inquiries Act 2005, Number SN06410, *https://researchbriefings.files.parliament.uk/documents/SN06410/SN06410.pdf*;   Scottish Government, *Covid-19 Inquiry* (2 November 2022), *www.gov.scot/publications/covid-19-inquiry/* (accessed on 21 February 2023).

33 This inquiry has not commenced as Lady Poole resigned on 3 October 2022: BBC, Covid in Scotland: Judge Lady Poole resigns from inquiry role (3 October 2022), and BBC, Scotland Covid inquiry, Lord Brailsford appointed new chair (27 October 2022), *www.bbc.co.uk/news/uk-scotland-63118187, www.bbc.co.uk/news/uk-scotland-63416975* (accessed on 21 February 2023).

34 Section 28(5) of the 2005 Act.

Chapter 11

Public Access to FAIs

This chapter as originally drafted was based on discussions and research conducted with the National Records Office of Scotland (NRS) and the Scottish Courts and Tribunals Service (SCTS). In February 2023, the SCTS closed all FAI records at the NRS to conduct a review of the public access arrangements.

As at June 2023, the review was completed. The purpose of the review was to assess a range of issues 'in order to strike a balance between protection of personal data of living individuals whilst maintaining access to archived [FAI] Records.' Following that review, 90% of FAI records held at the NRS have been re-opened. Where such records remain closed, a Freedom of Information request to access closed records may be made and processed by SCTS. Such records will be opened in response or released with information being redacted.

All FAI records older than 100 years held by the NRS will become an open record.

All FAI records can be searched using the NRS Online Public Access catalogue. Those researching should be aware of any data protection and the General Data Protection Regulation requirements as published on the NRS website and the FAI section on the SCTS Guide to Information.

It is recommended that anyone seeking access to historic FAI records on a public basis clarifies the position in advance. It is suggested that this is discussed with SCTS and the National Records Office of Scotland. There were over 150,000 entries in the National Records Office of Scotland spanning from 1895 (Schedule 2). More recent FAI records may be accessible with SCTS or on their database at https://www.scotcourts.gov.uk/search-judgments/fatal-accident-inquiries. Only the last 50 FAI determinations are available in chronological order – others require some information such as the name of the deceased in order to search, there are not ordered in relation a generic search for deaths falling into a category such deaths in custody.

1.   GENERAL

11.01   FAIs are held into deaths that arise in Scotland with the systems substantially differing from that in England and Wales where coroners' inquests are held. **Chapter 1** covers the circumstances of how investigations into sudden deaths and FAIs are held into deaths in Scotland and how they fall within the responsibility of the Lord Advocate, operating through COPFS and their procurator fiscals.

11.02   All sudden, unexpected, unexplained or suspicious deaths are required to be reported to the procurator fiscal. Some of these deaths will thereafter form the basis for either a mandatory or discretionary FAIs being held as set out under the Inquiries into Fatal Accidents and Sudden Deaths etc. (Scotland) Act 2016 (the 2016 Act).

11.03   The purpose of this chapter is to provide basic information and guidance as to what kind of information about any FAI may be available for public access. It is envisaged that members of the public may be interested to source this information for relatives who may have died, or for historical research.

2.   INFORMATION AVAILABLE IN CONNECTION WITH FAIS

11.04   Information that may be available in connection with FAIs for these purposes is referred to as (1) the determination and (2) general papers.

Determination

11.05   At the conclusion of the FAI held into the death following the leading of evidence with witnesses, usually in a court (though FAIs have and can be held at other venues),[1] a determination will be issued by a sheriff. The determination is the formal record issued by the sheriff which contains certain information as required under s 26 of the 2016 Act. (Earlier legislation required similar findings to be made but are referred to as a verdict since prior to 1976 a jury was involved.)

---

1   The Lockerbie FAI was held at Crichton Royal Hospital Dumfries.

11.06 Once the evidence being heard in any FAI is completed in court, SCTS retain the papers until such time as the determination is issued. Thereafter once the determination is issued, SCTS retain papers in storage until these records are passed to the National Records of Scotland[2].

11.07 All sheriff's determinations have been published since the 2016 Act commenced in 2017 as that was a statutory requirement under Section 27(1) of the 2016 Act though it provides discretion to SCTS as to how that publication is to be effected by the incorporation of 'in such manner as it considers appropriate.' Their choice is to provide a database showing the last 50 published chronologically. Prior to 2017, a determination might have been made available publicly on the internet but this was not necessarily the standard process adopted in all FAIs. There seems to have been no consistent or standard policy followed, with the decisions as to publication being left to the respective sheriff's discretion as to whether publication should be undertaken or not.

11.08 To source a recent determination, since publication is now required, the best access is through the SCTS website.[3] This details the last 50 FAIs that have been published in chronological order. Thereafter, for earlier determinations, there is a search function if the name of the deceased or other relevant information is known. SCTS has moved to the electronic publication of determinations so all FAI determinations should now be available electronically.

11.09 If a search electronically does not identify the relevant determination, contact can be made with the local Sheriff Court[4] where the FAI was originally held. They should be able to source the determination and to make it available for public access. Many of these records are held offsite so access presumably would and could not be immediate.

General papers

11.10 In addition to the issue or publication of the determination, other papers may have been retained in connection with any FAI that was held.

11.11 These FAI papers may comprise all documents that were led in court. This may include, but is not restricted to, witness lists, witness statements, photographs of the location and the deceased, the records of courts proceedings such as minutes, precognitions and letters to the sheriff. It is not possible to be prescriptive about what

---

2   National Records of Scotland, *www.nrscotland.gov.uk/* (accessed on 21 February 2023).
3   Scottish Courts and Tribunals, Fatal Accident Inquiries, *www.scotcourts.gov.uk/search-judgments/ fatal-accident-inquiries* (accessed on 21 February 2023).
4   A record of all sheriff courts can be found at https://www.nrscotland.gov.uk/record-keeping/ guidance-for-depositors/courts-and-legal-bodies/sheriff-courts#:~:text=There%20are%2039%20 sheriff%20courts%20throughout%20Scotland. This refers to 39 though remember some of these may have merged

information may be held as each FAI will vary both as to what evidence was led as well as what was subsequently retained.

11.12   As far as SCTS is concerned, when the determination is issued, and before the papers are retained, they will return documents to COPFS. This is on the basis that these are the Crown's documents as they were produced in the FAI. This would include photographs of the deceased and the locus as examples. Presumably, a similar rule would apply to all papers belonging to any party represented at the FAI and having led evidence since what was lodged would in effect belong to them though once the documents were entered in court, they would have formed part of the court process.

3.   ACCESS TO HISTORICAL FAIS

11.13   FAI papers are publicly available in respect of historical FAIs. As FAIs are a matter of public interest, and form part of Scotland's historical records, the responsibility and source for such FAI papers lie with the National Records of Scotland.[5]

11.14   The National Records of Scotland (NRS) is a non-ministerial department of the Scottish Government based in Edinburgh whose purpose is to collect, preserve and produce information about Scotland's people and history. They make papers available for the current and future generations. FAI papers form an important part of their collection and can be sourced through their catalogue, where a guide is available as to what is available and how best to search their collection.

11.15   The NRS is responsible for the selection, preservation and provisions of access to public records. Access to data is governed by the Data Protection Act 2018, which is the UK's implementation of the General Data Protection Regulation (GDPR). and covers the protection of individuals regarding their processing of personal data.

11.16   Where anyone seeks to source any FAI papers, contact would need to be made with the NRS where public examination facilities are available, using their services at their Historical Search Room at HM General Register House. Any FAI papers would need to be ordered electronically and requested in advance. A current readers' card is required with a limitation on the number of items which can be requested on a daily basis.

---

5   National Records of Scotland, *Fatal Accident Inquiry Records, www.nrscotland.gov.uk/research/ guides/fatal-accident-inquiry-records* (accessed on 21 February 2023).

4. THE RECORDS THAT ARE RETAINED

11.17 From 1895 onwards, following the Fatal Accidents Inquiry (Scotland) Act 1895, these FAI, as public inquiries, were undertaken by a sheriff and jury, following a petition made by the procurator fiscal. These early FAIs related to fatal accidents that had occurred during industrial employment. The death of John Hardwick which was the subject of an FAI in 1895 has been included under the **Appendix 2**.

11.18 The earliest COPFS FAI is from 1937. This was an FAI into the deaths of Patrick McNeela, Owen Kilbane, John McLoughlin, Martin McLoughlin, Michael Mangan, John Mangan, Thomas Mangan, Thomas Cattigan, Patrick Kilbane and Thomas Kilbane[6] which was held at Dumbarton Sheriff Court. They were Irish potato pickers who died in fire in a bothy at Eastside, Kirkintilloch, on 16 September 1937. On the catalogue, the entry has been linked to the relevant Sheriff Court FAI – SC65/25A/1937/14, so access can be obtained to both sets of papers.

11.19 From 1906, the Fatal Accidents and Sudden Deaths Inquiry (Scotland) Act 1906 (c.35) which amended the 1895 Act widened the scope to include inquiries into sudden or suspicious deaths in Scotland where an FAI should be held.

11.20 From 1976, the Fatal Accidents and Sudden Deaths Inquiry (Scotland) Act 1976 (c.14) dispensed with the need for a jury, widened the Lord Advocate's powers and brought in deaths in prisons and of persons in legal custody within the FAI system. Jurisdiction was extended to include the offshore oil industry.

11.21 From 2016, with the 2016 Act, mandatory FAIs may be held into deaths which arise while the deceased is acting within the course of their employment or occupation and legal custody or a child in secure accommodation as well as service custody premises. Discretionary FAIs arise where the death was sudden, suspicious unexpected or unexplained and where there are circumstances giving rise to serious public concern and the Lord Advocate decides it is in the public interest for an FAI to be held into the death. FAIs can also be held into deaths that occur outside the UK where the person was ordinarily resident in Scotland at the discretion of the Lord Advocate, though none as yet have been held.

11.22 FAI records have been retained since 1895 in a relatively piecemeal fashion. These are indexed under the respective Sheriff Courts Series where each Sheriff Court is allocated a number. To search, this should be carried out under the name of the deceased or, where the FAI involved more than one death, it may be searchable under its name. An example of this would be the Cairngorm disaster involving multiple deaths.[7]

---

6   AD2//1937//1.
7   **Appendix 2B**.

11.23 From approximately 1950 to the mid-1990s, the process to retain FAI papers became more systematic with more records becoming available and being preserved.

5. HOW TO FIND THE RECORDS

11.24 All Sheriff Court FAIs are open and available for public inspection[8]. FAI records that are held are listed individually. There is an online catalogue with the records which can be consulted in the Historical Search Room. (Several courts have recorded minutes of FAIs in their record of criminal jury trials, and some may be found in the Ordinary Court act books.)

11.25 For Sheriff Courts, each court is given a number ie Aberdeen is SC1. If SC1 is entered into the catalogue, it shows the series level description which lists the groups of records within the court series.

11.26 For each court, there will be a separate section for FAI records – for Aberdeen this is SC1/16.

11.27 Within the FAI series, each item will be listed by year, then by case number that year. Looking at Aberdeen FAIs in 1945, the catalogues show:

11.28 **Table showing catalogue entries:**

SC1/16/1945/1	Fatal Accident Inquiry: James Clark, tractor driver, 7 Church Street, Turriff, died on 7 December 1944 when he fell off the tractor he was driving and was crushed in a stubble field on the Lotted Lands, Greengate, Turriff	26 February 1945
SC1/16/1945/10	Fatal Accident Inquiry: James McDonald Pithie, watchman, 4 Sandilands Drive, Aberdeen, drowned on 16 or 17 January 1945 when he fell off the steam trawler "Kernevel" berthed at Balaclava Harbour, Fraserburgh	11 April 1945
SC1/16/1945/11	Fatal Accident Inquiry: James Coutts, fumigator, 6 Huntly Street, Canonmills, Edinburgh, died on 4 February 1945 on board HMS 'Stina' at Albert Quay, Aberdeen Harbour, when he was poisoned by hydrocyanic acid	11 April 1945
SC1/16/1945/12	Fatal Accident Inquiry: Hugh Falconer, post office survey officer, 66 Rosemount Place, Aberdeen, died on 21 January 1945 in a road traffic accident	12 June 1945

---

8   National Records of Scotland, *https://catalogue.nrsscotland.gov.uk/nrsonlinecatalogue/search.aspx* (accessed on 21 February 2023).

11.29 Each item has a title which details the deceased, their address, date and location of death, and if different, the date the injuries were sustained. The description will detail what is included in the papers, which will usually be the minutes and verdict/determination.

6. WHERE ARE THE FAI PAPERS OBTAINED?

11.30 The NRS obtain their FAI papers from the sheriff courts, now SCTS. From SCTS's storage, the NRS will collect the records on a national basis. (It appears that some procurator fiscal records are held by Shetland Archives and for Kirkwall by Orkney Library Archive.) Collection is undertaken on a rolling schedule, so some courts may take slightly longer to collect from. The most recent FAIs which are retained are from 1997.[9] The NRS will index them before they are made available to the public as outlined above. The records will be available up to the mid-1990s as the policy is for 25 years to have elapsed before the records are made publicly available.

11.31 A Protocol[10] Schedule of Sheriff Court Records For Preservation and Destruction 2017 (version 1) has been agreed where the requirements for retention of FAIs records are set out. It requires the retention of all records.

11.32 Records are also obtained from COPFS where they are selective about what is retained as these are records which would not normally come to the NRS. The NRS take FAIs from COPFS in nationally significant cases where the case precipitated a change or was a historically significant case. In effect, that recognises that these specific records are in the public interest.

11.33 Since 2017, NRS have an input into the decision whether to retain. As highlighted above, all FAI determinations are the responsibility of the sheriff court, such records that are agreed between the NRS and COPFS to be retained would be additional to the retention of these determinations.

11.34 These FAIs are catalogued under AD references, for advocate depute, and are within series AD27. These are the same as SC records and are catalogued by year and reference number ie AD27/1994/2. The only difference is that there are not so many. Items within the records are usually listed.

11.35 All COPFS FAI records are currently closed. The contents can contain more personal and sensitive information so the cases are reviewed by the COPFS Freedom of Information (FOI) review team before access will be granted. Parts of each case will be made available but items such as personal letters or highly sensitive items

---

9   The National Records Of Scotland Catalogue allows all FAIs records to be searched. https://catalogue.nrscotland.gov.uk/nrsonlinecatalogue/overview.aspx?st=1&tc=y&tl=n&tn=n&tp=n&k=fatal+accident+Inquiry&ko=a&r=&ro=s&df=&dt=&di=y (accessed 31/8/2023)

10   National Records of Scotland, *www.scotcourts.gov.uk/docs/default-source/default-document-library/sheriff_court_records_schedulepdf?sfvrsn=6* (accessed on 21 February 2023).

(ie secure plans of airports or letters from governments) can be closed under FOI legislation.

11.36   These will be available after 100 years – but applications can be made for earlier access which will be considered. An example of an open Crown Office FAI is AD27/1969/1, where COPFS have already reviewed it and deemed the majority of the papers open, with the NRS catalogue stating:

> 'The majority of this file has been opened following a request under the Freedom of Information (Scotland) Act 2002. Some parts of this file have been digitally imaged and will not be produced for readers. The digital images may be seen in the NRS Search Rooms on the "Virtual Volumes" system. Some information is exempt from release under the Freedom of Information (Scotland) Act 2002. This information has been redacted (blocked out). To request access to the redacted information whilst the exemption is current, please contact the NRS Freedom of Information Officer. For further details please look in the Freedom of Information (FOI) section of our website or ask a member of staff. For details of which parts are open and which are exempt, please consult the catalogue entry for each part.'

11.37   In the James Watt Street fire in Glasgow, the record displays:

> 'Under reference AD27/1969/1/1- AD27/1969/1/19 –
>
> "Fatal Accident Inquiry into the deaths of Thomas Whyte Turner, Henry Fulton Brown, James Monaghan, Joseph Greig, Thomas Daly, Elizabeth Taylor, Mary Leghorn Taylor, Harry Ure, Janet Taggart, Freda McCulloch, Christopher Kelly Duffy, Elizabeth Doyle Grant, Lewis Judah Radnor, James McArthur McDonald, John McCarroll, Alexander Goldberg, Julius Stern, William McGeachy, John Joseph Walker, George Bennedetti, Lawrence Ward Fleming and George Jesner held at Glasgow Sheriff Court with various dates showing as well as the status of the records. In this case they are marked as open.[11]"
>
> Clicking on the listing of the papers provides the description of the item which is retained. AD27/1969/1/15 refers to the COPFS correspondence file.'

7.   OTHER SOURCES

11.38   There are also a small number of FAI-related records held within the NRS HH series, which form the records of the Scottish Home and Health Department.[12] These are more specific records detailing parts of the Scottish Home and Health departments dealings with FAI inquiries, and include items such as papers and correspondence

---

11   Access status is categorised in three levels: Green is open, red is closed, yellow means that conditions apply.
12   Prior to 1995 and now part of the Scottish Government.

covering legal representation for the Scottish Home and Health department at an FAI, arrangements for publication of reports from FAIs, and transcripts.

11.39   An example is HH95 (HH95/1-HH95/48)[13] which contain the records relating to 21 deaths in the Lanarkshire E-Coli Outbreak FAI conducted in 1998. It includes a full set of records from the case and could be used if researching this FAI. Some of these records are open and some are closed, depending on the nature of the contents, the closure status and the relevant period is noted on the catalogue.

11.40   The SCTS Lockerbie papers are under review by SCTS as they contain very sensitive material and pictures. These have not been fully catalogued yet and are not currently available. Other major FAIs are the Ibrox disaster catalogued under SC36/30/1971/1 – 66 victims died on 2 January 1971 at Ibrox Stadium at the end of the Rangers v Celtic football match held on 2 January 1971, when the steel barriers gave way on Stairway 13. These records are all open.

11.41   With regard to any inquiries that took place before 1895, not many sources exist though the records of the Lord Advocate's department include registers of sudden deaths, fatal accident inquiries and accidents in mines, 1848–1935. There may be records available from local newspapers or local libraries, the National Library of Scotland and the British Library in London.

8.   WHAT HAPPENED DURING WORLD WAR II?

11.42   It appears during World War II, in England and Wales, it was not necessary for coroners to hold inquests into the death of air raid victims. It can be seen how a number of victims such as police and air raid precautions wardens would have been killed as the result of enemy action during their course of employment. Under the Emergency Powers (Defence) Act 1939, a number of defence regulations were made, including Defence Regulation 1939 No 30 that provided a body might be interred and the death registered if a certificate was given by an authorised person that the death was due to war operations which required that '… a coroner shall not be obliged or authorised to take any action in relation to any death if he is satisfied that the death occurred in consequence of war operations'.

11.43   This was amended by Regulation 30A on 14 March 1941 which required that an inquest should be held if an authorised person had reason to believe that a death might have occurred in consequence of war operations, but the body could not be recovered or could not be identified and they are satisfied that the death occurred in consequence of war operations.[14]

---

13   National Records of Scotland, *https://catalogue.nrscotland.gov.uk/nrsonlinecatalogue/overview. aspx?st=1&tc=y&tl=n&tn=n&tp=n&k=&ko=p&r=HH95&ro=m&df=&dt=&di=y* (accessed on 21 February 2023).

14   London Metropolitan Archives Collections Catalogue, *41 – Coroners records for London and Middlesex, https://search.lma.gov.uk/scripts/mwimain.dll/144/RESEARCH_GUIDES/web_detail_ rg/SISN+65?SESSIONSEARCH* (accessed on 21 February 2023).

11.44   It is assumed that similar processes applied in Scotland but it has not been possible to track the equivalent Defence Regulations – a great number would have been made at the outset of the War which dealt with the practices to be followed where there was the expectation of significant casualties. The practical impact of the war on Scotland was seen with the removal of juries from FAIs for the duration. FAIs continued to be held in cases of tragic domestic incidents such as the deaths of two boys (brothers) aged 7 and 8 from electrocution in Saltcoats on 6 December 1940 from an overhead power cable lay across a garden with a finding made that the owner of the cable or who was responsible for it was negligent in the discharge of the duty of examination of the cable.[15]

11.45   Explosions in factories turned over to manufacturing processes in war time were the source of a number of FAIs that concerned an Explosives Factory the property then of ICI (then Imperial Chemical Industries) at Stevenston. These FAIs were mandatory as those killed were acting in a civilian capacity in the course of their employment, separate FAIs were held including two who were killed on 9 November 1939 with their cause of death as multiple injury, and with notification given to the HM Inspector of Explosions Home Office London, 21 killed including 2 HM Inspectors on 28/9/1939, and one death on 29/5/41 as a result of extensive burns and multiple injuries. There were no verdicts or findings – only the deceased being named as well as the cause and time of death-so that compliance with the formal findings.

9.   SUMMARY

11.46   If seeking out an FAI, checking the NRS catalogue under the deceased's name is step one. It will be catalogued if held. If it does not appear the NRS may not have collected these records so an access request should be made to the sheriff court where the FAI was held. All FAIs at NRS are catalogued as soon as they arrive so they can be tracked on the catalogue.

11.47   For records since 1994, such as 2020, an approach should be made to the relevant sheriff court, who should still hold the papers.

11.48   For direct information from SCTS or COPFS, the relevant sources to contact are:

dpo@scotcourts.gov.uk (Information and Governances) and FOI@copfs.gov.uk (COPFS).

---

15   SC7/19/1941/1.

Chapter 12

Statistical Background to the FAI System

1. INTRODUCTION

12.01 **Chapter 1** outlined the system of reporting of sudden deaths in Scotland, involving a range of organisations, including the medical organisations and COPFS. It focused mainly on the process from the date of the death to the certification of deaths. This chapter looks beyond the certification of the death in these cases where this does not complete the State's involvement in the death investigation.

12.02 However, in order to provide some perspective, this section provides an analysis as to the number of deaths where the circumstances require to be further investigated by COPFS. In some cases, these deaths will go on to require a mandatory Fatal Accident Inquiry (FAI) to be held whereas in others, the Lord Advocate's discretion will determine that a discretionary FAI is to be undertaken.

2. NUMBER OF DEATH REPORTS

12.03 The following table provides information as to the number of deaths arising annually in Scotland. It then considers those that are reported to COPFS. What does not exist, at least publicly from one source, is that information, so that the information is required to be compiled from different reports.

Information provided	Numbers supplied	Additional information where available
Number of deaths in Scotland annually[1]	64,093 deaths (2020)	N/A
Number of deaths reported to COPFS (These statistics are further broken down into 2,759 accidental deaths of which 679 were self-harm, 47 from assault, and 1339 died from drug related deaths)	15,739 deaths (2020–2021)	Comparison with 2019–2020, 2019–2018, 2017–2018, 2016–2017 shows the number of reports by COPFS received respectively as: 10,931, 10,865, 10,397 10,921[2]

12.04   These statistics show an increase from 10,921 deaths being reported in 2019- 2020 rising to 15,739 deaths in 2020/2021, which presumably is related to the Covid-19 pandemic. This ties in with the COPFS Annual Report and Accounts 2020–21 which states that '…[they] saw a significantly increased number of reportable deaths which required further investigation. A dedicated Unit was established to investigate Covid-19 deaths that required to be reported.'[3]

These statistics do not provide any information as to the number of reportable deaths that do not require further investigation into the death by COPFS. **Chapter 1** provided a number of examples where the death, though requiring to be reported, might not need COPFS to do more than clear the cause of death and allow certification to take place. The only source of information comes from the COPFS Annual Report and Accounts where they indicates a key target for them in relation to the investigation of deaths. Where a death requires further investigation, they will conduct the investigation and advise the next of kin of the result within 12 weeks of the death being reported to the procurator fiscal. The COPFS Business Plan 2020–21 indicates that this has a performance target of 80%, which was not then achieved with performance then recorded at 70%.

12.06   However, what does this target actually mean? It does not state how many reported deaths are under investigation. If this means that all investigations are completed following the notification of the death and no further action is required by COPFS, this still leaves approximately 20% of cases to be further investigated beyond 12 weeks. Does this figure include foreign deaths which are now required to be reported to COPFS? The suggestion was made that this alone would bring in an additional 50 cases annually that required to be reported from abroad.

---

1   Scottish Government, *Standards for mortuary services: guidance published by the Scottish Ministers, Police Scotland and the Crown Office and Procurator Fiscal Service* (12 August 2022), *www.gov.scot/publications/standards-mortuary-services-guidance-published-scottish-ministers-police-scotland-crown-office-procurator-fiscal-service/pages/10/* (accessed on 21 February 2023)

2   *https://www.parliament.scot/-/media/files/committees/covid-19-recovery-committee/annex-a-copfs-statistics-on-case-processing-last-5-years-201621.pdf*

3   Annual Report and Financial Statements: For the year ended 31 March 2021, Laying number SG/2021/224, *www.copfs.gov.uk/media/u1bmwtmj/annual-report-and-accounts-2020-2021.pdf* (accessed on 21 February 2023).

12.07   That 20% of cases which do not meet the target of being closed within 12 weeks of the notification of the death, presumably include cases which are going to be the subject of further investigation and possibly, thereafter, the subject of FAIs. However, by way of explanation provided, is that 'many of these deaths require a post-mortem examination to be conducted. The examination process includes toxicological analysis. Pathologists are unable to conclude their examinations and submit their final reports to COPFS until they receive the toxicology results.'[4] That suggests the inability to meet the target relate in part to deaths where the cause of death may take more examination, though the cause of death in some cases will still remain unascertained. Presumably, acceptance of the cause of death, albeit unascertained, will conclude the investigation stage.

12.08   What this leaves is that the remaining 20% refers to a mixed bag of death investigations, some awaiting the final cause of death, while others are awaiting the conclusion of investigations and relevant decisions being made as to the holding of an FAI. That would mean in 2020–2021, that there was approximately between 3,000 to 4,500 reportable deaths still falling to be processed. Not all of these will then of course result in the holding of FAIs.

12.09   Covid-19 has been mentioned above. Further information can be analysed to see how Covid-19 has impacted on the death investigation system. COPFS undertook to report on Covid-19 deaths where the report was published in February 2022.[5] Their focus was on concluding death reports – however the information outlined in this Table below does not go on to indicate where these deaths will require the holding of any mandatory FAIs and the timescales for these FAIs being undertaken or completed. Indeed, there would be scope for such common interests in deaths for the FAIs to be conjoined to look at the system operating as an entity.

	Category of death	Number of death reports received 1 February 2022– 28 February 2022	Number of death reports dealt with
1	Care home deaths after 21 May 2020[6]	67	2,156
2	Worker deaths after 21 May 2020[7]	0	27
4	Deaths in custody	0	14
5	Other deaths[8]	24	1,033

---

4   Annual Report and Financial Statements: For the year ended 31 March 2021, Laying number SG/2021/224, *www.copfs.gov.uk/media/u1bmwtmj/annual-report-and-accounts-2020-2021.pdf* (accessed on 21 February 2023).

5   Covid Deaths Investigation Team (CDIT) monthly stats, Reports of Covid deaths received – February 2022, *www.copfs.gov.uk/media/xa0ij0x1/cdit-monthly-stats-february-2022.pdf* (accessed on 21 February 2023).

6   On 21 May 2020 guidance was issued that stipulated all Covid-19 or presumed Covid-19 deaths where the deceased was resident in a care home when the virus was contracted should be reported to COPFS.

7   On 21 May 2020 guidance was issued that stipulated all Covid-19 or presumed Covid-19 deaths where the deceased might have contracted the virus in the course of their employment or occupation should be reported to COPFS

8   Reference is made to the criteria for reporting other deaths to COPFS.

12.10   Mandatory FAIs are required to be carried out in relation to categories 2–4 of the deaths set out in the Table. Those falling within category 1 are discretionary and are forming part of the scope of the Scottish Covid-19 inquiry. Under category 5, it is, in theory, possible that a death from Covid-19 could be the subject of an FAI where other circumstances have arisen, such as a suggestion of poor medical or hospital care.

12.11   The COPFS's Briefing Note indicates that 'in over 90% of the 11,000 deaths reported to COPFS in a year, the Procurator Fiscal completes their investigation and is able to close the case within 12 weeks'.[9] That figure is not supported by their own performance target nor by the performance report. It is true that investigations into certain deaths may be complex and take longer than 12 weeks. However, the absence of statistics or performance targets as to the timescales for completion of investigations into deaths and/or the holding of FAIs is an omission – which is highlighted when looking in **Chapter 7** at the suggestion of including a requirement for COPFS to report on their progress of death investigations in line with the coroner system of mandatory reporting of inquests of delays over a six-month period.

3.   DEATH INVESTIGATIONS RESULTING IN FAIS

12.12   Where FAIs are instructed into deaths in Scotland, the numbers are relatively low. It is said to represent 0.6% of deaths investigated between 2016/17 to 2018/19.[10] However, there is a difference between instructing an FAI and holding an FAI – as there may well be a delay in allocating an FAI to a court. It is suggested ascertaining how many FAIs are held in a year would be a better statistic to consider for comparative purposes. However, this information is hard to ascertain.

12.13   Since the commencement of s 29 of the Inquiries into Fatal Accidents and Sudden Deaths etc. (Scotland) Act 2016 (asp 2) (the 2016 Act), a report is made to Scottish ministers as to the number of FAIs that took place in the previous financial year. It should then be possible to correlate the number of FAIs held in each year with the publication of determinations on the SCTS website, since the publication of determinations has been mandatory since the 2016 Act. These cannot be reconciled as determinations are neither required to be completed by the sheriff (the date appearing on the issue of the determination) nor published within any set timescale. Furthermore, as outlined in **Chapter 11**, the SCTS website tends to only show the

9   Crown Office & Procurator Fiscal Service, *Briefing note on investigation of deaths and FAI* (24 December 2018), *www.copfs.gov.uk/about-copfs/news/briefing-note-on-investigation-of-deaths-and-fai/* (accessed on 21 February 2023).
10   Scottish Government, *Fatal Accident Inquiries: follow up review* (7 August 2019), *www.gov.scot/publications/follow-up-review-fatal-accident-inquiries/pages/3/* (accessed on 21 February 2023).

last 50 determinations that have been published in chronological order. The number of determinations published in any financial year do then not correspond with the information being produced by COPFS.

12.14 Furthermore, what is meant by 'ended', as this is undefined? This is not a unique problem with the publication of justice statistics. In criminal justice, COPFS considers the end or completion of a prosecution when the case reaches a verdict. SCTS treat the end of a case when the sentence is passed as that concludes the court process and the utilisation of the court estate.

12.15 Does 'ended' mean when all evidence has been led in the FAI and the publication of the FAI determination is awaited? That would seem logical from the COPFS perspective as the publication of the determination lies out with the control of COPFS – their role concludes with the evidence gathering and the submissions then made to the sheriff in the FAI.

12.16 Seeking clarification of what the COPFS means by 'ended' would provide some clarity but on its own, that information is relatively meaningless. What seems of much more importance is an understanding of how many days that an FAI took in court, as that would help to show the required resource implications such as COPFS's staff time, the use of SCTS court estate as well as the use of judges' time.

12.17 FAIs can be in relatively short to hear as on occasion, several FAIs into deaths in custody have been heard on one day. Other FAIs extend to the hearing of many days of evidence and submissions such as the FAI into Shaman Weir's death at 46 days, which was described then as having been 'the longest running medical Fatal Accident Inquiry so far in Scotland', with its complexity noted as having had 'the highest number of professors attending to give expert evidence'.[11] More detailed and accurate production of statistics would provide greater transparency as to the adherence to timescales for holding FAIs – as the timescale taken from the date of the death including the investigation of the death, the holding of the FAI and the publication of the FAI should be able to be monitored and broken into sections as to the time taken for each section to be completed. The process culminating in an FAI is set out below.

---

11   Inquiry into the Death of Sharman Weir, *www.scotcourts.gov.uk/search-judgments/judgment?id=13c286a6-8980-69d2-b500-ff0000d74aa7* (accessed on 21 February 2023).

12.18   Process of death investigation

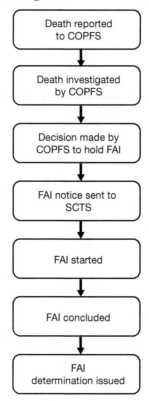

12.19   Furthermore, there should be set timescales for publication of FAI determinations by sheriffs which could then more accurately identify how many FAIs were concluded in any year. A further difficulty arises as the FAI itself may cover a number of deaths, such as the FAI into the Puma helicopter crash in the North Sea in 2009 where 16 men died.[12] Should the statistics not record the number of deceased in any report as the more deceased such as in a major accident there will inevitably be more complex requiring more evidence to be led and take longer in court.

4.   HOW MANY FAIs ARE HELD IN A YEAR?

12.20   The following Table has been taken from different sources, so does not provide a fully accurate picture. The data from 2012–2019 is taken from the Scottish Government's review, and the information from 2019–2021 comes the report to Scottish ministers.

---

12   [2014] FAI 5.

Year	FAIs held
2012/13	40
2013/14	33
2014/15	74
2015/16	53
2016/17	41
2017/18	53
2018/19	37
2019/20	54
2020/21	61

12.21   Looking at the type of FAI, that were held, there were 37 mandatory FAIs concluded in 2016/17, 45 in 2017/18 and 37 in 2018/19. Out of the 119 mandatory FAIs, 45 related to deaths that occurred in the course of employment and 74 when the deceased person was in legal custody. For discretionary FAIs, there were 12 held over 2016–2019. No further classification was completed as to what circumstances gave rise to these discretionary inquiries, which again may have provided a useful background. The report to the Scottish Parliament in relation to the 2016 Act does not require any breakdown into which type of FAI was held – whether mandatory or discretionary FAIs. The most common type of FAI relates to deaths in custody relating to those in prison. This is discussed in more detail in **Chapter 7.**

What do FAIs cost?

12.22   This is virtually impossible to discern as the FAI costs need to factor in all the relevant organisations' staff time in undertaking them. An FOI response from COPFS relating to costs provided the following information indicating that their staff costs could not be ascertained. The information provided then is as follows:

Financial Year Total Cost Associated with FAIs

Year of FAIs	Cost
2007/08 from 1/1/2008	£1,781.85
2008/09	£31,183.31
2009/10	£30,377.91
2010/11	£46,935.18
2011/12	£28,710
2012/13	£621.20

12.23   These represent the costs for expert and ordinary witness expenses, including the costs for doctors attending court, travelling expenses, report writing costs and forensic services. Again, this information is of limited use, as this will depend in any year on the number of FAIs held and the number of witnesses in each FAI that are to be called. Other parties to the FAI will bear their own costs of expert witnesses whom they wish to call; it is very common in FAIs into medical deaths to have a number of expert witnesses called.

12.24   COPFS will be responsible for the costs of their witnesses and accordingly, the majority of witnesses to the FAI will require paid for by them. A complex FAI involving a number of expert witnesses will impact significantly on the total financial cost in any year – however straightforward non-contentious deaths will not incur these significant costs.

12.25   A background outlining the costs can be obtained from the Financial Memorandum to the 2016 Act.[13] Interestingly, it indicates at para 6 that the Financial Memorandum (FM) gives 'an overview of the impact on the Scottish Government, COPFS, SCTS, and the other affected bodies as a result of the provisions in the Bill. However, many of the provisions will have no impact or financial element as they are a restatement (in modern drafting style) of the current provisions.'

12.26   That indicates that the changes brought in by the 2016 Act were not considered to be radical in affecting either the numbers of FAIs held and/or the scope of the number of FAIs to be held. The FM went on to highlight however that there may be an additional one or two FAIs held per year due to the change in definition of the mandatory categories of FAIs and by adding in that discretionary FAIs could be held into deaths abroad. However, there does not seem to have been any additional FAI held since the 2016 Act falling in either category which is notwithstanding that the FM included additional costs of investigating deaths abroad of 50 cases.[14] How many such deaths have been reported is unknown.

12.27   The FM also reflected on the 'volatility of FAI numbers due to the unpredictable nature of deaths requiring investigation and inquiry'.[15] Though that is true with regard to the nature of the FAIs that are held, there has to be a finite number of FAIs capable of being held in any year. The staff resources in COPFS, SCTS and the judiciary are not ring-fenced to cover costs of FAIs that are undertaken in any year. In order to increase the number of FAIs conducted in response to an increase in the numbers of FAIs, such as Covid-19 or to deal with the backlog, would require either additional resources allocated by the Scottish Government or indeed, if

13   Inquiries into Fatal Accidents and Sudden Deaths etc (Scotland) Bill, SP Bill 63–EN, Session 4 (2015), *https://archive2021.parliament.scot/S4_Bills/Fatal%20Accidents%20(Scotland)%20Bill/ b63s4-introd-en.pdf* (accessed on 21 February 2023).
14   Inquiries into Fatal Accidents and Sudden Deaths etc (Scotland) Bill, SP Bill 63–EN, Session 4 (2015), *https://archive2021.parliament.scot/S4_Bills/Fatal%20Accidents%20(Scotland)%20Bill/ b63s4-introd-en.pdf* (accessed on 21 February 2023), para 19.
15   Inquiries into Fatal Accidents and Sudden Deaths etc (Scotland) Bill, SP Bill 63–EN, Session 4 (2015), *https://archive2021.parliament.scot/S4_Bills/Fatal%20Accidents%20(Scotland)%20Bill/ b63s4-introd-en.pdf* (accessed on 21 February 2023), para 8.

prioritised, would need to be allocated at the expense of other civil or other criminal litigation taking place in the courts.

12.28   What was envisaged was that 'the existing costs of an FAI will not change as a result of the Bill' as the 2016 Act would 'not affect or change the long-standing common law duty of procurators fiscal to investigate sudden, suspicious or unexplained deaths in Scotland'.[16] Paragraph 91 of the FM indicated that 'it was anticipated' that these costs should be recorded and statistics maintained by COPFS 'so that there can be an assessment of the reforms'. This could be usefully undertaken in a review of the 2016 Act to evaluate how successful the 2016 Act has been in improving efficiency and effective performance.

12.29   Table 2 of the FM shows an estimation of the costs of holding an FAI. What costs have been factored in are specified with some riders that the costs for SCTS are based on the actual court sitting days for the hearing and do not include preparation work, including preliminary hearings.

12.30   As can be seen later, there is a level of judicial management of FAI cases undertaken at the preliminary hearing. There are cost and resource implications, though there appears little consistency in establishing just how long or how many preliminary hearings have been held in relation to any FAI.

12.31   Costs were excluded if held the FAI was at an outside non-court venue. When considering the FAI system under the 2016 Act, outside venues have always been used. Factors such as the size of the FAI, the number of victims and the proposed length of the FAI will determine its choice of location when using out of court facilities. The Lockerbie FAI was indeed held at Crichton Royal Hospital, Dumfries.[17]

12.32   It does not clarify when COPFS costs are taken to start. Does this include the administrative and legal staff time, including that of Crown Counsel from the date of death, in undertaking the investigation, the reporting the death which then results in the decision that an FAI is to be held and the costs of all notices and citing required prior to the start of the FAI?

12.33   Table 3 of the FM provides some breakdown on COPFS costs over the period but does not provide any clarity on the figures below. It does confirm that the COPFS costs on deaths administration and staff in the Deaths Unit in 2011/12, 2012/13 and 2013/14 were respectively £105,604, £104,456 and £106,095. These costs of course are generic but have not been divided into figure for out of court as compared to in court for legal staff.

---

16   Inquiries into Fatal Accidents and Sudden Deaths etc (Scotland) Bill, SP Bill 63–EN, Session 4 (2015), *https://archive2021.parliament.scot/S4_Bills/Fatal%20Accidents%20(Scotland)%20Bill/b63s4-introd-en.pdf* (accessed on 21 February 2023).

17   FAI relating to the Lockerbie Air Disaster, *www.vetpath.co.uk/lockerbie/fai.pdf* (accessed on 21 February 2023).

Name of organisation	1 day FAI	1 week FAI	Lengthy FAI (based on an estimate of 45 days)
SCTS Based on the basic approximate cost of an FAI sitting in a sheriff court, which includes judicial, and staff costs as well as running costs. These follow as being described as the impact on SCTS relates to the accommodation, services, staff and judiciary.	£2,000	£10,000	£90,000
COPFS These costs include administrative, precognition, victim information and advice (VIA), legal, pathology and witness costs.	£ 9,494	£13,122	£94,701

5.   TRAINING

12.34   One aspect which the FM considered was that of training. There were changes made to allow sheriffs principal to designate sheriffs as specialists in relation to FAIs and decide if an FAI should be allocated to a specialist sheriff. Since the 2016 Act, though the provisions exist, neither process has been followed. An All-Scotland specialist personal injury court[18] has now been established and recent reforms have called for the establishment of a specialist sexual offences courts,[19] with dedicated sheriffs and trauma informed agents to appear in them. Looking to considerations as to potential areas of reform, development of specialist practices might benefit the FAI process.

12.35   Judges' training falls to the Judicial Institute for Scotland (JIS) to arrange and it should include the law and practice of FAIs in its seminars. There is no information as to what training is being provided. Training costs were not mentioned with regard to either COPFS staff but training in what is a different inquisitorial system of law as compared to adversarial would seem to be equally pertinent to procurator fiscals as for the judges.

---

18   All-Scotland Sheriff Personal Injury Court, *www.scotcourts.gov.uk/the-courts/sheriff-court/personal-injury-court* (accessed on 21 February 2023)

19   Incorporated in draft Victims, Witnesses and Justice Reform Bill, currently before the Scottish Parliament (Stage 1): *https://www.parliament.scot/bills-and-laws//bills/victims-witnesses-and-justice-reform-scotland-bill.*

Chapter 13

Conclusion

13.01   In considering the Scottish system for investigations into deaths and the holding of FAIs, there is an opportunity to assess what is working well and to suggest where possible improvements may lie. The year 2009 provides a good base from which to start as this was when Lord Cullen extensively reviewed the FAI system, making a number of recommendations aimed at its overall systemic improvement. The majority of these recommendations were taken forward and implemented by the Inquiries into Fatal Accidents and Sudden Deaths etc. (Scotland) Act 2016 (asp 2) (the 2016 Act). A Table is included at the conclusion of this chapter to provide a broad overview of what has changed since with reference to his specific recommendations. It helps to suggest areas where the FAI system would benefit from further review in the light of the conclusions discussed below.

13.02   The overriding aim of the 2016 Act was to modernise the FAI system. In many ways, to that extent, the 2016 Act has been effective. However, specific details of the reforms, such as the holding of an FAI into a death abroad or further inquiry proceedings, have not yet been tested.[1]

13.03   However, the FAI system in Scotland today appears to be struggling at times to cope. Delays in the FAI system, which underpinned the need for the reforms in

---

1   2016 Act, ss 6 and 35.

the 2016 Act, have continued and are frequently referenced in press coverage with headlines specific to FAIs still to be held: 'No details of the date or location for the FAI have been announced by COPFS, which has been roundly criticised for delays in other inquiries.'[2] No examination of the current FAI system can be undertaken without considering the background and possible cause of these delays. Delay though is not the only way in which the FAI system appears to be encountering significant operational issues. Overall, the FAI system seems to lack available, accessible and reliable sources of public information, relevant training of and for those involved, and the public provision of data/statistics. It is suggested that it requires increased and better public reporting with enhanced support for the affected families who are central to the FAI system. The conclusion is that better transparency of the FAI process needs to be provided.

13.04 Reforms to these processes would not all necessarily require legislation. Lord Cullen's review had identified that an overhaul of the internal COPFS's systems needed to be in place before the legislative changes in the 2016 Act were implemented. Crucially, these areas outside of the legislation in the main still seem to be a source of these ingrained problems outlined above.

13.05 Quite simply, without changes being made, vital opportunities to learn lessons from these deaths continue to be lost. The public interest factor in death investigations cannot then be satisfied. There needs to be a successful operation of an effective, efficient, robust and thorough system for investigations into sudden deaths and the FAIs in Scotland. Improvements are needed.

1. GENERAL REVIEW OF THE FAI SYSTEM

13.06 The FAI system in Scotland is unique. It has evolved differently from other countries. However, in identifying reforms, reference needs to be made to the coroner's system in England and Wales where its purpose is the same in determining what can be learnt from the circumstances of a death. Specifically, it carries the same responsibility for discharging the UK's obligations under Art 2 of the ECHR, by considering the circumstances of the deaths of those in custody in prison or in detention from the police. Given the increase in the number of deaths arising in the circumstances of custody, now comprising the majority of FAIs that are now held, how these FAIs can be undertaken more efficiently and effectively should be a priority in Scotland.

13.07 Earlier chapters considered the evolution of the historical development of investigating sudden deaths by way of FAIs into their current form now held under

---

2   The Scotsman, *Cemfjord disaster: Sheriff to probe death of eight sailors in Pentland Firth tragedy* (2 May 2022), *www.scotsman.com/news/cemfjord-disaster-sheriff-to-probe-death-of-eight-sailors-in-pentland-firth-tragedy-3677149* (accessed 21 February 2023). This relates to the FAI to be held into the deaths of eight sailors in the Pentland Forth in 2015 when the Cemfjord went down.

the 2016 Act. The FAI system has developed from the earliest published FAI, held under the Fatal Accidents Inquiry (Scotland) Act 1895 (1895 Act) into the death of John Hardwick in July 1895.[3] FAIs have been held over a period of nearly 130 years where they have involved the investigation of all manner of deaths. Each of these deaths in itself has represented a tragedy for the respective family concerned.

13.08 FAIs have achieved much, highlighting weaknesses within working practices, such as at Quintinshill in 1915[4] where soldiers headed for the Western Front died as a result of a train signaling failure. FAIs included a gas explosion at Clarkston, Glasgow in 1971,[5] killing those out for an afternoon's shopping, and a tragedy for teenagers on the Scottish mountains at Cairngorm in 1971.[6] Place names too remain synonymous with disasters with, as examples, FAIs held into Lockerbie (the terrorist bombing of the Pan Am plane in 1988) and Dunblane in 1996 (in a primary school shooting).

13.09 It is crucial for all involved in the death investigation process and in undertaking FAIs to remember that sympathy must be extended to all relatives involved. The families frequently maintain that it is not a blame culture; it is about change. They do not want other families to suffer deaths in similar cases.

13.10 Investigation into sudden deaths and the holding of FAIs by the State is about finding out what and why the death happened, not only for those families involved but when acting in the public interest. The public interest in deaths allows society to learn from mistakes in the past so that there should be no, or a reduced, risk of repeating them.[7] FAIs are therefore quite rightly a matter of public scrutiny. This is reflected by the press coverage which will fully report on FAIs which are being held or on which a determination has been issued.

13.11 Their objective is that the circumstances of the death are subject to due judicial investigative process. They conclude with the issue of a determination identifying when, where and the cause of the death or accident took place. If relevant, it will identity any precautions which could reasonably have been taken and, had they been taken, might realistically have resulted in the death, or any accident resulting in the death, being avoided. It includes identification of any defects in any system of working which contributed to the death or any accident resulting in the death, and any other facts which are relevant to the circumstances of the death.[8] Any FAI system operated by the State must be robust and the examination processes thorough and transparent to ensure that necessary scrutiny of deaths is undertaken effectively and

---

3   **Appendix 2** shows the determination of the FAI held into John Hardwick's death, which appears to be the first FAI held under the 1895 Act.
4   **Appendix 2** includes some brief details on that FAI.
5   **Appendix 2**.
6   **Appendix 2**.
7   'Those who cannot remember the past are condemned to repeat it.' – George Santayana, *The Life of Reason*.
8   2016 Act, s 2.

efficiently. Only by that means can FAIs achieve and promote public confidence in the operation of the FAI system.

13.12   That requires each organisation involved in the FAI process, which includes COPFS, SCTS and the judiciary, to work together in a streamlined manner. That principal responsibility for the FAI system lies with the Lord Advocate and COPFS who are crucial to achieving the effective administration and delivery of the FAI process. Their responsibility starts from the date of the death that is reported and continues until the conclusion of the FAI.[9] The role of SCTS in providing adequate court estate and supporting administrative processes is essential.

13.13   However, what must be remembered is that an FAI is an inquiry conducted in an inquisitorial manner. 'Inquisitorial' means 'a system of justice in which the judge conducts an inquiry developing the facts of the case'. The role of the judge must ensure that the FAI is robust for them to discharge that responsibility successfully. That means more than mere acceptance of the evidence presented at the FAI by the parties. Their role is to act on behalf of the State and to ensure that the public interest in the investigation of the death has been achieved. **Chapter 5** dealt in detail with some of the issues arising in relation to the way in which evidence is presented to FAIs; the process of agreeing evidence is tending to stray beyond the factual and uncontentious information that is required to establish the actual detail of the findings in the determination and into acceptance of opinion evidence. Care is needed to understand why that is not what was envisaged when introducing more efficient processes in the 2016 Act and the 2016 Rules to provide the sheriffs with discretion in admitting evidence to the FAI. Reference is made to r 4.11.3 where it sets out categories of what is understood to comprise formal evidence. It does not include the acceptance of reports outlining the conclusion to internal inquiries conducted by the Scottish Prison Service (SPS) or in medical FAIs. These should be subject to the usual robust scrutiny of evidence.

13.14   That aspect of evidence and robust inquiry could be best picked up under the call for more training for the relevant organisations where the necessary balance of how to obtain formal, as compared to opinion, evidence at an FAI could be discussed. Just where the representation of the family of the deceased fits into agreement of evidence also remains a matter of concern. As highlighted the families tend frequently not to be represented at FAIs so when there is any agreement of evidence they are not involved. How then that any concerns which have been expressed by them are to be dealt with is therefore unclear.

---

9   Within the context of the statutory framework which the 2016 Act created, along with the Rules underpinning the process by which the FAI is held.

2. DELAY IN THE PROCESS

13.15   Today, there is a general climate of dissatisfaction from both the public and politicians on the operation of the FAI system. This is seen from headlines such as 'Fatal accident inquiries taking almost three years to complete'.[10] The politicians too are concerned with the observation made that '[t]hese long drawn-out inquiries cannot continue any longer. That is why I am pressing ahead with my plans to introduce a statutory time limit for inquiries to complete as part of my Victims Law.'[11]

13.16   FAIs are not being held and completed within reasonable timescales. There are different relevant factors at play, such as a lack of resources and the inherent complexity of some FAIs. However, these factors do not feature in all FAIs. It is challenging to identify just where the delays arise, due to an absence of published data/statistics from all organisations in exploring and understanding the source of issues. What appears surprising is that there seems little, if any, public acknowledgment on just how many FAIs are currently outstanding and require to be completed.

First, evidence of the length of delays in holding FAI can be seen from the following:

- The FAI held into the fire at Cameron House Hotel, where evidence was completed in 2022 into two deaths that took place in December 2017. the determination was issued in January 2023[12].
- Preliminary hearing dates were announced for December 2022 in respect of the FAI to be held into the deaths on the M9 of Lamara Bell and John Yuill in 2015 (eight years). The FAI is now due to start in September 2023[13].
- The mandatory FAI to be held into the death of Katie Allan[14] in June 2018 which is still awaited (four years).

13.17   Second, publication of determinations on the SCTS website illustrates a similar pattern that includes:

10   STV News, *Fatal accident inquiries taking almost three years to complete* (17 November 2022), *https://news.stv.tv/scotland/fatal-accident-inquiries-in-scotland-taking-almost-three-years-to-complete-foi-reveals* (accessed on 21 February 2023).
11   James Greene MSP with a requirement that the strict deadlines for FAIs to be completed would guarantee that the families of victims would not have to wait years for closure: STV News, *Fatal accident inquiries taking almost three years to complete* (17 November 2022), *https://news.stv.tv/scotland/fatal-accident-inquiries-in-scotland-taking-almost-three-years-to-complete-foi-reveals* (accessed on 21 February 2023).
12   Determination under The Inquiries Into Fatal Accidents and Sudden Deaths Etc (Scotland) Act 2016 Into The Death Of Simon Midgley and Richard John Dyson, *www.scotcourts.gov.uk/search-judgments/judgment?id=cee66ffd-ccb6-41e2-ac20-9722dd9f6bb9* (accessed on 21 February 2023).
13   BBC, Fatal accident inquiry into M9 crash deaths delayed, *www.bbc.co.uk/news/uk-scotland-tayside-central-64347748* (accessed on 21 February 2023).
14   A suicide in prison at Polmont.

- The FAI into the death of Roderick MacLean[15] in March 2012 was completed in May 2021 (ten years).
- The FAI into the death of Pjero Kurida was completed in February 2022 into a death that arose in June 2012[16] (ten years).
- The FAI into the death of Clare Shannon was completed June 2020 into a death that arose in April 2014[17] (six years).
- The FAI into the death of the Steven Connolly[18] in December 2016 was completed in June 2021 (five years).
- The FAI into the death of Sophie Anne Parkinson[19] in March 2014 was completed in September 2020 (six years).

13.18   Lord Cullen Report's report identified that COPFS should 'review its application of resources and expertise in order that FAIs are held as promptly as possible after the death'.[20] The 2016 Act did not seek to introduce any mandatory timescales on completion of FAIs. The only timescale from the 2016 Act that was included is included in the COPFS Family Liaison Charter that relates to making a 12-week report to the family on the progress of their investigations.[21] There is no requirement on COPFS to adhere to any other timescales for deciding on or holding an FAI.

13.19   Delay has an impact on all those involved in the FAI. Criticism is regularly made in criminal cases, quite rightly, of delays where witnesses struggle to remember what happened. Holding FAIs a long time after the incident has a similar effect on witnesses. They are being asked to relive traumatic events which include not only the eye witnesses but also members of emergency services responding to what will have been very challenging and difficult circumstances. The risk of re-traumatisation to them all should surely not be ignored. For the families, delay also causes continued grief, uncertainty and anguish. For professionals involved whose actions may be under scrutiny, such as doctors, this will be a source of continuing worry. These delays impact on all, as well as causing delay to any changes to the system being brought in or introduced.

---

15   The Times, Apology for inquiry delay over sea death (17 May 2021), *www.thetimes.co.uk/article/apology-for-inquiry-delay-over-sea-death-kxgm0mnks* (accessed on 21 February 2023).

16   FAI into the death of Pjero Kurida, *www.scotcourts.gov.uk/docs/default-source/cos-general-docs/pdf-docs-for-opinions/2022fai016.pdf?sfvrsn=d61c9754_1* (accessed on 21 February 2023).

17   FAI into the death of Claire Shannon [2020] FAI 26, *www.scotcourts.gov.uk/docs/default-source/cos-general-docs/pdf-docs-for-opinions/2020fai026.pdf?sfvrsn=34eab0d2_0* (accessed on 21 February 2023).

18   FAI into the death of Stephen Connolly [2021] FAI 41, *www.scotcourts.gov.uk/docs/default-source/cos-general-docs/pdf-docs-for-opinions/2021fai041.pdf?sfvrsn=95e68982_1* (accessed on 21 February 2023).

19   FAI into the death of Sophie Anne Parkinson 2020 FAI 32, *www.scotcourts.gov.uk/docs/default-source/cos-general-docs/pdf-docs-for-opinions/2020fai32.pdf?sfvrsn=19b648dd_0* (accessed on 21 February 2023).

20   Lord Cullen, para 10.17.

21   Crown Office & Procurator Fiscal Service, *The Family Liaison Charter* (September 2016), *www.copfs.gov.uk/publications/the-family-liaison-charter/* (accessed on 21 February 2023).

3. PROVISION OF DATA/STATISTICS

13.20 Reconciling the Scottish Government's publication of statistics on the number of FAIs held annually is difficult, as discussed in **Chapter 12**. There continues to be a backlog in FAIs being held which it is suggested needs to be accepted. Only in this way can the extent of the delay embedded in the system be truly understood. There is then a need to work together to identify what is required by way of prioritisation and allocation of adequate resource to manage that backlog. Though the holding virtual FAIs may be one way to expedite the process, that appears not to have continued much since the Covid-19 pandemic has receded with the courts reopening. How much that could or should feature as a means to resolve the backlog is difficult to establish as there are definite disadvantages in the absence of face-to-face contact in what can be highly charged and emotive circumstances.

13.21 More than just COPFS are involved in resolving the issue of delay as there are other sources of potential delays inherent within the FAI system. That makes it a challenge to work out exactly where the delay has come from. The suspicion is that the delays probably have multiple sources. Delay may result from:

- Administration:
  Where there is a lack of court time, court space or the Crown, court and/ or judicial personnel being available to undertake FAIs, this can cause timetabling delay once a decision to hold an FAI is taken. Where a complex FAI is held, such as the fire at Cameron House, these will definitely require significant staff resources and manpower, but this seems not to have been a specific explanation for the cause of delay to date. For instance, at the FAI into the Cameron House fire, there were many parties' interests included within the FAI; that alone required a large court room to accommodate all parties as well as the length of time to hear the evidence to be led in the FAI. In June 2021, the Scottish Government rejected a call from Liam McArthur MSP that there should be 'an independent expert review with a remit to include considering the options for removing FAIs from [COPFS's] responsibilities'. The Scottish Government response was that Parliament had 'agreed to substantial reforms for the inquiries into fatal accidents and sudden deaths in 2016… Additional resources have been applied and that is having an effect.'[22] COPFS had established an Operation Performance Group Committee whose minutes are publicly available and refers to the management of FAIs from time to time. Timetabling issues may be highlighted here, such as in August 2022[23] where it was acknowledged that: 'there has been a sharp increase in

---

22   The Scottish Parliament, Meeting of the Parliament (Hybrid) (10 June 2021), *www.parliament. scot/chamber-and-committees/official-report/search-what-was-said-in-parliament/chamber-and-committees/official-report/what-was-said-in-parliament/meeting-of-parliament-10-06-2021?meeting=13236&iob=119960* (accessed on 21 February 2023).

23   Operational Performance Committee, *www.copfs.gov.uk/media/jg1gwvf0/opc-minutes-3-august-2022.pdf* (accessed on 21 February 2023).

instruction for discretionary Fatal Accidents Inquiries… From March to date there has been 50% increase with anticipation 4 more to be marked soon. Discretionary FAIs are more complex, and take more time to prepare and so puts pressure on teams. Anticipate seeing his [sic] as a continuing trend. This in turn will put pressure on the estate on SCTS identifying court space for some of these FAIs which can take some weeks in court.'

- Management:

FAIs take time in court. This is much better managed now with the introduction of preliminary hearings following the implementation of the 2016 Act. These will allow discussions as to how long the FAI may take so that management of resources can be considered along with the projected timescales. However, the form of determination issued by sheriffs does not routinely give all the information as to when the first notice of the FAI was received, as well as the procedural history of the FAI. Were this to be included, as a matter of style and practice, this would allow the length of time that an FAI takes from its first notice to the conclusion with the issue of the determination to be easily ascertained.

- Writing/publication:

Once the hearing of evidence and submissions from the parties have been completed, the sheriff needs to issue the determination and then it is a matter for SCTS to make arrangements to publish it. There are no set timescales on sheriffs to write up or similarly on arranging for it to be published. It might be hard to impose a blanket timescale again on the issue of determination given the length and complexity of some FAIs. However, just how long this takes cannot be assessed.

In conclusion, delays appear at all points in the FAI system from the date of death to the FAI being instructed. Were the system to confirm publicly the number of FAIs which are outstanding and still to be held, this would help to demonstrate where the issues outlined above lie. That review process is undertaken regularly by COPFS and SCTS[24] when measuring the current criminal case backlog. Why should FAIs be treated any differently?

How could this change? The following system is suggested. When a death occurs which is reportable under the sudden deaths system, it is almost inevitable that an FAI will be instructed into all deaths that give rise to a mandatory FAI in terms of s 2 of the 2016 Act.[25] Therefore a system could be devised to collate the following sources of information from:

- Scottish Prison Service (SPS): SPS publish quarterly the number of deaths in prison which show 35 deaths have occurred from 1 January

---

24 Scottish Courts and Tribunals, SCTS News (22 September 2022), *www.scotcourts.gov.uk/about-the-scottish-court-service/scs-news/2022/09/22/updated-modelling-on-criminal-court-backlog-published-today* (accessed on 21 February 202322).

25 There are circumstances where the Lord Advocate may not hold a mandatory FAI but these will arise rarely, if ever.

2022 to 30 September 2022.[26] To these figures need to be added those deaths where FAIs are still outstanding from previous years.

- Police Scotland: From 1 April 2014 to 17 March 2021 (inclusive), there have been 26 deaths in custody and 89 deaths following police contact recorded by their Professional Standards Department.
- Health and Safety: They report the deaths that occurred in the course of employment with their report of 17 deaths that arose in 2021/22.[27] All of these deaths will be likely to result in the holding of a mandatory FAI.

13.22 These figures can only provide a snapshot projection of the number of mandatory FAIs that would appear to still be due to be held.

13.23 It is accepted that the numbers of discretionary FAI are inevitably harder to prepare for. That ties in with concerns being voiced of the relatively few discretionary FAIs that are apparently being held. That may well be due to circumstances beyond COPFS's control. The reasons for the few numbers may include: that appropriate deaths in which an FAI should be held may not have arisen, criminal investigations may still be under way, no decision on holding an FAI has been reached or a public inquiry is being held. For instance, there have been no FAIs into deaths abroad where holding an FAI into such deaths have been competent since 2016 Act was commenced.

13.24 There probably needs to be more investigation into why the figures for discretionary FAIs have fallen to ensure that there is no failure as to the deaths which are being reported or if reported, not investigated adequately in cases where discretionary FAIs might have been held in the past. Any trends in the types of discretionary FAIs being held and explaining their decline in numbers could be a matter to research, report on and evaluate going forward.

13.25 A review of the method of publication of statistics for parliamentary and public scrutiny would provide a means for ascertaining how efficient the FAI process is, allowing for comparisons to be made over time and ensuring the adequate allocation of funding and resources. That overhaul was called for in Lord Cullen's recommendations at 10.1 and 10.14. Making that information available on an annual basis would include the number and type of FAIs being held, and that were held, and identifying the time taken to complete the process from the date of death to the holding and completion of the FAI. That information would include all court hearings until its conclusion is reached with the publication of the determination.[28]

---

26   Scottish Prison Service, *Prisoner Deaths, www.sps.gov.uk/Corporate/Information/PrisonerDeaths. aspx* (accessed on 21 February 2023).

27   HSE, *Workplace health and safety statistics for Scotland, 2022* (March 2022), *www.hse.gov.uk/ statistics/regions/scotland-statistics.pdf* (accessed on 21 February 2023).

28   G Mawdsley, 'Why should the publication of fatal accident inquiry statistics be reviewed?' (2020) SLT 30, 197–200.

4.   INCREASED PUBLIC REPORTING

13.26   Delay is also a theme tackled in the Proposed Victims, Criminal Justice and Fatal Accident Inquiries (Scotland) Bill, which aims at 'putting the victims at the heart of the system'. The Bill was introduced by James Greene MSP[29] and seeks to 'expand the criteria for mandatory fatal accident inquiries, and set maximum timescales for mandatory and discretionary fatal accident inquiries'. Proposing to introduce a timescale for completing an FAI may not be practical for reasons of their complexity, the number or availability of witnesses, and operational constraints such as lack of court facilities. However, it is suggested that the monitoring of progress of FAIs is what is needed, similar to what currently exists within the coroner's system.

13.27   There, the coroner has a duty to hold an inquest[30] under r 8 of the Coroners (Inquest) Rules 2013. They are required to complete an inquest within six months of the date on which the coroner is made aware of the death, or as soon as is reasonably practicable. If a coroner has not completed their investigation within 12 months, they must report that to the Chief Coroner, giving reasons for the delay under s 16 of the 2009 Act and reg 26 of the 2013 Rules.[31]

13.28   Information as to the delay is required to be supplied, which includes (a) the factual dates of the case; (b) the nature of the investigation; (c) the reason for the delay; and (d) the likely date of completion.[32] The Chief Coroner's Annual Report provides that information, so what is reported states that:

> 'In total, there were 2,278 cases in England and Wales not completed within 12 months of being reported to the coroner as at 2019. This is in the context of 220,600 deaths reported to the coroner in 2018 and 29,100 inquests being opened. The figures for 2020 are set out where they have been provided.'[33]

13.29   The introduction in Scotland of a public system of similar reporting would not adversely affect COPFS. It would allow the resource implications to be clearly seen and monitored. It should be noted that, on its own, this would not resolve all the issues, as the inquest system is one which still attracts criticism. Inquest Co-Director Helen Shaw also recognised delay as an issue there in stating that 'One of the biggest

---

29   Proposed Victims, Criminal Justice and Fatal Accident Inquiries (Scotland) Bill, *www.parliament. scot/-/media/files/legislation/proposed-members-bills/jamie-greene--consultation--final.pdf* (accessed on 21 February 2023).

30   2009 Act, s 6.

31   Affects deaths after 25 July 2013 Guidance No 9 Opening Inquests: *https://assets.publishing.service. gov.uk/government/uploads/system/uploads/attachment_data/file/932518/chief-coroner_s-annual-report-1920.pdf* (accessed on 21 February 2023).

32   MoJ, Guide to coroners statistics (13 May 2021), *www.gov.uk/government/statistics/coroners-statistics-2020/guide-to-coroners-statistics* (accessed on 21 February 2023).

33   Chief coroners combined annual report 2018 to 2019 and 2019 to 2020 (5 November 2020), *www. gov.uk/government/publications/chief-coroners-combined-annual-report-2018-to-2019-and-2019-to-2020,* para 21 (accessed on 21 February 2023).

problems with the delay in the system is lessons aren't being learnt and ...families can wait for years for an inquest.'[34] This observation applies equally to Scotland.

5. TRAINING

13.30   A training needs assessment should be undertaken to ascertain what training is currently available on an organisational basis for those involved in undertaking FAIs. An overhaul of the skills and training should be carried out to ascertain how well that training currently equips those involved to undertake their current roles successfully. This would lead to better understanding of each other's roles and greater cohesion among organisations. These suggestions also echo Lord Cullen's recommendations at paras 10.3 and 10.17. The best way that this can be illustrated is by identifying what appear to be gaps at present where there is a lack of transparency as to how training is being conducted, its content, the allocation of the necessary and appropriate resources and stressing the importance of training.

13.31   Review of that training should include ensuring the inclusion of the important perspective of the deceased's family and what they want from the system. It should promote a better understanding of working practices within the medical profession and prison service, such as an understanding of internal investigations such as Serious Adverse Event Reviews (SAERs) within medicine and Death In Prison Learning, Audit and Review (DIPLAR). This would help ensure that, where recommendations are being made, they are directed to the appropriate organisations.

13.32   What is also absent in Scotland is the equivalent of the Coroner's Bench Book, issued by the Chief Coroner and the Judicial College (the Scottish equivalent is the Judicial Institute of Scotland).[35] Though that may be currently under review, it provides valuable information to those involved in the process. It aims at 'provid[ing] coroners, especially newly appointed coroners, with a guide to their use of words in court, although coroners will use their own words, tailored to the particular facts and circumstances of the individual case'. This Bench Book is available along with the Chief Coroner's Guidance covering many practical and legal issues. There is nothing that seems equivalent to that book or indeed any publicly issued guidance as to judicial practice currently existing in Scotland.[36]

---

34   BBC Radio 4's *Face the Facts*: that delays in the system meant that for many people, the grieving process simply stopped.

35   The Chief Coroner, *The Coroner Bench Book*, *www.judiciary.uk/wp-content/uploads/2022/07/coroner-bench-book-jury-inquests-revised-june-2016-1.pdf* (accessed on 21 February 2023).

36   Courts and tribunals Judiciary, *Chief Coroner's Guidance, Advice and Law Sheets www.judiciary.uk/courts-and-tribunals/coroners-courts/coroners-legislation-guidance-and-advice/coroners-guidance/* (accessed on 21 February 2023).

6. AVAILABLE AND ACCESSIBLE SOURCES OF PUBLIC INFORMATION

13.33   It is hard to find up-to-date, reliable information on sudden deaths and FAIs that is publicly available. There is no common website; though COPFS has some general information, it does not have similar webpages as the system in England and Wales have published available on the Coroner website. Overhauling all the publicly available information and ensuring that it is reviewed regularly would assist in making the public aware of the existence of the sudden deaths and FAI system, what an FAI is and importantly, what their role and interest as the public is when an FAI is held. An FoI request to COPFS dated 3 November 2022 produced an outdated Chapter 12 of the COPFS Book of Regulations, the COPFS internal manual on their processes. It appears to relate to the repealed 1976 Act. Accordingly, there appears to be no current internal or publicly available information on the number of aspects of COPFS processes relating to sudden deaths and the FAI system. What is available is limited and usually requires some kind of research – since not all the information is collated under the COPFS or the SFIU nor updated systematically.

13.34   Using the opportunity to inform the public as to the nature of an FAI and its purpose would help the public understand the role of COPFS within the FAI system and would allow them to measure their expectations as to what an FAI can and cannot do. The public need to be able to understand that it is not a prequel to the civil or criminal proceedings into the death which may also be involved at some stage. In short, it is a public inquiry – funded by the State, though interested parties can of course attend, participate and be represented privately or publicly.

13.35   Though determinations from FAIs are now systemically published, the SCTS website is not fully searchable and is limited to merely the last 50 FAIs showing chronologically. Paragraph 10.31 of Lord Cullen's recommendation recommended this change to ensure that publication took place but it has only had limited impact. Review of the website and its search engines would ensure that this valuable resource is fully searchable and access to the published FAI is easier to obtain.

13.36   If the Scottish Government were to set up and maintain the website in relation to the State's involvement in sudden death, this would ensure that all kinds of information could be easily available for the public. They would need relevant links to other websites to be included which would take on the information currently maintained by COPFS and SCTS. This is in line with Recommendation 10.33 of Lord Cullen's Report which outlined that 'the Scottish Government website should be revived and upgraded' with specific details. Time and resource need to be in place to ensure that information is regularly reviewed in line with changes to legislation and updated on a regular basis to ensure that it relevant. It should also provide information on the role and rights of the deceased families at an FAI which would include their rights of access to legal aid and to the Scottish Legal Aid Board's webpage.

7. SUPPORT FOR THE FAMILIES

13.37 FAIs are still, predominantly, held in courtrooms across Scotland. Competent as it is to hold them elsewhere, this does not tend to be the norm, except where practical logistics demand such arrangements should be made. This is what happened with the Lockerbie FAI, which was dictated by its sheer complexity and scale involving the investigation into the terrorist bombing of the Pan Am plane in 1988. The Covid-19 pandemic too has played a role in the operation of FAIs and indeed, in introducing provisions to allow remote FAIs to be held, practices which continue to operate.

13.38 The location of the holding of the FAI in a court emphasises the nature of their judicial inquiry status. However, when reviewing how FAIs are operating today, the court may lose the connection at times with those that have been principally affected by the death or deaths requiring an FAI into a death to be instructed and then held. These are the bereaved families whose lives have been affected by the death.

13.39 Lord Cullen had identified that in order to promote confidence in the FAI system that a specialist court should be established, similar in operation to the personal injury court that has now been established. This was not taken forward on the grounds of cost, but consideration could again be given to this suggestion.

13.40 In considering the creation of a dedicated facility, this would allow an overhaul of the FAI system to be undertaken, with a better focus being made on judges, COPFS and SCTS staff all being specifically trained for their roles. These should now recognise that there is a need to include and provide for trauma informed training. Those involved in FAIs are not immune from the circumstances of the deaths which are the subject of the FAI. They are required to deal with what at times can be harrowing accounts of what has taken place. FAIs are not the same as adversarial proceedings which form the basis of the criminal court system. They should not be treated as an add-on and should be given a role and job specific training . That means specialist training and skills need to be developed along with that gained from specialist practice – with the experience of undertaking them. That overhaul of the training would help all to focus on the kind of issues which may regularly arise in court, especially where a number of the deaths which are involved in FAIs have common features. This can best be seen in relation to the number of deaths which require investigation, such as suicides which have taken place in prison. That would help ensure and understand where recommendations in relation to the circumstances of such deaths might best be made or directed.

Support would underpin the Scottish Government's commitment to having 'effective, modern person-centred and trauma-informed approaches to justice in which everyone can have trust, including as victims, those accused of crimes and as individuals in civil disputes'.[37]

---

37 The Vision for Justice in Scotland – this is now included in draft Victims, Witness and Justice Reform Bill, currently before the Scottish Parliament (Stage 1): *https://www.parliament.scot/bills-and-laws/bills/victims-witnesses-and-justice-reform-scotland-bill.*

8.   TRANSPARENCY OF PROCESS

13.41   Many of the issues that have been highlighted identify a lack of transparency and clarity in relation to the processes in relation to sudden deaths and FAIs. These result from the best information, knowledge or understanding not being easily available or regularly updated. Where delays in the holding of FAIs arise, the factors involved need to be clearly understood and not accepted as being ingrained or forming part of the system that cannot be revisited or reviewed. In contrast, there may be times following the judicial inquiry (FAI) when what appears to have been a lengthy delay is in fact justified. That will only become apparent when the full knowledge of the facts surrounding the circumstances of the death can be examined, understood and accounted for.

13.42   In the FAI into the deaths of George Thomas Allison, Sarah Helen Darnley, Gary McCrossan and Duncan Munro,[38] Sheriff Principal Pyle at para [49] recognised that '[there was] no period over the last seven years during which the Crown failed to perform its duties diligently and expeditiously…the delay which did occur was beyond the Crown's control'. There seemed to be a recognition that resource allocation of staff had been a factor which had lead to the setting up of the COPFS Operational Performance Committee (OPC) who had devised a Case Management Panel process. Its purpose was to improve the operational of the system and to:

- provide a framework for senior management oversight and influence in significant, high-profile cases;
- better understand the risks in relation to those cases; and
- ensure a level of appropriate scrutiny, challenge and support, with an identified chain of escalation if required.

13.43   It was recognised that this should allow for much better scrutiny of the investigation process, promote a greater understanding for those tasked with oversight of the investigation, and of the direction of travel and the proposed investigative strategy from the investigating agency, the legal manager and allocated Crown counsel, greater transparency of progress and identification of impediments/blockers, and assessment of required resource. This Case Management Panel process/policy as outlined in the FAI does not seem to be publicly accessible.

13.44   However, if this information was published, this would allow for identification of relevant cases and where a proper assessment of where cases should be managed, effectively, which includes those FAIs which are due to last two months or more; high-profile cases, particularly those attracting or likely to attract substantial media attention; where there was perceived risk that the case had potential to cause significant reputational damage to COPFS; excessive delay in the circumstances of

---

38   FAI into the deaths of George Thomas Allison, Sarah Helen Darnley, Gary McCrossan and Duncan Munro [2020] FAI 34, *www.scotcourts.gov.uk/docs/default-source/cos-general-docs/pdf-docs-for-opinions/2020fai34.pdf?sfvrsn=3b655add_0* (accessed on 21 February 2023).

the case; and any other reason where the Panel considered a review would be of benefit.[39]

13.45   The Case Management Panel process does not deal with the delay in holding FAIs into the multiple and increasing number of deaths in prison from suicide and from those who died in prison from Covid-19. As there are means to investigate multiple deaths, being clear how that backlog is to be tackled and the allocation of resources to be made should be identified to understand how the reference in that FAI to a 'a plan to tackle the legacy work and to establish a legacy caseload team to tackle those cases with key milestones and timelines'[40] is being adhered to and managed.

9.   CONCLUSION

13.46   In conclusion to the examination of the sudden deaths and FAIs system reference needs to be made to a number of reports that have focused on the running of FAIs since the 2016 Act commenced. These include:

- The HM Inspectorate of Prosecution:
  They published a follow-up report on FAIs looking again at the issues raised in their FAIs report published in August 2016.[41] Michelle McLeod, HM Chief Inspector,[42] acknowledged that after three years (2019),

  > 'Undoubtedly resourcing has been an issue for the Scottish Fatalities Investigation Unit (SFIU) and we acknowledge that it is not yet at full complement following additional resource that was secured in 2018 and that it takes time to induct and train new staff. The ongoing modernisation project should also improve the effectiveness of their processes and procedures… Given the number of recommendations that remain in progress and the continuing concerns regarding delays in dealing with mandatory FAIs and the new recommendations made in this report, the Inspectorate plans to revisit the investigation of FAIs in a further follow-up report next year.'

  That further Report has not been undertaken or at least published as yet .It was due in 2020.

---

39   FAI into the deaths of George Thomas Allison, Sarah Helen Darnley, Gary McCrossan and Duncan Munro [2020] FAI 34, *www.scotcourts.gov.uk/docs/default-source/cos-general-docs/pdf-docs-for-opinions/ 2020fai34.pdf?sfvrsn=3b655add_0* (accessed on 21 February 2023).

40   Operational Performance Committee, Minutes of meeting held on 26 June 2019, *www.copfs.gov.uk/media/gcudorta/26-june-2019-operational-performance-committee-minutes.pdf* (accessed on 21 February 2023).

41   Scottish Government, Fatal Accident Inquiries: follow up review (7 August 2019), *www.gov.scot/publications/follow-up-review-fatal-accident-inquiries/* (accessed on 21 February 2023).

42   Scottish Government, Inspectorate of prosecution publishes follow-up report on Fatal Accident Inquiries (7 August 2019), *www.gov.scot/news/inspectorate-of-prosecution-publishes-followup-report-on-fatal-accident-inquiries/* (accessed on 21 February 2023).

- The Independent Review of the Response to deaths in Prison Custody: This was published in November 2021[43] and was followed with the setting up of a Deaths in Prison Custody Action Group.[44] They recommended that 'a separate independent investigation should be undertaken into each death in prison custody. This should be carried out by a body wholly independent of the Scottish Ministers, the SPS or the private prison operator, and the NHS.'[45]

13.47   Exactly where that body would sit and interact with COPFS who are responsible for the investigation into such deaths remains for the future.

13.48   Perhaps, being visionary, having the SFIU set up as a separate division under the Lord Advocate, where its resources are ringfenced both in relation to staffing and funding, might give it the necessary independence of governance, accountability and transparency. It would separate any perception of its connection with crime, which may be a practice which would rest with the deceased's family more happily.

13.49   Many involved in FAIs encounter the courts system and COPFS for the first time on the death of a relative, inevitably bewildered and upset by the strange environment in which they find themselves. In the short term, looking at some of the changes that can be made now, as outlined above, would go some way to seeking out improvements and achieving the necessary transparency. However, there seems some distance to go to achieving Lord Cullen's vision in 2009 as to providing a sudden deaths and FAI system in Scotland for investigating fatalities that is effective, efficient and fair.

---

43   *Independent Review of the Response to Deaths in Prison Custody* (November 2021), *www. prisonsinspectoratescotland.gov.uk/sites/default/files/publication_files/Independent%20Review%20 of%20the%20Response%20to%20Deaths%20in%20Prison%20Custody%20p6%20%281%29%20 WEB%20PDF.pdf* (accessed on 21 February 2023).

44   Scottish Government, Deaths in Prison Custody Action Group, *www.gov.scot/groups/ deaths-in-prison-custody-action-group/#:~:text=The%20Independent%20Review%20of%20 the,recommendations%20made%20by%20 the%20review* (accessed on 21 February 2023).

45   *Independent Review of the Response to Deaths in Prison Custody* (November 2021), *www. prisonsinspectoratescotland.gov.uk/sites/default/files/publication_files/Independent%20Review%20 of%20the%20Response%20to%20Deaths%20in%20Prison%20Custody%20p6%20%281%29%20 WEB%20PDF.pdf* (accessed on 21 February 2023).

The status of Lord Cullen's Recommendations considered

Number	Recommendation	Observation/Comment
10.1	An FAI should, where possible, not be held in a sheriff courtroom but elsewhere in other appropriate premises; and, where it is unavoidable that the FAI should be held in a courtroom, care should be taken to select one which, along with its ancillary facilities, such as waiting rooms, has the least connection with criminal proceedings. I also recommend that in FAIs sheriffs and practitioners dispense with the wearing of wigs and gowns, and that sheriffs discourage the hostile questioning of witnesses save where it is essential for ascertaining the true circumstances of the death (paragraph 3.13).	Legislative changes were made in the 2016 Act. However, few FAIs are held outside a court venue. Sheriffs still use court dress. Practitioners also still wear court dress and observe the formalities in court. Comment: There could be more use of outside court facilities which when focusing on the families might be advantageous so that the connection that may be perceived between a court and criminal process is not part of the system.
10.2	Where an FAI likely to involve matters of some complexity, a sheriff who has adequate experience is assigned to it, and, where necessary, is enabled to sit in the sheriffdom in which the FAI is to be held (paragraph 3.17).	In practice, complex FAIs are assigned to sheriffs with experience. See the FAI into the deaths of George Thomas Allison, Sarah Helen Darnley, Gary McCrossan and Duncan Munro,[46] where Sheriff Principal Pyle had been involved in other North Sea helicopter FAIs. Comment: There could be greater use of specialism made as many of the FAIs are undertaken by summary sheriffs. With the number of suicides in prison, there would be benefit in having a pool of sheriffs who specialise in this work.

46　FAI into the deaths of George Thomas Allison, Sarah Helen Darnley, Gary Mccrossan and Duncan Munro [2020] FAI 34, *www.scotcourts.gov.uk/docs/default-source/cos-general-docs/pdf-docs-for-opinions/2020fai34.pdf?sfvrsn=3b655add_0* (accessed on 21 February 2023).

Number	Recommendation	Observation/Comment
10.3	[The Judicial institute for Scotland] should include the law and practice of FAIs in their seminars, and sheriffs should be encouraged to take advantage of attending them (paragraph 3.18).	What training is provided to any involved in the process is unknown. Basic training should be included in induction training for shrieval appointments. Comment: There is a call for a training needs assessment to be undertaken and for there to be greater join up of training among the relevant organisations. For transparency, consideration should be given to guidance and a handbook being issued similar to the Coroner's processes in England and Wales.
10.4	It should continue to be mandatory that an FAI should be held into work-related deaths (paragraph 4.7).	Continued in the 2016 Act.
10.5	The legislation in regard to lawful custody (i) should be updated so as to refer to the Prisons (Scotland) Act 1989; and omit reference to borstal institutions; and (ii) should be extended to cover the death of a child while being kept in secure accommodation and the death of any person who is under arrest, or subject to detention by, a police officer at the time of death (paragraph 4.14).	Implemented by the 2016 Act.
10.6	The category of cases in which an FAI is mandatory should include the death of any person who is subject at the time of death to compulsory detention by a public authority within the meaning of section 6 of the Human Rights Act (paragraph 4.20).	Largely implemented by the 2016 Act. Comment: Deaths of patients detained in mental health facilities is not mandatory.
10.7	The category should also include the case of the death of a child who at the time of death was being maintained in a residential establishment (including secure accommodation) for the purposes of the Children (Scotland) Act 1995 or the Social Work (Scotland) Act 1968 (paragraph 4.27).	Implemented by the 2016 Act.

Number	Recommendation	Observation/Comment
10.8	The Lord Advocate power to make an exception under the Act should be extended to cases in which the Lord Advocate is satisfied that the circumstances of the death have been sufficiently established in a public inquiry under the 2005 Act (paragraph 4.31).	Implemented by the 2016 Act.
10.9	The Lord Advocate should be enabled to apply for a single FAI into multiple deaths in more than one sheriffdom; to direct which procurator fiscal will lead the investigation of the deaths, and in which sheriffdom the FAI is to be held (paragraph 4.35).	Implemented by the 2016 Act.
10.10	There should be an extension to the Act to make provision for the Lord Advocate to have a power to apply for an FAI into the deaths of persons normally resident in Scotland where the body is repatriated to Scotland, excluding cases for which provision is to be made in the [Coroners and Justice Act 2009]. The power of the procurator fiscal to investigate such deaths should be clarified, if necessary by legislation (paragraph 4.43).	Provision made by the 2016 Act but the provision remains untested. No FAIs into deaths involved have been instructed.
10.11	Where the Lord Advocate decides not to apply for an FAI, written reasons for the decision should be provided to relatives of the deceased when requested by them (paragraph 5.11).	Implemented by the 2016 Act.
10.12	There should be a central FAI team, led by an Advocate depute or a senior prosecutor, for ensuring that the knowledge, skills and experience of procurators fiscal for FAI work are adequate; for overseeing the training of procurators fiscal in such work; and for the setting of performance standards (paragraph 3.44).	The SFIU was established but any changes to their working and training processes appear not to be transparent. Chapter 12 of the Book of Regulations is being updated and still refers to the repealed 1976 Act. Comment: There is a need for an overhaul of training for all organisations – processes and procedures are best to be clerly understood by all. To promote confidence, setting out what training is provided might be useful.

Number	Recommendation	Observation/Comment
10.13	The central FAI team should also have the responsibility for overseeing progress from the outset in all cases for which an FAI is mandatory or is likely to be recommended for exercise of the Lord Advocate's discretion. The main functions of the team should be to (i) track cases and record their history, with details such as the dates of death, the report to the procurator fiscal, any report by a specialist agency, any prosecution, the completion of investigation, and any report to Crown Office; (ii) ensure that the investigation and preparation by the procurator fiscal of each case is supported by adequate resources (including advice, staff and expertise), supplementing them where appropriate; (iii) give guidance to the procurator fiscal in the light of previous FAIs, including as to the choice of expert witnesses; and (iv) ensure that preparation proceeds as expeditiously as possible (paragraph 6.15).	The SFIU (central FAI team) has been set out to rationalise the process within COPFS. A number of these changes appear to have been made but there are still considerable delays in holding FAIs. The reasons for these delays continue to be multifaceted and not always clearly understood. Comment: There is an inspection awaited from the HM Inspectorate. There are still press reports on FAIs delays.
10.14	The central FAI team should also be responsible for maintaining statistics relating the different types of case, their progress and timing (paragraph 6.17).	The SFIU was set up. Comment: There are a lack of statistics published to identify the extent of the backlog and to identify and ascertain the steps being taken to prioritise and to tackle the issue.
10.15	One of the duties of the central FAI team should be to confirm that a contact point with the COPFS has been established and maintained (paragraph 6.56).	Implemented by the production of the COPFS Family Liaison Charter.
10.16	(i) VIA officers should be trained in FAIs and that at least one officer should be a member of the proposed central FAI team, and liaise with the family and the local VIA officer; and (ii) VIA officers and procurators fiscal dealing with deaths should receive training on dealing with bereavement (paragraph 6.57).	It is not known what training is received by the Victim Information and Advice or if training includes bereavement training. There is reference made when considering a training needs assessment for the inclusion of vicarious trauma training to be mandatory.

Number	Recommendation	Observation/Comment
10.17	The COPFS should review its application of resources and expertise in order to ensure that FAIs are held as promptly as possible after the death (paragraph 6.14).	Delays continue to beset the FAI system. Comment: There is a backlog where provision of more information would help the public to understand and deal with the issues.
10.18	In cases in which an FAI is mandatory, the procurator fiscal should be required to apply for an FAI at an early stage after the death, so that the sheriff, the relatives and other interested parties can be informed as to the state of investigation, the expected timescale for the FAI and any factors likely to affect progress (paragraph 6.22).	Delays still continue within the FAI system. Comment: The lack of information as to the procedural history of an FAI within the published determination makes it hard to identify at times just how long the process has taken for the FAI to be held and to identify where the delay has arisen.
10.19	A preliminary hearing should be held in every case, save where the sheriff, on cause shown, dispenses with it. Its purpose is to ensure that the FAI is effective in achieving the object of determining the circumstances, and doing so in a manner which is fair, expeditious and efficient (paragraph 6.29).	Implemented by the 2016 Act and the 2016 Rules.
10.20	At the preliminary hearing the sheriff should fix the date for the commencement of the hearing of evidence, approve and settle the issues, and identify the extent to which any issues or matters are capable of being resolved (paragraph 6.30).	Implemented by the 2016 Act and the 2016 Rules.
10.21	Prior to the preliminary hearing the procurator fiscal should circulate copies of the documents to which he or she intends to refer at the FAI, a list of the persons whom he or she intends to lead as witnesses, and copies of the reports and police statements made by them. Leaving aside police statements, the same should apply to the interested parties. At the preliminary hearing the sheriff should deal with any questions relating to disclosure of, and access to, documentary evidence (paragraph 6.31).	Implemented by the 2016 Act and the 2016 Rules.

Number	Recommendation	Observation/Comment
10.22	The sheriff should be empowered, on cause shown and after hearing the procurator fiscal and the interested parties, to transfer the case to a different sheriff court in the same or a different sheriffdom (paragraph 6.32).	Implemented by 2016 Act.
10.23	In regard to legal aid, relatives of the deceased should not have to justify the reasonableness of the granting of legal aid for their representation at the FAI and the Scottish Ministers should consider increasing the limit for legal aid in FAIs and the extent to which legal aid is available within that limit. Legal aid should, as a matter of course, be granted in any case where the participation of the relatives is necessary in order to comply with article 2 of the ECHR (paragraph 6.46).	The potential changes to the provision of legal aid have been consulted on but no changes as yet have been made. Comment: It is also about representation for family at the FAI, as without the appropriate provision of legal aid questions as to access to justice can and do arise.
10.24	The recognised participants who have the right to appear and adduce evidence at an FAI should be extended to include civil partners and cohabitants (paragraph 3.50).	Implemented by the 2016 Act.
10.25	Rule 10 of the [earlier] Rules should be replaced by a general provision for the receipt in evidence at an FAI of a written statement (including an affidavit) admissible under section 2(1)(b) of the Civil Evidence (Scotland) Act 1988; and that such provision should be the same as that in an ordinary cause in the sheriff court (paragraph 7.10).	Implemented by the 2016 Act and the 2016 Rules.
10.26	There should be a comprehensive self-contained set of rules for FAIs (paragraph 7.22).	Implemented by the 2016 Act and the 2016 Rules.
10.27	The sheriff should have power to order that such part of the FAI as he or she considers appropriate should not be open to the public (paragraph 7.24).	Implemented by the 2016 Act.

Number	Recommendation	Observation/Comment
10.28	Sheriffs should use a standard form of determination, incorporating, according to the nature of the case, findings in fact, findings related to section 6(1) of the Act, a note on the evidence and issues, and such recommendations, if any as he or she considers appropriate (paragraph 8.7).	There is no standard style of determination though sheriffs do tend to adopt a variation of a form. Comment: This should be part of the overhaul of training that is called for to ensure that the FAI that is conducted is as robust and thorough as required. The determination is crucial to achieving that result as this reflects the conclusion of the judicial inquiry and is the document that forms the historical record.
10.30	Where, in the light of the circumstances of the death, the sheriff is satisfied of the need to take action to prevent other deaths, the sheriff should have the power to make recommendations for this purpose to (i) a party to the FAI; and (ii) any body concerned with safety which appears to the sheriff to have an interest in those circumstances (paragraph 3.32).	Implemented by the 2016 Act. Comment: There is a need to ensure that the importance of making recommendations and to the correct party is observed. Adopting a public register under a Scottish Government website similar to the England and Wales process would be a practice that might be followed as it would provide the necessary cohesion and transparency. The SCTS webpage is restricted to merely the publication of the last 50 determinations published at any time so that the recommendations, where made, cannot be clearly located and identified. Though there is reporting to the Scottish parliament, there is no information as to why the number of FAIs in which recommendations are made and which are key to lessons being learnt is so low.
10.31	Subject to such redaction as may be appropriate, the Scottish Courts website should contain all determinations; and that the website should be fully searchable (paragraph 8.21).	The SCTS webpage is up and running. Comment: It is restrictive in how determinations can be found – also the provisions only relate to determinations published after the 2016 Act came into effect. Other determinations can be located but publication was undertaken in a piecemeal practice – as it was a matter for the individual sheriff were they to agree to the publication of the determination.

Number	Recommendation	Observation/Comment
10.32	When a recommendation is made by a sheriff, the entity or body to whom it is directed should be under a duty to make a written response to an appropriate department of the Scottish Government within a period set by the sheriff, stating whether and to what extent it has implemented, or intends to implement, the recommendation, or, if not, for what reason or reasons. Where implementation is stated as intended, there should be a further duty thereafter to confirm its implementation (paragraph 8.25).	Implemented by the 2016 Act. Comment: However, see paras 10.30 and 10.31.
10.33	The Scottish Government webpage should be revived and upgraded. It should show, under reference to the sheriff's determination, the text of the recommendation, to whom it was directed and its reasons, with a link to the full text of the determination on the Scottish Courts website. It should also show the text and date of the response or responses. The relevant department should also be responsible for publishing an annual report of the recommendations and the responses to them. The report should also be laid before the Scottish Parliament and the United Kingdom Parliament (paragraph 8.26).	Implemented under the 2016 Act. A Report is made annually to the Scottish Parliament.
10.34	When issuing the determination the sheriff should have power to direct to whom a copy of the determination should be sent for the dissemination of the lessons of the FAI (paragraph 8.28).	Implemented by the 2016 Act.

Number	Recommendation	Observation/Comment
10.35	It should be open to the Lord Advocate to apply for fresh FAI proceedings in regard to a fatality where he or she is satisfied that (a) as to the existence of evidence (i) which was not reasonably available at the time of the original FAI; and (ii) which, if available and accepted, would have been likely to affect the determination of the sheriff in regard to one or more of paragraphs (a) to (e) of section 6(1) of the Act; and (b) it is in the public interest that such evidence should be considered in such proceedings (paragraph 9.8).	Implemented by the 2016 Act.
10.36	The fresh proceedings should take the form of a re-opening of the original FAI, save where the sheriff is satisfied that it is more appropriate that there should a further FAI (paragraph 9.9)	Implemented by the 2016 Act.

Appendix 1

Miscellaneous Forms and Reports

PART A – FORM EF5

Form eF5	
NOTIFICATION OF DEATH	
Reported by	«Next Record»
Contact details	
(phone + page + mobile number)	«Next Record»
Date & time of reporting	«Next Record»
Please provide details of who to contact if doctor reporting death is unavailable (name and telephone number)	«Next Record»
Supervising consultant and secretary or GP Practice Manager (Name and telephone number)	«Next Record»

PARTICULARS OF DECEASED	
Full name	«Next Record»
Age	«Next Record»
Date of birth	«Next Record»
Address	«Next Record»
Locus of death	«Next Record»
Date & time of death	«Next Record»
General Practitioner (name + address + telephone number)	«Next Record»
Please highlight any religious/cultural requirements relating to the deceased of which you are aware	«Next Record»
NEAREST RELATIVES	
Name	«Next Record»
Relationship to deceased	«Next Record»
Special Needs e.g. Interpreter	«Next Record»
Address and telephone number including mobile number of nearest relatives	«Next Record»
HISTORY	
Relevant past medical history and relevant medication (include prescribed medication and any alcohol / illicit drug abuse history)	
Summary of main events prior to death (where available please include copies of discharge summary; operation notes; etc)	
Reason for referring the death to the Procurator Fiscal? (Are there specific clinical questions /concerns to be addressed?)	
Have the circumstances of the death been discussed with nearest relatives?	«Next Record»
Name of person who discussed death with nearest relatives	«Next Record»
Date of discussion	«Next Record»
Have nearest relatives expressed any concerns about the circumstances surrounding the death? (If yes, please specify)	«Next Record»
Have nearest relatives been advised that the death has been reported to Procurator Fiscal?	«Next Record»

Have you any concerns? (Please list)	«Next Record»
Willing or unwilling to issue death certificate. If unwilling please explain why not	«Next Record»
Cause of death if certification being offered.	1(a) «Next Record»
	1 (b) «Next Record»
	1 (c) «Next Record»
	II «Next Record»
If certification is not being offered please provide the presumed cause of death in general terms, if known	«Next Record»
Has consideration been given to carrying out a hospital post mortem examination?	«Next Record»
Certifying doctor	«Next Record»
If this is a suspected asbestosis/ mesothelioma death please confirm whether a biopsy or other test has been taken in life which has confirmed this diagnosis. (Please provide details)	«Next Record»
For PF Office Use Only	
PF to whom reported	«Next Record»
PF instructions (remember to request medical records; admission/ pre-transfusion blood samples if applicable)	«Next Record»
Date of PF instructions	

PART B – EXAMPLE OF THE MEDICAL CERTIFICATE OF DEATH

Extract of an entry in a REGISTER of DEATHS

DG 10789978

(Section 37(2) of the Registration of Births, Deaths and Marriages (Scotland) Act 1965)

DEATH Registered in the district of Aberdeenshire					District No. 332	Year 2022	Entry No. 819

1. Forename(s) Elizabeth Alexandra Mary							2. Sex F

Surname(s) Windsor

3. Occupation Her Majesty The Queen

4. Date of birth	Year 1926	Month 4	Day 21	5. Age 96 years	6. Marital or civil partnership status Widowed

7. When died	2022 September Eighth 1510 hours

8. Where died	Balmoral Castle, Ballater, AB35 5TB

9. Usual residence (if different from 8 above) Windsor Castle, Windsor, SL4 1NJ

10. Cause of death	I (a) Old Age
	(b)
	(c)
	(d)
	II

Certifying registered medical practitioner   Douglas James Allan Glass

11. Forename(s), surname(s) and occupation of spouse(s) or civil partner(s) His Royal Highness The Prince Philip, Duke of Edinburgh

12. Forename(s), surname(s) and occupation of father/parent	13. Forename(s), surname(s) and occupation of mother/parent
Albert Frederick Arthur George Windsor King George VI (deceased)	Elizabeth Angela Marguerite Bowes-Lyon (ms) or Windsor Queen Elizabeth The Queen Mother (deceased)

14. Signature of informant, how qualified to give information and address	
(Signed) Anne (Transcribed)	HRH The Princess Royal, Daughter
Gatcombe Park Minchinhampton Stroud GL6 9AT	

15. When registered	Year 2022	Month 9	Day 16	16. (Signed) Lynne Driver
				Registrar

17.

18.

Extracted from the Register of Deaths

on Twentysixth September 2022   *Geul Edward Law.* Registrar General.

The above particulars incorporate any subsequent corrections or amendments to the original entry made with the authority of the Registrar General.

Warning

PART C – FAI INTO THE DEATH OF PAWEL KOCIK[1]

- In terms of section 26(2)(a) of the 2016 Act (when and where the death occurred)

  The late Pawel Kocik, born 20 June 1983, died at around 12.00 hours on 17 May 2017 at Kishorn Quarry, near Lochcarron, while in the course of his employment.

- In terms of section 26(2)(b) of the 2016 Act (when and where any accident resulting in the death occurred)

  The accident which resulted in Mr Kocik's death occurred at some time after 09.30 hours and before 11.35 hours on 17 May 2017 at Kishorn Quarry, near Lochcarron.

- In terms of section 26(2)(c) of the 2016 Act (the cause or causes of the death)

  Mr Kocik's death was due to chest and abdominal injuries, sustained as a consequence of being struck by an excavator boom and dipper arm resulting in a fall while working on a quarry stone crusher machine.

- In terms of section 26(2)(d) of the 2016 Act (the cause or causes of any accident resulting in the death)

  The cause of the accident resulting in the death of Mr Kocik was inadvertent contact by the excavator operator with the left-hand control joystick of the excavator at a time when the safety control lever was not engaged, resulting in the unintentional movement of the boom and dipper arm which then struck Mr Kocik.

- In terms of section 26(2)(e) of the 2016 Act (any precautions which (i) could reasonably have been taken and (ii) had they been taken, might realistically have resulted in death, or any accident resulting in death, being avoided)

  The following precautions could reasonably have been taken and, had they been taken, might realistically have resulted in the death, or any accident resulting in the death, being avoided, namely:

  (a) a discussion between Mr Morgan and Mr Kocik about the task in hand before Mr Kocik entered the feed hopper might have prevented the need for Mr Morgan to communicate with Mr Kocik during the task and the accident would have been avoided;

  (b) had Mr Morgan engaged the safety control lever when Mr Kocik was working in proximity to the boom when inserting the wedge and, in particular, had he done so prior to opening the cab door and attempting to communicate with Mr Kocik then the accident would have been avoided; and

---

1   [2022] FAI 35.

(c) had the sides of the hopper been modified so they were fixed in place, with no folding mechanism as per their current design, then the accident would have been avoided.

- In terms of section 26(2)(f) of the 2016 Act (any defects in any system of working which contributed to the death or the accident resulting in death)

  The system of work employed to raise the feed hopper sides was defective in that it lacked an instruction or step that required an excavator operator to engage the safety control lever when at rest or when others were in proximity of the boom.

- In terms of section 26(2)(g) (any other facts which are relevant to the circumstances of the death) the risk from the inadvertent operation of operator controls in excavators was widely recognised in the construction industry, but not so recognised in the quarrying and extractive industry. Industry training did not expressly include or record the correct use of the safety control lever in excavators on the approach or persons or when the machine was at rest. The operator's manual for the excavator in question did not specify that the safety control lever should be used when a person is within the danger zone of the excavator and when the machine is at rest. It is possible for the safety control [l]ever to be interlinked to an external warning red beacon so that those working in close proximity to the excavator can see when the safety control lever has been activated, the excavator controls are disabled and it is safe to approach the machine.

  It is possible to modify crushers of the type involved in this fatal accident so that the feed hopper sides do not require to be lowered and raised to allow road transportation.

- Recommendations: in terms of sections 26(1)(b) of the 2016 Act (recommendations (if any) as to (a) the taking of reasonable precautions, (b) the making of improvements to any system of working, (c) the introduction of a system of working, (d) the taking of any other steps, which might realistically prevent other deaths in similar circumstances)

  It is recommended that the Health and Safety Executive consider issuing a Safety Bulletin Alert to the quarrying and extractive industry to further raise awareness of the correct use of the safety control lever fitted to excavators, especially when using excavators in lifting operations. It is further recommended that the Product Safety Team of the Health and Safety Executive consider raising with the manufacturers of excavators the issue of how the use of the safety control lever is addressed in operator manuals for excavators.

PART D – THE DEATH OF KEITH RUPERT DIMOND[2]

Date of report: 22/10/2022

Coroner name: Sonia Hayes

Coroner Area: North East Kent

Category: Hospital Death (Clinical Procedures and medical management) related deaths – Other related deaths

This report is being sent to: East Kent Hospitals University NHS Foundation Trust

ANNEX A REGULATION 28: REPORT TO PREVENT FUTURE DEATHS (1) NOTE: This form is to be used after an inquest.

REGULATION 28 REPORT TO PREVENT FUTURE DEATHS THIS REPORT IS BEING SENT TO: 1. Chief Executive of East Kent University Hospitals NHS Trust

1   CORONER I am Sonia Hayes assistant coroner for the coroner area of North East Kent

2   CORONER'S LEGAL POWERS I make this report under paragraph 7, Schedule 5, of the Coroners and Justice Act 2009 and Regulations 28 and 29 of the Coroners (Investigations) Regulations 2013.

3   INVESTIGATION and INQUEST An investigation was commenced into the death of KEITH RUPERT DIMOND. The investigation concluded at the end of the inquest on 22 August 2022. The conclusion of the inquest was Natural Causes. The medical cause of death was 1a Haemorrhage, Pulmonary Thromboembolism & Infarction 1b Iliac Artery Aneurysm Rupture, Post Ileostomy Reversal & Atrial Fibrillation (Anticoagulated) II Peripheral Vascular Disease, Colitis, Polymyalgia Rheumatica.

4   CIRCUMSTANCES OF THE DEATH Keith Dimond died on 24 November 2021 at Queen Elizabeth Queen Mother Hospital of Haemorrhage, Pulmonary Thromboembolism and Infarction due to Iliac Artery Aneurysm Rupture, Post Ileostomy Reversal and Atrial Fibrillation (Anticoagulated) in a background of Peripheral Vascular Disease, Colitis and Polymyalgia Rheumatica. Mr Dimond developed new onset atrial fibrillation during a successful ileostomy reversal on 11 October 2021, commenced on anticoagulation and discharged home 19 October 2021. Mr Dimond was readmitted on 22 October 2021 with an abdominal bleed. Mr Dimond developed multiple bilateral pulmonary thromboembolism and advice was sought from haematology. Mr Dimond was diagnosed with an Abdominal Aortic Aneurysm and Iliac Artery Aneurysm in August 2019. Mr Dimond was treated with a direct oral anticoagulant discontinued on 22 October and recommenced on 16 November with a dosage

2   *https://www.judiciary.uk/wp-content/uploads/2022/Keith-Dimond-Prevention-of-future-deaths-report-2022-0338-published.pdf.*

for a thrombotic event. Mr Dimond died from a sudden catastrophic bleed from his ruptured iliac artery aneurysm with anticoagulation contributing to his excessive bleed.

5   CORONER'S CONCERNS During the course of the inquest the evidence revealed matters giving rise to concern. In my opinion there is a risk that future deaths could occur unless action is taken.

In the circumstances it is my statutory duty to report to you.

The MATTERS OF CONCERN are as follows. – Evidence was heard that there were communication issues: (1) Treating Clinicians stated they were not aware of the diagnosis of Iliac Artery Aneurysm previously made at the Trust in August 2019 even though this was set out in the medical records and made at the same time as the diagnosis of Aortic Abdominal Aneurysm that was known. Abdominal surgery and anticoagulation were undertaken without consideration of this information. (2) The patient was discharged on 19 October 2022 with a new diagnosis of Atrial Fibrillation and prescription of Direct Oral Anticoagulant Apixaban was prescribed. The patient was not given any written advice on the risks as to bleeding on this medication and the risks were not shared with family on discharge. This led to advice being sought from 111 and a long delay before 999 was called when the patient deteriorated on 22 October 2022. (3) Anti-coagulation on readmission was considered complex and the advice of a Consultant Haematologist was sought but not followed on two occasions: (a) Beriplex and Vitamin K was administered. There was no rationale noted as to why advice to withhold Beriplex was not followed. (b) There was no record as to why advice to give prophylactic clexane was not administered. (4) The Consultant Haematologist confirmed that if information of the existence of an Iliac Artery Aneurysm had been shared, they would have sought the advice of a Consultant Vascular Surgeon.

6   ACTION SHOULD BE TAKEN In my opinion action should be taken to prevent future deaths and I believe you and your organisation have the power to take such action.

7   YOUR RESPONSE You are under a duty to respond to this report within 56 days of the date of this report, namely by 18th December [2022] I, the coroner, may extend the period.

Your response must contain details of action taken or proposed to be taken, setting out the timetable for action. Otherwise, you must explain why no action is proposed.

8   COPIES and PUBLICATION I have sent a copy of my report to the Chief Coroner and to the following Interested Persons, (Wife). I am also under a duty to send a copy of your response to the Chief Coroner and all interested persons who in my opinion should receive it. I may also send a copy of your response to any other person who I believe may find it useful or of interest. The Chief Coroner may publish either or both in a complete or redacted or summary

form. He may send a copy of this report to any person who he believes may find it useful or of interest. You may make representations to me, the coroner, at the time of your response, about the release or the publication of your response.

9   22nd October 2022 Signature: Assistant Coroner North East Kent

PART E – IOPC REPORT DEATHS DURING OR FOLLOWING POLICE CONDUCT: STATISTICS FOR ENGLAND AND WALES – CLASSIFICATION OF CATEGORIES OF DEATHS[3]

Category 1: Road traffic fatalities: These include deaths of motorists, cyclists or pedestrians arising from police pursuits, police vehicles responding to emergency calls and other police traffic related activity. This does not include deaths following a road traffic incident where the police attended immediately after the event as an emergency service.

Category 2: Fatal shootings: These include fatalities where police officers fired the fatal shot using a conventional firearm.

Category 3: Deaths in or following police custody include deaths that happen while a person is being arrested or taken into detention. It includes deaths of people who have been arrested or have been detained by police under the Mental Health Act 1983. The death may have taken place on police, private or medical premises, in a public place or in a police or other vehicle. This includes deaths that happen: during or following police custody where injuries that contributed to the death happened during the period of detention, in or on the way to hospital (or other medical premises) during or following transfer from scene of arrest or police custody, as a result of injuries or other medical problems that are identified or that developed while a person is in custody, while a person is in police custody having been detained under s 136 of the Mental Health Act 1983 or other related legislation This does not include: suicides that occur after a person has been released from police custody and deaths that happen where the police are called to help medical staff to restrain people who are not under arrest.

Category 4: Apparent suicides following police custody: These include apparent suicides that happen within two days of release from police custody. This category also includes apparent suicides that occur beyond two days of release from custody, where the time spent in custody may be relevant to the death.

Category 5: Other deaths following police contact: This includes deaths that follow contact with the police, either directly or indirectly, that did not involve arrest or detention under the Mental Health Act 1983 and were subject to an independent investigation by the IOPC (related to the most serious incidents causing the greatest

---

3   *https://policeconduct.gov.uk/sites/default/files/Documents/statistics/deaths_ following_ police_contact_202021.pdf* (accessed on 25 November 2022).

level of public concern, have the greatest potential to impact on communities, or have serious implications for the reputation of the police service). This may include deaths that happen: after the police are called to attend a domestic incident that results in a fatality, while a person is actively attempting to avoid arrest. This includes instances where the death is self-inflicted, when the police attend a siege situation, including where a person kills themselves or someone else, after the police have been contacted following concerns about a person's welfare and there is concern about the nature of the police response, where the police are called to help medical staff to restrain people who are not under arrest.

PART F – THE CORONIAL PROCESS – REPORTABLE DEATH TO THE CORONER

The coroner considers information and decides whether an inquest is required. The coroner either requests more information (and opens a preliminary 'investigation') or decide that an inquest is required. The inquest is 'opened and adjourned for further investigations'.

If the investigation or inquest is opened, a post mortem examination is performed to establish the probable medical cause of death.

If the post mortem shows an inquest is not necessary, the process concludes.

If an inquest is necessary, the coroner reviews and decides:
- Whether a referral to Police/Crown Prosecution Service is needed for possible criminal prosecution.
- Where there are no criminal issues, sets timetable and calls for evidence.
- A Pre-Inquest Review (PIR) is held where interested persons discuss relevant issues.
- When investigations are complete, the inquest date is fixed and the witnesses notified to attend to give evidence and answer questions.
- Inquest hearing are held in public. The coroner gives the conclusion. The coroner completes paperwork with the death then able to be registered.

PART G – EXAMPLES OF REGULATION 28 REPORTS

Example 1 – Death of Ella Roberta Adoo Kissi-Debrah)[4]

The coroner's conclusions were heard on Wednesday 16 December 2013. The Record of the Inquest provided the following information, including the statutory determination and where required the relevant findings.

4   London South Coroner's Court, Inquest touching the death of Ella Roberta Adoo Kissi-Debrah www.innersouthlondoncoroner.org.uk/news/2020/nov/inquest-touching-the-death-of-ella-roberta-kissi-debrah (accessed on 21 February 2023).

The deceased was nine year old Ella Roberta Adoo Kissi-Debrah, where her cause of death was certified as being (a) acute respiratory failure, (b) severe asthma and (c) air pollution exposure.

Under how, when and where death arose: The record noted that she had severe hypersecretory asthma which caused her episodes of respiratory and cardiac arrest that required her frequent hospital admissions.

She died on 15 February 2013 in hospital of a cardiac arrest after an asthma attack at home.

'Air pollution was a significant contributory factor to the induction and exacerbations of her asthma.' She was exposed between 2010–2013 to levels of nitrogen dioxide and particulate matter in excess of World Health Organisation's (WHO) Guidelines. The source of the admissions was traffic emissions.

There was a recognised failure to reduce the nitrogen dioxide (NO_2) within EU and domestic law over this period 'which possibly contributed to her death'. Information about the health risks of air pollution and its potential to exacerbate asthma had not been given to her mother so she was unable to have taken steps which might have prevented her death.

The conclusion was that she died of asthma contributed to by exposure to excusive air pollution.[5]

This Report[6] in respect of her (Ella Roberta Adoo Kissi-Debrah's) death was sent to a range of Government departments and medical colleges in order to prevent future deaths. The Coroner's concerns outlined were that there was a risk that future deaths could occur unless action is taken. The matters of concern included:

(1) The national limits for Particulate Matter are set at a level far higher than the World Health Organisation guidelines. The evidence at the inquest was that there is no safe level for Particulate Matter and that the WHO guidelines should be seen as minimum requirements. Legally binding targets based on WHO guidelines would reduce the number of deaths from air pollution in the UK.

(2) There is a low public awareness of the sources of information (such as UK-Air website) about national and local pollution levels. Greater awareness would help individuals reduce their personal exposure to air pollution. It was clear from the evidence at the inquest that publicising this information is an issue that needs to be addressed by national as well as local government. The information must be sufficiently detailed and this is likely to require enlargement of the capacity to monitor air quality, for example by increasing the number of air quality sensors.

5   *file:///C:/Users/gilli/Downloads/mnizari_16-12-2020_10-28-00%20(1).pdf.*
6   Paragraph 7, Schedule 5, of the Coroners and Justice Act 2009 and Regulations 28 and 29 of the Coroners (Investigations) Regulations 2013.

(3) The adverse effects of air pollution on health are not being sufficiently communicated to patients and their carers by medical and nursing professionals. The evidence at the inquest was that this needs to be addressed at three levels:

    a.   Undergraduate. I am informed that undergraduate teaching is the responsibility of the GMC, Health Education England and the NMC.

    b.   Postgraduate. I am informed that postgraduate education is the responsibility of the Royal Colleges, in this case the Royal College of Physicians, the Royal College of Paediatrics and Child Health, the Royal College of General Practitioners, and the NMC.

    c.   Professional guidance. In this case relevant organisations are NICE and the British Thoracic Society.

EXAMPLE 2 – DEATH OF BILLY LONGSHAW

2. The Regulation 28 Report relating to the death of Billy Longshaw[7] who died on 7th March 2021 at Stepping Hill Hospital, Stockport. This was sent to Great Western Hospitals NHS Foundation Trust and the General Medical Council. An inquest was heard on 21st February 2022.

A Narrative Conclusion was given that Mr Longshaw died as a consequence of complications of an undiagnosed sigmoid volvulus. The circumstances of his death were that he had a complex medical history, including significant learning disabilities. His cause of death was certified as 1) Acute bowel obstruction; b) Ischaemic sigmoid volvulus. 2) Cardiomyopathy due to D2-Hydroxyglutaric aciduria.

He was taken to the Emergency Department of Great Western Hospital, Swindon, following experiencing sudden onset abdominal pain and vomiting on a car journey. Following examination, he left without basic blood tests being taken, any diagnosis being made, or serious abdominal pathology being fully excluded.

The Matters of Concern were addressed to:

1.   The NHS Trust

That Mr Longshaw died within 24 hours of being seen in the Emergency Department at Great Western Hospitals, Swindon, in these circumstances. The Trust did not undertake a detailed investigation into the care and treatment provided to him. "Prompt, rigorous and effective investigations into serious clinical incidents are essential to deriving learning and improving patient safety."

The '48 Hour Report for Significant incidents resulting in Moderate Harm and above' prepared by an Emergency Department Consultant and others was fundamentally and

---

7   *https://www.judiciary.uk/prevention-of-future-deaths-reports/billy-longshaw-prevention-of-future-deaths-report.*

Example 3 – Death of Molly Russell

obviously flawed with an assumption made that 'the patient self-discharged against medical advice'. The review missed an opportunity to consider vital issues such as the presentation of patients with significant learning disabilities to the Emergency Department, and the practical application of the Mental Capacity Act 2005 in a clinical setting.

2. To the GMC

His death raised issues as to the adequacy of education provided to medical students as to the Mental Capacity Act 2005, and to doctors of familiarity with the practical application in clinical settings, and accompanying guidance produced by the GMC.

A copy of the report was sent the Care Quality Commission, the Independent Regulator of Health and Social care in England as well as to the NHS Hospital Trust and the GMC.

Response under Regulation 29

This Response was received from the GMC who set out their role under the Medical Act 1983. This includes setting the outcomes for graduates of UK medical schools leading to their entry to the medical register and in approving the curricula and programmes for postgraduate training of doctors. They quality assure all undergraduate and postgraduate medical training against their standards for the management and delivery of medical education and training. Their response advised that their Undergraduate Outcomes and Postgraduate training requirements include those relating to the Mental Capacity Act 2005 and relate to 'caring for, safeguarding, and communicating with patients with learning disabilities.' They indicated that the recommendation may be better addressed by bodies such as Health Education England or NHS England. They went on to outline resources to help doctors apply the principles of their guidance into practice. They conclude that the death outlines the complexity of making decisions about mental capacity in the context of learning difficulty.

PFD Reports in these cases have clear implications extending to a possible review of medical training as it affects the whole of the UK. Mental health issues with patients affect all doctors whether based in Scotland or England and the GMC is the professional medical body where conduct issues are directed.

EXAMPLE 3 – DEATH OF MOLLY RUSSELL

Molly Russell committed suicide aged 14 years on 1 December 2017. Molly Russell died from an act of self-harm whilst suffering from depression and the negative effects of on-line content. The medical cause of death was 1a Suspension.

The circumstances of the death were such that Molly had become depressed which worsened into a depressive illness as she subscribed to a number of online sites. Some of these sites were not safe, allowing access to adult content that should not have been available to be viewed by her. The way that the platforms operated meant that Molly had access to images, video clips and text concerning or concerned with self-harm, suicide or that were otherwise negative or depressing in nature. The platform used algorithms as to result, in some circumstances, of binge periods of images, video clips and text some of which were selected and provided without Molly requesting them.

These binge periods, if involving this content are likely to have had a negative effect on Molly. Some of this content romanticised acts of self-harm by young people on themselves. Other content sought to isolate and discourage discussion with those who may have been able to help. In some cases, the content was particularly graphic, tending to portray self-harm and suicide as an inevitable consequence of a condition that could not be recovered from. The sites normalised her condition focusing on a limited and irrational view without any counterbalance of normality.[8]

It is likely that the above material viewed by Molly, already suffering with a depressive illness and vulnerable due to her age, affected her mental health in a negative way and contributed to her death in a more than minimal way.

The Coroners' concerns outlined in the Regulation 28 were that:

1. There was no separation between adult and child parts of the platforms or separate platforms for children and adults.
2. There was no age verification when signing up to the on-line platform.
3. That the content was not controlled so as to be age specific.
4. That algorithms were used to provide content together with adverts.
5. That the parent, guardian or carer did not have access, to the material being viewed or any control over that material.
6. That the child's account was not capable of being separately linked to the parent, guardian or carer's account for monitoring.

There was a recommendation that consideration is given by the Government to reviewing the provision of internet platforms to children, with reference to harmful on-line content, separate platforms for adults and children, verification of age before joining the platform, provision of age specific content, the use of algorithms to provide content, the use of advertising and parental guardian or carer control including access to material viewed by a child, and retention of material viewed by a child.

'I recommend that consideration is given to the setting up of an independent regulatory body to monitor on-line platform content with particular regard to the above. I recommend that consideration is given to enacting such legislation as may be necessary to ensure the protection of children from the effects of

---

8 *www.judiciary.uk/wp-content/uploads/2022/10/Molly-Russell-Prevention-of-future-deaths-report-2022-0315_Published.pdf* (accessed 21 February 2023).

harmful on-line content and the effective regulation of harmful on-line content. Although regulation would be a matter for Government I can see no reason why the platforms themselves would not wish to give consideration to self-regulation taking into account the matters raised above.'

The Regulation 28 Report was directed to a number of parties including the Secretary of State for Digital, Culture, Media and Sport and the media companies including Pinterest, Meta Platforms, Snap Inc and Twitter International Company.

PART H – INQUEST INTO THE DEATHS OF CAROL CULLETON (66), ANASTASIA KUZYK (36), AND NATHALIE WARMERDAM (48) (CHAPTER 8)

The inquest was held at Pembroke Ontario from 6–28 June 2022 Leslie Reaume, Presiding officer for Ontario. All died on 22 September 2015.

- Carol Culleton died from upper airway obstruction by means of homicide
- Anastasia Kuzyk died from a shotgun wound of the chest and neck by means of homicide.
- Nathalie Warmerdam died from shotgun wound of the chest and neck by means of homicide.

The jury made the following recommendations directed to:

The Government of Ontario– The recommendations were extensive and detailed covering topic including:

1. Oversight and accountability to declare "declare intimate partner violence as an epidemic"

They were to establish an independent Intimate Partner Violence Commission dedicated to eradicating intimate partner violence (IPV) and acting as a voice that speaks on behalf of survivors and victims' families, raising public awareness, and ensuring the transparency and accountability of government and other organizations in addressing IPV in all its forms.

They were to engage in meaningful consultation with IPV stakeholders and experts in the field, to determine the mandate and responsibilities of the IPV Commission. Reference was made to the United Kingdom's Domestic Abuse Commissioner model in developing the Commission.

2. System approaches, collaboration and communication

They were to ensure that IPV issues were addressed by an all-of-government approach across ministries, and cooperate and coordinate with federal, provincial, and territorial partners in seeking to end IPV. This included working with IPV survivors, training and engagement in a trauma-informed approach to interacting and dealing with survivors and perpetrators. They were to review policies to ensure the timely, reliable, consistent, and accurate dissemination of information, including the use of emergency alerts and media releases, where the police are aware of circumstances that could put the public in danger, and that the focus is on safety when developing policies regarding what information to share with whom and when. They were to establish clear guidelines regarding the flagging of perpetrators or potential IPV victims in police databases, immediate dispatch and police access to the identities and contact information of potential targets, and how to notify those targets.

3. Funding

They were identifying how recommendations from the inquest would be implemented which included the need for adequate and stable funding for all organizations providing IPV support services. They were to draw on best practices in Canada and internationally, and adopt and implement improved, adequate, stable, and recurring funding that incorporates the following:

4. Education and training

They were to develop and implement a new approach to public education campaigns to promote awareness about IPV, including finding opportunities to reach a wider audience in rural communities. The training goes on to include review of existing training programmes and providing professional education and training for the justice system

5. Measures addressing perpetrators of IPV

They were to establish a province-wide 24/7 hotline for men who need support to prevent them from engaging in IPV.

6. Intervention

These looked at risk assessment and developing training to deal with managing risk.

7. Safety

Other recommendations were made to:

- the Chief Firearms Officer:
- the Office of the Chief Coroner
- the Information and Privacy Commissioner of Ontario
- the Government of Canada:

Reconvene one year following the verdict to discuss the progress in implementing these recommendations.

Appendix 2

Examples of FAIs in Scotland since 1895

INTRODUCTION

Appendix 2 includes a number of examples of FAIs where the information has been taken mainly from the publication of the determination.

These examples provide an opportunity to understand how FAIs have evolved, and the different findings that have been made historically and were made by the jury prior to the 1976 Act when juries were abolished. Appendix 2 has been divided into different sections in order to categorise and provide examples of different types of FAI.

Part A includes FAIs that were undertaken from the inception of the original legislation in 1895 to 1950. These FAIs were chosen as they were the deaths which were themselves interesting from a historical perspective. They include the earliest FAI determination in the case of the death of John Hardwick and Jessie Cargill or Jamieson, the earliest determination into a woman's death.

Part B includes the FAI into the Cairngorm Disaster which is an example of what was at the time a very high-profile FAI into the deaths of school children and their leader on a winter mountaineering expedition. That FAI considered the safety of school children on school trips as well as the dangers inherent in mountain safety in Scotland which also provide the background to two subsequent FAIs. These FAIs continue to show the focus of FAIs on matters of public interest and lessons to be learnt, as well as looking at issues of considerable public and societal interest.

293

Part C includes FAIs and discussion of their role in relation to deaths resulting from any apparent failures in medical care. These FAIs will usually be instructed as discretionary FAIs by the Lord Advocate where the holding of an FAI is merited as the death is a matter of public interest.[1] What should be stressed is, that the FAI can make no findings of civil or criminal liability, as these are matters for a separate court, but the findings tend to be influential where the provision of medical treatment is found to have been less than satisfactory.

It is important to recognise that medical staff do make mistakes; that on their own mistakes do not justify the holding of an FAI to be instructed. The more appropriate action may be to raise a medical negligence action against the appropriate hospital trust. Where an FAI is likely to be instructed, it should be more focused on the circumstances where systemic failures have arisen. In many cases, it is the hospital system as an entity which failed and not the actions of any individual doctor. The FAI into the death of Nicola Welsh examined below illustrates this.[2]

Part D includes examples of mandatory FAIs held into deaths arising from persons in prison or in police custody.

In conclusion these FAI examples have all been provided as the study of FAIs is important as it provides a snapshot of society at various times and the type of deaths which have resulted in FAIs being held. It has been possible to consult these with the help and support of the National Records Office of Scotland.

Part E includes for completeness an example of the high-profile inquiry held into the Piper Alpha disaster. The discussion of that disaster illustrates the much wider framework provided in the case of an inquiry under the Inquiries Act 2005 than is possible in a FAI.

PART A – HISTORICAL FAIs
Death of John Hardwick (FAI held under the 1895 Act)

The oldest FAI[3] was held on 22 July 1895 into the death of John Hardwick, quarryman, Templand Village, Lochmaben who died in an accident at a quarry in Lochmaben on 9 July 1895.

The determination (Image 1 below) is recorded in the Court Minute book. What is remarkable is its brevity. Only several years later, the issue of the determination was to be accompanied by more information, that included the names of the witnesses who formed the jury. The records of FAIs were evolving.

---

1   Inquiries into Fatal Accidents and Sudden Deaths etc. (Scotland) Act 2016 (Asp 2), s 4.
2   *www.scotcourts.gov.uk/search-judgments/judgment?id=043e87a6-8980-69d2-b500-ff0000d74aa7* (accessed on 21 February 2023).
3   SC15/27/1895/1.

Image 1 The Determination

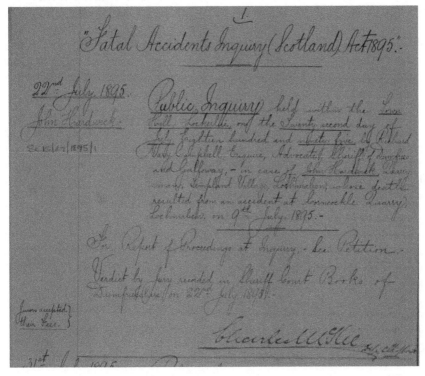

Death of Jessie Cargill or Jamieson[4] (FAI held under the 1895 Act and 1906 Act)

This FAI has been included as this is an example of an early FAI held into the death of a woman. Most FAIs held from 1895 onwards featured accidents at work, which was the primary reason for the introduction of the 1895 Act, followed by the widening of the scope with the 1906 Act to provide that overview separate from that of employers when investigating into deaths at work (see **Chapter 2**).

The FAI relates to the death of a domestic servant at the White Hart Hotel, Arbroath. She died on 8 October 1915 in Arbroath Infirmary. The jury verdict pronounced that she 'died engaged in the course of such employment attending to household duties in the kitchen of White Hart Hotel so severely injured by her clothing being set on fire in the open range of kitchen and burning her that she died in consequence of injuries'. Her injuries had been sustained on 3 October 1915.

---

4   SC27/10/1915.

Deaths of Frances William Scott, James Hannah and Samuel Stephen Lyn (held under the 1895 Act and 1906 Act)[5]

This FAI relates to the Quintinshill disaster that occurred on 23 May 1915 when 230 train passengers were killed. This railway collision resulted when the local train was stopped in the way of the troop train, carrying the Royal Scots battalion to their embarkment for the front at Gallipoli. Then, an express train hit the wreckage.

The mandatory FAI on 4 November 1915 was held only into the deaths respectively of the driver and fireman of the troop train and the railway saloon attendant on the express train. These were in effect mandatory FAIs being held into the deaths of the railway companies' employees. Subsequent successful criminal convictions for culpable homicide were thereafter obtained against the signalmen.

The determination shows that there were errors in signalling. However, it does not focus on what must have been other factors at the time such as the use of priority transport in wartime. The deaths of military personnel at the time did not result in the holding of any FAI nor is there any reference to these deaths, made in the FAI determination, given presumably the inevitable implications for public morale during wartime.[6]

Death of Fritz Saalbach[7] (held under the 1895 Act and 1906 Act)

This FAI was held on 11 July 1946 and referred to the death of a German prisoner of war (POW) that occurred on 25 June 1946. This FAI was held after World War 2 had ended, though POWs remained imprisoned in the UK for some time thereafter.

Various factors can be noted. The emergency powers under which FAIs were held in wartime continued still to operate with no jury as the requirement for juries had been abolished during the war and were not restored until later. This looks as if this was held as a discretionary FAI under s 3 of the 1895 Act as amended in that 'the Lord Advocate may, whenever it appears to him to be expedient in the public interest, direct that a public inquiry into such death and the circumstances thereof shall be held'. However, the obvious similarity with inquiries into deaths in custody and prisons can be seen from the terms of his captivity/detention.

---

5   SC15/27/1915/9.
6   National Records of Scotland, *Quintinshill Disaster 22 May 2015*, *www.nrscotland.gov.uk/research/ learning/first-world-war/quintinshill-disaster* (accessed on 21 February 2023). The National Records Office has much more in relation to this disaster.
7   SC25/15/1946/1.

His death was found to have been due to suicide by hanging with reference made to his suffering from mental depression.

Interestingly, the FAI included no expert medical evidence which would have been expected so as to allow a finding being made as to his mental health.

What is of relevance too is that the determination found that 'the ordinary camp procedure when a member requires medical attention was duly observed and that no blame is attributable to anyone but would recommend in special cases of this kind special attention should be given'. That finding of fault or liability in FAIs was not possible after the 1976 Act was passed.

Death of WGH and AM (held under the 1895 Act and 1906 Act)

This FAI was held on 20 November 1953 and has been included as it relates to an accident on a ferry crossing from North to South Queensferry. It was held into the deaths of a baby aged nine months and a deckhand. The deckhand, AM was employed by the shipping company, William Denny & Sons and his death during his employment gave rise to the holding of a mandatory FAI.

The baby fell from the ferry 'Robert the Bruce'. AM went in after him. As an observation, the list of jurors, which included women as well as men, show that it appeared only to be men who were chosen to sit as jurors. On the list of the Jury Assize, there were women but they appear without any specification of occupations in contrast to the men.

The death had only occurred two months before the FAI was held, providing a sharp contrast with the speed of those FAIs that are held today. The determination makes for uncomfortable reading now as it finds that the unanimous verdict of the jury was that the death of the child was 'accidently caused by the negligence of the mother who was suffering at the time from acute emotional stress, the jury commend the actions of the AM and Mr Strachan on their gallant efforts to effect a rescue and [the] jury find that a lifeboat should have been lowered and from the evidence which they heard they deplore this lack of organisations to meet an emergency such as this and recommend that regular inspection of life saving apparatus and training of crew are essential.'

The mother, but not the father, gave evidence to the FAI. A child gave evidence and is noted as having been admonished to tell the truth. The mother appears to have no legal representation as the only legal representation recorded relates to the shipping company, William Denny & Sons, presumably in respect of their employee. In conclusion, the finding of the mother for negligence is a finding that was not possible after the 1976 Act was passed and continues today in the 2016 Act where no findings as to civil or criminal liability may be made in any FAI.

Deaths of Alexander Cameron Boswell (11) George Samuel Murdoch Gibson (14) George Allan Penman (13) Harry Low (13) Thomas Thomson Bunt (14) and George Sinclair (13) (held under the 1895 Act and 1906 Act)

This FAI has been included as it provides a societal perspective of the 1940s. All six boys were pupils at Balgowan Approved School, Dundee. They escaped from the school during a recreational session in the evening by climbing over the roof of an outbuilding on 4 November 1947. They made their way to the Dundee docks where they managed to go aboard an Admiralty Motor launch boat. Once there, they played with a fire extinguisher which ultimately resulted in their deaths from the inhalation of poisonous fumes of methyl-bromide. What is telling is that 'the jury are of the opinion that the accident cannot be attributed to any persons other than Thomas Thomson Bunt and his companions but are further of the opinion that in future extinguishers containing the said or similar poisonous substances should very clearly marked poison'.

The factors that might be thought significant today are that the boys went missing at night with no apparent concern about their whereabouts on a winter evening. Two boys (one died) went back to the school in the morning, which is what brought the attention of the authorities as to their location. The finding on one boy's responsibility appears to come from the evidence of the only two who survived. Exactly how marking the extinguisher with poison would have avoided the boys playing with it is unknown. The fact that the boys reached a launch without detection at the docks would seem to be relevant too.

At the FAI the fathers of the boys gave evidence but were not asked about any concerns over their treatment, or supervision at the school, but were merely asked about the identity of their sons and when they last saw them, usually too late as they were already dead by the time they reached hospital. Image 2 shows a notification to the father as to the holding of the FAI into the death of his son.

Image 2 Notification

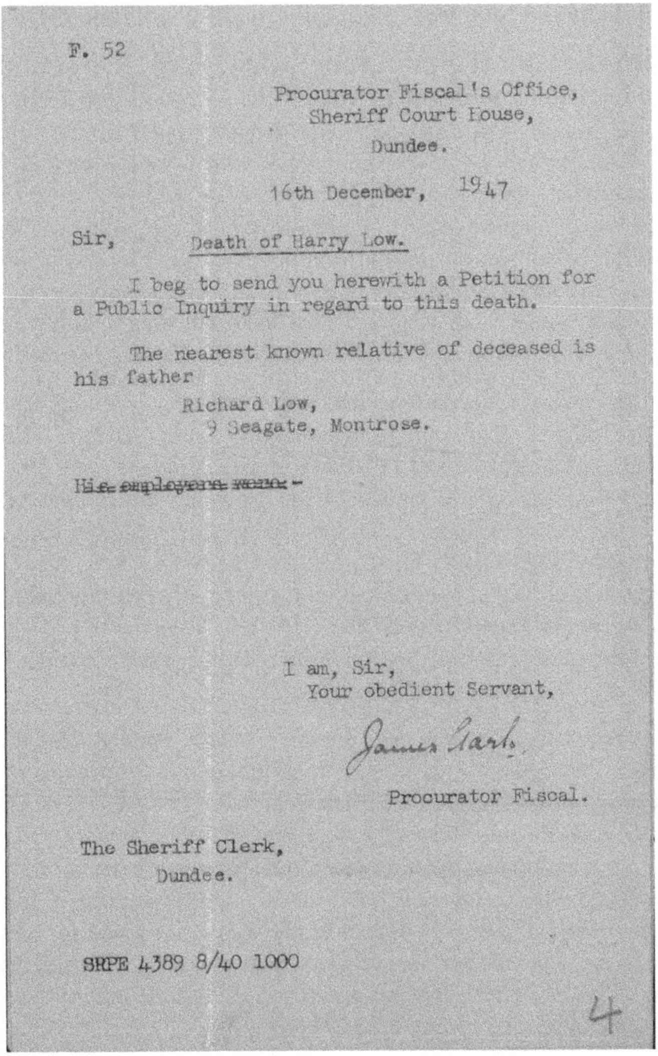

F. 52

Procurator Fiscal's Office,
Sheriff Court House,
Dundee.

16th December, 1947

Sir,   Death of Harry Low.

I beg to send you herewith a Petition for a Public Inquiry in regard to this death.

The nearest known relative of deceased is his father

Richard Low,
9 Seagate, Montrose.

His employers were -

I am, Sir,
Your obedient Servant,

James Clark

Procurator Fiscal.

The Sheriff Clerk,
Dundee.

SRPE 4389 8/40 1000

4

PART B – HIGH PROFILE FAIs CONCERNING SAFETY ON SCHOOL TRIPS AND MATERS OF PUBLIC INTEREST

Cairngorm Disaster (Feith Buidhe) – Deaths of five school pupils[8] and their teacher (held under the 1895 Act and the 1906 Act)

The name Cairngorm is an FAI synonymous with the disaster that occurred in 1971 that influenced the subsequent organisation of outdoor school trips and the design of parental consent forms. It also had significant implications for mountain safety concerning the location of high-level bothies,[9] being shelters provided on the mountains in Scotland. This FAI has been chosen as both mountain safety and the safety of youths' outdoor activities provided the focus then and they continued to feature as topics of public interest in subsequent FAIs discussed below.

The school trip in November 1971 started from Lagganlia Outdoor Training Centre, Kincraig and planned to head south from Cairngorm to Ben Macdhui. There were two groups of children, one group led by an experienced guide and the other group led by the other two inexperienced guides. The original aim was to practice navigation and emergency bivouac techniques, but that changed to include an overnight stay at the Carrour bothy. The weather for the trip deteriorated badly so that the leader of the second group decided to bivouac out on the plateau, worried about her ability to find the emergency shelter, given the depth of snow. This was to prove to be a fatal mistake. By the time search parties found her, on the mountain side, her original group was dead, except one boy who survived.

No one was found to be responsible for the accident. Section 2 of the 1906 Act provided that a jury could, 'after hearing the evidence and the persons … [to] return a verdict setting forth, so far as such particulars have been proved, when and where the accident and the death or deaths to which the inquiry relates took place, the cause or causes of such accident or death or deaths, the person or persons, if any, to whose fault or negligence the accident is attributable, the precautions, if any, by which it might have been avoided, any defects in the system or mode of working which contributed to the accident, and any other facts disclosed by the evidence which, in the opinion of the jury, are relevant to the inquiry.' Possible findings as to fault and negligence were to be removed by the 1976 Act

This absence of attributing blame given the inherent duty of care and responsibility provide a sharp contrast to both the earlier FAIs discussed above in relation to the baby's death and the deaths of the children at Balgowan Approved School. Findings of fault were made in both these FAIs, in effect blaming the mother and the children respectively. In the Cairngorm FAI, this absence of any such finding being made may have been due to the jury not wanting to curtail or restrict youth outdoor activities.

---

8   Carol Bertram, Susan Byrne, Lorraine Dick, Diane Dudgeon and William Kerr and Shelagh Sunderland, aged 18, Lagganlia volunteer trainee instructor.

9   *www.mountainbothies.org.uk/* (accessed on 21 February 2023).

That type of finding might have potentially inhibited other schools and outdoor centres from taking children out of school to undertake such activities, due to concern about the risks of potential litigation.

However, the FAI made recommendations for the organising of parties of young children in undertaking outdoor activities to have special regard to their level of fitness and training. The lack of experience of the group in this case was obvious in relation to the then prevailing conditions in the Cairngorms mountains, described as 'climatically, geomorphologically, and biologically the most extensive 'arctic' area in the UK'.[10]

The parents had been unaware of the extent of the expedition as the consent forms did not indicate that there would be any winter mountaineering. In the event too of any disaster, they found that closer liaison should be kept between authorities and the parents concerned. The families only became aware of the party being overdue on the Sunday night, by which time they had been overdue for some time.

The Cairngorm FAI was held in part to highlight risk, safety and to raise public awareness of the dangers of mountaineering in Scotland. It generated quite a vigorous discussion on the existence of high-level bothies, with arguments that they should be removed, which later many were, as they provided a false sense of security, encouraging inexperience out into the mountains.[11]

That was not to be the only FAI held into fatalities in school trips.

FAI into the death of Graham Greig Paterson (held under the 1976 Act)

Safety issues in the mountain trips were to provide the focus too of the FAI held into the death of Graham Greig Paterson,[12] who died between 27 and 29 December 2012. He was a leader in charge of a party in a mountain activity in Skye when he was killed. That FAI resulted in recommendations being made to the Scottish Government[13] to discover a means, whether statutory or otherwise, to ensure that mountain guides in Scotland were properly qualified and equipped to provide a commercial mountain guiding service for adults. Additionally, the relevant authorities[14] should inform the public of the importance for amateur climbers and hill walkers of having at least two

---

10   *https://cairngorms.co.uk/discover-explore/landscapes-scenery/the-mountains/*   (accessed   on   21 February 2023).
11   *www.cairngormclub.org.uk/journals/PDFs/Articles/J096/The%20Cairngorm%20Club%20 Journal%20096%20-%20The%20Cairngorms%20high%20level%20bothies%20WM.pdf* (accessed on 21 February 2023).
12   FAI into the death of Graham Greig Paterson 2014 FAI 37, *www.scotcourts.gov.uk/search-judgments/ judgment?id=ba0fbba6-8980-69d2-b500-ff0000d74aa7* (accessed on 21 February 2023).
13   Described vaguely as 'relevant stakeholders'. This shows the need for recommendations to be specific, as permitted now under the 2016 Act.
14   Ditto observation about clarity in footnote 6.

members of any party being fully equipped to deal with the possibility of an accident occurring to the leading member of the party.

FAI held into the death of Laura McDairmant (held under the 1976 Act)

The FAI held into the death of Laura McDairmant[15] in 2006 also considered the similar issue in providing safe outdoor activities for youths. She had been killed in a gorge jumping activity, conducted under the 'apparent' supervision of the Abernethy Trust. Considerable criticisms were made of the Abernethy Trust, which was also convicted of breaches of the Health and Safety at Work Act 1974. That provides a contrast with the Cairngorm disaster in that finding of criminal responsibility. It should be observed too that this FAI was in advance of the passing of the Corporate Manslaughter and Culpable Homicide Act 2007. Though to date, no convictions have ensued in Scotland, under such legislation companies and organisations can now be found guilty of corporate manslaughter where serious management failures have resulted in a gross breach of a duty of care.

That FAI recommended that a comprehensive review should be undertaken by the Health and Safety Executive of the statutory scheme for the regulation of the provision of adventure activities to persons under the age of 18 years, set up under the terms of the Activity Centres (Young Persons' Safety) Act 1995 and the regulations of 1996 and 2004 made under that Act. That review included a need to look at 'the training and level of qualifications appropriate for persons involved in the management and delivery of adventure activities to young persons': an echo again of 40 years' earlier regarding youths' safety and training requirements for those involved.

FAI into the death of Kaylee McIntosh (held under the 1976 Act)

At the FAI held into the death of Kaylee McIntosh (aged 14) in 2007,[16] risk and safety again featured. She drowned during an Army Cadet Force expedition on South Uist. No appropriate risk assessment had been made of the weather, which was too bad for the exercise to be held safely. This resonates too with Cairngorm disaster. That error was compounded by others, including failures over the equipment issues being used as only being suitable for adults rather than children, the lack of processes for accounting when raising the alarm and the checking of numbers after the launch had capsized.

---

15   FAI into the death of Laura McDairmant 2010 FAI 29, *www.scotcourts.gov.uk/search-judgments/judgment?id=fb3786a6-8980-69d2-b500-ff0000d74aa7* (accessed on 21 February 2023).
16   FAI into the death of Laura McDairmant 2010 FAI 29, *www.scotcourts.gov.uk/search-judgments/judgment?id=a45687a6-8980-69d2-b500-ff0000d74aa7* (accessed on 21 February 2023).

Interestingly, at this FAI, Major George McCallum, Territorial Army, who was in charge of the expedition, was 'the subject of much scrutiny, and criticism, during the inquiry'.[17] He had not been legally represented, due apparently to his own lack of funds. This illustrates some of the potential legal aid issues discussed in **Chapter 9**.

PART C – MEDICAL FAIs

FAIs may be held into any type of medical death. A quick overview of FAIs provides some examples of medically related FAIs that were held into deaths arising from:

- pre-eclampsia during pregnancy;[18]
- Instrumental perforation of the duodenum during an endoscopy, resulting in septicaemia secondary to sepsis;[19]
- bronchopneumonia following on hypoxic-ischaemic encephalopathy. The severe encephalopathy that caused the death of a baby of five months[20] was because of acute severe ischaemic insult in the brief period before his delivery when his mother's uterus ruptured. The death might have been avoided had he been delivered by Caesarean section;
- peritonitis from a perforated diverticulum as a result of an intestinal obstruction due to an internal hernia of a 13-year-old.[21] A reasonable precaution would have been if her current physical observations, readily available, had been considered before deciding upon her discharge from hospital.

Many prison deaths too are in fact medically related, as an FAI will be held where a prisoner has died from natural causes, such as an existing medical condition. Such deaths inevitably give rise to the holding of a mandatory FAI, caused because the deceased person is in prison, not necessarily through any concerns over the circumstances of the death (though there could be). From an ECHR perspective, it is important to ensure that the quality of medical treatment given in prison is no less than that which would have been provided to the deceased prisoner had they been at liberty.

The UN Standard Minimum Rules for the Treatment of Prisoners[22] r.24 state that prisoners should receive the same standards of health care that are available in

---

17   FAI into the death of Laura McDairmant 2010 FAI 29, *www.scotcourts.gov.uk/search-judgments/judgment?id=a45687a6-8980-69d2-b500-ff0000d74aa7* (accessed on 21 February 2023).

18   FAI into the death of Sharman Weir, *www.scotcourts.gov.uk/search-judgments/judgment?id=13c286a6-8980-69d2-b500-ff0000d74aa7* (accessed on 21 February 2023).

19   FAI into the death of Norma Haq 2011 FAI 34, *www.scotcourts.gov.uk/search-judgments/judgment?id=4c5386a6-8980-69d2-b500-ff0000d74aa7* (accessed on 21 February 2023).

20   FAI into the death of Elijah Stirling 2015 FAI 10, *www.scotcourts.gov.uk/search-judgments/judgment?id=d063cfa6-8980-69d2-b500-ff0000d74aa7* (accessed on 21 February 2023).

21   FAI into the death of Kirsty Rutherford Thompson, *www.scotcourts.gov.uk/search-judgments/judgment?id=fd8786a6-8980-69d2-b500-ff0000d74aa7* (accessed on 21 February 2023).

22   The 'Nelson Mandela Rules'.

the community. 'Prisons should have a health-care service tasked with evaluating, promoting, protecting and improving the physical and mental health of prisoners, paying particular attention to prisoners with special health-care needs or with health issues that hamper their rehabilitation; the service should consist of an interdisciplinary team with sufficient qualified personnel acting in full clinical independence and should include sufficient expertise in psychology and psychiatry.'[23]

As discussed in **Chapter 6**, this is an area which may not always be fully appreciated in the FAI when providing evidence by means of Joint Minute. It should be a specific aspect of the investigation into the death about which the sheriff should be satisfied as to the adequacy of the medical treatment provided to the deceased prisoner. It is part of the State's compliance in undertaking the FAI in accordance with the requirements of Art 2 of the ECHR.

FAI into death of Nicola Welsh (held under the 1976 Act)

Nicola Welsh[24] died at 9.15am on 25 September 1999 at Ninewells Hospital, Dundee. The cause of her death was (i) Raised Intercranial Pressure; (ii) Acute Hydrocephalus; and (iii) Posterior Fossa Mass Lesion (probable cerebellitis).[25] The circumstances of her illness were described as 'unusual and her probable illness a very rare one'.[26] However, there were faults in the investigation processes which should have alerted the medical profession to the cause of her illness, namely intercranial pressure. However, she had not exhibited obvious signs of raised intercranial pressure, displaying 'only what the experts described as "softer" more subtle ones'.[27] It was important to gather all relevant medical information together to seek an early CT scan which should have been carried out in her case. Had a CT scan been instructed in the late afternoon on 22 September or the morning of 23 September 1999, it was unlikely to have been normal. That would have alerted staff to her having raised intercranial pressure, treatment would have started and the 'coning' of the brain leading to brain stem death would have been avoided.

Implications from the sheriff's determination

Scan: A scan should have been instructed timeously. This would have been justified, based on her symptoms on which the expert evidence agreed at the FAI. She had made repeated complaints of headaches, regular vomiting, disturbed sleep and occasional

---

23   UN Standard Minimum Rules for the Treatment of Prisoners r.25.
24   FAI into the death of Nicola Welsh, *www.scotcourts.gov.uk/search-judgments/judgment?id=043e87a6-8980-69d2-b500-ff0000d74aa7* (accessed on 21 February 2023).
25   Section 6(1)(b) of the 1976 Act.
26   At para [79].
27   At para [79].

bouts of double vision, dizziness, temporary loss of vision and photophobia. These should have alerted medical staff of the need to carry out a CT scan. Increasingly, strong medication was given to treat her. However, medical staff thought that Nicola's headaches might be attention seeking which appeared to have affected her diagnosis.

Note taking and recording: When she died, she had been in hospital for less than four days (87 hours). At least 17 doctors had seen her. Due to the changes in shift staff, accurate note taking and briefing for other staff was critical so they could review notes and scrutinise the processes. Accurate, clear, consistent, and uniform notes were essential. Guidelines needed to be promoted to ensure that the doctor in charge of ward round checked, countersigned and, if necessary, amended the junior doctor's ward round case notes.

The FAI had difficulty in ascertaining what information had been considered, the examinations that were carried out and the diagnoses made, due to the brevity of these notes. The sheriff recommended that the consultant/doctor in charge of the ward round should see and, if necessary, amend the note at a convenient time after the ward round.

Now that the 2016 Act allows for recommendations to be made, these comments over note taking and junior doctors could have referred to the need for training, applying to both undergraduate and for doctors in training and could have wider implications. This is not a finding that relates solely to this hospital trust or to this area of medicine. Presumably, the death then would then have triggered the Scottish Mortality and Morbidity programme processes.[28] These processes have similar aims to the FAI process in providing learning and training and to the sharing of learning across the wider NHS Scotland. Such processes consider the review of the incident and the standard of care to allow for 'open examination of adverse events, complications, and errors that may have led to illness or death in patients'. Both these internal processes and the holding of the FAI are about patient safety, which is clearly a significant matter of public interest.

Reporting of deaths: In this FAI, this aspect of the reporting of the death came under scrutiny. As stated in **Chapter 1**, doctors need to know when and how to report sudden deaths to the procurator fiscal. This was also a focus in the FAI into the death of Norma Haq where a finding was made that 'In terms of Section 6(1)(e) of the [1976 Act] Act, the death ought to have been reported to the procurator fiscal in terms of the literature "Death and the Procurator Fiscal"; ... NHS hospitals; management in NHS and private hospitals should ensure that all doctors treating patients are aware of the terms of "Death and the Procurator Fiscal"'.[29]

---

28   Healthcare Improvement Scotland, *Scottish Mortality and Morbidity Programme*, *www. healthcareimprovementscotland.org/our_work/patient_safety/scottish_mortality__morbidity.aspx* (accessed on 21 February 2023).
29   FAI into the death of Norma Haq 2011 FAI 34, *www.scotcourts.gov.uk/search-judgments/ judgment?id=4c5386a6-8980-69d2-b500-ff0000d74aa7* (accessed on 21 February 2023).

In Nicola Welsh's case, her death was erroneously not reported to the procurator fiscal. Had the death been reported, this would have allowed a post-mortem examination to be carried out of her brain and neck area. This would have allowed organ donation to have taken place in keeping with what the family wanted. Instead, the family were left to 'decide'[30] between reporting the case to the procurator fiscal or allowing arrangements to be made to donate Nicola's organs. This was described as an 'invidious position' to have been placed in.

Chapter 1 outlined how important that it is that doctors are trained to be aware of the Scottish system of reporting of deaths. It also requires accurate information to be readily available, on how and when to report deaths whether it is available the COPFS or the Scottish Government website (if set up). Such information needs to be kept fully up to date.

PART D – FAIs INTO PRISON DEATHS AND POLICE CUSTODY

Prison deaths

Chapter 2 discussed the obligations of the State under Art 2 of the ECHR regarding investigations into deaths arising from those in prison or detained in police custody. **Chapter 6** looked specifically at the FAI system dealing with deaths in prison, promoted by the fact that most of the FAIs that are carried out presently are in relation to deaths that occurred in prison. The numbers dying from suicide in prison are increasing[31] so that the focus is justified on such FAIs due to public interest in such matters. It is appropriate therefore to consider some examples of FAIs held into deaths that occurred in prison. Many of these prison deaths result from natural causes, the issues of which were considered under Part 3 – Medical FAIs. The main concern in these deaths is the quality of the medical treatment provided to the deceased person in prison. It should not be inadequate just because they are in custody.

FAI into a death from natural causes (held under the 1976 Act)

An FAI was held into the death of Alexander James[32] (age not provided) on 16 November 2008, who died in hospital when he was a serving prisoner at HM Prison, Peterhead. His cause of death was held as having resulted from natural causes, which was pneumonia following a pneumonectomy for carcinoma of his left lung.[33]

---

30 At para [121].
31 BBC, *Deaths in Scottish prisons at record high* (30 November 2022), *www.bbc.co.uk/news/uk-scotland-63780998* (accessed on 21 February 2023).
32 2012 FAI 20.
33 Section 6(1) (b) of the 1976 Act. No family member is recorded as being present at the FAI.

By the time he was imprisoned in 2004 (though the FAI does not record his sentence or the nature of his conviction), he had suffered from angina and had had three heart attacks. He was later diagnosed as suffering from Chronic Pulmonary Obstructive Disease and a cancerous left lung. He had been in hospital undergoing an elective operation to remove the cancerous lung.

The operation was carried out on 11 November, but on 13 November 2008, his other lung deteriorated through infection, with his condition then deteriorating, leading to secondary multi-organ failure from which he died.[34] In this case, the death was the direct consequence of the cancer from which he was suffering, so the mandatory FAI was required as he died when he was in prison. No concerns as to the medical treatment which he received were recorded or any reference made to any family or to them expressing any concerns.

Murder in prison (held under the 1976 Act)

Where a murder was committed in prison, though a successful prosecution took place, resulting in the conviction of those involved, the death in prison of the victim itself generated the holding of a mandatory FAI.[35]

The FAI was held into the death of Michael Peter Cameron (21) on 17 June 2006,[36] which occurred in hospital, following an attack in Cell Ward 4 of the Health Care Centre of HM Prison, Kilmarnock on 16 June 2006. The cause of his death was blunt force trauma of the head and neck, sustained as the result of 'the murderous assault inflicted upon him by David Martin and Andrew Kiltie'.[37]

The sheriff found that no reasonable precautions could have been taken, nor were there any defects in the system of work that contributed to his death or other facts found relevant to the circumstances of the death. The death of a serving prisoner was however a matter of considerable 'public' concern. The sheriff indicated there had been failings regarding accurate form filling and strict adherence to the Prison Rules about the segregation of prisoners. By the time that the FAI was held nine years later, changes had been made to the system, including that very few young offenders were now being housed in that prison.

The sheriff's view was that 'the violence offered against Michael Cameron was unexpected and in [the sheriff's) view unforeseeable'. Little more could therefore be achieved in making any other findings in this case.

---

34   FAI into the death of Alexander James 2012 FAI 20, *www.scotcourts.gov.uk/search-judgments/judgment?id=205086a6-8980-69d2-b500-ff0000d74aa7* (accessed on 21 February 2023).

35   Now under the 2016 Act the Lord Advocate could exercise his discretion not to hold an FAI.

36   FAI into the death of Michael Peter Cameron [2016] FAI 8, *www.scotcourts.gov.uk/search-judgments/judgment?id=e1f115a7-8980-69d2-b500-ff0000d74aa7* (accessed on 21 February 2023).

37   FAI into the death of Michael Peter Cameron [2016] FAI 8, *www.scotcourts.gov.uk/search-judgments/judgment?id=e1f115a7-8980-69d2-b500-ff0000d74aa7* (accessed on 21 February 2023).

FAIs in deaths by prison suicides (held under the 2016 Act)

Chapter 6 recognised that the number of suicides occurring in prison are rising. It is apparent from SPS's records[38] that a number of FAIs have still to be held into deaths over the past few years that have resulted from suicide. These FAIs into the suicide deaths should be prioritised as there appear to be a number of common factors arising in relation to these deaths, such as the detention of young prisoners, and mental health issues when considering the circumstances in which prisoners have taken their own lives. Practices are aimed at the assessment and monitoring of prisoners' mental health to determine risk where, if ascertained, so that when identified this would lead to a reduction in the incidence of these kind of deaths.

The FAI[39] into the death of Gary Gallagher (aged 39)[40] at HM Prison Glenorchil at 9am on 12 October 2020 is an example of a prison suicide death. A subsequent post-mortem examination found that the cause of death was suspension by the neck by means of a ligature made from a dressing gown cord (hanging). The sheriff made no findings about any reasonable precautions or identified any defects in the system of working or any other matters that would have prevented the death.

A Joint Minute of Evidence detailed the circumstances of Mr Gallagher's death and his care and treatment within HM Prison Glenochil.

The FAI recorded that none of the parties to the FAI made any criticism of the care which had been provided to the deceased within HM Prison Glenochil. Presumably, the sheriff meant to reference SPS, COPFS, NHS Forth Valley and the Scottish Prison Officers Association Scotland, who were present, but realistically none of these parties were likely to have expressed concerns. The concerns should have come from the FAI if the facts presented in evidence had indicated any such concerns. The family, as appears often to be the case in such FAIs, were unrepresented. However, it indicated that the deceased had been in telephone contact with his sister, Julie Gallagher, who noted no change in his health or mood on 9 October 2020.

The circumstances of the death showed that the deceased had had regular contact with his personal officer prior to his death. He had not expressed any suicidal thoughts or thoughts of self-harm to him and was not subject to any observations at the time of his death. However, no independent medical evidence was presented at the court perhaps to conclude that there had not been any failings in the care provided by the mental health nurses.[41] While in no way indicating that the converse is true, it seems material when considering the actions of mental health nurses for the court to receive that separate assurance as to the quality of care that was provided.

---

38   Scottish Prison Service, *Prisoner* Deaths, www.*sps.gov.uk/Corporate/Information/PrisonerDeaths. aspx* (accessed on 21 February 2023).
39   Section 4(a) of the 2016 Act.
40   [2022] FAI 29.
41   [2022] FAI 29 at para [17]: *www.scotcourts.gov.uk/docs/default-source/cos-general-docs/pdf-docs-for-opinions/2022fai029.pdf?sfvrsn=377ee932_1* (accessed on 21 February 2023).

Actions involving the mental nursing staff seemed relatively limited in that a referral was made on 1 June 2020 as Mr Gallagher was not eating prison issue meals, but showed no evidence of distress or distraction. As he had highlighted feeling symptoms of grief since his brother died in 2017, bereavement counselling was provided by the prison chaplain. Though Mr Gallagher presented frequently as 'quite down and gloomy, this was normal for him'. There had been no indication of any suicidal thoughts or thoughts of self-harm.

Following his death, a DIPLAR [42] was undertaken. It set out the deceased's medical history, including his engagement with the health care services within the prison. It had considered the circumstances surrounding Mr Gallagher's death and confirmed that there were no causes for concern. There were no indicators of risk. (This was an internal report commissioned by SPS.)

The sheriff concluded that there were no prior signs or clues to indicate any risk of suicide. He was serving a sentence imposed in July 2016 for an Order for Lifelong Restriction with a punishment part of five years' imprisonment. His Parole Board hearing had been refused on 1 June 2020.

Mr Gallagher had been diagnosed with Charcot Marie Tooth disease which affected his mobility and was declared medically unfit for work within HMP Glenochil for periods. 'Assessment on Mr Gallagher's cognitive functioning concluded that Mr Gallagher functioned on a borderline level. He had difficulties with verbal comprehension, perceptual reasoning, and processing speed. However, he managed day to day tasks well.'

SPS had a suicide prevention policy known as 'Talk to Me' in place. Though mentioned, exactly how this would have engaged with the deceased is not then outlined.

In conclusion, some of the factors which are common with deaths in prison can be noted. In seeking to answer whether there was perhaps more that could have been done to have avoided the death, there are possible gaps highlighted from the findings made based on the evidence which appear to have been led. There seems to be a need for independent assurance to be obtained about the provision of medical services rather than this being covered by the DIPLAR. There are mental health assessment processes in the prison where clarity on their relevance to this death would help — as in examining such deaths, it is about lessons to be learnt.

There was no apparent undue delay in the FAI being held. However, factors such as the Covid-19 pandemic, isolation from family and the refusal of a parole hearing might all be possible indications of heightened risk of mental health issues. How were these factors assessed, bearing in mind that in findings that can be made that there must be a causal link with the death. The sheriff conducting the FAI is 'entitled

---

42   Death in Prison Learning, Audit and Review, which was discussed in **Chapter 10**.

to examine much wider issues, including areas of practice, and is entitled to direct criticism in such terms as seem appropriate if satisfied upon examination of the facts that it is right to do so. The making of such criticism has no necessary implication for any other proceedings in which issues of professional standards may be properly focused.'[43]

No FAI has yet been held in relation to any of the prisoners who have died of Covid-19. The cause of death, just as with the FAI into the death of Alexander James above, will presumably result in a finding from natural causes. There may be wider concerns however about the policies operating when the pandemic was at its height and the implications of the multiple lockdowns in prisons with the risk of infection that still require to be explored in due course. The pandemic required many prisoners to remain on remand for longer periods and were affected by similar delays in the holding of their trials' sentencing due to numerous court closures. The link up too with issues in relation to suicides in prison is pertinent as a possible significant source of mental health issues as prisoners were unable to maintain a level of contact with their families during this time.

Deaths in police custody

There are fewer FAIs held concerning deaths arising in police custody than deaths in prison. For completeness, it is appropriate to include an example of one, which by chance is also an example of a remotely held FAI due to the Covid-19 pandemic.

The FAI held into the death of Shania Collins (aged 19) was treated as a mandatory FAI in terms of s 2(4)(a) of the 2016 Act.[44] Ms Collins' death was caused by a cardiac arrest which occurred when she was being arrested[45] by a police officer around 11.55am on 22 December 2020. She had become unconscious and was taken to Aberdeen Royal Infirmary, where she died on 28 December 2020. Her cause of death was certified as (a) global ischaemic brain injury and bronchopneumonia and (b) presumed butane abuse.[46]

Ms Collins was unmarried but was in a relationship with 'Paul Wilson' with whom she had a baby son, who was under the care of Aberdeenshire Council in terms of a child protection order. She had a history of low mood, drug misuse and self-harm. The narration of her partner 'Paul Wilson' at para [33], with whom she was in the car when it was pursued by the police, summed up what took place:

---

43 Lord President pointed out in *Black v Scott Lithgow Ltd* 1990 SLT 612 quoted in the FAI into the death of Gordon Scott Niven, *www.scotcourts.gov.uk/search-judgments/judgment?id=2fc286a6-8980-69d2-b500-ff0000d74aa7* (accessed on 21 February 2023).
44 [2022] FAI 4.
45 Explained further at para [19] as being under s 2(5)(b) of the 2016 Act ('police custody' as a form of 'legal custody' for these purposes) and s 64 of the Police (Scotland) Act 2016 (the matters which may constitute 'police custody' for these purposes).
46 After post-mortem examination and toxicology reports.

'... Shania was excited due to the events of the 22nd of December 2020. This was due to her arguing with the Social Work Department then not getting a visit to see our son. We were then in a car being chased by the Police and Shania was aware that I was a disqualified driver and that if caught I would be arrested and would go to prison. It was a strange situation it was like a last hurrah as we thought we would not see each other for a while and she was taking the gas quicker than usual and drinking whisky at the same time.'

The pursuit itself lasted around 25 minutes and covered around 27 miles. It was not a high-speed pursuit, but it occurred in a rural area where it was impossible for the police vehicle to safely force it to stop. When Ms Collins exited the car, the police officer ran after her. She turned and threw something at the police officer, which was found subsequently to be a butane gas canister. She struggled with him but lost her balance and fell to the ground. When she did not get up, he rolled her onto her side. Immediately, he noted that her eyes were wide open, her pupils were dilated and that she appeared drowsy, though breathing. Help was then summoned.

The accident[47] resulting in Ms Collins' death was caused by her actions in inhaling a significant quantity of butane gas on 22 December 2020, prior to and during the lawful pursuit by the police of the motor vehicle being driven by Paul Wilson in which she was the front seat passenger. When the pursuit ended, she ran from the vehicle, attempted to strike, and struggle with a police officer. The accident[48] resulting in her death would have been avoided had Ms Collins not inhaled butane gas or having inhaled butane gas, behaved in the manner which she did.

Butane is a commonly recognised volatile gas, abused through inhalation/sniffing with potentially fatal side-effects. These affect the central nervous system depression, cause respiratory depression, coma and death and cardiac arrhythmia. A hyperadrenergic state caused by stress, illness and physical activity lowers the threshold for a fatal arrhythmia.

There was no family representation at the FAI. This is an FAI where there was great effort by the sheriff to record the efforts made to ensure the family could appear if they wanted because of course, this was being held remotely. Her mother had expressed that there were no complaints about the conduct of the police officers involved and was grateful for the attempts made by police officers to assist when Ms Collins collapsed.

The societal interest in the circumstances of Ms Collins death can be seen, as it involved a police pursuit, a struggle with police and timely medical attention when she took unwell. No concerns were found regarding the police conduct or the appropriateness and adequacy of the response of police which demonstrates the benefit and effectiveness of the FAI system.

---

47 Section 26(2)(d) of the 2016 Act.
48 Section 26(2)(e) of the 2016 Act.

PART E – EXAMPLE OF A PUBLIC INQUIRY
Piper Alpha[49]

In the evening of 6 July 1988, explosions ripped through the Piper Alpha platform in the North Sea. There was a fire with most oil rig topside modules collapsing into the sea. 167 men died with many more injured. It was the world's biggest offshore oil disaster. It affected 10 per cent of UK oil production and led to financial losses of an estimated £2 billion.[50]

In a Minute dated 13 July 1988, the Secretary of State for Energy under the Mineral Workings (Offshore Installations) Act 1971 and The Offshore Installations (Public Inquiries) Regulations 1974[51] determined that "a public inquiry should be held to establish the circumstances of the accident and its cause". He appointed The Hon. Lord William Douglas Cullen "to hold the inquiry and to report to him on the circumstances of the accident and its cause together with any observations and recommendations which he thinks fit to make with a view to the preservation of life and the avoidance of similar accidents in the future".[52] This appointment process can be contrasted with the process under the FAI system of the Lord Advocate calling for the FAI to be held and arranging for a sheriff to be appointed to hear the FAI. This was the first inquiry that was held under these regulations – this inquiry would now presumably fall under the scope of the Inquiries Act 2005.

On 14 July 1988, the Secretary of State had explained that the public inquiry should be as full and far reaching as possible. The Report was subsequently published in November 1990 (180 days of evidence having been held.)

Lord Cullen posed two questions:

- What were the causes and circumstances of the disaster of the Pipa Alpha Platform on 6 July 1988?
- What should be recommended with a view to preservation of life and the avoidance of similar accidents in the future?

His view was that it was not a 'roving excursion into every aspect of safety at work in the North Sea or into every grievance, however sincere or well-founded that was

---

49 Cullen, The Hon. Lord William Douglas, *The Public Inquiry into the Piper Alpha Disaster, Presented to Parliament by the Secretary of State for Energy by Command of Her Majesty (Report)* (1990, London: HM Stationery Office), *www.hse.gov.uk/offshore/piper-alpha-public-inquiry-volume2.pdf* (accessed on 21 February 2023).

50 The Chemical Engineer, *Piper Alpha: The disaster in detail, www.thechemicalengineer.com/ features/piper-alpha-the-disaster-in-detail/* (accessed on 21 February 2023).

51 SI 1974/338.

52 Cullen, *The Public Inquiry into the Piper Alpha Disaster*, para 2.4: *www.hse.gov.uk/offshore/piper-alpha-public-inquiry-volume1.pdf* (accessed on 21 February 2023).

entertained'.[53] There should be a 'tenable' connection with the line of evidence and the events that had occurred. The inquiry comprised two parts which covered:

- Part 1 related to how and why the disaster had occurred. This considered the physical conditions, events and human conduct which contributed to the occurrence of (a) the initial and later explosions and fires and (b) the loss of or danger to life. His aim was to ensure that no FAI was required to be held (s 6(5) of the Mineral Workings (Offshore Installations) Act 1971).[54]
- Part 2 related to the observations and recommendations with a view to the preservation of life and the avoidance of similar accidents in the future.[55]

Conclusion

Lord Cullen clearly defined how he came to a making a recommendation. A recommendation must be needed in the interests of safety and that it was reasonably practicable to implement it and there was an adequate basis for it in the evidence at the inquiry.[56]

The initial condensate leak was the result of maintenance work being carried out simultaneously on a pump and the related safety valve. It criticised Piper Alpha's operator, Occidental, who were found guilty of having inadequate maintenance and safety procedures, though no criminal charges were to be brought against the company. There were 106 recommendations[57] for changes to North Sea safety procedures made that included:

- 37 that covered procedures for operating equipment;
- 32 that related to the information of platform personnel;
- 25 that referred to the design of platforms; and
- 12 that related to information of emergency services.

As far as the responsibility for implementation, 57 lay with the regulator, 40 with the operators, eight for the industry as a whole and one for stand-by ship owners.

Legislation followed the inquiry with the passing of the Offshore Safety Act 1992 and the making of the Offshore Installations (Safety Case) Regulations 1992.

---

53 Cullen, *The Public Inquiry into the Piper Alpha Disaster*, para 2.15: *www.hse.gov.uk/offshore/piper-alpha-public-inquiry-volume1.pdf* (accessed on 21 February 2023).
54 Now repealed.
55 Cullen, *The Public Inquiry into the Piper Alpha Disaster*, para 2.21: *www.hse.gov.uk/offshore/piper-alpha-public-inquiry-volume1.pdf* (accessed on 21 February 2023).
56 Cullen, *The Public Inquiry into the Piper Alpha Disaster*, para 2.32: *www.hse.gov.uk/offshore/piper-alpha-public-inquiry-volume1.pdf* (accessed on 21 February 2023).
57 Cullen, *The Public Inquiry into the Piper Alpha Disaster*, Vol 2, *www.hse.gov.uk/offshore/piper-alpha-public-inquiry-volume2.pdf* (accessed on 21 February 2023).

Why was this held as an inquiry?

Chapter 10 discussed the system of public inquiries and their place in comparison with the holding of FAIs. Holding a public inquiry such as that into the Piper Alpha deaths would be anticipated where there were multiple deaths and indeed, the circumstances of the deaths were complex, as can be seen from the number of extensive recommendations made and the significance to the international oil and gas industry in such a high-profile disaster.

The costs in holding an inquiry are met by the government, with the government selecting the judge to lead the inquiry. An inquiry's scope has specific advantages over those of holding an FAI – as the inquiry was not restricted by the narrow framework of what was then the 1976 Act and now the 2016 Act. The conclusions to the inquiry are also published in an extensive report which is provided to government. Here, the effect and the impact of the report can be seen in the legislation which was then to follow.

A public inquiry while judge led is not a court of law and similarly to the FAI system cannot determine civil or criminal liability.

Given the wide-ranging remit of the Piper Alpha inquiry, no subsequent FAI was held. Its scope does illustrate one of the reasons for the passing of the 1976 Act,[58] which had recognised that reform in the 1970s was needed to ensure that there was jurisdiction for investigating deaths arising on North Sea oil platforms.

The success of the inquiry can be ascertained in the substantial changes that were made which related to design issues; personal safety over processes; permit to work and isolation for maintenance (the pump was re-started before maintenance complete); handover (inadequate transfer of information between crews, shifts and disciplines); interconnection as the oil rig connected elsewhere; emergency response (evacuation) and no doubt in common with many other industrial FAIs, that there had been reliance on existing safety culture or complacency.[59] This shows quite clearly the purpose that was achieved in identifying and implementing lessons learnt.

---

58   Including within the 2016 Act.
59   The Chemical Engineer, *Piper Alpha: The disaster in detail*, *www.thechemicalengineer.com/features/piper-alpha-the-disaster-in-detail/* (accessed on 21 February 2023).

Index

[All references are to paragraph number.]